Advance Praise for *Social Media Marketing: An Hour a Day*

"In a world where 'authenticity' matters, Dave's the real deal. I first met him when I launched PlanetFeedback: He's one of the smartest and most passionate leaders around the business issues of social media. Dave's book, a practical, step-by-step guide for marketers looking to expand their skills, shows you how to tap the Social Web the right way."
  —PETE BLACKSHAW, Chief Marketing Officer, Nielsen|Buzzmetrics

"Dave has incredible insight into the customer perspective and his passion for social media is contagious. He has the remarkable ability to see the broad overall vision but is willing and eager to get into the details so necessary for successful execution. Dave doesn't just give you the magic answer—rather he gives you the essential insight and perspective so you are empowered to leverage social media to reach your business goals."
  —LAURA PINNEKE, Senior Community Manager, Meredith Publishing

"Marketers are falling behind as their audience increasingly turns to social media as part of their daily media mix. Social Media in an *Hour a Day* lays out a practical path for marketers to catch up and make social media a vital business tool."
  —JIM NAIL, Chief Strategy & Marketing Officer, TNS Media Intelligence/Cymfony

"Dave Evans's book presents a clear case for fully aligning your efforts in social media with your overall business objectives and measures. Now more than ever, congruency is vital to your marketing plans."
  —DAVE ELLETT, President, Belo Interactive Media

Social Media Marketing

Social Media Marketing

An Hour a Day

Dave Evans

Wiley Publishing, Inc.

Senior Acquisitions Editor: WILLEM KNIBBE
Development Editor: HILARY POWERS
Technical Editor: JAKE MCKEE
Production Editors: LIZ BRITTEN AND MELISSA LOPEZ
Copy Editor: KATHY CARLYLE
Production Manager: TIM TATE
Vice President and Executive Group Publisher: RICHARD SWADLEY
Vice President and Executive Publisher: JOSEPH B. WIKERT
Vice President and Publisher: NEIL EDDE
Book Designer: FRANZ BAUMHACKL
Compositor: CHRIS GILLESPIE, HAPPENSTANCE TYPE-O-RAMA
Proofreader: CORINA COPP, WORDONE
Indexer: NANCY GUENTHER
Project Coordinator, Cover: LYNSEY STANFORD
Cover Designer: RYAN SNEED
Cover Image: © PATAGONIK WORKS/ DIGITAL VISION/ GETTY IMAGES

Dear Reader,

Thank you for choosing *Social Media Marketing: An Hour a Day*. This book is part of a family of premium-quality Sybex books, all of which are written by outstanding authors who combine practical experience with a gift for teaching.

Sybex was founded in 1976. More than thirty years later, we're still committed to producing consistently exceptional books. With each of our titles, we're working hard to set a new standard for the industry. From the paper we print on to the authors we work with, our goal is to bring you the best books available.

I hope you see all that reflected in these pages. I'd be very interested to hear your comments and get your feedback on how we're doing. Feel free to let me know what you think about this or any other Sybex book by sending me an email at nedde@wiley.com, or if you think you've found a technical error in this book, please visit http://sybex.custhelp.com. Customer feedback is critical to our efforts at Sybex.

Best regards,

NEIL EDDE
Vice President and Publisher
Sybex, an Imprint of Wiley

To my friends Jack and Dewey, for showing me how to see what's out there, and to my family, for the drive to chase after it.

 # Acknowledgments

Social media and the rise of the Social Web is by definition a collaborative effort, and so the ideas in this book have came from everywhere. Dr. Richard Mancuso (Physics) and Dr. Kazumi Nakano (Mathematics) put me on a path seeking a quantitative understanding of the world around me. You'll see the connection in Chapter 13, "Objectives, Metrics, and ROI." Dr. Anthony Piccione (Poetry) gave me an appreciation for the written word. Steve Tufts pulled me from R&D into marketing and product management, and then Phil Ashworth pulled me into the space program. Xray introduced me to the "Why?" committee, and Roy Fredericks provided a social context for understanding business as it applies to earning loyalty in the Millennial generation. You'll see these connections too.

Susan Bratton and everyone at ad:tech, Pete Blackshaw, and Jim Nail provided the mentoring and thought leadership that led me into noninterruptive, trust-based marketing. My experience with the Word of Mouth Marketing Association formed the underpinning of my interest and exploration of social media as a formal marketing discipline. Special notes to Robert Scoble, for his commitment to business blogging and his conceptualization of the social media starfish, to Christopher Locke, a.k.a. Rage Boy and his Entropy Gradient Reversal (he's never heard of me, but I've been reading his stuff for years), and to Dave Ellett for his connection of the purchase funnel and Social Web through the social feedback cycle. My thanks to Hilary Powers of Powersedit and everyone at Wiley|Sybex, in particular Kathy Carlyle, Liz Britten, Melissa Lopez, and Willem Knibbe. As a first-time writer, they were essential to me and no doubt endured a lot of "first-time writer" pain without complaint.

I am indebted to Jake McKee, the Technical Editor for this book. Jake is an evangelist for customer collaboration, online communities, and fan groups. Jake was the Global Community Relations Specialist for the LEGO Company, where he spent five years on the front lines of customer-company interaction, building social projects and programs. Jake has a rich background in web development, community management, business strategy, and product development that gives his community work and insights into the subject matter of this book a unique spin. Jake is currently the Principal and Chief Ant Wrangler at Ant's Eye View, a Dallas-based customer collaboration strategy practice. I highly recommend talking with him.

Where would I be if not for Austin, TX, declared by city charter to be a multimedia industry–supportive city in 1994. My colleagues in Austin's city government, especially Jim Butler, and the professionals and partners I worked with at GSD&M and FG SQUARED, all contributed to this book. My sincere appreciation to each of the businesses and organizations who contributed case studies: Without you and the work that you've shared, this book would be significantly less valuable. In the same way, to Warren Sukernek and the rest of my community on Twitter, many of whom reviewed various chapters and stages of this book, thank you all.

Finally, to my wife Jennifer and son Broch. Writing a book while launching start-ups and running a consulting practice around a discipline that has been exploding since mid-2006 is often toughest on those who are closest. For them, my love always.

About the Author

"If I couldn't interrupt you, how would I reach you?"

That's the question that Dave starts with as a communications expert focused on social media and its application in marketing. His passion is tapping the power of the Social Web through connected networks and consumer-generated media. His expertise lies in his ability to match business objectives, current marketing and operations programs, and consumer preferences as to how and when they would like to be reached.

Dave founded Digital Voodoo, a marketing technology consultancy, in 1994 and later, the business-to-business podcasting service HearThis.com. As both a consultant and Strategy Director with GSD&M IdeaCity, Dave has developed technology and integrated communication strategies for such clients as Microsoft, Hewlett Packard, Southwest Airlines, AARP, U.S. Air Force, AT&T, Wal-Mart, Dial, PGA Tour, Chili's, Meredith Publishing, and many more.

Dave is a ClickZ columnist, and frequent conference speaker. He has served on the advisory board for ad:tech and the measurement and metrics council for the Word of Mouth Marketing Association.

Prior to his work in advertising and digital media, Dave was a Product Manager with Progressive Insurance Company and a systems analyst for the Voyager deep space exploration program with Jet Propulsion Laboratories/NASA. Dave holds a B.S. in Physics and Mathematics from the State University of New York/College at Brockport.

In the event that you'd like to interrupt Dave, the easiest way to do it is via Twitter (evansdave) or email (dave.evans@digital-voodoo.com).

Contents

Foreword

Pick one. Test-drive a few luxury sports cars. A Ferrari, a Lamborghini, a Maserati maybe? Or compare the top First Growth Bordeaux from 2005. Maybe an Haut-Brion, Latour and Mouton-Rothschild? Alternatively, go play in a social media application. Perhaps creating your profile on Facebook or blogging about your passions or sharing your expertise on Spire.com. Would you choose the car, wine or to engage in social media?

Chances are you'll be tempted by the sexy cars or the exquisite wines, but I promise, social media will bring you more pleasure.

How can that be? The technology and the overwhelming range of social media options seem daunting, don't they? Yet our innate desire to connect with each other at a human level is richly rewarded by social media.

It wouldn't be half as much fun to peel out in that red Ferrari without a friend riding shotgun. Imagine comparing a flight of tongue-titillating Bordeaux without a tasting buddy with whom to wax poetic. Social media can extend your business goals while more deeply connecting you to your customers and prospects and connecting you personally to old and new friends alike.

Dave Evans, the author of this exemplary book, has a personal mission to see his son, Broch, "grow up in a world without interruption." This from an ex–ad agency guy? Gutsy. Social media creates the possibility in marketing to move from blasting our messages to interacting with our prospects. And Dave is going to show you how to apply these connective concepts to your business goals.

Speaking of kids. Recently my daughter, struggling to memorize prepositional phrases for her grammar class, made up a song and choreographed a dance with her friends where each child represented a phrase and they sang them while dancing together. This kind of kinesthetic learning is powerful. She aced the test, and so can you.

Dave has laid out an "hour a day" (OK to cheat—an hour whenever works too) program to give you an experiential learning tour of the myriad social media constructs. This brilliant plan gives you approval to get your fingers dirty on your keyboard, "learning" about social media. How fun. It's justified playtime. Thanks, Dave.

With this book, you get solid examples of the most important trends of the Social Web deftly laid out by Dave, and the encouragement to take a tour of your options to formulate your plan. Avail yourself of his exercises and worksheets and you'll be choreographing your own social media dance in no time.

—SUSAN BRATTON
Chair Emeritus, ad:tech Conferences and CEO, Personal Life Media, Inc.

Introduction

"I had (and still have) a dream that the Web could be less of a television channel and more of an interactive sea of shared knowledge. I imagine it immersing us as a warm, friendly environment made of the things we and our friends have seen, heard, believe, or have figured out. I would like it to bring our friends and colleagues closer, in that by working on this knowledge together we can come to better understandings."

—TIM BERNERS LEE, 1995

This book is for marketers wanting to combine social media skills and expertise with their existing, established capabilities. Much of the book is based on my experience as a marketer and product manager, positions where success is largely dictated by what others, *outside your direct span of control*, think of you. That is, more or less, how the Social Web works.

My motivation for exploring social media and its use *in business* arrived one day as I was feeling particularly overwhelmed by the rate of change in advertising and marketing and simultaneously exhilarated by the pure rush of consumer-generated information flowing to me off the Internet. I decided that day that I wanted to see the next generation—my son was about two years old at the time and beginning to make real use of his first iMac—grow up in a world without interruption, where the information needed to make an informed choice was readily available.

Marketing—the thing that most of us do all day—has its roots in the word-of-mouth conversations that have linked buyers with sellers over the past few thousand years. Reputations were built based on experience. With the advent of mass communications and contemporary advertising and PR, the individual voices that had once powered the sales cycle were effectively buried. Professionally created ads, taglines, and PowerPoint decks, each in some small part exerting and consolidating control over the message, slowly took over.

Now the pendulum is swinging back: The voice of the *individual* is again asserting its fundamental value, this time expressed through its role in building the *collective* conversation as it now occurs online. The Social Web—the combination of social networks, photo and video sharing, blogs, and early conversational communities such as Twitter and Seesmic—is bringing the consumer voice to the fore in a big way. More than a few Chief

Marketing Officers are in a tough spot as a result. Not only do marketers—at all levels—have to deal with the complexity of fragmentation in traditional channels, they are now faced with the outright takeover of brand communications by consumers as they remix, restate, and then republish their version of anything that comes their way. When they agree and amplify your message, it's wonderful. When they don't, it can get ugly fast.

Building on the personal empowerment and liberation that the Internet offers, consumers are actively connecting with each other and sharing information about everything from cars and health to scrapbooking techniques and pool chemicals. In the process, they are either reinforcing marketing efforts or beating marketers at their own game by directly sharing their own experiences and thoughts with each other. Because consumers tend to trust conversations between themselves more than they do advertising, marketers are now finding their messages routinely held up for verification in forums over which they and their ad agencies and PR firms have little, if any, control. For these industries—very much used to control—this is the game changer.

This book is about learning how to *properly* use the Social Web to your *business advantage* and about how to *effectively participate as a marketer* by adopting the underlying behaviors that power the Social Web and making them the basis for your business and marketing plans. It's about the fundamental paradox between *giving up control*—you can't control conversations that aren't yours—and simultaneously *gaining influence* by becoming a respected member in the communities that matter to you. This book is about realizing and putting to business use the powerful connection between participation and influence, and ultimately preparing for and embracing what's next.

How to Use This Book

I designed this book to be used in a variety of ways and by a variety of people. Some readers will have prior experience with social media, some will not. Some will want to jump right in, and some will want to understand what social media is all about before putting their name on a plan that integrates social media into their currently working marketing program. There is something here for everyone.

You can begin reading this book at any point you'd like: Here are some suggested starting points and tips:

- Are you already comfortable with social media and looking to jump right in? If you have a good handle on your social reputation, start with Part III, "The Social Media Channels." You'll quickly cover your primary social media options, and then get right into metrics and the creation of your plan. Do come back and read Parts I and II at some point, because they contain useful insights and best practices supporting what you already know.

- If you're ready to get started but want to first understand how the things you are doing now are driving the conversations you'll discover on the Social Web, start with Part II, "Prepare for Your Social Media Campaign." If you find you have questions about why social media is emerging, take a quick look at Part I as well.

- If you are a seasoned marketer, I'd suggest starting with Part I, "The Foundation of Social Media." The first three chapters are short, about half the length of those that follow. However, they also set the ground rules for the *business use* of social media and provide a solid transition for experts of traditional marketing looking to build new skills in social media. Read these on the train, on the plane, but please, not while driving your car.

- What if you're really new to marketing? What if you're a sole practitioner, looking to understand social media and develop a practice of your own? This book is certainly for you. My only assumption is that you have a basic marketing plan now. If not, then you may want to create that first, using the online planning guide written by marketing expert Shama Hyder. It is specifically for independent professionals and service firms. You'll find the guide at `http://www.afterthelaunch.com/` .

Regardless of where you start, beginning with Part II, each chapter includes a week's worth of exercises and is designed to be completed in sequence in about an hour each day. The result, depending on how you approach the exercises, is either your actual social media plan or a framework for a plan or RFP. If you'd like to skip the exercises—perhaps you are reading the book for "theory and understanding," or maybe you simply want an overview of social media and its application in marketing—you can do that. The issues, concepts, and techniques presented will still flow logically. Make no mistake though: If you don't do the exercises, you will not come out with a plan. Nonetheless, you will come away with a solid understanding of social media, and why it's an important part of contemporary marketing.

Finally, a note to established social media practitioners: You'll recognize the risk in writing about a subject as dynamic and broad as social media. There are as many ways to approach our emerging discipline as there are early pioneers helping to define it. My hope is that you will find this book useful, if only as a guide to help your clients understand the importance of your counsel on the critical issues of participation, transparency, and quantitative measurement. With those three right, the rest of the pieces tend to fall into place.

Mostly, enjoy this book. This is an exciting time, and opportunity is everywhere. Be a part of it.

Disclosure

Within this book, I have included references to over 100 companies and practitioners, a handful of which I am formally associated with—for example, as a co-founder, part owner, engaged within a client relationship, or in which I have a similar interest that deserves disclosure. If there is a number one best practice on the Social Web, it is being transparent. Let transparency start with me. As referenced in the book, these companies are:

Bazaarvoice

Digital Voodoo

FG SQUARED

HearThis.com

Jive Software

Lithium Technology

Mikons

Minggl

Pluck

ProductPulse

Wakesites

The Foundation of Social Media

Building on the personal empowerment and liberation that the Internet offers, consumers are actively connecting with each other and talking about everything from cars and health to scrapbooking techniques and pool chemicals. In the process, they are either reinforcing marketing efforts or beating marketers at their own game by directly sharing their own experiences and thoughts on the Social Web.

In Part I, you'll gain an understanding of not only the growing consumer attraction to social media but also the causes of consumer frustration with traditional media. These trends — each significant in their own right — amplify each other when combined. I'll end with a working definition of social media and a framework to understand how to apply social media to your business or organization.

I

Backlash

In 2004 I read an article written jointly by Jim Nail, at the time a Principal Analyst at Forrester Research, and Pete Blackshaw, then Chief Marketing Officer for Intelliseek. They quantified and defined the extent to which a sample set of trend-indicating online consumers were "pushing back" against traditional media. This was a turning point for me — I was working at GSD&M IdeaCity, an ad agency in Austin, TX, where I was helping develop the online and integrated marketing strategy team. This was also around the time when the first contemporary social networks began to gain critical mass, something that caught my attention and became the focus of my work.

In this opening chapter, I'll cover the origin of the Social Web and the events that ushered in the capabilities that consumers now enjoy as they make daily use of the information available to them.

1

Chapter Contents

The Early Social Networks

My first involvement with online services was in 1986. I had just purchased a Leading Edge Model "D" (so that I could learn about the kinds of things one might do with a personal computer). I signed up as a member of Prodigy, launched a couple of years earlier by CBS, IBM, and Sears. The underlying premise of Prodigy was that advertisers — attracted by members — would play a key role in the business success of what was called the first "consumer online service." On the typical Prodigy page, the lower one-third of the screen was devoted to ads. These ads — more or less untargeted by today's standards — were nonetheless a significant advancement in the potential for a marketer to directly reach an *individual*. Although it hadn't been put to use yet, that computer screen — unlike a TV — had a unique physical address. The opportunity for truly personal adverting took a step forward.

Prodigy, and in particular its contemporaries CompuServe and America Online, were in many ways the forerunners of present social networks and targeted online advertising. The thinking was that reaching a large number of *individuals* was not only potentially more valuable than reaching a homogenous mass audience, *but that through technology, marketers just might be able to actually do it.*

Individual, person-to-person connections have always been highly valued. The "real-world" community status of highly localized professionals — think of doctors, preachers, and insurance agents — comes from the fact that they are personally acquainted with each of the *individuals* that make up their overall customer base. This gives them the advantage of a highly personalized level of service. Assuming the service itself is acceptable (and if it's not, they are quickly out of business), this personal bond translates directly into *loyalty*, the ultimate goal of brand marketers. Rather than failing to recognize the value of one-to-one efforts — no rocket science there — it was a logistical challenge that thwarted market-wide adoption of highly localized, personal advertising. Simply put, a mechanism to efficiently reach *individuals* on a large scale didn't exist. In the early nineties, that changed.

Although it had been in development for a number of years, the Internet as we know it today began its climb when the National Science Foundation (NSF) and its forward-thinking National Science Foundation Network (NSFNET) program laid the ground rules for it. It was the NSF that championed the cause of an "open" Internet — a network that any entity, *including a business*, could use for any purpose, *including commerce.* Combined with the proliferation of low-cost personal computers, the opening up of the Internet set in place the path we are now on. Today, we are realizing the "Global Village," a term coined by Wyndham Lewis in 1948 and popularized by Marshall McLuhan in 1964 in his seminal work "Understanding Media." The Global Village is understood in both an historical and contemporary context through this partial excerpt from Wikipedia: The social and personal interactive norms preceeding the 1960s are "being replaced...by what McLuhan calls 'electronic interdependence,' an era when electronic media replace[s] visual culture, producing cognitive shifts and new social organizations." That certainly sounds familiar now.

The release of Prodigy and the significance of the potential of its integrated ad platform in targeting individuals is best understood in the context of the prevailing advertising mediums of the time and in particular television. Under the leadership and vision of NBC executive Pat Weaver, TV had shifted in the 1950s from a locally controlled, single-advertiser-per-show model to a network controlled, multi-advertiser (aka "magazine") model. While this was great for the networks, marketers, and ad agencies — reaching national-scale audiences was good for business as it provided operational and marketing efficiency — it also meant that viewers were treated more and more like a "mass" audience. With only four networks in place — CBS, NBC, ABC, and for a bonus point (see sidebar), name the fourth — mass advertising was clearly the wave of the future. To be fair, media planning and placement meant that Geritol was directed primarily toward an audience with an older skew or component. As a young kid, however, I saw plenty of Geritol ads while I watched Ed Sullivan and wondered how a person could ever need "more energy." Fifty years later, I know the answer: I now get my daily wings from Red Bull. Beyond big buckets such as "older" or "female," the targeting capability we now take for granted wasn't really possible. While some degree of targeting was achievable on early radio or locally controlled TV prior to the rise of the national networks, the ability to target a message to an individual was severely limited.

Bonus Point:

Name the fourth TV network active in the 1940s and '50s. Hint: It's *not* Fox, and I've given you a clue in Figure 1.1.

The fourth network, known for shows like Faraway Hill, Rhythm Rodeo, and Chicagoland Mystery Players was The DuMont Network.

Figure 1.1 The New York Headquarters of the Fourth Network

150 East 34th Street, New York. (Scott Murphy — http://members.aol.com/smurphy110/mid/515madsn.htm)

The Pushback Begins

During the early years of television, ads made up less than ten minutes of each one-hour show. The time devoted to commercials has more than doubled since then, with many half-hour shows now showing about equal amounts of program content and advertising. With this much time being devoted to what has become "content" in its own right — look no further than the Super Bowl ads for proof of the notion that ads are a distinct form of entertainment — it's not surprising that a "pushback" began. The pushback was driven in a large part by the confluence of two major factors: the rise of the Baby Boomers and the arrival of the Internet-connected personal computer.

Spurred on by Boomer spending on electronics and the proliferation of the personal computer, by the mid-nineties the number of Internet websites had climbed from the 6,000 or so of 1992 to more than 1 million — and that was just the beginning. Email — still considered to be one of the earliest "killer apps" — had taken off as well. A developing world it was, too: while it seems incredible, into the mid-nineties email servers around the world sat open and unprotected, an "oversight" that would prove pivotal in the advent of the Social Web. Back then, if you knew the IP address or name of the server, *you could use it to send mail*, no questions asked. We're talking about mail that recipients would actually get and read. Commercial mail hadn't really happened yet; however, the combination of the NSFNET lifting the ban on using the Internet for commercial purposes and the relatively unprotected nature of mail servers made what happened next inevitable. The big question of when — and not if — this new medium would be used for advertising and whether or not this would be accepted on a large scale was on more than a few people's minds. It was a question just waiting to be answered.

Hotel Exercise

Don't try this at home. Instead, try it in a hotel room. When you're in an unfamiliar city — and when all you have is a relatively crude remote control — try channel-surfing to find out what's on television. Unless you have a favorite channel and can jump right to it, the odds are higher that you'll find a commercial rather than program content. The ads can be so thick you'll find yourself "surfing commercials." Don't believe it? Try it.

A Big Boost from an Unlikely Source

On April 12, 1994, husband and wife Laurence Canter and Martha Siegel unknowingly gave social media — still more than 10 years in the future — a big boost when they provided an answer to the question of whether or not email could be used for advertising: It could. The "Green Card" spam that they launched is generally considered the first unsolicited email advertisement sent over the Internet. The result was explosive, on both sides. Enterprising minds quickly realized there was money to be made — lots of money — and relatively little actual regulation that could be applied to constrain them. The term "spammer" — loosely based, unfairly, on Hormel's canned meat — was coined to describe people sending email filled with questionable content. But if you could stand the heat coming from those who made it their business to thwart this new-found advertising channel, you could get rich. Real rich. Real fast.

Just as quickly, recipients and their Internet Service Providers (ISPs) realized that this practice — novel as it was — was fundamentally objectionable, so they went to work on countermeasures. Cancelbot—the first antispam tool developed to automatically cancel the online accounts of suspected spammers — launched an entire movement of antispam tools. In 1997, author and Austin resident Tracy LaQuey Parker filed and won one of the first successful antispam lawsuits. (If you'd like to read the judicial opinion, I've included a reference to it in the Appendix of this book.) A domain she owned — Flowers.com — was used by Craig Nowak (aka C.N. Enterprises) to launch a spam campaign falsely identified as originating from Flowers.com and Austin ISP Zilker Internet Park. Oops.

Why Does This Matter?

The arrival of spam — *on a communications channel that recipients had control over* — shattered a peaceful coexistence that had been in place for the past 30 years. Viewers had accepted interruptions more or less without complaint as the quid pro quo for free TV (and amazingly, albeit to a lesser extent on for-pay cable as well). Even if they objected, short of changing channels there was little they could do. Ads were part of the deal. The Internet — and in particular an email inbox — was different. First, it was "my" inbox, and "I" presumed the "right" to decide what landed in it, not least because I was paying for it! Second, spam — unlike TV ads — could actually clog my inbox, slow down the Net, and generally degrade "my" experience. People took offense to that, on a *collective* scale. Spam had awakened a giant, and that giant has been pushing back on intrusive ads ever since. *On the Social Web, interruptions do not result in a sustainable conversation. In their purest form, all conversations are participative and engaged in by choice. This simple premise goes a long way in explaining why interruption and deception on the Social Web are so violently rejected.*

The relevance of these particular events and those that have followed in driving the evolution of social media cannot be overstated. In one sense, the issues raised by spam — the practice of sending a highly interruptive, often untargeted message to a recipient — triggered a discussion about how advertising in an electronic age could, and more importantly *should*, work. At the same time, in the early days the messages weren't as bad, the emails not as junky, and the content not so disgusting. In the early days, it was about an annoyance for techies and a perceived (and misunderstood) opportunity for marketers. The questions were as much about how to make money as they were anything else, and not enough forethought was given to the recipient experience. Regardless, these discussions gave rise to the idea that *recipients should have control* over what was sent their way. The fact that their personal attention was worth money — something that ad execs had long known — was suddenly central in the discussions of the thought leaders who pushed all the harder against those who abused the emerging channels.

The offensive nature of spam, in particular, inflicted collateral damage on the ad industry as a whole. Ironically, and much to its own loss, the ad industry did little to stop it. Unsolicited email rallied people against advertising intrusion, and a lot of otherwise good work got caught in the crossfire. In contrast to TV ads, for example, spam fails to pay its own way, fails to entertain, and often contains deceptive messages. These are not the standards on which advertising was built. At GSD&M IdeaCity, the agency where I spent many years, agency co-founder Tim McClure coined the "Uninvited Guest" credo. The "Uninvited Guest" basically holds that a commercial is an interruption. As such, it is the duty of the marketer and advertiser collectively to "repay" the viewer, for example, by creating a moment of laughter or compassion that genuinely entertains. It is this quid pro quo that transforms the interruption into an invitation. This symbiotic relationship sat at the base of an ad system that had worked well, and with relatively few complaints, for 50-plus years. Beginning with Tide's creation of soap operas and the Texas Star Theater in the '40s up to the Mobil-sponsored Masterpiece Theater in the '70s, viewers readily accepted that advertisers were paying the freight in exchange for attention to their products and services. Measurable good will accrued to sponsors simply by virtue of having underwritten these programs.

No more. By violating the premise of the "Uninvited Guest," spammers brought to the fore a second and much more powerful notion among consumers: spammers raised awareness of the value of control over advertising *at the recipient level*. Spammers galvanized an entire audience (against them) and created a *demand* for control over advertising at a personal level. With TV, radio, magazines, and even direct mail — the United States Postal Service (USPS) has long enforced the rights of marketers to use its services so long as they paid for it — there was no viable means through which a recipient could select or moderate — much less block — commercial messages short of turning off the device. With digital communications, control elements are now built in; they are an expected part of the fabric that links us. If advertisers and network executives are experiencing angst over contemporary consumer-led "ad avoidance," they have, among others, Laurence Canter and Martha Siegel to thank. By introducing unsolicited messages into a medium over which recipients can and readily do take ownership and control, the actions of the earliest for-personal-gain commercial spammers created in consumers both the awareness of the need for action and the exercise of personal control over incoming advertising. Antispam tools ranging from blacklists to spam filters are now the norm.

As spammers continued to proliferate, spam became not only a nuisance but a significant expense for systems owners and recipients alike. It was only a matter of time before legislation followed. In 2003 the CAN-SPAM act was signed into law. This was significant in the sense that legislation had been enacted that in part had its roots in the issues of recipient control over incoming advertising. This further validated — and pushed mainstream — the idea that "I own my inbox." From this point forward, it would be more difficult as a marketer to reach consumers using email without some form of permission or having passed through at least a rudimentary inbox spam filter. It wasn't just email that felt the impact of growing consumer awareness of the control that now existed over interruptive advertising.

On the Web, a similar development was taking place. In 1994, HotWired ran what were among the first online ads. Created by Modem Media and partner Tangent Design for AT&T, these ads invited viewers to "click here." GNN was running similar ads on its network, and others would follow. That the HotWired ads ran less than two weeks after the initial-release version (0.9) of Netscape's first browser made clear that advertising and the online activities of consumers were linked from the get-go. The first online ads were simple banners: they appeared on the web page being viewed, generally across the top. Page views could be measured. DoubleClick founder Kevin O'Connor took it a step further: DoubleClick made the business of advertising — online anyway — quantitatively solid. With online advertising now seen as fundamentally measurable, marketers sat up and took notice. Online advertising quickly established itself as a medium to watch. One of the results of the increasing attention paid by marketers and advertisers to online media was an increased effort in creating ads that would "cut through the clutter" and get noticed. As if right out of *The Hucksters,* someone indeed figured out a way. It was called the *pop-up.*

Like an animated "open-me-first" gift tag, the pop-up is a cleverly designed ad format that opens up on top of the page being viewed. Variants open under the page or even after it is closed. Here again, it's useful to go back to TV, radio, and to an extent, print. Certainly, in the case of the TV, when the show's suspense is built to a peak… only to cut away to a commercial, that is a supreme interruption. But it was tolerated, and even desired. The interruption provided a way to freeze and "stretch out" the moments of suspense. The pop-up is different. It's not about suspense or entertainment. It's about obnoxious interruptive behavior that demands attention right now.

So, it wasn't long before the first pop-up "blocker" was developed and made available. Its development points out the great thing about "open" technology, and one of the hallmarks of the Social Web: open digital technology empowers *both* sides. As brands like Orbitz made heavy use of pop-ups, others went to work just as hard on countermeasures (described in Brian Morrissey's article "Popular Pop-Ups?" at www.clickz.com/showPage.html?page=1561411). Partly in response to marketers such as X10 and Orbitz, in 2002 Earthlink became the first ISP to provide a pop-up blocker free to its members. Again, the notion that an ad recipient had the right to control an incoming message was advanced, and again it was embraced. Pop-up blockers are now a standard "add-on" in most web browsers. The motivation for the Social Web and user-centric content *control* was going mainstream.

Heat Maps: Passive Ad Avoidance

Passive ad avoidance — the practice of sitting within view or earshot of an ad but effectively ignoring it — has been documented by Jakob Nielsen and others through visualizations such as the *heat maps* shown in Figure 1.2. Using eye movement detection devices, maps of eye movement during page scans show that most consumers now know where to look...and where not to look. The advertisements in Figure 1.2 are the least-viewed areas on the page. Complete information on Jakob Nielsen's "Banner Blindness" study may be found at www.useit.com/alertbox/banner-blindness.html.

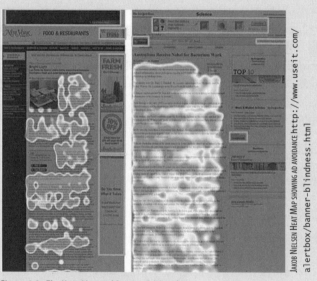

JAKOB NIELSEN HEAT MAP SHOWING AD AVOIDANCE http://www.useit.com/alertbox/banner-blindness.html

Figure 1.2   The Heat Map and Passive Ad Avoidance

It was therefore only a matter of time before the combination of formal ad avoidance and content control would emerge in the mainstream *offline* channels. It happened in 1999, with the first shipments of ReplayTV and then TiVo digital video recorders, launched at the Consumer Electronics Show. From the start, the digital video recorder (DVR) concept was loved by viewers. To say it was "controversial" among advertisers, programmers, and network operators is putting it lightly. While initial penetration was low — just a few percent of all households had a DVR — in the first couple of years after launch, the impact and talk-level around a device that could be used to skip commercials was huge. Most of the early DVRs had a 30-second skip-ahead button — a function now curiously missing from most. Thirty seconds is the standard length of a TV spot: this button might as well have been labeled "Skip Ad." Combined with the fact that a DVR can be used to record shows for viewing later, the DVR was disruptive to TV programming. In one easy-to-use box, a DVR brings control over *what* is seen — unwanted or irrelevant commercials can be skipped as easily as boring segments of a show — and control over *when* it is seen.

Right behind the changes affecting TV were those aimed at the telephone. Long a bastion for among the most annoying of interruptive marketers — those who call during dinner — the telemarketing industry felt the impact of consumer control as the Do Not Call Implementation Act of 2003 substantially strengthened the Telephone Consumer Protection Act of 1991. The Implementation Act established a list through which any consumer can register his or her phone number and thereby reduce the number of incoming telemarketing calls. There are some exceptions — nonprofits, political candidates, and a handful of others are still allowed to call — but in general the combined acts have been viewed as a success. In fact, nearly 150 million phone numbers have been registered on the Do Not Call Registry. In 2007, an additional act — the Do Not Call Improvement Act — was undertaken to remove the "five year renewal" requirement for those who have registered. Sign up once and you're on the list forever unless you take yourself off of it.

> **Note:** Are you on the Do Not Call list? Here's where to find out and to obtain information about the list: www.donotcall.gov.

The Backlash: Measured and Formalized

Think back to what was covered. A set of basic points that connect past experiences with email, online media, and traditional media to the present state of the Social Web emerges:

- The genie is out of the bottle: consumers and their thought-leading advocates recognize that they own their inbox, their attention, and by extension (rightly or wrongly) the Internet itself.

- Online, people are annoyed with spam, and with pop-ups. Spillover happened, and advertising in general got caught up in the fray.

- Offline, people are now looking around asking, "What other interruptive advertising bothers me?" The Do Not Call list was implemented as a result.

If you take these events together — antispam filters, pop-up blockers, DVRs, and the Do Not Call Registry — it's pretty clear that consumers have taken control over the messages directed their way. The genie is indeed out of the bottle, and it isn't going back in. At the same time, if you consider the number of *beneficial* product- or service-oriented conversations that occur on Facebook, MySpace, and elsewhere on the Social Web using content posted to services ranging from Flickr to YouTube to Twitter, it's also clear that consumers want information about the products and services that interest them. After all, no one wants to make a "bad purchase." Consumers want to know what works, and they want to share great experiences right along with bad ones. More information is generally considered "better," especially when the information originates with someone you know.

Which Brings Us to Trust

The idea of "trust" is perhaps the point on which most of the objectionable ad practices have common ground with each other — that is to say, they *lack* trust — and the central issue on which the acceptance of social media is being built. *It's all about trust.* It's as if the question that consumers are now asking is as follows:

> *"If you have to interrupt or annoy me to get your ad across, how valuable can what your offer really be? If you think I'm dumb enough to fall for this, how can I trust you?"*

The link between consumer backlash and the rise of social media first occurred to me in 2004. Recall that I was reading a report from Forrester Research, written by Forrester analyst Jim Nail. The Executive Summary of the report is as follows:

> *"Consumers feel overwhelmed by intrusive, irrelevant ads. The result: a backlash against advertising — manifesting itself in the growing popularity of do-not-call lists, spam filters, online ad blockers, and ad skipping on digital video recorders (DVRs). Marketing campaigns of the future must facilitate consumers' cross-channel search for information, going beyond the brand promises made in traditional advertising."*

The report further detailed some fundamental insights, all-the-more impactful given that the source of the data was a joint report done by Forrester Research and Intelliseek, now part of Nielsen. The audience was a very good cross-section of "savvy online users" — about two-thirds female, an average household income just more than $50K, 60 percent using broadband, and about 80 percent having five-plus years experience online. This audience was *not* a snapshot of what was then-mainstream, but rather a highly probable indicator of "what's next," of what "mainstream" would become: overwhelmed, with the result being a backlash.

Working in the ad industry at the time, as I read this report I thought, "Wow. This is simultaneously describing what I do as a professional marketer and how I feel as an ordinary consumer." Being a "glass-half-full" kind of guy, I saw in Jim's and Pete's work two distinct opportunities:

- The opportunity to develop a formal marketing practice based on information that consumers *would readily share with each other*

- Quite selfishly, the opportunity to ensure better information for me to use when evaluating my own options as a consumer

Social media and in particular its application in marketing and advertising is at least part of my response to the first of these opportunities. Implemented well, the second follows from it. What social media is all about, and again especially as applied to marketing, is the smart use of the natural conversational channels that develop between individuals.

These conversations may take a positive or negative path — something I'll spend a lot of time on in Chapter 6, "Touchpoint Analysis" and Chapter 7, "Influence and Measurement." Either way, they are happening independently of the actions or efforts of advertisers, with the understanding that just as a marketer can "encourage" these conversations by providing an exceptionally good (or bad!) experience, so too can an advertiser "seed" the conversations by creating exceptional, talk-worthy events. Around these events awareness is created, and a conversation may then flow. Word-of-mouth marketing, like social media, operates in exactly this way. Social media and word-of-mouth are fundamentally related in that both rely on the consumer to initiate and sustain the conversation.

Advertisers can of course play a role in this: advertisers can create images, events, happenings, and similar which encourage consumers — and especially potential customers — to talk or otherwise interact with current customers. Social media and word-of-mouth are also related by the fact that both are controlled by the individual, and not by the advertiser or PR agency. This has a deep impact on the link between Operations and Marketing, a discussion I will take up in Chapter 5, "The Social Feedback Cycle." This theme will recur throughout the balance of Part II of this book.

When you consider the issues that face traditional marketers, and in effect create the motivation for considering complementary methods such as the use of social media in marketing, it's not surprising that many of them are rooted in the core issues of trust, quality of life, value, and similar undeniable aspirations. The issue of trust can be understood best in terms of the word-of-mouth (including "digital word-of-mouth") attributes related to trust. Word-of-mouth is consistently ranked among the most trusted forms of information. As a component of social media, trust seems likely to follow in the word-of-mouth-based exchanges that occur in the context of social media. In fact, it does.

In addition to trust, from an advertiser's perspective, the primary challenges are generally clutter and fragmentation. The sheer numbers of messages combined with a short attention span (developed at least in part by watching stories with a beginning, middle, and end that together last for exactly 30 seconds) are challenges as well. In *Branding for Dummies* (Wiley, 2006), a claim is made that consumers receive approximately "3,000 messages per day." Other citations place that figure in the range of a few hundred to well in excess of a few thousand (one set of estimates is available at http://answers.google.com/answers/threadview?id=56750). Even at the low end of the scale, several hundred messages each and every day means that as humans we have to be actively filtering. That in turn requires some sort of associative decision-making process. In the preface of this book, I made the case that we are social beings and that we have adopted what would be loosely called "social behaviors" because we believe them beneficial. Our ability to deal with incoming information in anything like the volumes estimated makes apparent the need for *collaboration* in problem solving. Through social media — enabled by the Internet and the emergence of the Social Web — we are beginning to embrace those tools that significantly extend our collaborative abilities. These tools, taken as a whole, are the new tools of the social marketer.

Chapter 1: The Main Points

- The emerging role of the individual as a source of content used to inform a purchase decision is increasing as the role of the marketer and traditional media programmer in establishing the primary advertising message diminishes.

- A backlash developed when the practice of pushing ads to consumers moved to the digital platform, a platform over which consumers (end users) actually have control.

- The role of trust is central to marketing effectiveness in contemporary social conversations.

The Marketer's Dilemma

It's ironic that as a powerful force — the Social Web — is emerging, the overwhelming share of media spending is still directed to marketing channels that don't tap it. Part of this is metrics, something I cover beginning in Chapter 7, "Influence and Measurement." Part of it is newness, and part of it is the continued performance of mass media. Regardless, the primary challenge facing marketers remains: cutting through the clutter. From the consumer's perspective, marketers are the clutter. By comparison, the Social Web is an oasis. The challenge marketers face now isn't just competition from other marketers. It's from consumers themselves, turning to each other, avoiding ads. Savvy marketers are turning to social media and the opportunity to market without using ads at all.

2

Chapter Contents

The Roots of Avoidance

Growing out of clutter and media saturation comes a predictable viewer response: ad avoidance. Traditional marketers and media firms have largely ignored the issue of avoidance, favoring interruptive "tricks" such as the apparent volume boosts in the audio track of a TV ad, the use of an interstitial ad online, or an envelope promising savings on auto insurance based on a personal assessment when the contents are merely an impersonal pitch. Media mainstays like reach and frequency, neither a true measure of receipt or action taken have become surrogates for effectiveness, as if the simple act of *exposure* is somehow the same as *influence*. Viewership studies that confirm that Americans still watch plenty of TV too often add to the sense of complacency: According to Nielsen Media Research Study completed in 2006, American homes were connected to the TV for more time each day than a typical person spends in the office working.

As a kid, I sold boxes of all-purpose greeting cards door-to-door. I got used to "avoidance" early-on. I'd knock, someone would answer, and I'd introduce myself. I'd show my cards and ask if maybe someone was having a birthday or was sick or had passed away...and just about that time *SLAM* would go the door. Fortunately, there was always another house next door. But it did get me thinking about the product: How could someone not be excited to learn more about what I was offering? Perhaps I was selling the wrong thing, or maybe the sickness and death angle wasn't all that appealing. So I did what any smart marketer would do: based on customer data, I re-evaluated my product and changed my pitch.

I switched to Christmas cards, pre-printed with the customer's name and personal message. Bingo! All I needed to do was hold out that catalog and say "This year, you won't have to sign 100 cards." I was selling joy, and it was an instant sale. Even better, after ordering from me, they'd call their friends and refer me to them, too. What I discovered has stayed with me: If what you are offering has an obvious benefit and fully delivers on the promise, your customers will spontaneously engage and *talk with others about it*. The pure simplicity of genuine engagement, combined with the conveyance of real control *as they spread your word* to potential customers is at the root of the conversations that occur on the Social Web.

Ad avoidance isn't a new phenomenon. A study done in Canada between 1975 and 1978 found that almost 60 percent of those participating "left the room" when a commercial came on the TV. They grabbed a beer, they headed for the bathroom, they refilled the chips...they did everything but watch the ads. Filtering — separating what we need to know from what we don't need to know — is as old as humanity. That bad news travels faster than good news through an office is testament to our innate capacity to prioritize "lurking tiger" (bad news) over "tree full of oranges" (good news). Think back to the "3,000 messages" per day reference and the kinds of intense messaging that occurs in places like Times Square, shown in Figure 2.1, and in cities and along highways throughout the world.

Figure 2.1 Message Overload, Times Square

Even if it's only partially true, absent our ability to filter, our heads would explode. There is actually a medical term — *hypermnesia* — for people who "can't forget," people whose heads are so filled with extraneous details that they have difficulty processing a normal information flow. Avoidance, selection, filtering...all are necessary human abilities. It isn't at all surprising that they are applied to your marketing message.

What is surprising is that marketers in many ways refuse to accept this basic premise, or choose to operate in ways that seek to make avoidance impossible. *It can't be done.* Recall Alex DeLarge in the film *A Clockwork Orange*, eyes propped open with mechanical lidlocks as he is reprogrammed through the Ludovico Technique by forced exposure to video imagery and music. In much the same way, out-of-home advertisers like skywriters, shown in Figure 2.2, refer to beachgoers in crowded spots such as Rio de Janeiro or Fort Lauderdale, FL, as "captive eyeballs." As they see these potential consumers, there isn't enough room on the beach to roll over, so they pretty much have to look up!

While this may be a relatively humorous (but factual) example, the core issue is the contradiction between "consumer as king" or "consumer in control" versus "consumer as target" or even worse, "consumer as object." No one treats a king — especially a king who's in control — the way too many marketers treat too many consumers. When you stop and think about the language that most of us *in the marketing profession* use on a daily basis, it isn't surprising at all that consumers are expressing a fundamental objection to what they see as an encroachment on their personal lives. Customers once referred to by name have over time become "prospects" and are now called "targets." Captive audiences are especially prized. Reach and frequency culminate in "saturation," a measure of the brain's limit of meaningful absorption. Maybe lid-locks *are* what's next! According to Yankelovich, a firm known for its studies of consumer behavior, 65 percent of Americans say they are "constantly bombarded with too much advertising" and 61 percent think the quantity of advertising and marketing they are exposed to "is out of control." Likely as a result, 60 percent reported that their view of advertising is "much more negative than just a few years ago." Keep in mind that this was a 2004 study: this data is a few years old, to be sure, but I haven't noticed any decline in ad density since it was conducted.

Figure 2.2 Crowded beaches make a perfect venue for skywriters.

What all of this points to — and even more so when combined with the technology within easy grasp of mainstream Americans, online and off — is the growing "acceptance of ad avoidance." Network execs can cry foul all day long, but from a consumer's perspective there is nothing wrong with skipping ads. Recall from Chapter 1, "Backlash," that from 1930 to 1980 there was a relatively peaceful coexistence between advertisers and viewers. For 50 years, give or take, viewers accepted advertisements as a part of the otherwise "free" TV and radio programming that they enjoyed. Sponsors were central to the first shows. In fact, the "ad men" actually *created* the shows that the networks aired. From the movie *The Hucksters* comes the famous line, "If you [ad men] build the most glamorous, high Hooper rating show on the air, it ain't gonna do us a damn bit of good unless you can figure out some way to sell soap on it."

Pat Weaver, running NBC, changed this programming model when he moved content production to the network studios. In the process, he created contemporary network programming. In response, advertising agencies — and in particular those involved with TV and radio — increased the overall number of ads and products offered as many new shows were created. They reduced the length of spots and tied the advertising to *who was watching* rather than *what they were watching*. They created the current-day "ad pod," the collection of two to eight short spots that run back-to-back every two to five minutes during a show. By the late eighties and early nineties, commercials were essentially on par with actual programming in terms of both content production values and raw airtime. If this seems a stretch, consider that commercials account for 10 to 15 minutes of most 30-minute shows. With a DVR you can watch

"The Daily Show" and "Colbert," back-to-back, in about the same time as it takes to watch either one without the DVR. Ads became uninvited interruptions. Some "paid their way" by entertaining us. Others...were just "in the way." As the clutter-factor came to the fore, consumers began to push back: Adbusters Media Foundation — started in 1989 by Kalle Lasn — originated in response to the timber industry using TV to plant the term "forestry management" in the minds of the public. This outraged Lasn, and Adbusters was born. Today, Adbusters Media Foundation is ironically a brand of its own but also still true to its roots as a source of dialogue on the appropriate role of advertising. Adbusters Media Foundation and other forums like it offer a point for marketers to heed: Consumers have attained a level of expertise and sophistication with regard to their judgment of advertising that far surpasses that of their fifties and sixties counterparts. Mistrust and avoidance are predictable endpoints for messages and campaign methods that fail to respect contemporary consumer sensibilities. From *Advertising Age* in 2004 comes this thought:

> *"It is better for the industry to act voluntarily. Otherwise, after a long court battle, angry citizens will get rid of the commercial speech doctrine and replace it with the right to be left alone."*

> — Gary Ruskin, Executive Director of Commercial Alert, published in *Advertising Age*, April 26, 2004

Indeed.

Early Online Word-of-Mouth

Perhaps in direct response to the growing sophistication of marketing and advertising — and our own growing consumerism — people began tapping the fledgling Internet as a place where they could share and extend collective thought. Early member communities — CompuServe, AOL, Tripod, and Geocities, along with legions of focused efforts such as SmartGirl Internette (now `smartgirl.org`) — evolved as the forerunners of the Social Web. Common to all of these was the *exchange between members* of information across a range of topics. On CompuServe it was technical; on AOL it was largely personal interest. What mattered more though, in the long run, was that *members were talking to members* rather than reading scripted or editorial content provided by experts. These early communities were built on the premise that the *members would make the content.* Email was the original "killer app," a term describing an application of a technology that is itself so compelling that everyone simply has to have it. Email pointed the way for an interpersonal-communications-oriented network. Content is just now emerging as the primary activity for those online: Up through about 2006, communications — not content — led in terms of the share of time that people spent online. Think about the task-focused mom using the Web to compile and evaluate household needs or the family in search of a campground in the mountains. This type of use stood in contrast to media like TV, where entertainment and enter- tainment-style news ruled. The shift to content that happened in 2006 was driven at least in part by the growth of consumer-generated content (and a good dose of profes- sionally generated content) on sites like YouTube.

From a marketer's perspective, the important element driving the surge in word- of-mouth is "trust." Given the damage done by pop-ups and spam, along with the ad industry's relatively light response to the former and outright embracement of the latter, the value of "trust" between friends and colleagues gained in its role in purchase decisions. It is exactly this sentiment that drives word-of-mouth, and now social media. The dynamics of trust have long been part of the marketing conversation. Early studies on advertising and trust confirmed what many had suspected: advertising is a great way to hear about something new, but the information presented is not, by itself, considered "trustworthy." Hear about it in an ad, but then ask your friends if it's any good. Pete Blackshaw bought a Honda hybrid based on the ads and pre-purchase research. A whole lot of people since have purchased a Toyota Prius based on his well- documented post-purchase experience.

Word-of-mouth, from a consumer, is generally considered trustworthy. But what about when the source is a marketer? How can you use word-of-mouth in your own campaigns? This same question turns out to be fundamental to the use of social media. Parodies of "truth in advertising" aside, there is a basic, healthy human skepti- cism present whenever someone is making the case for why you need what he or she is selling. It's the cross-purposes of the transaction — in its most extreme an outright conflict of interest — that gets in the way. If I profit by your purchase, then I have at least one reason to push for closure that may not be aligned with my regard for your best interest. The interest in my *making a sale* invariably colors the transaction. Word-of-mouth marketing firms such as BzzAgent go to great lengths to ensure dis- closure on behalf of their clients; that they have to do this in the first place makes the case for why nontransactional word-of-mouth is considered "trusted." By comparison, marketers — regardless of otherwise positive attributes of the brand — always have an incentive to make the sale. This is why *transparency* — the outright, unambiguous disclosure that you are in fact a marketer — is so essential in both word-of-mouth and social-media-based campaigns. It is perhaps the most powerful point on which you can establish trust. *"If I am willing to disclose my own self-interest, then there is good rea- son to consider 'truthful' the balance of what I might say."*

Ironically, it's when the advertising and marketing is low-key or absolutely quiet that the "trust" factor is highest. "Here, I made this. It's for sale. Buy it and try it out. If you like it, great. If not, you can give it back and I will refund 100 percent of your money." More than a few brands have built themselves largely or purely on the combination of a great product and word-of-mouth: Starbucks, Red Bull, Hotmail, and Amazon come to mind. In the case of Amazon, while they advertised early on, they felt the return did not justify the expense. So, in 2003 they dropped the ads and offered free shipping on orders over $25. The result was explosive in terms of word-of-mouth. Instantly, everyone knew that "shipping was free" at Amazon, something that served them well on two counts. First, there was the obvious benefit of positive word-of-mouth. Second, the conversation centered on one of the central objections from the consumer perspective with regard to online shopping: the incremental cost of shipping versus buying from a store. By removing this objection from the conversation, Amazon had made itself the obvious place to buy. The rest is history.

In the same way, brands ranging from Old Spice to Craftsman have built themselves — *with* advertising — while following this same path: "If you don't like it, or if it breaks, we'll make good for it." It works with basic packaged goods: "Try Old Spice. If you don't like it, we'll buy you whatever you normally use." When I talked with Larry Walters, who created that campaign, he said he'd yet to be asked to buy a competing brand for a dissatisfied customer. This type of guarantee also works in more substantial purchases: Craftsman — the Sears in-house brand of hand tools — has long offered a simple guarantee: "If our tool breaks — if it *ever* breaks — we'll hand you a new one. Free." Remarkably, that guarantee will emerge in *any* conversation with *anyone* who uses Craftsman hand tools, *even though most have never had a Craftsman tool break*. Want proof? While I was writing, Hilary Powers, the developmental editor working on the book with me, shared the following:

> *"My mother had a pair of pruning shears break after 20 years of steady use, and she took them along to the store to make sure she bought the same thing again. The clerk pounced on her and sent her off with a new pair free — and that tale got told and retold."*

"Satisfaction Guaranteed" is a fundamentally powerful guarantee which at once conveys quality and largely removes the self-interest in the sales pitch. Yes, Sears wants to sell you a tool. But in the same transaction, Sears is also agreeing to enter into a lifelong, binding, irrevocable contract of performance. That is the kind of transaction that builds trust. That is the kind of experience that gets talked about.

Word-of-mouth applies to non-transactional campaigns as well: Advergaming— an early form of interpersonal media — is largely built on word-of-mouth. In 2003, Dial Corporation, working with our group at GSD&M Ideacity, released "Coast BMX Full Grind" (shown in Figure 2.3), a video game created by Wild Tangent based on the Activision title "Matt Hoffman's ProBMX." The game built on the action inherent in the underlying title, and featured added brand elements along with some new BMX tricks and riding areas created specifically for the advergame. High-score and "challenge boards" ensured that the game — made available for free — would receive wide circulation. The most telling aspect of the game in regard to word-of-mouth and trust came, oddly, in a *complaint* from a player. As the strategy director for this project, I wound up fielding the complaint. It is always a good test of the mettle and prowess of a social media team when the challenge of handling objections arises. A particular player was absolutely livid with the fact that we had "ripped off" his favorite game (Activision's ProBMX) and produced this "advertisement" based on it. He was personally writing to Matt (Hoffman) and urging him to sue us. I wrote him back, within an hour or so of the time he sent his email. I explained that we had worked with Activision, that the game was fully licensed, and that Matt was okay with this. I wanted to address first what he was upset about. But I also took a further step: I explained that we had built the game for him to share with his friends who didn't have the game that he loved so much, and that we had created some new riding spaces and tricks that he may not have seen before. In other words, I connected him to the underlying objective of the campaign: participation with friends in something that is genuinely fun and totally on the up-and-up. I clicked "Send." The same day, I got an email back. He not only apologized, he went on to become one of the highest scorers and biggest promoters of the game. He got the fact that we had thought about him and his friends, and built something for them to enjoy. As a result, we earned his trust, and he rewarded us by *talking about it.*

Figure 2.3 "Coast BMX Full Grind"

Compare this with examples where trust itself is feigned — only to be discovered as false. In 2002, Sony Ericsson launched a street campaign for its T68i that involved the use of actors presenting themselves as tourists visiting New York City. They got caught, and even then they tried to explain it away. Instead of two simple words — "I'm sorry" — the response tried to make light of the issue of transparency and reaction to the campaign. Given that response, they predictably made the same mistake again in 2006 with their "All I want for Christmas is a PSP" fake blog campaign. In 2005, Wal-Mart became entangled in a "fake blog" campaign. Dubbed "Wal-Marting Across America," couple Jim and Laura blogged about their drive in an RV across the country with nightly stops in Wal-Mart parking lots. Overnight RV parking is something Wal-Mart has always allowed. This particular policy makes for great social press: RVers — who get together and chat nearly every evening — save both money and time by spending an occasional evening at a convenient Wal-Mart. It's also a great business move for Wal-Mart. After all, RVers need supplies, right? Despite the "real" nature of Jim and Laura, the campaign nonetheless blew up as neither Wal-Mart nor its PR agency, Edelman, disclosed the connection between Jim, Laura, and Wal-Mart in the early stages of the campaign.

Figure 2.4 Wal-Marting Across America

Ironically, the Wal-Mart and Sony Ericsson campaigns probably would have worked if they had fully disclosed. "Hi. I work for Sony. Would you mind taking a picture of me and my friends?" Most people would have said "sure" and then *asked* about the camera phone. Wal-Marting Across America could have been really interesting, in the same way that any reality show or travel series is. On the Social Web, transparency is everything. For Wal-Mart, rightly or wrongly at the center of controversy over its internal and "secret" practices, getting caught in this campaign was doubly damaging. Not only did it tank the campaign — which could have played out through a contest or a variety of other cool and talk-worthy methods — it actually added credibility to those whose cause it is to *discredit* Wal-Mart.

Both examples — Wal-Mart and Sony Ericsson — point up not only the role of trust in word-of-mouth but also the degree to which campaigns that could have *succeeded* can take on larger-than-life proportions when trust is — *or even appears to be* — violated. This has huge implications for marketers interested in social media. Not only is trust the essential element, it is a sure bet that violators will get caught. The collective is simply too connected — and too skeptical. They'll dig in and ferret out the truth given even a slight indication that the setting for any given social campaign is not what it appears to be.

This happens on the Social Web for two reasons: first, calling back to "my ownership of my inbox," there is now a movement among people who actively seek out violators. Second, the connections back to the sponsoring brand tend to highlight themselves, in much the same way as the Wizard's true identity was revealed in Oz when Toto pulled the curtain back *out of simple curiosity*. On the Social Web, it is just too easy to make the connections to *not* notice who is in fact controlling the campaign. Disclosure is therefore an essential element of any social-media-based campaign.

One final point about word-of-mouth and trust. I've selected this example because it shows how "deception" can be used "properly," just as a creative writer properly withholds certain elements until the delivery of the punch line. To promote its "Madden 2004" release, Sega and its agency creative directors Ty Montague and Todd Waterbury created "Beta-7," *a classic hoax* designed to pull people in and generate word-of-mouth. That it did. With downloads estimated in the millions, the campaign was successful in both building awareness of the game and expanding the audience for the game. The campaign played on the notion of "beta test" downloads, and then added the twist that some early testers had experienced personal problems as a result of exposure to the beta release. Fueling the conversation, early "testers" who had downloaded the software were then sent strongly worded "legal cease and desist" letters from Sega demanding the return of this beta software! This of course only caused them to spread the campaign further...and the game was afoot. In the end, people figured it out, and Sega confirmed the ploy. Unlike Wal-Mart and Sony Ericsson, however, there was little if any negative backlash. Why not? Because the campaign was ultimately intended to be fully transparent. The deception was part of the allure and the campaign was so well done it was embraced by participants. If you are unclear on when or how to assure transparency, here is a simple rule to follow:

Tip: Create your disclosure plan first: make it a central part of your campaign.

If you can't disclose the campaign sponsor and motives, this is a clear signal that you are risking a public backlash on the Social Web.

Confused About Transparency?

Although it may be tempting to conclude "On the Social Web I can lie as long as I don't get caught or can pass it off as a joke," bear in mind that your audience is smarter than that. This is your reputation, and it is through the combination of transparency and actual experience that your reputation on the Social Web is built. Being known as the "nice guy who will try and pull a fast one" isn't necessarily the best positioning you can establish. Sunlight is the best disinfectant, as the saying goes, and nowhere is this more true than on the Social Web.

I mention the Beta-7 campaign simply to point out that the Social Web is filled with people who love to be entertained and who do have a sense of humor. At some level, they understand the difference between fake actors or evidently less-than-transparent bloggers and a game. Was the Madden campaign itself a deception? Yes. Are the light sabers used in *Star Wars* also a deception? Ditto. Last time I checked, both were major hits. Core to the efficacy of online word-of-mouth — and hence to social media and the related advertising and marketing forms it takes — is the combination of an *authentic experience* and *something to talk about*. The Wal-Mart blog, like the Sony Ericsson street campaign, did provide something to talk about. However, they both failed on the "genuine experience" count. Unlike the Beta-7 campaign that delivered on experience and talk-value, the desired outcome of the Wal-Mart and Sony Ericsson campaigns was to inform or persuade *without letting the subjects in on the game.* The sole objective was self-serving: bolstering a reputation and selling more products. The consumer was considered a pawn, and it was for this reason that the subjects reacted as they did when the truth came to be known. The Beta-7 campaign involved consumers as actual participants. The experience was created for their benefit as much as it was to generate awareness of the upcoming release. When the campaign was "fully revealed," the reaction was "Wow! That was a blast! Can we all ride it again?" In fact, we can and we will. These are the kinds of campaigns that can be augmented with consumer-generated content, and the kinds that will succeed as a result on the Social Web. Keep in mind too that your social campaigns are part of an overall integrated approach to marketing: it is the combination of what you say, and what your audience says, across all of the channels you use that determines the outcome of your overall marketing effort.

The Social Web Blooms

The backlash against traditional advertising that is powering the rise of the Social Web is a backlash against intrusions, against falsehoods, and against a lack of respect for the *individual*. Jack Myers, a writer for *MediaPost,* talked in 2004 about "the new media technologies that attack the foundation of intrusive advertising." Note the word "intrusive." Advertising is simply one way that consumers learn about new products and services. Advertising is, in a sense, a start into the process of learning about what is out there, about things you may want or need. The more we know about them, the better informed we are. No one sets out specifically to make poor choices when it comes to purchases. Instead, the real driver for social media and the marketing forms based on it is the near universal objection to intrusions combined with the belief — correct or incorrect — that the information needed to make a smart choice is available on the Internet.

Think about what is probably the number-one "social skill" development for a toddler: learning *not* to interrupt. "Please, not right now, I'm on the phone. I'll be just a minute." We practically make a ritual of this in preschool: sitting quietly, raising your hand, and not blurting the answer out. Then we turn on the TV. It's no wonder kids have a hard time understanding what we mean by "wait your turn." Every 3 minutes, with zero social grace, now arrives before us a commercial. Late night (not that kids should be watching late-night TV) it's even worse: the apparent sound level is boosted to pull you back from the sleep state you had nearly attained. Then comes the high-speed reader who in the last 0.7 seconds of the spot explains why none of what you just saw actually applies to you. It is these practices that people are pushing back on, and it's the Social Web that is emboldening them to do it.

So far in this chapter, I've provided a basis for the backlash against traditional advertising (but wait, there's more...) and made the case for the role of trust. I've hinted at what makes for a successful social campaign. My hope is that it's clear at this point that the backlash is *not* against mass media per se, nor is it really an objection to advertising. Two separate studies conducted by Ferguson and Perse on "Audience Satisfaction among TiVo and ReplayTV Users" — the first in 2000 and a follow-up in 2004 — speak to this. The 2000 study found that people with DVRs actually watched more TV each day — a finding confirmed again in a 2005–2007 Nielsen study — and used their DVRs for recording programs that they would otherwise not see and only to lesser extent for skipping commercials. The second study went on to note that commercials airing during recorded shows were often watched. Further, commercials aired during "live" viewing that piqued interest were often rewound and viewed again. Both underscored *the value of user control over content and the newfound ability to selectively watch "good" content while skipping over fluff.* Ad avoidance is less about skipping ads than it is about skipping irrelevant or intrusive ads. This is an important point to keep in mind as you consider moving onto the Social Web. On the Social Web, irrelevant equals invisible.

Apart from the Social Web itself — its content and its applications — it is important to note the manner in which the Social Web also connects more people than would be possible otherwise. LinkedIn.com and Spock.com are examples of the value *not of direct connections* — save the occasional hermit, we've all got at least a few direct connections — but rather *connections to connections*. These networks multiply the networks we've already built. Amazon directly leverages this: it's not the reviews that provide the real value. It's the *reviews of the reviews*. To be sure, for a lot of purchases the reviews themselves are in fact helpful. If they all say is "this is the worst product ever" then chances are a) it is, and b) you're not going to click "Add to Cart." However, for most purchases, there is a mix between "I love it" and "I hate it." To make sense of these, Amazon offers "reviews of reviews" along with insights of the reviewers themselves. *Amazon extends your network.* Using this extended network, you can actually go one social-level deeper and sort out for yourself which of the reviewers you are most like and pick out the reviews that most other people like you found helpful. This helps you make a better, more informed choice *given your specific needs*. It's that ability to connect as an "individual" that consumers had been looking for back in Chapter 1.

The Social Web, as it expands and exerts itself over at least a portion of contemporary marketing, is driving interconnectedness to new levels. This is the fundamental learning: your customers, using the Social Web, can talk with each other about you and about your products, services, and brand. You can't control it directly. Your messages are only present in these conversations if your customers choose to bring them there, or choose to bring you there. It's a party to which you *can* get invited, and it's on this point that I find so many otherwise solid marketers have difficulty. The most common objection that I hear when talking about "social media" is that "We aren't ready to let our customers talk about us in an open forum, and in particular one that we appear to endorse." In Sections 2 and 3, I will share specific strategies and tactics for seeing this challenge in a new way. For now, I'll simply say this:

Tip: Your customers are already talking about you. The fact that you aren't participating is your implicit endorsement of whatever it is that they are saying.

Not participating on the Social Web is effectively saying, "I know what is being said, and it's okay with me." I don't know about you, but as a business owner when I think about that, I sit up and take notice. How many times have you been in a meeting, been asked for comments, failed to comment, and then told later, "You had your chance to comment, and you didn't, so this project has gone ahead." Marketers, ignore *your invitation to participate* in the conversation at your own peril: This is your chance to be part of it and to influence the outcome through your participation.

Nielsen Shows the Way

I'd be remiss if I didn't talk about *media measurement*. Next to "How do I market on the Social Web," the most often-asked question I get revolves around three letters: ROI — the return on investment that's so important to everyone in business. Measurement is the first step in showing a return. One of the best things about the Social Web, social media, and social-media-based advertising is that like online media it is fundamentally measurable. Industry leaders like Nielsen have put real measurement practices in place. Beginning in 2006 and continuing today, Nielsen provides estimates of DVR usage in its standard reporting: in mid-2006, about 9 percent of the Nielsen households had DVRs. This projected adoption compares well with current data: Nielsen reports approximately 25% actual adoption in 2008. As shown in Figure 2.5, eMarketer goes on to project a DVR penetration of about 30 percent by 2010.

DVR and VOD-enabled Household Penetration in the U.S.
(% of TV Households)

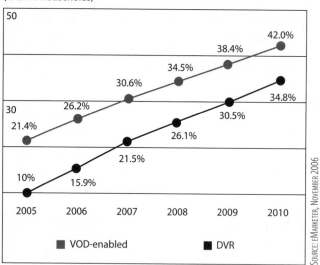

Figure 2.5 DVR penetration

When you consider the demographics of households with DVRs — for example, residents of Los Angeles are more likely than average to have a DVR, as are households with home theater and similar entertainment centers — the projected penetration will have significant impact in the ways in which TV and video-based advertising is viewed. That Nielsen and others are adding alternatives to traditional TV to their reporting mix is a very good thing.

For traditional marketers, it means that there is a path from the data you are used to getting to the data you'll be getting and using as you develop your social media metrics. Firms like BuzzMetrics (now part of Nielsen), New Media Strategies (now part of Meredith), Intelliseek (now Nielsen as well), and Cymfony (now part of TNS Media Intelligence) all made early contributions as innovators in the measurement of online conversations. Each of the these firms offers a robust platform that provides the data you need to gauge effectiveness in a way that is similar to the measures you are used to in traditional media.

For example, traditional media metrics address questions like "How many people saw this?" Combined with planning tools, you can launch campaigns with the expectation of very specific delivery parameters, among them being reach and frequency and the degree to which your intended audience received your message.

While social-media-based campaigns are not "purchased" in the traditional sense — you can't order X-million people to talk about you — you can measure who is talking, what they are saying, and how often they are saying it. For example, using the Cymfony metrics platform you can measure the degree to which your message is positively or negatively received by looking for specific phrases in the blogosphere coincident with the nearby occurrence of words or phrases that suggest polarity. Using the BlogPulse tool from Nielsen|BuzzMetrics, you can quickly gauge the degree to which your message is getting picked up in blogs. Using this data, and then trending it over time, you can build "best practices" around your use of social media. I'll go into measurement in depth in Chapter 13, "Objectives, Metrics, and ROI." Rest assured that measurement will be part of the social media campaigns you'll be building.

Chapter 2: The Main Points

- Marketers are facing a dilemma: Giving up control in order to gain a presence in the conversations that matter.
- It is the *interruption* that is driving the backlash that advertisers are feeling.
- The importance of disclosure as a means to establish trust cannot be overstated.
- Trust is essential to any form of conversation on the Social Web.
- Robust metrics and measurement are available that can be used to track and prove the effectiveness (or lack thereof) of social campaigns.

What *Is* Social Media?

Social media involves a natural, genuine conversation between people about something of mutual interest, a conversation built on the thoughts and experiences of the participants. It is about sharing and arriving at a collective point, often for the purpose of making a better or more-informed choice. Beginning with this simple focused concept, this chapter will explore social media in more detail. First, I'll define it more precisely (and demonstrate something about social media in the process) and then move into how you can use social media to complement the marketing activities you are using in your current campaigns.

3

Chapter Contents

Social Media Defined

Think back to school: When you wanted to know what something was, you went to the dictionary for words and the encyclopedia for most everything else. So where do you look for a "current" definition of social media? How about the reference that is itself built on the principles of social media. That is, of course, Wikipedia. This socially built online encyclopedia is an example of both "social media" and the social processes that make this emerging form of media so powerful. You may be thinking, "Hey wait! Who says Wikipedia is accurate? I've heard that people can write anything, whatever they want!" That much is true: in Wikipedia you can write whatever you want. However, it's also true that just as soon as you do — often within a few minutes — someone else will look at what you just wrote and either validate it or revert the passage to its prior state.

Fact: Wikipedia and the Encyclopedia Britannica both have errors. In a study conducted by the scientific journal *Nature,* Wikipedia was found to have 162 errors across 50 articles, compared with 123 for Britannica. Wikipedia tends to get corrected quickly, as does the online version of Britannica, so these online versions actually fare better over time than their print counterparts. A better way to view Wikipedia — and in fact, any encyclopedia — is to imagine a group of interested participants, fastidiously reviewing the content entries and guiding a discussion, arriving at an agreed-on result. More often than not, and true to the promise of social media and the tapping of the collective, the resulting Wikipedia entry is dead on. In June of 2008, Britannica Online announced its new program that recognizes the potential in a collaborative approach to the development of its content. You can read more about this at the Britannica blog (http://britannicanet.com/?p=88).

The Wikipedia process for arriving at a definition of "social media" is an excellent example *of* social media: social media is used in this context to tap the collective expertise and arrive at an acceptable conclusion. It is the wisdom of the crowd, with all caveats fully present. Think about this a bit if you're still skeptical: it's actually a rather insightful look into social media. The Wikipedia process provides a great example of why social media is useful to you as a marketer.

When I first started writing this book, Wikipedia did not have an agreed-to definition of social media. Instead, Wikipedia had an emerging, in-process definition of what more accurately described activities on the "Social Web" — the total of all of the applications and uses of online tools aimed at enabling consumer-generated and shared content, and facilitating conversations relating to that content between people. This short definition was *followed by an intense discussion of what social media might or might not be.* This discussion, which began late in 2006, only recently stabilized with a fairly solid definition.

Here is how Wikipedia defined "social media" on Friday, January 12, 2008:

Social Media: Participatory online media where news, photos, videos, and podcasts are made public via social media websites through submission. Normally accompanied with a voting process to make media items become "popular."

Social Media Expanded Definition: Social media is the democratization of information, transforming people from content readers into content publishers. It is the shift from a broadcast mechanism to a many-to-many model, rooted in conversations between authors, people, and peers. Social media uses the "wisdom of crowds" to connect information in a collaborative manner. Social media can take many different forms, including Internet forums, message boards, weblogs, wikis, podcasts, pictures and video. Technologies such as blogs, picture-sharing, vlogs, wall-postings, email, instant messaging, music-sharing, group creation and voice over IP, to name a few. Examples of social media applications are Google (reference, social networking), Wikipedia (reference), MySpace (social networking), Facebook(social networking), `Last.fm` *(personal music), YouTube (social networking and video sharing), Second Life (virtual reality), and Flickr (photo sharing).*

From the Wikipedia entry come these fundamental elements that merit notice.

1. Social media involves a number of different *social* channels and especially online social channels, just as traditional media utilizes a number of different channels.

2. Social media changes over time. The Wikipedia entry will continue to evolve as our collective understanding and acceptance of just what constitutes "social media" evolves.

3. Social media is participative: the "audience" is assumed to be part of the creative process or force that generates content.

Herein are found the most important aspects of social media from a marketer's perspective: social media isn't a "thing" in the sense that direct mail or TV advertising are, but is rather a *collaborative process* through which information is created, shared, altered, and destroyed.

Featured Case: Fiskars

Fiskars Brands needed to build an emotional connection with their customers. They engaged Brains on Fire for the development of an online and offline brand ambassador movement. They were able to not only increase emotional connections, but increase online chatter about their brand 600 percent, bring new voices into the blogosphere, and grow sales rates in key regions by 300 percent.

Is Social Media Accurate?

This may seem the question of the day but it's really a red herring. Consider that the same line of thinking that results in the dismissal — rather than attempted understanding — of Wikipedia because "anyone can contribute" can do the same for the collective message in a social conversation. After all, all of this is really nothing more than "a few comments from the people on the Internet" right? Don't make that mistake. This is not to say "believe everything you read..." but rather that if you build a solid process around *listening* via the Social Web — in good part what this book is about — then you can learn a lot about your products and services *directly from your customers*. This is knowledge that you can put to good use as a marketer, in applications ranging from product development and evolution to practical applications like increasing average sales in your online checkout process or reducing expenses by lowering return rates.

 Tip: When your customer base rejects your product or service, you really do have to fix it if you want to succeed as a marketer on the Social Web.

To get the most out of this book, following these ground rules will be helpful:

1. Social media uses the collective, the wisdom of the crowd; it is seldom *entirely* wrong. In fact, more often than not, it is more than reasonably accurate and therefore constitutes a measurable, trackable feedback point with regard to the acceptance and performance of your product or service.

2. Social media is used effectively through participation and influence, not command and control. In each of the upcoming chapters, I will highlight the opportunities for participation and show how your participation can lead to influence, influence that helps you achieve your business and marketing objectives.

As you think through all of this — your mind jumping to things like inaccurate perceptions, uncontrolled forums, loss of control over your brand or message — it can appear pointless and intimidating, even a bit scary. The response is often "OK, fine, we're not going to use these channels. Our brand isn't ready to engage customers on this level. We don't want to appear to be endorsing these conversations." Here's the problem: social media exists, and social media is real. It gets used by people who are thinking about buying your product *because* it was created by people who have already purchased your product. Social media is utilized in the conversations that occur between your customers — conversations that you may not even know about and certainly will not be part of unless you are present and listening. Choosing not to participate is tantamount to *endorsing* — by your own absence — the messages that are ultimately formed in social channels. You can choose whether or not your customers will see you on TV. You cannot choose whether or not your customers will see you on the Social Web. They will, because *they will put you there*. You can only choose whether or not you will *join* them there. As such, for contemporary brands aiming for long-term success, not participating is not an option.

Featured Case: Home Depot

What happens when you choose to participate? Consider Home Depot and the Social Web. If you search blogs, YouTube, Flickr, and similar sites for entries relating to Home Depot, you'll find plenty of negative content. Home Depot has its followers and detractors through no fault of its own: It's basically impossible for a business the size of Home Depot, and in particular a "big box" retailer for someone, somewhere, not to say something negative. The Social Web makes this even easier, and so there is negative content about Home Depot in circulation, and there is little if anything that Home Depot can do about this negative content. Instead, Home Depot participates on the Social Web itself: it provide how-to videos and allows the use of cameras (or at least looks the other way) when parents want to take pictures of their kids building a bird feeder or wooden fire truck at one of Home Depot's "Kids Workshops." Those same people can then upload and share their pictures from Home Depot on sites such as Flickr, shown in Figure 3.1.

continues

Featured Case: Home Depot *(Continued)*

These workshops are offered the first Saturday of each month, and they are free. You'll find plenty of pictures documenting various projects online, created and uploaded by kids and parents right along with success stories based on the use of Home Depot products in renovation and remodeling projects. By participating on the Social Web in this way, Home Depot ensures that there is plenty of "positive content" to counter the "negative" and thereby brings a balance to the content on the Social Web. The result is a more balanced reflection that includes the positive contribution Home Depot makes within its local communities.

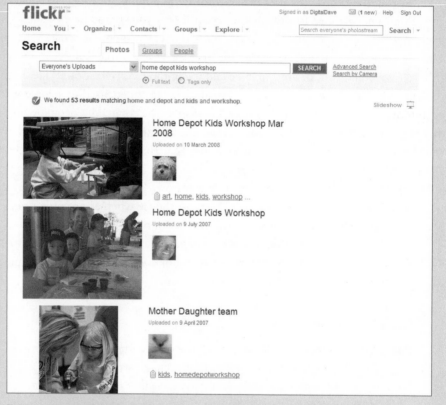

Figure 3.1 Home Depot Kids Workshops

Social Media and Marketing

From a marketer's perspective, the premises I've asserted with regard to the application of social media in marketing are daunting. Assume that what the crowd says is valid, and that you have limited control over what they say. Scary as this may seem, if you learn how to "influence the crowd" effectively you can actually create a significant and defensible market position based on solid social acceptance. The Social Web, used correctly, is all about what your community of supporters can do to help you build your business. Keep in mind too that all of your other channels still exist; social media is a complementary extension of all of your other marketing efforts. Social media is, after all, more of a mind-set than a true channel; however, throughout this book I will show you practical ways through which you can approach social media as if it were a marketing channel.

So how do you influence a crowd? Well, given that you can't tell "it" what to think, going the *direct control* route is probably a loser. Instead, *listen* to it. Tap it. Learn from it. And then "do that." One of the characteristics of social media is that you can listen to it, measure it, and track it over time. You can use what you learn to modify and improve *what you offer*, and in so doing influence the online conversation.

Take a look back at the primary elements of the Wikipedia definition:

Social Media: Participatory online media where news, photos, videos, and podcasts are made public via social media websites through submission. *Normally accompanied with a voting process to make media items become "popular."*

Social media is characterized largely if not completely by the content trail — ratings, reviews, comments, and more — that it leaves on the Social Web, and by the voting processes and related assessments that clearly mark what the crowd thinks of this content. So, right off, you've got a measurable "pulse" that you can use to guide your efforts in near real-time. Listening to and responding to your customers by paying attention to their conversations is a great way to use social media to "influence" these discussions. But just how do you *influence* them? This question brings us to the heart of what social media is, and how to use it properly as a marketer.

Featured Case: Hallmark Idea Exchange and Project HaHa!

Hallmark has always been a company to watch in the greeting card and retail gift industry — and they were one of the first companies to work with an online customer community. They have been true pioneers in the consumer space. In 2000, the Hallmark/Communispace team launched the "Hallmark Idea Exchange," where 200 mothers with young children were recruited to brainstorm ideas, help Hallmark rethink the retail experience and merchandise, and react to pricing. They effectively became an extension of the marketing team as close advisors on just about everything Hallmark was working on — including how to get a handle on what's funny to baby boomers (turning 40 is not the same for boomers as for their parents). In 2004, Hallmark introduced "Project HaHa!" to better understand how people's sense of humor was changing — and how to retune its Classic Humor and Shoebox card lines.

At the start of this chapter, I established a basic concept: that social media is based on a natural, genuine conversation between people about something of mutual interest. Because social media gains its power from sharing and consensus, if you influence it by any means other than transparent, genuine participation, you taint the outcome. The results are effectively meaningless.

Instead of trickery, coercion, or control, when I talk about "influencing the crowd" I am talking about giving them an experience that they will want to talk about, positively, and then using the resulting conversation to continuously improve. If you follow this approach, over time you will separate yourself from competitors who don't tap social media, and especially from those who opt for shortcuts.

 Tip: As a marketer, you *do not* want to control your audience. If that is your only recourse, you are better off not using social media at all.

Social Media as a Guidepost

One of the most valuable aspects of social media from a marketer's perspective is in building and maintaining a feedback loop. It is through this feedback loop — and your measurement of it — that you can learn *where and how* to influence the social conversations that are important to you. Firms like Cymfony, Intelliseek, and BuzzMetrics built practices around this application of social media, focusing on blogs and similar text-based conversations. Of course, getting the data is only part of the equation: doing something with it is where the real action is. The remainder of this chapter focuses on the elements of social media, and how they play into the purchase process via the social feedback cycle — simply, the feeding back of the post-purchase experiences of *current* customers into the purchase funnel at the point of consideration for use by *potential* customers when making a purchase decision. Later chapters cover in detail the actual use of social media and the metrics that are available to you for measuring and managing your social campaigns.

What If You Don't Run in Nikes?

One of the more interesting pieces of user-generated content that I've seen is the "How To" on converting any brand of running shoe into a "Nike Plus" compatible shoe. The content — which includes instructions, photos (Flickr), and video (YouTube) — provides the step-by-step process to cut away a section of the inner sole of the shoe and install the Apple transponder that tracks and stores details of your last run for upload when you're back home. Whether these modified shoes really work or not, here is a group of runners who found the *idea* of this type of running

To get an idea of how the social feedback loop that you'll create, tap, and measure is set up, look at the classic purchase funnel shown in Figure 3.2 from the traditional media perspective. The three stages — awareness, consideration, and purchase — define a pathway along which you move potential customers toward the ultimate goal, the sale.

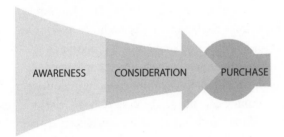

Figure 3.2 The Classic Purchase Funnel

The purchase funnel offers both an insight into why traditional media works so well, and why marketers who rely on traditional media exclusively have difficulties when first thinking through the potential application of social media. The purchase funnel is a model that characterizes the process that leads from awareness through consideration to purchase *as if it existed in a vacuum*. It treats your marketing program — and in fact your entire business — as if it were a closed system. If it ever was — debatable in itself — it isn't anymore. A more contemporary representation of the purchase funnel incorporates the Social Web and accounts for the impact of consumer-generated media during the consideration stage. It is an open model that recycles the experiential data generated by current customers for the benefit of the next wave of shoppers. The feedback loop that connects the post-purchase conversation back to the purchase funnel is the key to the application of social media. This is the subject of the next section.

Social Media's Impact on the Purchase Funnel

Traditional media is a time-tested workhorse when it comes to awareness. Marketers can literally "buy" market share through awareness-focused media. To this day, spending on traditional advertising is often expressed as "dollars per point," meaning not only that a certain spend level buys a certain exposure (e.g., ratings points) but also that "X dollars" spent will or did generate "Y market share points" in the business sense of market share. To be sure, someone who sees your ad — the "ad spend" part of the equation — has to actually buy the product in order to realize those market share points. But for many industries, there is an accepted sense of cause and effect between advertising spend and market share. Think especially about Hollywood and the movie business where a relatively robust formulaic approach often predicts the opening weekend gross based on up-front ad spending. It's not surprising that Hollywood is likely already feeling the direct impact — both positively and negatively — of social media. Two insightful film-opening events suggest that this is in fact the case. The first, *Gigli* — pronounced "ZJEE-lee" and released a few years ago — was one of the those "should have been a bigger open" that simply wasn't. Even though ad spend was significant, the opening weekend was a disappointment. *Gigli* wasn't the first movie — and certainly won't be the last — to perform poorly at the box office. What is notable about this case is that the box-office performance fizzled on Friday night, *between the early and late screenings*. Typically, if a film bombs — or soars, for that matter — it does so *after* the opening weekend, not *during* the opening weekend. People need time to gather (for example, in the office on Monday) or to go home and write online reviews after seeing the film during the opening weekend. In the case of *Gigli,* the culprit was "texting" (SMS). During the early shows, influential viewers were letting their late-show friends know that they could safely skip this film. They did.

Social media, like any other form of expression that takes its roots in word of mouth, cuts both ways. It can boost viewership and purchase by reinforcing the underlying marketing message just as easily as it weakens intent and the likelihood of successful conversion. Early films that demonstrated the beneficial impact of social media — spurring more recent use of the channels — include *Superbad* and *Resident Evil: Extinction.* Think back to when these were released: they were the first films released by Sony/Columbia Tristar where spending levels for online marketing — including through social media — edged out traditional forms of advertising as the primary spends associated with driving *awareness*. Both went on to box-office success: *Superbad* grossed in excess of $160 million while *Resident Evil* pulled in more than $100 million. Dwight Caines, Columbia Tristar EVP, Worldwide Digital Marketing, had this to say at the time: "The tools for people to use social networking and collaborative site building are now commonplace. As a marketer, you have to find new ways to stay on top of those trends."

Social media sits at the pinnacle of the current trends in consumer-to-consumer conversation and marketing effort amplification. The takeaway here for marketers across all categories is that in the examples presented here, the marketing teams "gambled" on social and digital media as the primary awareness tool, and turned down the spend on traditional media channels. The results speak for themselves. As you set up your social media program, don't hesitate to experiment. Don't be reckless, either: your brand may or may not be your life, but it's almost certainly your livelihood. Begin with your business objectives and solid preparation and a current review of your customer's online media habits using the tools and techniques presented in Chapter 5, "The Social Feedback Cycle," Chapter 6, "Touchpoint Analysis," and Chapter 7, "Influence and Measurement." Then, look at the various social media channels you have available: These will be presented in a systematic way beginning in Chapter 8, "Build a Social Media Campaign." Find the channels that build on or complement your current efforts or that fill a gap in your current marketing program and start there, building your social media program as you develop your capabilities.

The Social Feedback Cycle

In most organizations, a set of disciplines and capabilities that roll up under "operations" and ultimately report to the Chief Operating Officer (COO) or an equivalent are the point within that organization where the rubber meets the road — where the customer experiences that drive word of mouth and (now) social media actually happen. It may be a product use or store experience, an interaction with a field service professional, or a call to customer support. In general, these are all operations-based experiences. By contrast, marketing is charged with telling potential customers what these experiences are likely to be and why they matter, or reinforcing in current customers why making this same choice again is a good idea.

Tip: Marketing promises. Operations delivers.

The connection between operations and marketing — between promise and delivery — is central to social media. Social media — in the business context — is based on the degree to which the actual experience matches the expectation set. If you're wondering about the importance of social media, consider this: Recent studies have shown that of the estimated 3.5 *billion* word-of-mouth conversations that occur around the world *each day*, about 2.3 billion of them — roughly two out of three — make a reference to a brand, product, or service. Word of mouth is increasingly manifesting itself through digital social media, where it spreads both farther and faster. This use of the Social Web is increasingly important to marketers.

Many of the difficulties faced by contemporary CMOs are in fact issues that arise not in Marketing, but in Operations. Home Depot lost CMO Roger Adams after seeing more than its share of prior CMO departures in the recent past. In an *Advertising Age* article, Home Depot's need for operational efficiency was cited. *Advertising Age* noted that Home Depot's needs are (in order): "a better floor experience, better trained associates, and more traffic." The majority of the CMOs, CEOs, and COOs would be tempted to separate these, assigning floor experience and associate training to operations while hammering the CMO for traffic. In fact, these are all Operations issues that impact Marketing — people talk about each of these in conversations with friends and neighbors about experiences that originate in *Operations*. Beyond the first visit that any specific individual makes to Home Depot (and c'mon...who hasn't already been to at least one Home Depot?), the floor experience combined with the perceived level of associate competence *directly drives floor traffic*. It is not uncommon to see a customer asking for an associate in Home Depot *by name*, very likely the result of a prior, positive experience. Compared to providing a great experience with a knowledgeable associate, a flyer advertising a few cents off on Duracell batteries is a weak proposition for boosting sales, especially when what Home Depot sells — things to make your home or residence better — are things which are very likely to start conversations: "You have to come over for dinner next Saturday to see what we did to the patio this weekend!" That is the kind of conversation that will drive floor traffic at Home Depot.

Look back at the purchase funnel, and expand it to include "post-purchase" experiences of the overall marketing process as shown in Figure 3.3. Social media connects these experiences back to the purchase process in the social feedback cycle. Social media is effectively the product of Operations, given the expectation (the brand or promise) established in Marketing.

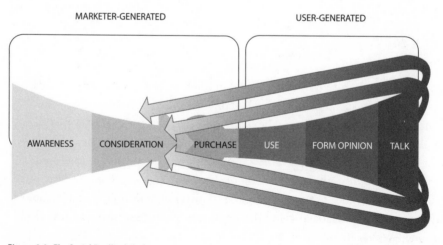

MARKETER-GENERATED   USER-GENERATED

AWARENESS   CONSIDERATION   PURCHASE   USE   FORM OPINION   TALK

Figure 3.3 The Social Feedback Cycle

The "consideration phase" of the purchase cycle is an area that marketers have typically avoided, primarily because it hasn't been — and still isn't — *directly* accessible. Instead they spend heavily on awareness and on point-of-purchase efforts — as an example, think of point-of-sale coupons or keyword campaigns — and then hope, generally correctly, that the consideration "gap" takes care of itself as consumers, charged up with awareness-inspired demand, head for the checkout lanes. Looking at the purchase funnel this way, it all makes sense: generate awareness and then supplement that at or near the cash register with point-of-sale marketing efforts as needed. A decent product — or at the least one with a clear promise — ought to be able to jump through the "consideration" phase.

In 2004, Dave Ellett, Jeff Petry (CEO and Sr. Director of Marketing, respectively, of the social media firm Powered), and I "extended" the purchase funnel conceptually to include the impact of post-purchase consumer activities. At that point, post-purchase was largely the domain of Customer Relationship Management (CRM) software and services. In many firms CRM was separated from Marketing, often seen as an Operations extension where it was all too often used to measure performance alone rather than the combination of performance and *delivered experience*. Word-of-mouth, especially the online variety that in part gives rise to social media, makes obvious the relationship that has long existed — more or less invisibly — between promise and delivery. The social feedback cycle is set in motion by a post-purchase opinion that forms based on the relationship between the expectations set and the actual performance of the product or service. This opinion drives word-of-mouth, and word-of-mouth ultimately feeds back into the purchase funnel *in the consideration phase*.

Wham!

Right between awareness and point-of-purchase comes customer-driven social media. It hits hard too: remember, word-of-mouth is considered to be the most trusted source of information, a fact again affirmed in a recent (2007) Zenith Optimedia study. If the experience is less than expected, your awareness efforts get short-circuited beyond the initial purchase wave. Think back to the mother of all film-industry "word of mouth" success stories, *The Blair Witch Project*. The social feedback cycle boosted uptake and created nothing short of a phenomenon. Social media does indeed cut both ways: Be sure you know which way the scissors are pointing before you start cutting.

Tip: The social feedback cycle is driven by word-of-mouth, itself driven by the actual post-purchase or trial/sampling experience. It is essential that Operations and Marketing be in sync.

You'll spend more time on the relationship between Operations and Marketing along with the social feedback cycle and the effective use of social media later in the book. For now, just keep in mind that they are related. It is through this relationship that you — as a marketer — influence the crowd. Getting the Operations + Marketing link right is the first step in successfully implementing social media.

The Elements of Social Media

So far, I've defined social media, and shown how it relates to the purchase funnel through the social feedback cycle. I've talked about the use of social media as a trend indicator, and how you can combine the efforts of Operations and Marketing to manage the behavior of crowds. The final section of this chapter covers specific social media channels.

Note: Throughout the book, I will refer to social media *channels*. What is meant by the term "channel" may be different from what you are used to, especially if you are thinking along the lines of something you can "buy" or schedule. Social media channels — e.g., blogging or photo sharing — as used throughout this book mean simply, "one of the methods or media forms through which social media is made available to Social Web participants."

Robert Scoble, a noted blogger and technology evangelist, introduced what he calls the Starfish model of social media. Robert lists a dozen social media channels, organized around *conversion*, that are themselves examples and embodiments of online social technology. The channels Robert lists, shown in Figure 3.4 in the context of traditional media and the other channels you are likely using now, are:

- Blogs
- Photo sharing
- Video sharing
- Personal social networks
- Events (face to face) and event services
- Email
- White label social networks
- Wikis
- Podcasting (audio)
- Microblogs
- SMS (texting)
- Collaborative tools

Two essential marketing elements arise out of Robert's starfish concept: First, social media involves a diverse set of activities — photo sharing, blogging, and so on. Second, the effective use of social media depends in part on the activities selected and the mix of the social and traditional channels that your audience is interested in or to which it is receptive. In other words, the effective use of social media — technology, control, and a few details aside — is essentially an *integration* problem. Guess what?

You already know how to handle that. As a marketer, you've been managing integrated campaigns for years. Social media, while certainly different in terms of how you approach it, is no different than anything else in your marketing toolbox: the channels may be different, but you still plan for it within the context of your business and campaign objectives and audience and channel mix.

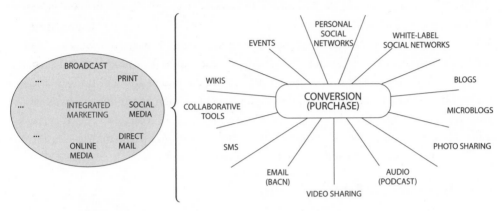

Figure 3.4 The Social Media Starfish

I will focus more on the various social media channels and the integration of social media into the larger set of channels available to you in Chapter 6, "Touchpoint Analysis." I'll dig into the networks themselves — including networks that you can build and implement — in Chapter 9, "Social Platforms." Chapter 10, "Social Content: Multimedia," Chapter 11, "Social Content: Reviews, Ratings, and Recommendations," and Chapter 12, "Social Interactions," will focus on content creation, ranging from text and multimedia to mobile services and events. I'll work through how these different social media channels can be linked with each other, and with the balance of what you're currently using from your overall marketing toolbox.

In the upcoming sections, you'll start building your social media program. Following the Hour a Day format, you'll do a little bit, each day, over a period of time. I believe that following this methodology will result in a success for you. Because you are only doing a small amount of work at any one time, you can learn as you go and combine what I present with the new innovations that will no doubt arise. Each chapter and each exercise builds on what came before it.

The challenges you will face will be along the lines of one or more of the following:

- Ceding control — real control — to your customers
- Building bridges into Operations
- Managing short-term performance expectations
- Getting a handle on technology in flux
- Allocating a budget for metrics and following through

The challenges you are most likely to face include the challenge of moving outside your comfort zone. My advice is to make your plan and then just do it. Follow the Hour a Day process, and stop and breathe when needed.

Think through the various examples you'll encounter in the upcoming chapters. Relate them to your business, and involve your coworkers. Build consensus. Above all, look at what you are selling or promoting. If it needs "fixing," then right now would be an excellent time to take care of that. When you hit Chapter 7, "Influence and Measurement," which discusses the Net Promoter Score and similar measures of acceptance, the response to your social efforts will be brutal if your product or service isn't all it's cracked up to be. If things are as they should be, you're going to find smooth sailing. Implemented correctly, social media will help set significant hurdles between you and your competition. If your product or service *isn't* all it should be — if there is a notable gap between marketing expectation and operational performance — and you don't take the time now to address that ... you've been warned.

Chapter 3: The Main Points

- Social media is defined as: Participatory online media where news, photos, videos, and podcasts are made public typically accompanied with a voting process to signal items considered "popular."

- Social media is an effective guidepost. Social media can be used to gather valuable information about how your product, service, and brand are perceived in the marketplace.

- The basic application of social media is as a consideration phase tool that connects post-purchase experiences with potential customers progressing from awareness to purchase.

- Social media is an activity that is based on the notion of *influence*.

- Planning and implementing channels associated with social media fits well with the concepts of integrated marketing.

Month 1: Prepare for Social Marketing

In Part II you'll begin building for your social media campaign. Following the Hour a Day format makes it easy. Because you will add to your skills sequentially, you'll first establish a solid base and working knowledge of the tools that are available to you as a marketer and only then add social media elements to your plan. Importantly, you'll also learn the etiquette and rules of social engagement. In social media–based marketing, perhaps more than any other single factor, the understanding and adherence to etiquette (along with emerging "best practices") will make or break the effectiveness of the campaigns you create. "What goes around comes around," and nowhere is this more true than on the Social Web.

II

Week 1: Web 2.0: The Social Web

4

This chapter offers specific examples of social media (a.k.a. "Web 2.0") tools and applications. In it, I pull out a few examples that are being used in business now. Each day, you'll spend an hour or so looking at the selected examples and applications so that by the end of the chapter you'll have worked through a range of social media applications, and seen first-hand how they fit together and can be used in a business context.

Chapter Contents

Social Networks: The Power of the Collective

Relax. This is not about communal living, although in a weird, virtual way it may seem close. The power of the collective is all about the power that arises directly from the ways in which the Social Web is organized and what it conveys to its participants as a result. Although this may seem a bit of a divergence — after all, the clock is running and you haven't started building a plan yet — pay attention here, as this chapter prepares you for the mental shift that will help you later when you get to the tactical issues of building your plan. Understanding how network organization affects the flow of information is central to your successfully making the case for social media within your organization. Ultimately, you need to be able to make that case, for the right reasons.

I am not going to try to sell you on the idea that social media is "good" simply because everyone is using it. That in itself does not make a business case for the investment of your time or marketing dollars. As often as not, "because everyone is doing it" actually makes the case for *not* doing it. What does make the case is being able to demonstrate that social media — done right — can offer a boost to your marketing efforts. Presenting this to your colleagues — and winning the discretionary budget dollars you'll need — means understanding how this "social" benefit comes about.

So, I am going to start with the fundamental notion of *network value*. Though it's a bit geeky, I'll answer — or at least frame — the question "Why is social media such an important phenomenon?" Three basic laws apply here — together they'll give you a sense of why the Social Web is becoming important even when compared to proven work-horse media like television, radio, and print. There are three network-value-governance laws: They speak to the fundamental value of a network from the perspective of those connected to it. These laws ascribe a potential value to any given network on the basis of how participants are connected: to a central source, to each other, and so on. The laws that govern the value of social networks and the Social Web itself are presented in order of increasing importance with regard to the use of social media.

Network Value

A quick word on "value" is important here. When I talk about "value" and "power," what I am really talking is about is the value of the network from the participant's perspective. There is certainly no guarantee that the economic value of an email list with 100 million unique, active, opted-in, etc. addresses is 100 times more valuable to a marketer than a cable program that reaches "only" 10 million viewers even though both are fundamentally broadcast implementations. Obviously, a lot of other factors enter into the economic value calculation. Instead, what I am referring to is the power or value of the network from a member's perspective. If I can reach anyone, anytime with a specific and personalized message, this is potentially more valuable from a marketer's perspective than one which constrains me to always reaching the entire network with a single message. Learning to leverage social media is the key to understanding how to translate this potential into reality.

Sarnoff's Law

David Sarnoff was a pioneer in the broadcasting business: He founded the National Broadcasting Company (NBC) and led the Radio Corporation of America (RCA). Sarnoff's law, which was framed to relate the value of a radio station to the number of listeners, holds that the value of the network increases in direct proportion to the number of listeners (or other participants, these days) on that network. This basic law, shown in Figure 4.1, underlies the *reach* component of most media pricing models: In the typical broadcast application, a single voice is sent to millions of listeners. A network with 100 people is therefore 10 times as valuable in terms of reach as a network with only 10, all other things being roughly equal.

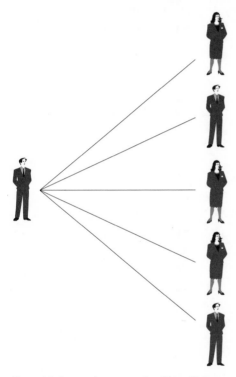

Figure 4.1 A network representative of Sarnoff's Law

Metcalfe's Law

Metcalfe's Law is named after Massachusetts Institute of Technology (MIT) graduate Robert Metcalfe, one of the co-inventors of Ethernet and founder of the networking firm 3Com. For networks that support communication between members — rather than only from a single source — the network value grows as the square of the number of users. Think of this as arising out of the fact that people can talk in both directions, and with more than one conversation occurring simultaneously. This is shown in

Figure 4.2. The telephone and basic Internet communications — email, minus email groups — are examples of networks that follow Metcalfe's Law. A network of 100 people is roughly 100 times as valuable as a network of only 10 members.

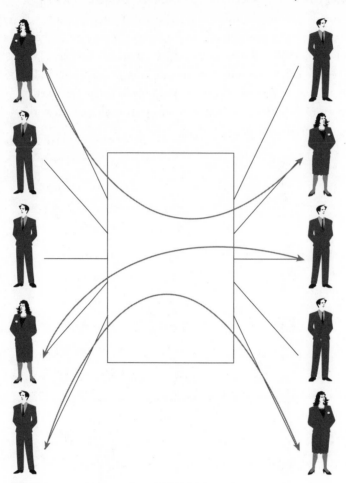

Figure 4.2 A network representative of Metcalfe's Law

Reed's Law

Computer Scientist David P. Reed is known for his work at MIT in the area of computer networking. Reed's Law — also called "The Law of the Pack" — holds that the value of the network grows more powerfully than either Sarnoff or Metcalfe would suggest with the formation of groups (which in turn give rise to communities) and the interconnections between them, as shown in Figure 4.3. Compared with a network of 10 people, a network of 100 people that can talk not only with each other as they would under Metcalfe but also within *groups* of people is 2^{90} (2 raised to the 90th power) which for all practical purposes is an exceedingly large number. Reed's Law applies to the typical social networks in use today.

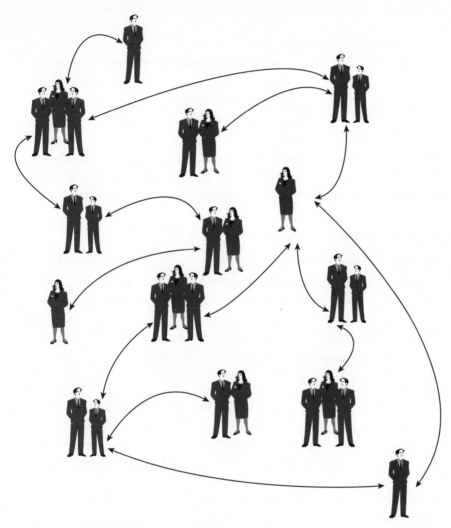

Figure 4.3 A network representative of Reed's Law

Tip: Contemporary social networks follow Reed's Law.

Look back at the three network types covered and consider two networks, one with 10 people and one with 100. Under Sarnoff, think TV, Radio, and most large-audience, centrally managed websites. The gain in value by attracting 10 times the (unique) members is of course 10×. Now consider your personal email or your mobile phone: These operate on bidirectional networks. I can talk to you while you talk to me, and while Chris is talking with Pat. For these networks — which follow Metcalfe — a tenfold member increase boosts their value by a factor of 100 compared to what it would have been for a simple one-way broadcast-style network.

Reed's Law adds another layer: groups. Specifically, Reed's Law speaks to the impact on network value by recognizing and supporting *groups* of members. The ability to talk in groups can result in more efficient filtering, vetting, and emphasis on "necessary" information. This may occur through well-connected power users, for example, who often exert a larger-than-expected influence on group behavior. Social networks — which encourage the formation of and communication between subgroups — follow Reed's Law. The incredible power of communities is in this sense "tapped" by fundamental organization and administrative policies of social networks.

The Impact of Control

Do you wonder what happens when a social network is strongly controlled by a central governing body? It devolves toward the most basic networking model, Sarnoff! Think about it this way: In an essentially anarchic social network, members are free to tap Reed's law to the fullest. As rules are imposed, and especially those that constrain self-expression, there is a throttling-down of the free flow of content between members. If you place constraints on who can talk *by permitting only a central authority or editorial body to post,* you devalue the network.

OK, enough theory and math. What does all this have to do with social media, and why should you care about it? It's simple, you know, like radar. Ordinary people — the kinds of people you are trying to reach — are finding that group-oriented (a.k.a. "social") networks are very effective when it comes to receiving and sharing information as compared with the largely one-way channels such as television, radio, and print that are still following Sarnoff's Law and early radio value models. These highly interconnected social networks are equally perceived as effective in vetting that information, and it is the combined impact that makes social networks along with user-generated content and social media so powerful from a consumer's perspective. *They are using these networks to evaluate everything you say.* It may have been true, as a trenchant *New Yorker* cartoon once pointed out, that on the Internet "no one knows you're a dog." With the newer social networks, however, dogs get pegged as dogs pretty quickly. Online community members are discovering that it is very easy to find, learn about, and share information that directly contributes to an *informed choice.* It is for this reason that people are moving en masse to the Social Web, and it is for this reason that you should be there, too.

Let Your Fingers Do the Walking

Want a simple example of why it makes sense to follow the information value of the network? Think back — way back — to the early campaigns touting the value of the Yellow Pages. "Let your fingers do the walking" spoke directly to the value of the "Yellow Pages community" — the collection of local merchants who supported a central, easy-to-use directory that was offered to consumers as an alternative to the time-consuming task of driving around town looking for someone who embroidered baseball caps. *For member merchants, the Yellow Pages served as a one-to-one network.* The Yellow Pages are an analog example of Metcalfe's Law: compared with TV advertising of the day, the Yellow Pages combined with the telephone allowed any merchant to connect with any consumer. The more recent tagline "We wrote the book on local search" underscores the present-day importance of the Yellow Pages and its use in marketing even in the face of *online* local search: In 2005, AT&T's Directory Services segment *net* income was about $2 billion, accounting for over 40 percent of AT&T's *total* net income.

Social Media Begins Here

Think back to the basics of integrated marketing and a concept or model that you've probably worked with: the *touchpoint map.* A hypothetical touchpoint map is shown in Figure 4.4. Note that this representation is not suggestive of *your* touchpoint map, though it is clearly intended to elicit a questioning response. *What if?* This simple diagram — which places the customer at the center of all potential brand-related experiences — is based on the Social Web reality that all of the communications that a particular individual is exposed to shape her ultimate perception of your brand, product, or service. You'll spend more time on the touchpoint map in the upcoming chapters. For now note that all communication — everything you say, along with everything that your customers say — plays a role. This includes your advertising and the actual product experience *as well as the conversations occurring on the Social Web.*

The touchpoint map delineates not only a collection of the media and marketing channels you are using now, but also a collection of social media components. These elements — combined — contribute to the formation of an opinion or perception. Specific to marketing and its core objectives, these perceptions generally (and certainly hopefully) contribute to a *conversion.* It is in this way that social media ties directly into your marketing toolbox: These social components — blogs, wikis, podcasts, and more — surround the conversion process and are central to the usefulness of social media in marketing. As you jump into social media, keep the following tip in mind.

Tip: Social media contributes to informed choices by aggregating and making available to an interested individual the collective experience and resultant conversation.

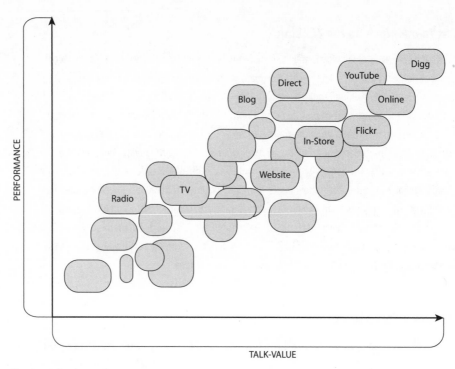

Figure 4.4 Touchpoint Map

Ready to jump in? OK, everyone in the pool. First up in your Hour a Day work (as if you've read everything up until now in your off-time!) is experiencing social networks. If you're already a member of one or more, that's great. You can use those and follow along or try the suggested networks in addition to social networks you are a member of now. This week's objectives are designed to get you familiar with a wide range of social applications. You'll no doubt recognize many of them, and you are probably using a few of those listed or applications that are similar to those listed.

Here is what you are going to do:

• Look at a variety of social media activities.

• Learn how these activities can be used to weave social experiences together.

• Review a sample of online social media tools that you can use through selected real-world business examples.

Note: Many companies have policies that prohibit or control the use of the Internet using company equipment. Check with your Human Resources (HR) or Information Technology (IT) groups to learn about your company's specific policies. If your corporate policies prohibit viewing or using any of the applications, services, or networks suggested in this book from the corporate network, either complete the exercise at home or ask your IT Director or Systems Administrator to suggest an alternative that you are permitted to use. Please do not place yourself at risk by circumventing established corporate policies.

Week 1: Engaging with Social Media

This week your exercises focus on a survey of the content that makes up the Social Web. There is a good chance that you have seen some of this, in which case you can use this time to visit other similar sites that you may not have made the time for. Following the Hour a Day format, each exercise is designed to be done in an hour...or less.

Tip: A set of worksheets covering this week's exercises can be found in the appendix of this book. In addition to these printed worksheets, you can also download electronic copies and access related resources at the website accompanying this book. Complete information regarding these resources and the website is included in the appendix.

Monday: The Written Word

The written word is a fundamental building block of "permanent" communications. Online, "permanent" takes on at least two meanings:

- It is something you can reference later, in its original form.
- It may live forever, *whether you want it to or not.*

The first meaning is generally considered good. It's that second one you'll want to watch out for.

Look at nearly any news article, blog, web page, super-slick Flash interface and you'll see mostly text. Given that the Web supports multimedia — recall its origins as both a structured document language and a replacement for the Gopher-esque "read the text and click here for the picture" forerunners of the contemporary Web — it's surprising that so much of the Web is still fundamentally text. But it is, so that's a great place to start exploring the world of social media.

Monday's One-Hour Exercise: Blogs and Wikis

Today you're going to spend an hour looking at several different blogs and wikis. If you have favorites of your own, feel free to substitute them for the examples but do note the different roles that the examples I've provided play in *creating* and disseminating shared information.

Let's first be certain about what blogs and wikis are, and how they differ from each other. As a marketer, you can use both. A *blog* is basically a diary *that others can comment on.* As it turns out, it is the "comment on" part that makes a blog so different from a diary or journal you may have kept yourself in the past. The *wiki* is similar in that it is also participative; however, rather than being a sequential journal that gives rise to a collective conversation, the end result of the wiki is a single entry that reflects the collective consensus. Like the blog, the wiki is built by a combination of its owners and readers. Unlike the blog — where each sequential owner-generated post (typically date-ordered, most recent first) is followed by reader-generated comments — the wiki allows readers and owners alike to directly modify the primary post.

Got that? Table 4.1 shows a simple illustration of the difference:

▶ **Table 4.1** Comparison of Blog and Wiki Entries

	Blog	Wiki
Original Post	New York is on the west coast.	New York is on the west coast.
Final Result	New York is on the west coast. [on 1/24/2008 daveevans said] Get a map. New York is on the east coast	New York is on the east [1] coast [1]Corrected 1/24/2008 by daveevans.

Where the blog is an ongoing diary that invites user-generated comments and thereby initiates conversations, the wiki is a collection of entries that evolve over time according to the consensus of the owners and readers acting together. In the case of the blog, the entire conversation is immediately visible: With the wiki, the discussion on the merits of each "correction" or update is often placed in a separate area or page with only the present status of the entry immediately visible.

Note the difference between these two types and the way each can be used in business. The blog is a great placed to start dynamic conversations about things that interest your customers. The wiki is a natural place to build your product FAQ: Post your frequent questions, or suggest an answer, and then *let your customers refine those answers over time based on their actual, collective experience.*

Using Blogs and Wikis

In the next hour, visit the suggested blogs and wikis and ask yourself the questions I've posed. As you do this, do your best not to judge the content itself — it may appear pure folly that someone has actually taken the time to create some of the entries you'll encounter. Let it go. Try instead to see the larger view — the Gestalt if you will — that underlies the experience of blog and wiki participation. *Focus on understanding why these sites exist and why they are popular.*

Fact: About 100 million hours have been spent, in total, building Wikipedia as it sits now. If that seems like a lot of time, and in particular if that seems to you like a waste of time, consider that Americans, taken together, spend the same amount of time, about 100 million hours, watching TV advertising *every weekend.*

Some examples of blogs to visit are suggested in the following list. For this exercise, limit yourself to 15 minutes. Don't get yourself fired for surfing. I just want you to get an idea of what blog *consumption* is all about. Reading — not writing — is what most users still do, so start with reading.

> **Tip:** I've included the URLs for this exercise; however, the easiest way to find the following blogs and wikis is by searching for them.

Blogs to visit:

- Boing Boing (http://www.boingboing.net)
- SocialMediaToday (http://www.socialmediatoday.com)
- Mashable (http://mashable.com)
- CommunityGuy.com (written by this book's technical editor, Jake McKee, at http://www.communityguy.com)

Questions to consider while reviewing these blogs:

1. What is the central theme?
2. Who would read this on a regular basis? Why?
3. Is this person (possibly) a customer? If so, what other blogs does he read?
4. What could you add to this conversation?
5. Are you getting drawn in — that is, are you starting to follow posts via comments and winding up in unexpected places?
6. How could you use this in your business?

Wikis to visit:

- Wikipedia (http://en.wikipedia.org/wiki/Social_media)
- One Laptop per Child (http://wiki.laptop.org)
- IBM Wikis (http://www-941.ibm.com/collaboration/wiki)

Questions to consider:

1. Are the entries evolving over time?
2. Who is in charge?
3. Is the Updates section or Discussion page visible? If not, how does not being able to see the entry evolve over time change your view of the end result?
4. How could you use this in your business?

Finding Social Content

So you're now about halfway or a bit more through your first hour. You've visited a few blogs and a wiki or two. It's likely — especially if this was your first exposure to blogs and wikis — that this was more or less a spectator sport. That's OK, although the real experience arises out of *participation*. Don't let today be your last experience. Find some blogs and wikis you like, and in particular look for some that provide examples of how these tools can be used in your business as marketing channels and relationship builders. Above all, participate.

So just how do you find more blogs? More wikis? I'm glad you asked: That's where you're going next. For starters, finding social media is as easy as using Google. Type in a phrase or keyword, and there is a very good chance that the first page of results will contain blogs and wikis along with typical web pages.

The following tools will help you find and make sense of social content. You'll spend the remainder of today's hour looking at them. At the top of the list is Technorati. Technorati is one of the more popular blog indexes and certainly one of the most useful. From Technorati comes this description of what it's all about:

> *Welcome to Technorati.*
>
> *Currently tracking 112.8 million blogs and more than 250 million pieces of tagged social media.*
>
> *Technorati is the recognized authority on what's happening on the World Live Web, right now. The Live Web is the dynamic and always-updating portion of the Web. We search, surface, and organize blogs and the other forms of independent, user-generated content (photos, videos, voting, etc.) increasingly referred to as "citizen media."*

Technorati isn't the only tool or course that helps you make sense of the *blogosphere,* as the collection of all blogs is often called. As with any set of tools, different tools are used for different purposes. Where Technorati gives you a "what's hot" view with the addition of search, analytical marketing tools like BlogPulse come at the problem of making sense of the Social Web from a different perspective. BlogPulse is an analytical social marketer's best friend — it allows you to quickly see the trend in the occurrence of specific words or phrases as used within the blogosphere. Launching a new product? Use BlogPulse to quickly find out who is talking about it.

For the rest of the hour (but do save a few minutes for the wrap-up) think of something related to your business and use the following suggested tools to research it on the Social Web. For example, search for a product you recently launched or the name of your company or that of your fiercest competitor. If you are working in or around politics, search for the various candidates in national, state, and local elections. Compare these results with those for your favorite pop culture icons (brands or people).

Social Media Content Tools:

- Technorati (`http://www.technorati.com/`)

- Google Blogsearch (`http://blogsearch.google.com`)

- BlogPulse (`http://www.blogpulse.com`)

- BlogPulse Trend (`http://www.blogpulse.com/trend`)

Monday's Exercise Guide and Wrap-Up

Based on today's exercise, you should have a better idea of not only how to find blog content and how to subscribe to it, but also how you might use a blog for your own business, or as one element of a social-media-based campaign. For example, you might create a blog that announces the launch of new product and then use that blog to elicit customer comments that inform the future versions of your product. Or, you could use the blog yourself and talk about the kinds of issues that your service or product is meant to address, giving your customers a way to talk back to you and let you know whether or not they agree, see the value, or have other ideas about what you could do to serve them.

Today you got your feet wet. You started with the text — blogs and wikis — and explored how they formed the *first* of the basic social media building blocks. Tomorrow you'll head into multimedia, and by the end of the week you'll have seen how everything is tied together with one of the most important advancements on the Social Web: RSS.

Tuesday: The Web Comes Alive with Multimedia

Among the original promises of the Web was the ability to read, see, and hear content simultaneously. This was both a part of the original intention for the Web and one of the earlier problems in the development of the HTTP protocol.

> **Note:** Geek Alert: The next section will be interesting for some, and less so for others. If you're into the history of the Web and how some of what we now take for granted came about, you'll enjoy it. If not, you can skip directly to Tuesday's One-Hour Exercise.

The following is an exchange between Marc Andreessen, founder of Netscape, who was at the time in school and working at the National Center for Supercomputing Applications (NCSA) in Chicago, and Tim Berners-Lee, credited as the primary inventor of the Web while working at CERN (Conseil Européen pour le Recherche Nucléaire, which in English is "European Council for Nuclear Research").

From Marc:

multimedia files over httpd

Marc Andreessen (marca@ncsa.uiuc.edu)
Fri, 5 Mar 93 00:15:36 -0800

Some people using NCSA Mosaic 0.9 have noticed that they can't put multimedia files on their own httpd servers and retrieve them correctly with Mosaic. What's happening in most cases is that the WWW Daemon is prepending <PLAINTEXT> to the head of those files.

Basically, if you hack this so it just sends back files with unrecognized extensions (or some set of extensions that your server would like to serve) without prepending anything, things will work.

The only gotcha I've found is that anything on the server without the extension .txt will no longer be given a free ride as <plaintext> from the server to the client.

An alternate solution is to put your images, sound files, etc. on your anonymous FTP server or (shudder) your Gopher server and then point to them at that location from your HTML documents.

Cheers, Marc

Reply from Tim:

Re: multimedia files over httpd

Tim Berners-Lee (timbl@www3.cern.ch)
Fri, 5 Mar 93 08:45:47 +0100

> Basically, if you hack this so it just sends back files with unrecognized extensions (or some set of extensions that your server would like to serve) without prepending anything, things will work.

This is a hack — the suffix is NOT supposed to mean anything in HTTP and there are servers which serve things with no suffix at all, and have totally un-filelike names for objects. So beware.

Or use the not quite released Daemon 1.0 which will MIME-wrap them according to HTTP2.

Sorry for the delay... I should answer [even] less mail :-}

Tim

Wow! Two of the most influential individuals with regard to the realization of the World Wide Web, sorting how out to manage the transfer of multimedia files. Now here we are — 15 years later — and it seems everyone is slinging homemade multimedia around the Web like child's play. In fact, it is child's play, or more accurately, schoolwork. I recently sat in on a conference at my son's first-grade class. They were engaged in an independent study of *animation*. They use digital video cameras (I know, big whoop — but wait, it gets better) to record vignettes at home, out-of-doors, at school, to do video interviews. They carry the files around on their USB drives (they wear them around their necks…) before uploading them where the class views them. They use MP3 recorders *in class* to record spontaneous thoughts because it's much faster and more "in the flow" than writing. I learned a new term, too, and found out it applies to me: DSL — as in "Digital as a Second Language." For my son and his buddies, "digital" is a *first* language. He was navigating his way through *Toy Story* on his iMac at 18 months, before he could speak, and he's hardly alone in that regard.

What's important about the prior discussion is this: if you have any doubt as to whether or not Millennials — and in particular teens to those near 30 — view the Social Web differently than Boomers or even Gen X…forget it. For the Millennials — who increasingly comprise and influence your markets — the use of the Social Web is simply part of everyday life. Think back to the touchpoint map and the ideas of integrated marketing. Add to the traditional forms of media a set of digital channels that fit as naturally into their daily experiences as watching TV does for Boomers.

On the Social Web multimedia plays an increasingly large role from both a consumption and production perspective. Multimedia makes up a large component of all social media — and sooner rather than later will likely account for the majority of social media. Think about it: Experience something and then find a keyboard or pad on which you can type an extended passage and blog about it…or grab your video phone, click record and then upload. The preferred path is pretty obvious. Flickr (purchased by Yahoo!), Photobucket (purchased by MySpace), YouTube (purchased by Google), Seesmic and others are the direct result.

Tuesday's One-Hour Exercise

The multimedia sites you will visit today are shown in the following list. Remember: this is a *survey*. Spend only 5 or 10 minutes on each site. This isn't enough time to fully explore and become part of the communities. Instead your goal is to get a sense for the content and the ways in which members of these sites are sharing and using this content to exchange everything from personal stories to viewpoints on the news to experiences with products and services. You're likely to confirm a couple of common thoughts about these sites — yes, there is content that doesn't legally belong there, and yes some of what you'll find is nonsense — but as well you'll also come away thinking,

"Hey, that's cool! I didn't know you could do that!" That's the "Aha!" you are looking for today: Those are the insights that consumers find valuable.

Multimedia sites to visit:

- Flickr (http://www.flickr.com)
- Photobucket (http://www.photobucket.com)
- YouTube (http://www.youtube.com)
- Seesmic (http://www.seesmic.com)
- Metacafe (http://www.metacafe.com)
- PersonalLifeMedia/DishyMix (http://personallifemedia.com)

Questions to consider:

- What service does this provide?
- Who would use this on a regular basis? Why?
- What content could you add to these sites?
- Are you getting "drawn in" — that is, are you starting to follow posts via comments and winding up in unexpected places?
- In addition to looking at the content in the site (for example, looking for product or brand information), ask yourself about the social motivation for the site.
- Pick out content that is interesting to you and think about why the person who posted this content did so. What was his or her motivation?
- What did you come away with as a result of the content you looked at having been posted?

Tuesday's Exercise Guide and Wrap-Up

As you are summarizing your work so far this week, take the time to think about any content that you may have uploaded and why you did this. If you've not uploaded content, and especially if you've never transferred content from a digital camera to the Internet, take a break here and try it.

Part of mastering social media is discovering the simple joy of seeing your own content online and in sharing it with other people. As you progress with later exercises, experience with the basics — like photo sharing — will help you get more out of this book and as a result will help prepare for the use of social media in your marketing program.

 Tip: In general, the newest digital cameras are much simpler when it comes to transferring content to a computer or even directly to the Internet than those just a few years old. Don't make yourself nuts trying this. Searching online for help is often a good idea if you get stuck. It's also a great way to experience support forums, something you will spend more time on in Chapter 9, "Social Platforms."

Today you covered a lot — multimedia accounts for much of the content that powers the Social Web — and came away with your first big, practical insight into the effective use of social media in business. The attraction of social media — as the name implies — has as much or more to do with how the content is connected and reinterpreted than it does the content itself. In other words, the focus is on the social connections, and only as a by-product on the media itself. The act of sharing is more important than what is being shared. This is the antithesis of the traditional advertising approach, where everything is tightly controlled and the focus is on the message.

As you roll into Wednesday, keep the idea of "social connections" forefront in your head. Connections will form the central theme of nearly everything you do from this point on.

Tuesday Bonus: An Additional Exercise

Having looked at a handful of content sites, you're probably thinking "OK, I see where I could have some fun and spend a lot of time." This is — in a serious way — certainly part of the social media dynamic as it impacts your current marketing programs. People who frequent these sites typically spend less time with other forms of media, most notably TV. But that is only half of it: The other question you're probably asking is "What can I do here *as a marketer*? How can I participate and in the process promote my product?"

The following links will help answer this. I've used the Nike+ Running Shoe as the example. The essential learning in today's remaining exercise is this: Like any integrated marketing effort, social media channels do not exist in isolation. In fact by definition they are connected: Users who participate in blogs also post pictures, and create videos and podcasts, and watch TV and listen to the radio. Often, they do all of this at the same time. The phrase is "continuous partial attention."

Look at these links, in the order presented. You'll start with a woman explaining the Nike+ and how it enables those who wear them to connect with each other around their shared passion of running. In her video, she also ties in well-known athletes, suggesting a connection to an additional community. After viewing this, you'll jump over to Flickr. Here, searching for "Nike" (I've provided the search result URL for you) you'll find a photo of a "hacked" running shoe. The owner of this hacked shoe has posted photos of how to "install" the Apple widget that powers Nike+ into his favorite (non-Nike) shoe.

Tip: Social Media isn't about the content itself: it is about the way in which consumers of content are connected and about the conversations that result.

Social Media Example: The Nike+ Running Shoe

- The Nike+ Explained on YouTube (`http://www.youtube.com/watch?v=rtFi5wlvP2k`)

- Nike on Flickr (`http://www.flickr.com/search/?q=nike`)

- The Running Shoe Modification (`http://www.flickr.com/photos/callumalden/347076681/`)

- The Discussion of the Modification (`http://www.metacomment.com/blog/2007/01/06/diy-nike-plus-hack/`)

Wednesday: Microblogs and Tagging

On Monday and Tuesday you surveyed some basic content. You looked at blogs, wikis, photo and video sharing, and more. You experienced a significant element in the attraction to social media and to its usefulness: It's the *connections* that count. On Monday you looked as well at how blog search tools and related analytical services help find or track content. Today you'll dive into microblogs and the concept of *tagging*. Microblogs are short sentences or thoughts: Think status updates. Tags are little descriptive bits that you apply to content so that you (and others) can find it again later.

If you're wondering how these concepts relate, it's the fact that both are quick, isolated actions that over time lead to something more substantive. The Social Web is built up of small, connected parts. The World Wide Web by comparison is certainly built up of connected parts, but they aren't necessarily *small*. Want proof? Go to your boss, right now, and request a meeting with IT. Tell everyone that that you want to rebuild your corporate website, you know, just to make it better. Watch them glaze over, and then look at the IT director squirming at the prospect of yet another year-long (or more!) project. No, the components of the traditional Web are *not* small. The Social Web, by comparison, is the world of quick comments, connections, and mash-ups: Small parts, connected, to do big things. The microblog is simply a word, a phrase, or a number that is injected into a stream of similar content and thereby adds meaning, clarification, or information to the stream. Think about the status updates in MySpace of Facebook, or social tools like Twitter. These streams can spark blog entries, articles, and even whole books! Or — if no one picks up on them — they simply vanish.

Tags are single words or very short phrases that are attached to social content to make it easy to find (increased utility) and easy to share (increased value). For example, if I am visiting a Formula 1 enthusiast website, I might tag it "motor sports." If I am visiting a pool chemical supplier's how-to page, I might tag that "green murky water." Perhaps you've been there too.

Tags are often organized into *clouds* or simple lists. Importantly, the tag collection around any specific content object is the result of a collective effort: If I tag something as "racing" and you tag the same object as "sports" then a third-party searching for either "racing" or "sports" will find the object. Because anyone can add tags, there needs to be some way to ensure relevance and prevent mischief, and the Social Web provides for that. Over time, the tags are ranked (the voting thing again…) by the use that each tag receives: those used most often to locate the object rise to the top, making that object more accessible to more people. Connections — and consensus — power the Social Web.

Wednesday's One-Hour Exercise

Today the assignment is easy. You're going to take a quick look at some popular micro-blog and tagging services. The point of today's exercise — as with all exercises this week — is to quickly survey the social media landscape and simply get a sense of what is available and how it is being used. By taking this time now, you'll have a firm basis and working knowledge across the range of activities that are available to you on the Social Web.

It is very possible that you are already participating in some of the activities covered on any given day. If so, you can either use this exercise as a review or extension, or you can use that tie to explore a similar activity that you may not have made the time to do. Regardless, for each of the exercises, do take the time to look, do, play, explore. The more you get involved yourself in social media *as a participant*, the more sense it will make when you consider the ways that social media can be used for marketing.

Microblog Services to Visit
- Twitter (`http://twitter.com/`)
- Pownce (`http://pownce.com/`)
- Tumblr (`http://tumblr.com/`)
- Plurk (`http://plurk.com`)
- Seesmic (`http://seesmic.com`)

Note: In the above URLs, there is no "www." That's on purpose. They aren't websites, per se. They are social media services.

As a starting point, Twitter is a good choice. First, it has lots of members, so there is a steady stream of content. Second, it has a nice public display of the main content stream — you don't have to sign up or do anything to look at what others are generating. You'll want to sign up though: it's easy and fast. A word to the wise: The raw stream itself probably won't make sense any more than randomly tapping into a phone switchboard would. However, in that analogy is the actual value. Imagine that instead of the raw stream you saw only a small subset of friends and colleagues with whom you really wanted to keep up-to-date. You'd see that Deb was heading for the beach or that Max was thinking about writing a book. You could jump into the conversation — or ignore it — as you wanted. Of course, instead of imaging this you could sign up and try it! C'mon, go for it. If you're like me, you won't get it at first. But then, over a few days...or a few minutes...as you add friends, family, colleagues, and start to build off of their connections, you'll figure it out as you become more connected with others. It's hard to explain, easy to experience.

 Note: At the time of this writing, another leading microblog service — Jaiku, recently acquired by Google — was not accepting new members and is instead in an invitation-only stage. Do check it out.

Questions to consider:

1. What is the attraction to following the activities of others?

2. How could you use these services? In your business? Internally? Externally? Personally?

Tagging Services to Visit:

- Del.icio.us (http://del.icio.us)
- Stumble Upon (http://www.stumbleupon.com)
- Ma.gnolia (http://ma.gnolia.com/)

Delicious is one of the core tagging services in a class called "social bookmarking." Users of Del.icio.us "tag" their favorite websites and add them to their personal, remotely stored bookmark list. If you are still maintaining a browser-based Favorites list, consider that your list is personal, to you only, and as such does not benefit your friends or colleagues. All of the work that you have done in building your list — the value that you have created by compiling resources and references — is off limits to everyone else. Likewise, the efforts of others who have similarly created local Favorites lists is off limits to you. How much better would it be if you pooled resources? This, by the way, is something that Millenials are generally very good at and do naturally: author Henry Jenkins made this point recently while speaking at South by Southwest Interactive Festival (SXSW) in Austin when he talked about the difference between the "we" language of contemporary political marketing versus the "me" language of more traditional campaigns.

At a more practical level, your browser-based Favorites are only available when you are using the computer on which your Favorites list is saved. At a friend's house down the street? Or an Internet café in Barcelona? Sorry, no Favorites for you! Del.icio.us solves this problem while at the same time bringing you not only the power of the collective in finding more sites like the ones you have bookmarked, but also an indication of the relative worth of each specific site based on how others have tagged or shared that same site.

StumbleUpon takes basic tagging and bookmarking one step further: Stumble-Upon combines a basic recommendation system with a website index: You find a site you have an opinion about ("like it, don't like it") and you rate it. Your fellow Stumblers — people whose interests match yours — then benefit from your recommendations when they look at similar sites, something you'll spend more time on in Chapter 11, "Reviews, Ratings, and Recommendations." For example, if you visit a site about an art exhibit and "like it," your friends who are into art will see that you liked this site the next time they look at art sites through StumbleUpon.

An Additional Exercise

If you haven't already, take some time to set up some of the social tools you've covered. Create a Twitter account, for example, or make a copy of selected bookmarks from your current Favorites list at Del.icio.us. If you're really bold, export your browser favorites and then delete them from your browser entirely: Make a clean break to social bookmarking. If you find yourself starting to shake after a week, you can always import and restore your list. But do try as many of the tools and services as you're comfortable with. Social media is, after all, a participatory sport. Like a high school dance, the action is out on the floor, not along the wall.

> ### Viral Marketing
>
> Here's a quick word on *viral marketing* as it relates to social media. The two terms are often used interchangeably, but they are *not* the same. Just as a room full of toddlers sets up the conditions under which a virus *can* spread, the Social Web is an environment through which your message *can* spread. However, just because you have a room full of toddlers does not mean that a virus *will* spread. They could all be washing their hands; stranger things have happened. I point this out because I often hear people say "We need to be on the Social Web so that we can infect it, so that our message will go viral." Don't count on it. Savvy Social Web citizens wash their hands frequently. Unless people — in large numbers — value and accept the content, viral campaigns have little chance of "infecting" anything.

Wednesday's Wrap-Up

Today you covered tagging, social bookmarking, and small quick text-streams called "microblogs." You looked at the role the collective plays — typically through the acts of filtering, compiling, and rating — in the culling of Web-based content. This has a direct impact on your business and your traditional offline/online marketing programs. Thumbs up, and your efforts get amplified as your message gets spread through social connections. Thumbs down...and you have to work a whole lot harder to achieve the same results.

Thursday: RSS

You started off your first week in the Hour a Day program looking at content. Mid-week you were looking at highly fluid, tiny conversations along with social tagging and recommendation services. Combined, the result is a Social Web that supports everything from impromptu, transient bursts to entries that develop a fixed permanence over time based on consensus. In a nutshell, you've looked at the content that's available to Social Web participants and at the tools that allow them to discover, rate, and share this content. I hope you've jumped in and participated.

Today's exercises focus on one thing, and one thing only: collecting and organizing social content. Today, you'll change your overall Web experience from "you go out and find it" to "it comes to you when it's fresh." You're going to learn about RSS (Really Simple Syndication). RSS is fundamentally important to the Social Web.

You're probably wondering something like this: "I have my Favorites list (hopefully maintained at Del.icio.us!). Why do I need to have this same stuff sent to me? I already get too much!" The answer is, RSS will make your life on the Social Web easier. Because it will make it so much easier, Chapter 12, "Social Interactions," is almost entirely devoted to the ideas and practices that originated in RSS. RSS provides two basic benefits, both of which are very important. Unlike email — where anyone can send you anything — RSS allows *you to control* what you receive, not like a filter but more like a smart magnet. Using RSS, you attract what you want rather than blocking what you don't. Think back to Twitter for a minute: The whole point of the service is to let you know what your friends and colleagues are up to. Who wants to run to the Web, or go to Twitter, and check to see if there are updates? To help with this, Twitter offers SMS-based text notices and an RSS feed. The SMS notices are useful if you want Twitter updates on-the-go. That benefit is clear. The RSS feed, however, duplicates the information you'll get if you simply go to Twitter and view someone you follow. So why set up RSS?

Multiply your use of social applications like "Twitter" by 10 and you'll start to get the idea. Social web users typically use more than one social application. Look at your own website Favorites list: In a study done in 2004, the *average* number of bookmarks was 184. *Now imagine that these were all social sites, and that they were all talking to you at random intervals.* Social sites are updated whenever participants feel like updating them. By comparison, typical websites are never updated. Social sites behave more like "breaking news" in that *updates,* which is to say content changes, are driven by random external factors. How would you keep up with this? Would you really want to log into each of your social sites every day or every week just to see if something had changed? Of course not. Instead, you'd instruct each site to ping you when something changes. This is what RSS, Atom, and similar protocols do. For simplicity, I'll use RSS in the following examples. The others operate in a substantially similar fashion.

To say that RSS powers the Social Web is an understatement. Without RSS, none but perhaps a handful of blogs would have survived. Without RSS, a blog — to the external audience — is no different than any other website. To read it, you have to go to it. Of all the websites in your Favorites list, how many did you visit last week? One? Three? Thirteen? Probably not 184. Without RSS, only the most popular blogs would have maintained any sort of traffic flow. The long tail...would get bobbed. Let's face it, if no one reads a blog what's the point of having it? But what if the audience could be made aware of new posts, as they are posted? That would change things. RSS allows blog posts to be sent *to its readers*, whenever it is updated or shortly thereafter. With an RSS reader — now built into most contemporary browsers email programs and dedicated tools like Google Reader — you simply subscribe to the blogs you want and then look periodically to see what's new. It's a lot like checking your phone messages: Rather than calling all of your friends to see if any had called while you were out, you press a button and hear something like "You have seven new messages." You can deal with them as you'd like, on your time.

So what about multimedia? Can RSS help with that, too? Would I be asking this if it couldn't?

Dave Winer, one of the architects of RSS, introduced a new feature called "enclosures" into RSS in late 2000. Think of enclosures as a way to package and deliver content other than text. Among the first uses of this new feature was sending audio files on a subscription basis. The *podcast* had been born. A podcast is after all nothing more than a scheduled sequence of audio files, typically downloaded to a computer and then transferred to a portable media device — initially via iTunes to the iPod, hence the name "podcasting." Audio podcasting and its relative, video podcasting, are now standard tools in the social marketers' toolkit.

Thursday's One-Hour Exercise

Today you're going to pull together everything you've done so that you're ready for tomorrow when you visit some social networks. Begin by opening your web browser: Let's look at where RSS feeds live and how to work with them.

Figures 4.5 and 4.6 show Internet Explorer, Version 7, and Firefox, Version 2. Open up your Feeds list (don't worry if it's empty, you'll fill it).

Sites to visit:

- Twitter (You have set this up, right?) (`http://twitter.com`)
- Boing Boing (`http://www.boingboing.net`)
- Seesmic (`http://seesmic.com`)

Things to do:

Locate the RSS/Atom subscription icons for each of the suggested services. Add these to your Feeds list. Although you won't see much right away, take a look at your feeds tomorrow and see what's new.

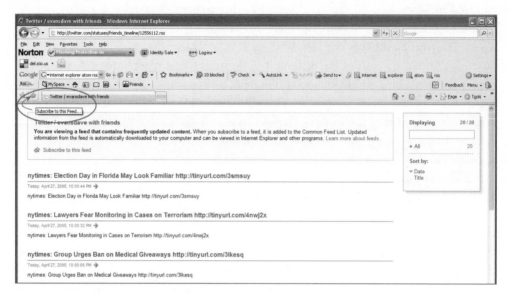

Figure 4.5 Subscribing to a Feed on Internet Explorer

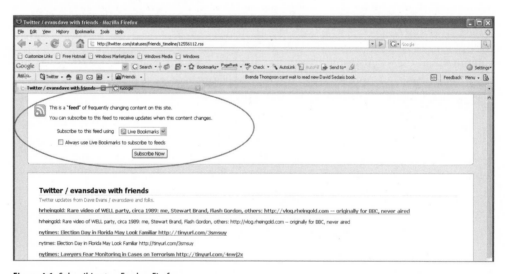

Figure 4.6 Subscribing to a Feed on Firefox

Thursday's Exercise Guide and Wrap-Up

Today you looked at RSS, the universal connector that sits between social content and content subscribers. RSS enables the scheduled delivery of the content you want, freeing you from having to go out and search for it again after you or someone in your social circle has located it once. You can think of RSS as a sort of digital labor-saving device. Importantly, RSS isn't simply for social content: It's for any content that is "better when delivered." This applies to news, service subscriptions, marketing updates, downtime alerts, and more.

Friday: Social Networks

I waited until Friday to introduce social networks for a reason: You've spent four days on social media and haven't visited a social network yet. What should be clear, then, is that the *Social Web* and *social media* are *not* the same thing as *social networks*. Social networks are simply one element of the Social Web. Social networks wouldn't exist — at least not in the context most people think of them now — without the technologies and broadly adopted online social practices associated with the social media services you explored earlier in the week. The usefulness of the featured services — along with RSS — have made joining and actively participating in social networks possible. To be clear, community members don't need a lot of what you've now seen if they are satisfied with belonging to *one* community — but who wants to spend all day in one community? If social media and its application to marketing were truly centered around single communities, you could buy banner ads on MySpace or Facebook and be done with it. Fortunately for everyone involved, there is much, much more to do on the Social Web.

Consider that AOL's membership peaked at about 26 million in 2002. AOL is proof of the size of the "walled garden" community — that is to say, a community that really does intend for its members to get the vast majority of service, experiences, and interactions within the confines of that community — that can be built with fairly basic community tools. At the same time, America Online (AOL) also makes a pretty good case for the impact of the richer toolset you've seen this week. By 2006, AOL's membership had dropped to about half of its peak levels driven at least in part by the realization that a wider set of social tools — Del.icio.us, blogs, Wikipedia, the things you've seen this week — and a growing number of increasingly focused online social communities exist outside of AOL. You name the interest and there is a community for it — these communities exist right alongside big mainstream communities such as MySpace and Facebook and compete for attention. The ability to easily manage subscriptions, to connect community experiences, and to efficiently keep track of the information flowing into, out of, and through multiple communities has made the

Social Web a reality. This is again an example of the long tail applied to social participation and the kind of participation in niche activities that develops as a result. This has carried an entire user base — led by the Millenials — into an online social world that is unprecedented in terms of scope, depth of experience, and ultimately, real world social impact. This is the larger social media framework that you are now facing as a marketer.

Friday's One-Hour Exercise

Today you'll visit the two leading social sites — MySpace and Facebook — and look at some of the methods and applications that marketers are using in them.

 Note: Be sure to check on existing policies regarding the use of social networks when using company-owned equipment. If in doubt, ask first.

Visiting Facebook, the first thing you will notice is that while you can see an abbreviated view of Facebook members, you need to create an account to see the sort of detailed personal information that makes Facebook what it is. Facebook is a relatively closed community and so the real content is largely unavailable outside of its membership. Facebook began as a private network — it was created for use at Harvard and then expanded first within the Ivy League (can you name all eight schools that make up the Ivy League?) and then to all colleges — before opening itself to anyone in 2006. It retains some of the exclusivity to this day even as it has evolved to be a much more open community.

By comparison, MySpace is largely open and available to all. While you can't do much without joining ("You must be logged in to do that!"), you can at least browse all of the member pages. Again, go back to the roots of MySpace — during its early days efforts were made to grow membership as fast and wide as possible. As a result, MySpace — with about 200 million accounts worldwide — commands nearly 80 percent of all social network page views. Facebook accounts for 15 to 20 percent, and *all other networks combined* make up the balance. Together, these two social networks account for over 95 percent of all social network traffic. You'll see this distribution of social networks and membership again in detail in Chapter 9, "Social Platforms."

Apart from the Big Two and other social networks, there are literally hundreds of business social networks. AdGabber — built on the Ning platform — is a great example. AdRants founder Steve Hall built AdGabber at home, in a couple of hours. The primary purpose of the network is to offer a space where advertising professionals can talk about and share industry experiences. LinkedIn and Plaxo Pulse are business connection services with lots of special features that professionals find useful. Today you get to survey these sites: Spend a few minutes on each and consider the questions I have framed for you.

Social sites to visit:

- Facebook (`http://www.facebook.com`)
- MySpace (`http://www.myspace.com`)

Business sites to visit:

- AdGabber (`http://www.adgabber.com`)
- LinkedIn (`http://www.linkedin.com`)
- Plaxo Pulse (`http://www.plaxo.com`)

Questions to consider:

- Look around at MySpace in particular. What do you think?
- Now imagine being 18 to 24 years old (or maybe you are!). What does it look like from this perspective?
- How is MySpace different from Facebook?
- Who is advertising? What is being advertised?
- Beyond the ads, what is being talked about?
- Compare the social sites with the business sites. What is the *common* element?
- How could you use the social sites?
- How could you use the business sites?

An Additional Exercise: ProductPulse

In 2007 Facebook introduced a significant innovation when it opened its platform to independent application developers. The first wave of applications included better ways of sending rich messages, offering vampire bytes, tossing sheep, the kinds of things that you'd expect as a "Version 1" attempt with a new toolset. Version 2, which is shaping up now, takes the learning from Version 1 and pushes it forward into much more sophisticated applications. Firms like Slide and RockYou — creators of early and innovative applications like "Fun Wall" — are serving as launch pads for this next wave of applications. Among them is ProductPulse (see Figure 4.7). ProductPulse allows subscribers to quickly rate products and services (love/hate/want/need info) and then share their list with Facebook friends. Applications like these have natural marketing uses within a permission-based, user-driven social context. Pay specific attention to these types of applications as it is very likely you will want to tap them when you set about building your social media marketing plans.

Figure 4.7 ProductPulse on Facebook

ProductPulse: Marketing on Social Networks

In mid-2007, Friend-to-Friend launched an embedded marketing application on Facebook. The embedded application — called ProductPulse — encourages participants to rate products, services, and brands. Ratings range from "Love It!" to "Hate It!" and include action-oriented expressions like "Want It" and "Need Info." Along with the core ratings tools, the application facilitates contests that feature specific items: Participants enter themselves into the contest to win the items as they talk about them through the application. Very importantly, a positive comment is an entry, just as a negative comment is also an entry. There is no filtering or screening because that would violate the basic terms of engagement between marketers and participants on the Social Web. Instead, marketers using ProductPulse rely on two things to prevent the kind of runaway bashing that can occur. First, they make good stuff. Mountain Hardwear, Northface, and Timbuk2 are known for the quality standards to which they adhere. Second, because the marketing action in the contests themselves is all around *winning that item*, the majority of contest participants tend to fall into the "I want it" camp. Nonetheless, in the contests' run to-date, there is always a subset of entrants who in fact do not like these products, and they say so. On the Social Web, that's all part of the game. In return, the participating companies get great exposure as friends tell friends about the contests. The fact that some negative comments exist actually *validates* the overwhelming positive conversation that occurs, a phenomenon that Bazaarvoice has documented through published studies. See Chapter 11, "Ratings, Reviews and Recommendations," for more on Bazaarvoice.

Friday's Wrap-Up

Today you spent an hour looking at two types of social networks and, if you did the additional exercise, an embedded social marketing application. With the exception of the embedded applications, the social networks — MySpace in particular — operate more or like traditional media websites. This is to say that they a) generate massive traffic, and then b) rely on interruptive advertising for revenue. You can play there — they have a rate card — but that's old school. The new school is beginning to emerge: The embedded applications first introduced on Facebook are part of the new wave of social media tools. These new marketing tools are monetized through their value to marketers *and* are *noninterruptive* from the perspective of audience. Over on the business site, it's a similar story with an additional source of revenue: Traffic generates ad revenue, which is then supplemented with fees for premium services.

From a marketer's perspective, social networks offer two things: traditional media-buying and ad placement opportunities — let's face it, getting your brand in front of a subscriber base of 200 million is worth something. At the same time, and growing in importance, is your forward-looking opportunity to develop noninterruptive, member-driven social campaigns. Hold that thought.

Chapter 4: The Main Points

- Social media derives its value simultaneously from the collective and the individual, not the mass. This is a reversal of traditional marketing and creative models where a single message is crafted and pushed out to a mass audience.
- *Network value* — that is, how efficiently it supports sharing and collaboration — is determined by the way in which members are connected. Networks that follow Reed's Law — where members are free to form groups and connections between themselves and these groups — are the types of networks of most interest to *social media* marketers.
- The touchpoint map and social feedback cycle are central to the successful application of social media.
- RSS allows content to be scheduled for delivery. This is much better than having to go and check on it. RSS powers much of the Social Web.
- Social networks are part of, but not the same as, social media and the Social Web.

Week 2: The Social Feedback Cycle

For the past fifty years media spending has been focused largely on awareness — where it drives demand — and point-of-sale — affirming pending purchases or shifting them to a competing brand. Under-utilized by too many marketers has been the consideration process through which consumers evaluate purchase options.

The consideration phase — in the middle of the purchase funnel — turns out to be the central link between the Social Web and Marketing. This is the Operations connection of social media based marketing, where conversations between consumers based on experiences carry further and with greater trust than traditional media.

Chapter Contents
Social Media in Marketing
Consideration and the Purchase Funnel
Consumer-Generated Media
Create Your Social Feedback Cycle
The Main Points

Social Media in Marketing

On the Social Web, consumers connect, share, and validate thoughts, arriving at consensus over time. Consensus on the Social Web may be fleeting or scattered — think of fads or small groups of ardent followers for products like the new designer energy drinks — or it may indeed manifest as "mass" popularity around long-standing power brands such as Red Bull, Apple, and Nike, all of which have a strong presence on the Social Web. Online marketing concepts such as *engagement* and *loyalty* morph into their social counterparts like *participation* and *reputation*. Why? With traditional and most online media, the interaction is generally one way: The end user gets to watch or play with something that someone in a position of control has put forth. Too often, that's about as far as it goes. With social media, it's truly participative: The end user gets to shape, create, and share the content. Through participation and response, social reputations are formed: When the context is marketing, these become the active social expressions of the brand. This participative development of reputation is a direct consequence of collective action, of *community*. Communities — whether formally built around a specific interest or cause, or informally built through more casual connections — sit at the center of the Social Web.

Featured Case: GlaxoSmithKline Consumer Healthcare

The desire to lose weight is one of the most universal and emotional issues in America. Millions of overweight women and men are constantly seeking a "silver bullet" that will rescue them from the torment of failed efforts. So when GlaxoSmithKline Consumer Healthcare set out to market alli, the only FDA-approved weight-loss product available to overweight adults without a prescription, they knew they were entering unusually challenging territory. They needed a way to understand the rational and emotional tugs of war overweight adults face every day in order to help the company develop, and inspire, a new behavioral model, while carefully managing consumer expectations.

A first-of-its-kind over-the-counter (OTC) drug launch required a new approach to listening to, and understanding, weight-challenged consumers — new ways that would get at consumers' hearts and minds and provide an intimate experience, which allowed the company to go deeper than ever before. GSK Consumer Healthcare partnered with Communispace, spanning over two years to create five private online communities that became the center of gravity for the entire multifaceted market launch of alli.

On July 25, 2007, GlaxoSmithKline released its second quarter earnings statement reporting that sales of over-the-counter alli hit $155 million in just six weeks, since its launch on June 14, 2007. On October 23, 2007, the company announced that it had sold more than 2 million alli starter packs at retail, and that alli users are enthusiastically embracing alli and its proven track record of helping people lose weight gradually.

In the physical world, people can engage and learn through direct experience. Then, based on that experience, they develop a "favored supplier" with regard to a particular product or service (for example, a restaurant or line of automobiles). Community — the collection of individuals acting together around a specific topic in conversations on the Social Web — doesn't operate in quite this way. In an online social community, loyalty and engagement are certainly possible, although they take a different form, and are much more easily lost given the power and presence of the collective. The online community — because it is measurable and therefore tangible — fosters *participation*, through which engagement at the individual level occurs. The community maintains — that is, acts as a curator for — the *collective reputation* of a brand, based on which an individual may develop or attest to personal loyalty. In other words, communities are the containers for the individual attributes you are familiar with and use when building mass campaigns. On the Social Web, it's the collective — not just the individual — that is of interest to marketers. This is not because "collective" is analogous to "mass" — it isn't — but rather because it is the tangible collective that the individual taps when making a decision. By influencing the collective, you reach the individual. Therefore, and arising directly out of this, active participation — not message saturation — drives your success on the Social Web.

Step back and look at most traditional forms of media: They are "push" and "tell" oriented. They place the marketer in control of the message and dictate for the consumer a subservient role. Social media tips this balance: On the Social Web, both the consumer and the marketer have an equal voice in terms of *permission to speak*. This not the same as implied trust, which is something else altogether, but it does serve to support the notion that as a marketer you need to participate in the communities of which your audience is a part in order to *gain* trust. On the Social Web, to *not* be present is to send a message that you don't really care enough to participate.

Tip: On the Social Web, your *absence* is conspicuous. Failing to participate retards the advancement of trust. In fact, it can increase the likelihood of *mistrust*.

From your perspective, social media may be outright scary, and the cautionary memos from your legal department don't help. *From the perspective of your audience, especially if they are using the Social Web already, participation is easy, simple, and natural.* Members of your audience may not grasp or even care about the complexities of the corporate policies that are causing you grief: For them, the Social Web is second nature. Just do it. Actually, for many, it's first nature: For younger Millenials, some of their first social experiences were very likely digital, not analog. I am making this point in a bit of detail here because it presents a significant challenge to the traditional marketing orientation. There are genuine issues relating to participation — including the fear that comes with ceding control — that require your thought and commitment prior to initiating a social campaign. At the same time, your audience may well expect you to be there. This is the subject of more than a few books and certainly will be the theme of many more. The good news is that if you work through these issues, following the framework that I am outlining in this book, you'll be able to operate on the Social Web with a very high degree of confidence and in ways that Social Web participants will tend to embrace. Ultimately, participation is key, and participation is what this book is all about.

Oddly, too many marketers still take the position that they are better off *not* participating so as not to appear to "approve" of the social conversations that include references to their brand. There is an obvious wrong-headedness in this logic, and the flaw here is actually two-fold. First, it implies that consumers care whether or not a marketer has approved *their* conversation. *Consumers don't care.* In fact, they are having these conversations themselves because marketers have *not* entertained them in the past. Second, choosing not to participate implies a now questionable belief that consumers don't have an alternative forum to share information. *Consumers have lots of alternatives.* Back in the day, robust, widespread mass communication may have muted casual conversation around brands. No more. Consumers are having these conversations between themselves, posting all sorts of content around the Social Web widely and easily, and regardless of whether or not what they post has been "approved" by your agency or public relations (PR) team.

Consideration and the Purchase Funnel

Savvy marketers have not only picked up on the existence of the Social Web but have found ways to use it to advance their interests by tapping into the consideration phase of the purchase process, something out of their reach with the traditional tools of marketing. How they've done this is what this section is all about.

The classic purchase funnel referenced in Chapter 3, "What Is Social Media?" is back. Figure 5.1 shows the purchase funnel and buying phases of awareness, consideration, and purchase. "Consideration" links the buying-process activities, connecting awareness and purchase. Consideration is the point where a consumer thinks through the purchase. Value, performance, applicability, reputation...are all "considered" factors surrounding a potential purchase.

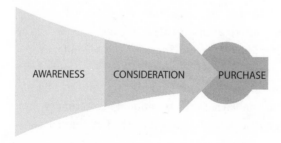

Figure 5.1 The Purchase Funnel

Traditional media and marketing practitioners approach the problem of inciting a purchase from the awareness perspective, leaving the consumer to make up her mind (consideration) albeit with lots of interruptive prompting. By comparison, social media simultaneously tackles awareness *and* consideration, and does so with a lower level of perceived interruption. To be sure, traditional media still plays a role in pure awareness. Again I'll stress that "social media" *is not* a technique that is applied in isolation. However, unlike traditional media, social media connects with and involves the consumer from awareness all the way through consideration. Just as with a TV spot, an interesting forum or blog post or a compelling homemade video may be the *starting point* through which a potential customer gains an awareness of a product or service. However, with the social channels, often right in the same conversation, a more substantive validation that supports the purchase decision takes place. Social media is applicable as both a prompt (awareness) and as a validation, something that works very much to your advantage if you apply it correctly.

It is important to understand the role of the social feedback cycle as a *purchase validation* tool. Note too that the *source of awareness* has little to do with it. Traditional media is still very much a part of the picture in terms of awareness. It's the validation step that is changing the equation. From a Forrester Research report comes the following consumer quote:

> *"No matter what I hear, read, or find on TV, radio, or in a magazine or newspaper, I can verify it on the Internet."*

Boom! There you have it: You talk about it, and they check it out. This validation impact of the Social Web via the content created and made available in the social feedback cycle is best understood though the mechanics of word-of-mouth. Figure 5.2 shows the purchase funnel with the addition of post-purchase word-of-mouth and consumer-generated media. It is the post-purchase conversation — built up and validated through the collective wisdom of the crowd — that ultimately drives word-of-mouth-based evangelism.

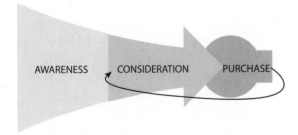

Figure 5.2 The Social Feedback Cycle

The Role of the Evangelist

Evangelists exert a significant impact on the buying process through the social feedback cycle via word-of-mouth and consumer-generated media. As consumers increasingly choose to block advertising in all forms, the impact of traditional advertising is bound to be diminished. By what degree remains to be seen. Nonetheless, it is happening. This is perhaps ironic: Consumers aren't opposed to learning more, and no one wants to make a poor choice. It's the intrusions and the interruptions that are driving this. In response, consumers are using the Social Web to talk with *each other* about potential buying decisions. These actions are often driven by evangelists.

The conversations built around word-of-mouth extend to the discussions of the company itself when the company chooses to participate in the conversation. Participation conveys a sense of trust, of caring, of involvement in the outcome. This applies even when the experience is negative: There are many cases of a "mistake" being righted in public, and of considerable goodwill being generated in the process. To this end, using the Social Web as a *listening* platform pays dividends in terms of a better understanding of what your customers want. Taking the next step — using the Social Web as a platform for talking and sharing — brings your company to the level of *participation*.

 Tip: The addition of consideration-phase marketing bridges a critical gap for marketers between awareness and purchase while opening the channel for effective word-of-mouth.

Consideration phase marketing is a toolbox essential. It forms the basis for effective social media campaigns. Participation in the consideration phase — using the tools available, offering and sharing content — is an essential "plus" in the awareness-consideration-purchase campaign integration process. Quantitative measurement — readily enabled on the Social Web — gives you the ability to track effectiveness as you add social elements to your existing campaigns.

Although there is a common misperception that social media is somehow unmeasurable, it is in fact quite measurable. Chapter 13, "Objectives, Metrics, and ROI," is devoted entirely to the connection of business objectives and social media measurement. Consider the impact of social media and the conversations that reference your brand, product, or service with your existing measures of customer profitability. You already know about the value of repeat customers in terms of their generally higher purchase levels. Take this a step further, and use the Social Web to gauge the impact of these same customers as "reference experts" for other customers. One of the benefits of using the Social Web as a measurable feedback loop is that you can see the impact of beneficial word of mouth. Your existing customers are — or should be — among your strongest evangelists. After all, they are buying your product again and again...they must like it! Your objective should be to get them to talk about their positive experiences. This gives you the double benefit of making the current sale — to them — and a future sale to the new customer that they create for you.

Social media measurement has a direct impact on the value calculation of current customers. It may be, for example, that an "expensive" customer — one that always seems to be asking for a special part or new feature — is actually the "hub" for your "profitable" customers. Identify, connect with, and tap this value through social media and its measurement. By taking account of the social feedback cycle, your calculation of your customer's "net profitability" changes dramatically. Customers who ask for favors can be expensive: But if they are *so delighted* as a result that they create three new customers for you, it may well be worth the investment. If it's favor after favor, followed by a never-ending stream of requests for price concessions with no detectable beneficial conversation being generated, then you're servicing yourself right out of business. Those are good things to know, and powerful distinctions to draw. The simple act of *listening* on the social web enables this level of understanding.

Shown in Figure 5.3, adding "Degree of Influence" expands the "profitable customer" segment, and, suggests strategies for converting selected noninfluential customers to influential customers. You will spend more time on this in Chapter 7, "Influence and Measurement," when you work with the Net Promoter Score and related measures of influence.

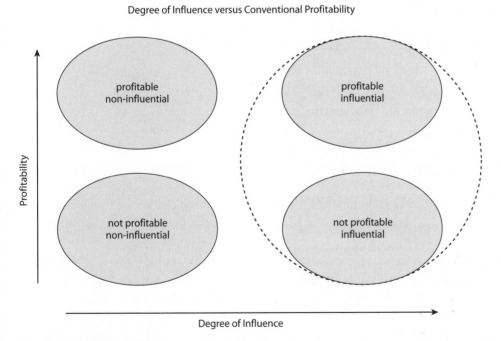

Figure 5.3 Profitability and Influence

In summary, marketing efforts focused on the social feedback cycle are less about what a marketer has to say and instead more about the consumer and what he wants to know right now. While it may be tempting to jump ahead to measurement or some other favorite chapter, take your time and work through the social feedback cycle, thinking about why it works and about its role in social media versus traditional media. This will be important later when you start building your social media plan. If you jump ahead and simply pick three social channels, you'll be fast out of the gate, as they say in horse racing. But there is also a good chance that one or more of your ideas will not work — that's to be expected with any new media form. If that's all you've got, it's going to be a short ride. On the other hand, if you work through the process I've established in this week's exercises and still happen to pick the wrong channel for a particular application, you'll quickly catch it, correct it, and move on toward a success. By tapping the social feedback cycle — and understanding how to build off of it — you create a powerful link between your awareness and point-of-purchase efforts based on the value of trusted conversations. Trusted conversations and the content associated with them — however casual or trivial they may appear — are essential to your successful use of social media.

 Tip: What you see on the social web may seem pointless, trivial, or otherwise lacking in conventional measures of editorial value. Avoid this mindset: Instead, think about the fact that someone actually took the time to create this content. To that person, what is being expressed through this content most certainly matters.

Consumer-Generated Media

The Internet has had a pronounced impact on how people view *their ability* to gather unbiased information, to *seek, find, and obtain* a wider range of products and services, and to talk with others about actual experiences both before and after purchase.

Coincident with the launch of the World Wide Web, content itself was changing from analog form (sheets of paper, vinyl records, VHS tapes) to digital forms (web pages and blogs, MP3 audio, MPEG movies) that lent themselves to distribution on the Internet checked to a large extent only by available bandwidth. These two developments — the realization of a global network and the digitization of content — multiplied each other, driving the growth in the use of the Web as an information and fulfillment platform.

As an example, consider Napster and its impact on music. If music were spread over a global network in *analog* form, it would quickly deteriorate in quality as successive copies were made. Think about the cassettes (or eight-track tapes!) that used to be made for use in the car from the vinyl albums: The sound quality was reduced in each successive copy. As a result, copies of copies weren't worth the effort. Alternatively, consider digital copies — each perfect — *but with no global network*. This is essentially the situation that existed for the first 20 years of digital audio: Compact discs (CDs) were not widely copied and passed around, other than in an analog form — e.g., as cassette tapes, very much subject to the aforementioned limitations. However, when the two came together — digital content plus a global digital network — the result was no less than a tectonic shift. The music business is still trying to recover, and the film and video businesses are being challenged now. Digital content spreads rapidly and perfectly, quickly becoming both everywhere at once — powering widespread distribution — and persistent over time — filtering into the niche markets and driving the long tail.

There is a second profound impact of the combination of digital content and a global digital network: It's the breakdown of the scale requirements that have prior to this point supported mass media. Not only did the Internet and digital content change the economics of distribution, it created a viable market for very small audiences. Where the transition from "three networks" to "four networks plus cable" split viewers into narrower segments, the combination of Internet-based distribution and the digitization of content fundamentally changed the ways in which consumers viewed, used, and shared information and digital content across a range of decisions and activities. Consumers are more connected, more informed, and more likely to *share experiences* with each other as a result.

Great recent examples of this are Dell's "Idea Storm" and Starbuck's "MyStarbucksIdea" forums, along with companies like Southwest Airlines and Zappos and their use of Twitter, a very casual form of blogging and community-like interaction. Dell and Starbucks are using a combination blogs and forums to provide current, past, and prospective customers with the ability to directly comment on the issues that matter, including the direction of future product ideas. Southwest Airlines and Zappos are using more casual channels — in this case, Twitter — to maintain an ongoing conversation that establishes a very basic level of personalized communication between the brand and its audience. All feature plenty of content — positive and negative — and stand as testaments to the willingness and desire for consumers to get involved in the brands that they are — or about to become — passionate about.

Figure 5.4 shows a typical Twitter dialog in which I happened to be involved. A friend was commenting on Southwest Airlines with regard to travel with children, and I responded with the information that I had (having flown Southwest in the prior week). Shortly after, a post from Southwest appeared on Twitter, directing people traveling with children to its online tips on how to make that travel easier. This is a really nice example of the smart use of social channels like Twitter: By simply being involved in the conversation, you can learn about what your customers like (and don't like) and you can respond right away, through that same channel. Not only do you get on converse directly with the person creating the original comment, you also get to do it in a forum that *influences* everyone else who is watching.

Figure 5.4 Twitter Conversations

Consumer-generated media — photos, blogs, videos, comments, ratings, reviews — is controlled by the *participants* in that media or conversation. They directly control the content and the path it takes. Consumer-generated media features the thoughts, hobbies, and interests of consumers. While the bulk of this content is created purely for fun, sharing experiences that relate to products, events, services — in short, many of the things that you sell — appears in the same channels and often with the goal of encouraging or dissuading a specific purchase based on personal experience. Think of the sites that enthusiastically support — or vehemently denounce — popular automobiles, stores, telecommunications providers, airlines, and of course restaurants. Firms like Nielsen|Buzzmetrics and TNS|Cymfony specialize in the measurement of online conversations through quantitative indexing of blogs and similar forums, giving marketers insight into what these consumers think about specific products and services. This information can be folded right back into the product development process, creating products "just for them" and thereby encouraging active, authentic evangelism.

The takeaway for marketers is this: participants on the Social Web engage in social activities. They talk about the things that interest them, and this talk can be measured. What interests them includes not only personal activities — birthdays, celebrations, and similar — but also the experiences that arise directly out of the things that you bring to them through the marketplace. Airline flights, concerts, movies, new cars, dealership service experiences, hotel stays…are all extensively documented on the Social Web.

Need a New Computer?

Consider the following personal story from Hilary Powers. Hilary is an editor, and just happens to be the developmental editor for this book. She writes, "My computer is showing signs of going belly-up, so I've got to think about a new one. Assorted discussion lists have persuaded me that the best thing to do is get someone trustworthy to build a machine locally — but who's trustworthy? I went online to check out the nearest store, only to find reviewers split about evenly between love and hate, with the latter more recent. On the other hand, a guy up the road had all enthusiastic reviews, so I went and talked to him and was very favorably impressed. Deal isn't quite done, but I expect to close shortly — and return from my speaking engagement in New York to a brand-new machine."

(Author's note: Hilary did indeed return to find a brand new machine, and loves it.)

So why the big interest in consumer content and all of the associated conversations now? Consumer-generated media is a reflection of the generational norms: as Millennials move into the center of the marketing power band, their online behaviors become increasingly significant. Websites, the first wave of online publishing, were (and many remain) largely one-directional, island-mentality prospects. That some sites still expect others to *ask permission* before linking is proof-positive of this. This first wave — developed and led early-on by Boomers in the early/mid-'90s tracks the Boomer mindset: It's all about me, and it's my property. More recently, blogs have exploded. They are in many ways an easier way for people to tell their own story. Others can comment — creating an "us" experience. Open publishing and truly collaborative platforms called "wikis" are now gaining popularity as their place in the overall landscape gets sorted out. Not coincidentally, the Millenials (which includes people ages 18 to 24) are gaining considerable influence. The Millennial mindset is "we" compared with the Boomer "me" — and nowhere is this more evident than wikis, the mashup — the connecting together of existing software services to make something new, as is often done with Google maps and various geographic or demographic data sources to create a richer map — and similar collaborative work products. These all invite participation, and are essentially controlled only by the collective. Generational norms are expressing themselves on the Social Web via the information structures they suggest.

The proliferation of consumer-generated media also tracks broadband adoption, users of which are more likely to create — or at the least share — content. The majority of broadband users create or share content with others compared to a minority of dial-up users. John B. Horrigan, Senior Research Specialist with the Pew Internet Project, put it this way in 2002 as broadband was emerging: "Broadband users drive in both directions on the information superhighway. With their tendencies to create and post online content, they value not only fast uploading speeds, but also an unconstrained Internet, a network on which they are free to publish and share whatever they want, with whomever they choose." Sites like Current TV — through a combination of video and web postings — bring the same opportunity to younger consumers seeking a broad-reach multichannel forum, allowing individuals to reach the widest audience for their content and offering them the greatest range of sources to satisfy their appetite for information.

 Tip: For a fun look at the world of banner ads, check out Current TV and search for "Man vs. Banner Ad." You'll find Current TV at `http://current.com`.

The net impact is a democratization of information, a relative loss of control for the established content distributors — including marketers, agencies, and PR firms — and a corresponding gain for consumers. *This has had an obvious and direct impact on marketing and advertising.* This democratization — and the tools supporting it — have enabled what is likely the largest driver yet of the changes in how consumers learn: *consumer-generated media.* What was a single voice being broadcast through centralized services is now a sea of individual voices — powered by consumer generated media — coming together in conversations. The key point is partially that the illusion of control, to the extent that it ever really existed, has been lifted. In its place, Social Web participants now have the power to make what they were already doing louder. From a marketing perspective, you're no longer competing just with your direct competitors for share of voice: You're also competing directly with *your customers.*

Create Your Social Feedback Cycle

Your exercises this week focus on establishing the feedback cycle for your chosen brand, product, or service. You'll start by identifying what you want to look at, and then you'll make a list of all of the things you are doing to generate awareness or encourage a sale at the point of purchase. Finally, you'll use existing tools to discover and capture what is being said on the Social Web as it relates to your current marketing program. The work that you do this week — along with the touchpoint map you'll create next week — will form the measurement framework for your social media marketing plan.

 Tip: A set of worksheets covering this week's exercises can be found in the appendix of this book. In addition to these printed worksheets, you can also download electronic copies and access related resources at the website accompanying this book. Complete information regarding these resources and the website is included in the appendix.

The Social Feedback Cycle

To understand how to apply social media, start by getting a handle on how social media is being applied to you! The reality of social media is that it is by and large something that happens *to you* as a result of a set of experiences that your brand, product, or service have set into motion. Go back to the purchase funnel: Social media is generated at the *output* end of the funnel. If you say "Our new formulation with XZ7 really gets whites whiter…" it has to do it, and the result has to be obvious. The conversation on the Social Web *is going reflect your claim*: "You've got to try this new XZ7 stuff…it really works!" Compare that with, "They claim it's a new formulation…I looked at the label and an online testing report (click here!): The product hasn't changed. They simply renamed the ingredients. It's no better than the old stuff." Which conversation do you want?

This is a key realization in the application of social media in marketing: Where you can craft and deliver your own message in traditional awareness and point-of-sale efforts, on the Social Web your participation is just one of many voices. Quite often participation is limited to gauging and responding to, or even facilitating the (positive!) conversations that occur there. Your ability to control the conversation — other than through your own behavior — is severely limited, if it even exists at all.

This week you'll create your own feedback cycle, including on it the consumer-generated media elements that contribute to the conversations that impact your brand. This may be a bit tougher than it sounds, so take the time to work through each of the steps. Creating your social feedback cycle will show you how your message — combined with the actual experiences of your customers and the larger conversations that occur — is being fed back into your campaigns at the point of consideration. This exercise will set the stage for understanding which social media elements are likely to be most effective in amplifying beneficial conversations versus addressing those that are offered by detractors.

To get started building a feedback cycle, you need to decide *what* to map. Ideally you'll use one of your own products or services that you are responsible for, or even your brand as a whole. If you are working through this book purely as an exercise or simply want to see how social media applies to an arbitrary or favorite brand, then you can pick any brand with which you'd like to work. The main point is this: You want to work with a brand, product, or service that you understand. In this exercise you'll need a more-than-passing familiarity with how the product or service is being marketed. If you make up or assume the answers, you'll miss the value of the exercise.

Once you've identified a product, service, or brand, you're going to make two lists. The first is a detailed list of your business objectives. Specifically defined objectives like "Turn a profit of X" or "Create a sustainable online presence as measured by Y" ought to be at the top of your list. But don't stop there: Dig deeper, and in particular dig into the things that *lead to* a profit or create a sustained presence. For example, your objectives may be increasing market share (new sales), promoting a new use of your product (new customers), or elevating the opinion of your brand (better reputation). The most important thing is to be clear about what you are trying to accomplish so that you can tie the measures you'll develop in later chapters to those objectives.

Monday's One-Hour Exercise

Today you're going to spend an hour reviewing and documenting specific objectives for your campaign. Work through the following questions, and think carefully through the answers you provide. It's not a test — however, the clearer you are about what you want (and how you will measure it), the higher your chances for success.

- What is the name of the product or service (or brand) with which you will be working?
- What is the business objective of this campaign?
- What are the metrics or objectives you are setting for this campaign? List them all.
- For each metric identified, what is the success value? What is the failure value? (In other words, what result would make you decide to double your effort or stop altogether? This could be either something that happens or something that fails to happen.)
- For each metric identified, what is the *current* value?
- In a short summary, write out what success looks like.

Some of the above may seem trivial, but you'll be surprised by how quickly you start to slow down and have to dig or think to come up with answers you could defend. There is a huge value in simply writing this out, so take the time to do it. Then, with your campaign objectives completed, consider the following:

- Are your objectives clear? If you handed them to someone else in your office, or better yet, a friend or family member who knew nothing about your business, would they make sense?
- Are your objectives specific? "More sales" is great, but it is hard to translate directly into action. "Reaching $100,000 in wake-sport-related sales by the end of the current quarter" is a more specific objective.
- Are your success metrics quantitative?

I have to admit to a certain bias here: I am a scientist and mathematician with a passion for marketing: For me, *numbers rule*. To quote engineer and physicist William Kelvin (for whom that particular temperature scale is named):

> *"When you cannot measure it, when you cannot express it in numbers, your knowledge is of a meager and unsatisfactory kind."*

Ouch! OK, so Lord Kelvin may have been a bit of a snob with regard to quantitative measures, but his point is well taken: If you can't measure success, how do know when you've achieved success? Even more to the point, for online media — and social media is granted no exception here — a robust measure of Return On Investment (ROI is) essential. Your colleagues, with whom you compete for budgets and around-the-office prestige, will expect you to possess a numerical justification for your social media projects. Ultimately, when you go up against the COO with your excellent idea for leveraging Twitter, you'd better have more in your arsenal than "It's cool" or "We need to be there." If you haven't gotten to the numbers, stop now, go back, and *find some*. Note here that by "numbers" I don't mean "17" or "112" — I mean having a quantitative basis for determining whether or not moving from 17 to 112 is getting you where you want to go. You need the actual measurements (e.g., 17 and 112), but you also need context and meaning. As a marketer, you are uniquely qualified to provide them. Here are some ideas that may help you:

- Count the number of comments your campaigns generate in the blogosphere and look for a trend.
- Track the positive references versus the negatives and trend that, too, noting your success and failure reference points.
- Count the number of inbound links to your site or campaign and tie your social campaign to the metrics that underlie your Search Engine Optimization (SEO) program.
- Conduct a pre/post awareness study, and then make this an annual benchmarking exercise.
- Compare (quantitatively) the study with the trends you just developed.
- Compare negative comments you find with Customer Service inquiries and begin to connect "operations" and "marketing."
- Connect your trends and studies quantitatively with sales. It may be primarily "correlation" at first (versus "causation," which is what you are ultimately after), but that is a start down a quantitative path.

Monday's Wrap-Up

Today you set up your objectives, and you took the time to ensure that they are specific and measurable. These are marketing basics, to be sure, but a lot of us are or have been guilty of glossing over this critical step. You are heading into the uncharted seas on the Social Web: Having a map is a good idea. You will face critical reviews. Some of what you propose will not work, and some will. In all cases, numbers — right along with your trusty gut — are your best friend. There are a lot of ways to quantitatively assess marketing performance. The previous listing is just a small sample. The takeaway for Monday's exercise is this: Put your campaigns on a solid, metrics-oriented base that is closely tied to your business objectives. Otherwise, you'll end up floating with the tide, rising in good times and sinking in bad. That might float your boat, but it won't put you ahead of the competition.

The Awareness Phase

Today you're going to dig into your current marketing program, beginning with *awareness*. Yesterday you clearly articulated your objectives as you defined what success looks like and how you'll measure it. Today's exercise involves assessing what you are doing *now* to build awareness and how you are measuring it.

Awareness drives the purchase funnel, and "awareness" is just as important on the Social Web as any place else. This reality points up one of the governing factors of contemporary marketing: it remains an *integration* challenge. You can't switch to "social media" and dump everything else any more than you can build a brand purely on TV. Building awareness means placing your "introductory" message where it will be seen; building *sustained awareness* means anchoring your message across a variety of channels, and then tapping the social feedback cycle to pull social media and social conversations back into the loop where they can do you some good.

Tuesday's One-Hour Exercise

For today's exercise, identify all of the channels that you are currently using to generate awareness. Use the following questions as a guide and as you did yesterday answer each, taking care to make sure that what you write down is specific and where appropriate, measurable.

- List each of the channels you are using currently or have used in the recent past.
- For each channel identified, what is the success value? What is the failure value?
- For each channel identified, what is the *current* value?
- For each channel identified, what did you have to do to justify its use? When will this decision be next reviewed?

Look back at the list you have developed. The first big question is "Do they all have defined, quantitative success goals?" To the extent that they do, how many are currently in the success range? This is more than an academic exercise: As a consultant, when I go through this analysis with clients, I often find that there are channels that are accepted on faith or simply because they have always been used. To be sure, there is a certain amount of "correct wisdom" and "gut knowledge" that is part of the DNA of every successful marketer and the campaigns she produces. At the same, on some level you are exploring a new approach to marketing — one that introduces the consumer conversation as an integral part of the overall process. This will upset some "conventional truths." Take some time here to discover and validate your own "accepted beliefs."

Tuesday's Wrap-Up

The main goal of today's exercise is to be specific about what you are doing to generate awareness, and to identify the conventional or accepted practices that are a part of your overall marketing program. At this point, you simply want to be aware of what you really do know versus what you believe but don't necessarily know. Of course, you also want a solid handle on all of the awareness channels you are using, regardless of why or how justified.

The Point-of-Sale

If yesterday was all about purchase funnel input, then today is all about the output, the transition point to a relationship. The last step of the purchase funnel has traditionally been viewed as just that: the *last* step. "We've got your money. Who's next." It's as if the purchase funnel was a landing strip that ended at the cash register, as if your business sales cycle operated in a vacuum. Look back at the social feedback cycle: The purchase phase is the gateway to the Social Web, the transition point at which you shift from courting a customer to building a durable relationship. The relationships you build will set in motion the conversations that occur on the Social Web, expressed through social media and fed back into the purchase funnel in the consideration phase. If the conversation helps you, you'll have less to do at the point of purchase. If the conversation is hurting you, then you have to make up for that, for example through a coupon or in-store promotion. In any event, what you do — or have to do — to make the actual sale is what you will be working on today.

Like yesterday, today is a survey, not an analysis. The objective is to get a complete understanding of what you are doing and how you are defining and measuring success.

Wednesday's One-Hour Exercise

For today's exercise, identify the channels that you are using at the point-of-sale. Use the following questions as a guide, as you did yesterday.

- List each of the channels you are using currently or have used in the recent past.
- For each channel identified, what is the success value? What is the failure value?
- For each channel identified, what is the *current* value?
- For each channel identified, what did you have to do to justify its use? When will this decision be next reviewed?

    Look at your list and consider:
- Do they all have quantitative success goals? Are they delivering?
- Which of the above are you using *offensively* (for example, to side-track a competitive sale in favor of your own product) and which are you using *defensively* to protect *your* sale?
- Which of the above are driven by direct market forces (recognizing that to some extent everything you are doing is driven by market forces)?

Finally, think about what conditions would have to exist in the mind of your customers that would change the tactics you have identified. That is where you are headed tomorrow.

Wednesday's Wrap-Up

Today you gathered the remaining information needed to map the traditional purchase funnel. This provides a solid baseline for your marketing activities going forward and especially for the integration of social media. Integrating social media involves developing a clear plan of attack. Like any marketing plan, your social media plan is based on your business objectives and the channels you are currently using. To your current plan add your point-of-purchase efforts needed to push the ball across the line. Then you can gauge the conversations likely to form around your brand, product, or service and make some decisions about what you want social media to do for you. For example, do you want to start a new conversation, sustain or amplify an existing positive conversation, or respond to and address a negative one? Tomorrow you'll be looking at what the current conversations are like. On Friday you'll complete your map and set your initial objectives with regard to the use of social media.

Let the Games Begin

You're now about a week and a half into a three month process. Today you're going to use the tools you've already looked at to generate "intelligence." Simply put, you're going to see what people are saying about you.

As you start gathering intelligence, relate it back to your purchase funnel and social feedback cycle. However, as you do this *switch your perspective from a marketing view to a customer view.* Why? Because the intelligence you are gathering is the equivalent of customer feedback. It may or may not be what you want to hear. The key is this: Put yourself in your customer's place and ask how these comments arose rather than judging what you find. Don't dismiss critical reviews or immediately accept positive comments as if they were gospel. Ask yourself if these comments are isolated, and think about existing customer service calls you may have listed to or for which you may have internal data. What you find in terms of intelligence on the Social Web is largely the result of the consistency between your awareness campaign promises and the experience actually delivered. Anything different is in a large part driving your point-of sale efforts. In other words, a very simple (and yes, simplistic but insightful nonetheless) relationship emerges:

 Tip: Your promise minus your delivery drives what you do at the point-of-sale.

What you are currently doing at the point of sale has a cost: If you are rebating or running sales, you are losing margin. If you are creating displays or buying search terms to get noticed, you are increasing your expenses. To be sure, either of these can result in incremental gain, at a profit. There is nothing wrong with that. What's important to identify is whether you are primarily running defensive or offensive point-of-sale programs. The key to tapping social intelligence — part of the larger landscape called social media — is suddenly obvious: This intelligence allows you to proactively "tune" your promise *and delivery* so that you can focus your point-of-sale on *offense* rather than defense.

Thursday's One-Hour Exercise

Today you're going to spend an hour gathering as much online intelligence as you can find. The following tools will help you. As you find references or competitive comparisons, subscribe to feeds if they are offered and use Del.icio.us to collect, save, and share bookmarks to these items. While you may not be able to do this next item "in an hour," at some point spend some time looking at the services offered by BuzzMetrics, Cymfony, Techrigy, and others. Each is different, and each is particularly useful in a different role. They may be attractive to you as part of an ongoing intelligence program. Listening is one of the easiest and most practically valuable ways to utilize the Social Web.

Google's Blogsearch

Start here and go for the wide view. Blogsearch will quickly bring you into the conversation. Use Blogsearch to follow the conversations around competing products — for example, to get an idea of what that exists on the Social Web in the market around you.

        http://blogsearch.google.com

Nielsen | Buzzmetrics BlogPulse

Jump over to Blog Pulse. Look for two things: the trend in the number of mentions that relate to you, and the trends around competing products or general terms of art within your specific industry segment.

BlogPulse will take you into the conversations (which Blogsearch will do as well), and will give you a picture over time of the activity level. You'll be able to see, for example, the dates of press releases or major announcements.

        http://www.blogpulse.com

Planet Feedback

Be sure to check out one of the original consumer-generated content sites specifically focused on company ratings. Developed by Pete Blackshaw, PlanetFeedback covers a lot of companies, all at the initiation of customers.

        http://www.planetfeedback.com

YouTube

Don't forget video! Start with YouTube and search for your branded terms — you may be pleasantly (or otherwise) surprised by what you find. YouTube and similar video content sites often contain references, new uses, and critiques that are immensely helpful.

    http://www.youtube.com

Online Reviews

Depending on your industry, there are very likely one or more online review sites that pertain to your product. Again, look at competitors, too.

Google Alerts

One of the easiest ways to monitor your brand, products, or services is through Google Alerts. This service is free, very quick to set up, and provides daily (near real time) notices of references to the terms or trademarks in which you are interested.

 Tip: Use Google Alerts to monitor your competitors.

Presenting Video Offline?

Wondering how to present multimedia content to your team or a client whose Internet connection is slow or nonexistent? If you'll install RealMedia's latest media player, you can save many forms of online video to your desktop with a single click. That way, you can show it as a part of a presentation when your Internet connection isn't all it should be. Not that it ever happens!

Thursday's Wrap-Up

You've now gotten your first real sense of what social media brings to your toolkit from a marketing intelligence perspective. Hopefully, you're happy about what you've found. If not, it's still good: By opening yourself to the conversations that are happening around you, you've gathered the critical information needed to *change* the conversation by discovering, documenting, and then proactively working with Operations to address the issues raised through what you've learned on the Social Web.

Your Social Feedback Cycle

Today you put it all together: awareness, consideration, and purchase. Today you'll draw your social feedback cycle and examine the way in which *what you promised* was reflected back on the Social Web. Assuming that your marketing plan is working reasonably well, your awareness efforts combined with the consideration phase and social feedback cycle should validate your point-of-purchase efforts. If not, then you have your first opportunity to use social-media-based intelligence to refine your awareness and point-of-purchase efforts.

Importantly, keep in mind that you *cannot change* the conversation by *fiat*. Instead, you've got to look at how well your product performs, the expectations you are setting, and the competitive landscape to understand why the social intelligence gave rise to what you found. If it's negative — in other words, if you have to work harder to overcome the information circulating on the Social Web — then you can use this same information to reformulate your offering, not just your message. If it's positive, you can use what you've learned to refine your supporting advertising and to establish the beneficial attributes of your current offering that you want to protect.

Friday's One-Hour Exercise

Today you're going to spend an hour pulling together what you've gathered this week. This includes:

- Monday: Business objectives and success measures
- Tuesday: Awareness efforts and performance metrics
- Wednesday: Point-of-sale efforts and performance metrics
- Thursday: Summarized social intelligence

Start with the funnel included on the worksheet for this chapter, or create your own. Start with your business objectives and then connect your awareness efforts with them as they support promotion, trial, connection, or initiation of the relationships that lead to success in terms of your objectives. Then, add your point-of-purchase efforts. If you can, tie these directly to actual sales. You now have a "map" of your purchase funnel, similar to that shown in Figure 5.5. Starting with your business objectives, you can see how you are generating awareness and what you have to do to actually close or realize your sales.

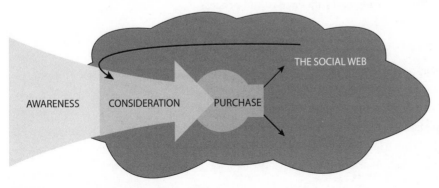

Figure 5.5 The Social Feedback Cycle and Social Web

Next, add to this what you've learned through your social media intelligence efforts. Note that the social feedback intelligence is being developed in several places. Social media content that enters the purchase funnel at the point of consideration can be developed after the purchase, for example by your customers based on an actual product experience. It can also arise as a part of, or because of, advertising: Burger King's "King" and "Subservient Chicken" campaigns, along with competitor Wendy's "Red Wig" campaigns are examples of this. As well, conversations and content postings on the Social Web can result from what Paul Rand, Partner, President, and CEO of Zócalo Group, refers to as a "brand detractor."

 Tip: A *brand detractor* is not the same as someone who simply doesn't like you. A brand detractor is someone who has made it his personal cause to impact you negatively, generally out of a strong belief that what you are doing is wrong. By comparison, an upset customer is someone who is open to a change in viewpoint: Generally speaking, a brand detractor is not.

Paul describes the detractor as the person whose mission it is — regardless of what you do, short of shutting down — to impede you. Think of tobacco or trans fat, or any other polarizing brand, product, or service. Rightly or wrongly, the detractors are out there, and their voices are part of the conversation.

The combined experiences — as shared by your customers, by people exposed to your ads, through the content generated by brand detractors, and more — are then fed back to your potential customer. The entry point to the purchase funnel is the point of consideration that occurs during the research and social discussion phase. Look at your completed map and see if it makes sense. What you should see is a consistent progression, from awareness to purchase, with a predictable effort applied at the point of sale that is more or less driven by what is entering the funnel at the point of consideration. Assuming that your map shows something like this, you've isolated the impact of social media: It may be helping, hurting, or both. By isolating it, you can develop a plan to add your understanding and influence to the process.

My Map Doesn't Tell Me Anything

If your Social Feedback Cycle map is empty, disconnected, or otherwise a jumble, take a break. Remember, no single technique is perfect, and sometimes it takes a few tries to get it right. Go back through this exercise and make sure that you've uncovered enough detail. Check that you are mapping actual results and not assumptions. It may be too that no one is talking about you…in which case consider yourself fortunate. It could be worse! Seriously, if the conversation is nonexistent, just note that. You'll get into "starting a conversation" in upcoming chapters.

Friday's Wrap-Up

Look at what you are saying in your awareness campaigns and at the point-of-sale. Look as well at the intelligence you have gathered via the Social Web. Compare these: The difference between your messages and the conversations you find is what is happening in the consideration phase. By isolating the social feedback cycle contribution, you've effectively modeled the macro-impact of social media on your current marketing program. You may not be able to see into the individual channels — yet — but you can at least point to the specific contributions or impediments to your current campaigns that arise on the Social Web.

You did a lot this week, and you took your first big steps in harnessing the Social Web. By looking at your current awareness and point-of-purchase efforts and then connecting the two with the conversations that consumers are having about your products and services, you are now able to identify your opportunities and challenges in the application of social media.

Chapter 5: The Main Points

- Social media plays a significant role in marketing: The conversations that take place on the Social Web determine how easy — or difficult — your task in driving conversion will be.

- The social feedback cycle is built on the post-purchase feedback and conversational loop that augments your traditional purchase funnel activities.

- Consumer-generated media, and in particular photos, audio, and video that supplement text (blogs), are in mainstream use now, even if concentrated in the Millennial and Gen X segments.

- The determined detractor is an individual who plays an important role in the evolution of markets but nonetheless will not (normally) be "won over" and therefore is generally best viewed as a participant with whom you will "respectfully agree to disagree." Your best response is to simply ensure that *your story* is also being told.

- Your social feedback cycle, developed and maintained over time, is a key planning tool as you develop your social media plan.

Week 3: Touchpoint Analysis

How many marketers have gone to great lengths at considerable expense to devise and implement campaigns that conveyed a strong customer service orientation with regard to their brand only to see their efforts hobbled by a customer service team that was measured by how quickly representatives could end a call? When you see that scenario as it's presented here, it is obviously contradictory. No one would really do that, right? Actually, it happens a lot, and much more often than it should.

In this chapter, you'll continue with the product or service you selected in Week 2. You'll build a touchpoint map and then learn to use it to build your action plan internally (where you'll work to resolve problem spots) and externally (where you'll turn your focus to the touchpoints that matter to your customers).

6

Chapter Contents

Touchpoints and the Social Web

Identifying Touchpoints

Quantifying Touchpoints

The Main Points

Touchpoints and the Social Web

The Social Web is particularly good at pointing out differences between promise or expectation and the actual experience delivered. On matters of customer satisfaction, the Social Web can be like a magnifying glass, with each customer success or failure replayed in exacting detail via one or more forms of social media. Figure 6.1 shows an example of how this can occur. Using a mobile phone, Seesmic founder Loïc Le Meur recorded a video of his "less-than-Hilton" experience at Hilton's Schiphol (Amsterdam, Netherlands) airport location. Within minutes of check-in, he created a review, posted it to YouTube, and spread it through his community via Twitter. You can watch the review on YouTube here:

http://www.youtube.com/watch?v=zLBiSSRzGqo

Figure 6.1 Loïc Le Meur's Schiphol Hilton Video Review

What's the big deal about a seemingly random video? The main point is this: When your customer can post a video review of an actual experience with your product or service in real time, in minutes, and from any place in the world, the difference between what you promise and what you deliver (positive or negative) will drive a very visible social conversation. The Hilton video has been seen a couple of thousand times — a small number by most standards. But consider that most of those who viewed it are probably people who either know Loïc or saw his comments on Twitter or some similar forum. There is a good chance that — compared with a million or so TV viewers — a higher percentage of Loïc's friends will be considering a stay at a Hilton in the near future. This is one of the characteristics of the way information spreads on the Social Web: It tends to end up in the hands of the people who will actually use it.

When you look at the difference between what you are saying about your brand — in other words, the "beef" in your awareness and point-of-purchase campaigns — versus what you hear coming back off the Social Web, any differences can often be traced to the difference between what you actually delivered and the expectation you set (or that was set for you). It works both ways, too. In fact, experiences of joy (and especially positive reviews) actually outnumber negative stories and reviews.

Nonetheless, if you are over-promising and under-delivering, expect to hear about it on the Social Web. When Marketing and Operations crank along with not quite enough contact with each other, they are on a sure path to a problem. Generally speaking, *disconnects* between the two are not planned: Nobody of any lasting business or social reputation ever actually sat down and said, "Tell our customers all of this, but when they do buy, do something less instead." Plans like that make for a short career and an even shorter brand trajectory. The problem is that too often nobody plans the *connection*, either. Nobody made it his or her job to reach over the department walls and get in touch with the issues and objectives of the holistic organization. Instead, two separate groups, both of which are fundamentally important within the organization — one reporting through the CMO and the other reporting through the COO — simply went about their business, honestly and intently doing what each thought best. A customer-level disconnect that works against both Marketing and Operations is too often the *unplanned* result.

Rebates: A Tricky Touchpoint

C'mon: Who doesn't like a deal? Rebates are a great example of unplanned (or in my most cynical mind, totally planned) consequences. Rebates set the expectation of savings, but only a fraction of the actual savings is ever realized by consumers. If you are using rebates, pay special attention to the social feedback cycle. Rebates have long been used as a sort of "come-on," as a way to lower the *apparent* price without lowering (by nearly as much) the actual price paid. While estimates vary from 2 percent to 80 percent, the fact is that only a portion of all rebates are ever actually collected by consumers owing in part to the often complicated redemption process. Using rebates? Beware of the social backlash. On the Social Web — where people retell their stories far more effectively than they've been able to in the past — one upset person can easily tip off a few hundred — or a few thousand — others. As I noted previously, consumers will talk just as they have always done. The difference is that now — on the Social Web — while it may not necessarily be louder, it will be much more likely heard.

Touchpoint analysis — the rigorous discipline of carefully evaluating each point of contact between a firm and its customers has been used in traditional marketing to catch the divergence between what you want to convey and what you are actually conveying. Touchpoint analysis has been typically applied within the *Marketing* department to ensure a consistent message across a range of channels. What you'll come to appreciate as you work through this chapter is that this same discipline can and should be used to map the consistency with which your brand promise is turned into action. This is critical when social media is involved: Because your customers have the ability to freely exchange information, any disconnect *can and will show up on the Social Web.*

Tip: Your marketing message, expressed through one or more touchpoints, is instantly picked up, validated, and modified as appropriate by those creating and participating in the conversations circulating on the Social Web. The post-purchase, operations-driven conversations that they create are now just as much a part of your message as the tagline and ad content that you create. Therefore, you have to analyze both the touchpoint and the associated conversations simultaneously in order to understand the total information on which your potential customer is acting.

Touchpoint analysis — applied simultaneously to marketing and operations — uncovers and quantifies the relationships between promise and delivery, between "what I thought I'd get" and "what I'll tell my friends I got." With a solid understanding of this difference — positive or negative — you can act decisively, protecting and building on what works while addressing what's falling short. At its core, touchpoint analysis is all about syncing Operations and Marketing, about understanding the perception of your product or service based not on your claims or customer needs, but by the degree to which your present customers (and to a certain extent prospective customers) feel that you've delivered what you said you'd deliver.

Touchpoint Analysis: Two Great Blogs

Two of the blogs that I recommend are Susan Abbott's "Customer Crossroads" (`http://www.customercrossroads.com`) along with Ben McConnell and Jackie Huba's "Church of the Customer" (`http://www.churchofthecustomer.com/blog/`). Both blogs feature great posts on touchpoints and the development of a great customer experience.

Speaking of touchpoints, Figure 6.2 shows the parking signs that alert Chili's patrons that a particular space is reserved for "To Go" customers. These signs are typically used to mark the spot immediately outside the dedicated "To Go" entrance, another Chili's innovation (the separate entrance, not the idea of take-out) and very favorable customer touchpoint. Reserving parking spaces is always tricky — it's easy to irritate customers roaming the lot, looking for a space so that they can park, go inside, sit down, and eat. At the same time, "To Go" is all about convenience, and having to hunt for a spot a quarter mile from the door is *distinctly not* the desired experience. So, Chili's takes a humorous approach: You may be annoyed that you can't park in this otherwise open space unless you are getting food to take out, but at the same time you'll also laugh about it. "Fun" is a brand anchor and key touchpoint experience of the Chili's casual dining experience. "To Go" customers, of course, love this special parking space, and cite this among reasons why they prefer Chili's for take-out.

Figure 6.2 Chili's "To Go" Parking Sign

Identifying Touchpoints

Understand from the outset that touchpoint analysis is a quantitative approach to understanding your strengths, weaknesses, opportunities, and challenges from a marketer's perspective. This is not an exercise in "about right" and "pretty close." It is about establishing a robust measurement base and then tracking that over time, thereby driving continuous improvement.

Touchpoint analysis is also about more than marketing. On the Social Web, the conversations reflect the *actual customer experience* as much as they reflect your underlying promise. Touchpoint analysis, expanded as we've defined it here, is a *holistic* approach that includes Operations, Human Resources, and more. The quantitative information you generate through touchpoint analysis can be applied throughout your organization.

For example, a lot of airline marketing concerns itself with on-time performance. Through phrases like "the most on-time flights to New York of any airline," the airline offering this message sets an expectation of punctuality. From a flyer's perspective, it looks different. If the airlines running these ads were really focused on timeliness, there would *always* be a clock right behind the service agents at check-in and at the gate. They would make a big deal of what the time is right now and what time the flight is likely to actually leave. I asked a friend who works for an airline about this: She said that airlines in general were very concerned about being on time but also felt that installing clocks would be a waste of money. After all, most travelers wear a watch.

From a customer's perspective, this explanation actually *predicts* the gap between the claim that on-time flights are important and the reality of the flying experience, which often suggests otherwise. When your customers are doing "A" and you are doing "B," there is a marketing disconnect. *Customers* are obviously concerned about punctuality: That's why they are wearing watches. A lot of airlines are primarily concerned with managing costs — that's why they don't buy the clocks. People would have no problem believing that such an airline was "one of the leading cost-managers" in the world. But that is not the claim made in the ads about punctuality. As a demonstration of the power and importance of touchpoints, think about Southwest Airlines. For all of the knocks they endure about their boarding process (which, by the way, is consistently applauded by their core flyers), they can actually board a full plane and pull away from the gate in about 15 minutes. The "agent talk" in the gate area is all about "hustle" — they understand that *you are flying because you are in a hurry and want to get there fast.* If you were looking to occupy your time and enjoy some scenery, you'd have taken the train! On a touchpoint level, the next time you're in an airport look at the Southwest Airlines "Bin Hog" and the motives for this campaign. Aside from the comic relief provided as someone tries to fit a life-size artist's mannequin, two cases of rum, and a flea market rocking chair into the overhead bin, not being ready to walk on, stow luggage, and *sit down* wastes an incredible amount of time. Southwest gets this, and creates a series of touchpoints expressed through a combination of processes, signage, and actions that reinforces their understanding of the fundamental brand value points that connect Southwest Airlines with its customers.

For most of the rest, the touchpoint disconnect comes down to the basic realization that *ads* and mission statements about on-time performance will not make flights take off and land on time, and that ads in particular will actually raise the level of negative conversation when they don't. By comparison, putting a clock in plain view and instilling in *all* employees — including the people who plan the routes, handle the bags and ensure that the ground activities are running correctly, and the lobbyists who press for air traffic improvements — a commitment to honoring the posted time just might make a difference. This is exactly the sort of approach that Starbuck's founder Howard Shultz has recently adopted: back to basics, back to the customer promises, and back to the excellent delivery of the core product or service. Touchpoint analysis taken to its ultimate is about running a business based on holistic principles. This is why touchpoint analysis matters in setting out to tap social media.

Starbucks

On Tuesday, February 26, 2008, at 5:30 PM, Starbucks founder and CEO Howard Schultz closed 7,100 locations for three hours. After several years of questioned expansions, the conversion of the "coffee" experience into a retail experience, issues of consistency, long waiting times, and similar difficulties that tarnished the company's reputation, Schultz "pulled the cord" and stopped the line. Everyone participated in a program designed to reinvigorate a commitment to 100 percent satisfaction, and a return to a focus on a great *coffee* experience. At the same time, MyStarbucksIdea was launched, giving consumers a direct voice in the future direction of Starbucks. Regardless of how it plays out — early results are positive, if measured only in terms of favorable PR — the commitment of leadership combined with company-wide buy-in has put Starbucks back on track.

Apart from claims that fail validation, or the discovery of touchpoint experiences that, like biting into a warm Krispy Kreme, are pure joy, through careful analysis you may discover misaligned practices. I recall a financial services brand that found — through touchpoint analysis — that a primary advertised service benefit was actually seen as worthless by the firm's own representatives. In touchpoint testing, test customers were shown the new ads, after which they called or visited the office. There they were told, "Here is something better (that also happens to cost more)." Had this gone live, how do you think it would have gone over? From a purely practical perspective, what do you suppose the return would have been on the campaign investment had it gone forward? In this case, performing the touchpoint analysis during testing pointed out the potentially negative perception and the campaign and branch practices were changed. The changes involved internal training (HR), service support (Operations), and retiming the campaign itself (Marketing). *Social media-based marketing reaches across internal departments and organizations.*

This again points to the cross-functional nature of contemporary marketing and the dilemma that many CMOs face. The Social Web reflects a holistic view of the product or service based on the combined efforts of Marketing, HR, Operations, and Finance. In Chapter 3, "What *is* Social Media?" I made a reference to Home Depot and the challenge, as *Advertising Age* noted, of providing a better floor experience and better trained associates, and thereby driving more traffic. These issues span Marketing and Operations and require a collaborative solution.

Quantifying Touchpoints

This week you'll create a basic touchpoint analysis. Recognizing that you will do this in a week — I've spent months on similar assignments with clients — the focus will be on the mechanics and the application of touchpoint analysis to a specific area of your business. Once done, you can expand this as needed or guide a team or your agency through this to build a larger, holistic view that can guide your entire organization. You'll start by picking a focus area and gathering some data. Throughout the week you'll build on that, completing a basic touchpoint analysis on Friday.

Tip: A set of worksheets covering this week's exercises can be found in the appendix of this book. In addition to these printed worksheets, you can also download electronic copies and access related resources at the website accompanying this book. Complete information regarding these resources and the website is included in the appendix.

Featured Case: Inbound Communications at Nestlé

As a highly visible, global brand, Nestlé continuously reevaluates its customer touchpoints. Marketers typically consider outbound touchpoints — in-store experiences, TV, print, online, live events, and similar. However, Nestlé has literally converted its inbound customer call centers — once seen largely as an expense to be minimized — into high-performance customer touchpoints and beneficial brand assets.

Beginning in 2003, Consumer Services Director Beth Thomas Kim engaged internal constituents to reposition and reorient Nestlé's inbound phones into a listening unit, offering a less-expensive solution for ideas and suggestions that generated measurable results including a larger package size for Coffee-mate lovers and clearer colors on the packaging to address confusion at the store shelf. In order to do this, Beth and her team worked with Operations, Marketing, and even Quality Assurance to reshape the view of what was possible and what was not being communicated through typical focus groups and other traditional research methods. The contact center is a rich source of interaction with your most valuable customers. Those who take the time to reach out and connect with a company are typically the most loyal or most highly engaged with the product or service. Leveraging this connection leads to deeper understanding and a stronger appreciation for your most valuable consumer.

As Beth passionately advises, "Allowing these opportunities to languish or worse yet, ignoring them, is a short-sighted and potentially damaging exercise in today's highly connected and influential consumer-driven environment. Don't delude yourself into thinking that you have a real handle on your consumer until you take the time to *listen **and** talk* to them. These people are easily found. All you need to do is reach out to your Customer Service department."

The opportunity that was grasped at Nestlé and put to use exists in nearly any company: Engage your customers, and listen and respond to what they say. They will reward you with loyalty, beneficial word of mouth, and a nice boost to your brand.

Gather Your Touchpoint Data

The first step in conducting a touchpoint analysis is deciding what you will measure. The easiest and often quickest way to do this is to grab a note pad and take a trip through an actual customer experience. If you sell your product or deliver your service in physical stores, go and take pictures. If you're marketing online, use screen grabs. If your business is telephone-based, use recordings.

Figure 6.3 shows a sampling of typical, well-known touchpoints. Some — such as the Southwest Airlines and Sea World brand integration created by painting Shamu on one Southwest's 737s — create a highly visible, promotional touchpoint that calls out to the kind of innovation and fun that these firms are all about. Others — such as Nike+ and Apple, or the interior of a produce market — are aspirational or tactile expressions that operate in an experiential context. The result is an expectation of a high degree of satisfaction: When delivered, the combined experience and touchpoints reinforce and amplify your marketing efforts, especially on the Social Web and through social media where these touchpoints are talked about.

Figure 6.3 Typical Touchpoints

Photos, Recordings, and Touchpoint Analysis

Oddly, in an era of consumer-generated media, most businesses with a direct consumer-facing presence still do not allow photographs. For whatever reasons such policies may exist, respect them and *make sure that you have permission to take pictures before doing so.* On more than one client assignment — even after identifying myself — I found myself quickly surrounded by employees wanting to know why I was taking pictures. It's unpleasant for everyone. Above all, do not photograph or record actual customers — this can be uncomfortable for them and may land you in a hot water later. Instead, capture the experience of being a customer through your own eyes.

The most important aspect of your initial "data gathering" exercise is to capture everything, and to do so without bias, without a personal agenda. If you set out to show how clean or dirty your store is, then that is exactly what your analysis will conclude. You won't have actually learned anything. That's not what you want. What you want is an objective assessment of what it feels like to be a customer or to actually purchase and use your product. In general, you won't know what you are looking for at this point: This is why you are starting with *observation*. Touchpoint analysis is about discovery and subsequent quantification. After all, if you had a list of the "disconnects," you could just go and fix them. Chances are you do not have such a list: Through this week's exercises, you'll make one. This includes documenting the positive aspects: Not only are these an obviously important part of your current service delivery, but you also want to identify what works well so that you don't inadvertently mess it up while "fixing" something else.

With your photos, screen grabs, product marketing samples, and whatever else you've collected in hand, you can now begin to sort out the customer experience.

An Hour a Day

Importantly, the hour that you are spending each day following the approach suggested in this book is designed to acquaint you with social media, with how it works, and with how you can use it in marketing. For any of the exercises contained in this book you could, if you chose, jump in and do an exhaustive treatment. At some point you'll want to, either directly or through the services of a retained expert practitioner. Throughout this book, the Hour a Day exercises are designed to provide valuable real-world insight into how you can incorporate social media into your current marketing program. Like all learning activities, there is always more that you can do after you've established your basic skills.

Monday's One-Hour Exercise

Today you're going to spend an hour identifying all the places your current and potential customers directly experience your brand. For the purpose of keeping the exercise to an hour, start by simply reviewing the brand and marketing materials you have on hand, including copies of recent ads or TV spots. For extra-credit (because it will take you more than an hour), go out and experience the delivery of your product or service directly, recording your experience as suggested earlier. Either way, you'll quickly get value out of this exercise.

With your marketing materials in hand — complemented by whatever "through the experience of the customer" materials you may have gathered — spend the balance of this hour looking through them. Get a handle on the primary promises you are making and on the supporting details. As appropriate, write out your answers to the following questions as you review these materials:

- What are the primary promises?
- How are these promises related to the needs of your customers?
- How are these promises supported?
- What is the actual delivery mechanism that validates each promise?
- What are the actual customer experiences that demonstrate successful delivery?
- What channel has been used to convey each particular aspect of your promise or brand?
- How important to your customer are each of the promises and points and delivery?

When you have completed this exercise, go back and review and then write out or otherwise expand on your answers. Instead of writing, use an MP3 recorder to take notes. I highly recommend this technique: It's quick, easy, and you can use it "remotely" to capture ideas to build on later. Again, avoid filtering or being subjective. This is a research exercise, so keep an open mind.

Monday's Wrap-Up

Today you pulled together the materials you are using to set expectations and convey the promise or value of your brand, and perhaps a handful of artifacts that indicate what actually happens when your customers experience your product or service in the marketplace.

Organize Your Data

Monday you collected; today you'll make sense of it. Looking at the materials you pulled together, the goal today is to connect the touchpoints through which you are telling your story to the touchpoints where your customers are likely to set an expectation or form an impression. In other words, you are going to break into its component parts the process of setting an expectation and then actually delivering on that expectation. That way, you can evaluate things such as consistency. Are you telling the same fundamental story everywhere? Is that story applicable, relevant, and important? Most important, are you continuously evaluating the performance of your various touchpoints from the perspective of a customer? These are the things that ensure success on the Social Web.

Ultimately, the purpose of this exercise is influencing social conversation. I've talked about this in earlier chapters: Making social media work means influencing the crowd. But remember, you cannot do this by edict, at least not in the same way that you can tell your agency what or what not say. Successfully using social media depends on your learning to *correctly* influence the crowd. If you want the conversation on the Social Web to reinforce your paid-media messages, you have to start with a promise that you can deliver on (to generate positive talk) and one that matters to your customer (to generate the interest that drives that talk in the first place). It sounds simple; but like all things "marketing," what might be simple in theory quickly becomes complex in practice. You may find that you are spot-on in your alignment between promise and delivery — unfortunately, however, you may be aligned on a point of customer contact that your customers don't consider important or don't typically notice, *much less talk about*. That usually means you are wasting money — or at least failing to earn credit — and who can afford *that*?

Being able to validate your claims is equally important. The Social Web is quite good when used as a verification tool. Consider this: Does your marketing claim "leadership" as a provider of whatever it is that you do? If so, ask yourself how you measured this. Go to your competitor's site, and see if they are making the same claim. Two competing firms can't both simultaneously be "the best." Moreover, outside of your C-suite, it might not even matter. Lots of perfectly acceptable goods and services from less-than-leading firms are purchased every day. Plenty of positive conversation that supports brands, products, and services *that simply do the job* exist on the Social Web. Figure 6.4 shows the HGTV Forums, where discussions about leaky faucets, septic systems, washing machines, and many more everyday activities and products take place.

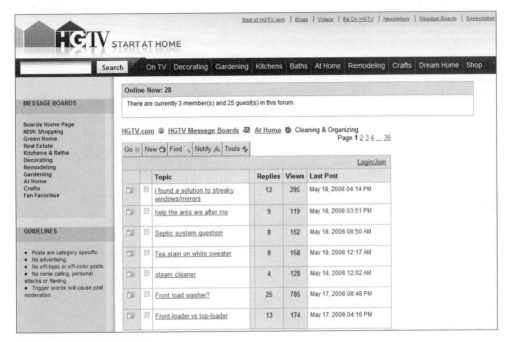

Figure 6.4 HGTV Discussion Forums

One of the Leading

The number of firms that claim to be "one of the leading…" amazes me. What does this claim even mean? Students of formal logic will recognize that "we're not the worst" is the logical equivalent. I haven't seen too many brands sporting that as a tagline. When someone reads "one of the leading," the message is discarded. Money spent, touchpoint lost. If the product, service, or brand is not *the* leader, and if the claim can't be backed up, it's best if the claim is simply avoided. Find something else to talk about. The audience is smarter than that.

Today you're going to spend an hour organizing your touchpoint data. There are a variety of ways to do this: Your data will likely suggest one or two methods that make the most sense, and then you can pick one. Here are some typical methods that I've used: You may find that one of these is directly applicable, or you may create your own method. What matters is that the method you choose be something that leads to insights you can use in strengthening your marketing programs.

Following are some of the ways in which you can organize your touchpoints. You are always welcome to create an organizational system that makes sense for you.

Organize by Channel

If your marketing programs are channel-specific with separate teams heading each, then one of the easiest first steps is to simply evaluate message consistency. Look across channels at the touchpoints you've selected: Do they tell the same story? Or is one touting the use of your product as a dessert topping while another is claiming superiority as a floor wax? If so, watch out: It's hard to be both. More seriously, many of your messages may be properly tuned to a specific channel: You may well be emphasizing different aspects of your value proposition across multiple channels. In that case, the question to ask is "Do the messages add up to and support your underlying core value or operational principles?"

If you've chosen to organize your materials this way, create "buckets" for each of your channels and place the appropriate materials into these buckets.

 Tip: When organizing by channel, your touchpoint map's vertical axis will be "consistency" and your horizontal axis will be "talk value."

Organize by Function

If the issues that you uncover (or otherwise know to exist) relate to a specific mismatch between promise and delivery, then one of the best organizational techniques for touchpoint analysis is according to the department or function most closely associated with that touchpoint. I've talked about Home Depot in earlier sections: My family has been in the hardware business since the 1800s, so I have a particular passion for this business and appreciate the convenience Home Depot brings. Many of my weekends begin at Home Depot.

The challenges that Home Depot CMOs are often tasked with are in fact more operational than marketing. For example, the CMO is generally charged with driving floor traffic. However, particularly for a business that is primed for social media (more on this in a minute), it is critical to realize that floor traffic is driven less by awareness and point-of-sale efforts — what we'd all call "marketing" — than it is by the actual floor experience and number of times that what is needed is in stock and available when the customer walks in. *These are operations issues. When the things you need are in stock and a trained associate helps you make the right choice, you tend to go back, often to that associate.*

I mentioned Home Depot being primed for social media. Here's why: Home Depot sits at the center of the American Dream — home ownership and more specifically the pride we take as homeowners. This is a pride that by extension applies to nearly anyone — homeowner or otherwise — who has at one time or another thought, "If I planted something right there, or refinished that wall, or added a fireplace, or..." then my residence, my little spot on this planet, would be nicer for it. When people successfully do this, *they tell other people*. They invite their friends over. They upload before-and-after photos to online communities such as "Better Homes and Gardens" or "Kitchen and Bath Ideas." Go and look at the discussions on those sites: It is amazing how many times Home Depot is referenced. Home Depot truly is — whether it chooses the role for itself or not — a player on the Social Web.

> **Tip:** When organizing by function, you are evaluating relative performance versus promise. Your touchpoint map's vertical axis will be "relative performance" and your horizontal axis will be "talk value."

Organize by Customer

For many businesses, a common product or service may be tailored to fit multiple specific customer groups. Tire manufacturers are an example: Applications range from minivans to construction vehicles to sports cars and racing. In this case, one would expect diversity in messages, in touchpoints, and in resultant conversations. For this type of analysis, organize by customer group and then evaluate the applicability of core messages. Does Michelin's racing program matter to a mom driving a minivan the way it would to a sports car owner? Probably not, so you wouldn't really expect anything more than a passing reference in the ads for moms. Instead, Michelin's history of performance and safety would be featured.

When organizing by customer, look for potentially contradictory claims — especially when low-cost commodity versions exist alongside premium products. Strategically, these product introductions are often forced by market conditions, and so marketers don't always have the luxury of designing the perfect campaign for what are often very difficult product launches. Cadillac suffered when it released its Cimarron in 1981, essentially a rebadged mid-size Chevrolet Cavalier. Customers saw through it, and the prestige of "Cadillac" was compromised. Reportedly, General Motor's president at the time warned Cadillac's general manager that he "didn't have time to turn the lower-line car...into a Cadillac." He was right, and Cadillac was pushed close to bankruptcy as a result. The Cimarron was discontinued a few years later.

In comparison, Mercedes faced similar challenges when it launched its 190-class (precursor to the C-Class), the very car that in fact put the pressure on Cadillac to introduce the Cimarron. In the case of Mercedes, they built a great car at a low entry-price point. In their own words, the 190 was "massively over-engineered" because they were keenly aware that a failure could significantly damage the Mercedes-Benz brand. To this day, they've anchored the entire brand in the promise that "No matter which

Mercedes you choose...you'll always get a Mercedes." They back it up, too. Where a lot of brands have introduced "baby" versions of premium automobiles, the Mercedes C-class is a screamer. Instead of a case study or photo as a proof point, try this: Go to a nearby Mercedes dealership this weekend and drive one. Test drives in what amounts to a rolling touchpoint are free.

Now it's General Motors' turn again, this time with the Chevy Volt. Where Toyota effectively own the hybrid market, the Volt — an all-electric vehicle — is designed to redefine the ownership experience via the environmental impact and fuel costs associated with a car. One way or another, both GM and the world need this car.

If you're organizing by customer, look for contradictions, potential leverage points, and general alignment with specific customer values that may or may not be associated with the flagship or primary brands.

 Tip: When organizing by customer, you are evaluating the relevance and importance of the message to each specific customer. Your touchpoint map's vertical axis will be "importance" and your horizontal axis will be "talk value."

Organize by Stage

As an example of the more creative side of touchpoint analysis, you might consider the customer life-cycle stage. I used exactly this technique when performing a touchpoint audit for AARP while working at GSD&M Idea City. I collected promotional and fulfillment material, and then started tacking it up on the walls in one of the war rooms at the agency.

As I did this, a natural framework for the analysis became apparent. The customer life cycle: pre-sales, sales, renewal, upgrade, etc. If your business has a strong life-cycle element, consider organizing your analysis according to stage. How do the messages produced for acquisition square with messages (and actual product delivery) after fulfillment? How is the purchase and subsequent experience with one product leveraged to encourage trial and consideration with another? These are the types of marketing challenges to which a touchpoint analysis — organized by life-cycle stage — can be applied.

Tuesday's One-Hour Exercise: Ready? Set? Organize!

Over the next hour:

- Look at materials and data you've collected and decide how you want to structure your analysis. You can follow one of the above or define an alternative that is more applicable to your specific business.

- As you organize your data, think about how the results will be used to guide the improvement over time of your current marketing program, and how you can begin to tap the Social Web in driving this improvement.

Tuesday's Wrap-Up

You should now have a nice collection of marketing materials and photos or similar proof-points with regard to the actual customer experience that you — meaning your entire firm — are creating. These elements should be organized according the analytical framework you've selected, one which you can relate to the business objectives for the product or service you are working with as you progress through this book. Don't worry about drawing conclusions yet — we've got one more day (tomorrow) to set things up first.

Evaluate and Rank Your Data

You've got your touchpoint materials, and you've selected a structure for your analysis. Today you're going to make sense of the data by looking at two key parameters: performance and relevance, both of which you will gauge from the perspective of a customer.

First, assess performance (and what will be our vertical axis) as it applies to the organization scheme you have selected. To do that, you need a few things, so gather them up. You need something to measure: For this, pick one of the primary promises, for example, as delivered through one of your selected touchpoints. Second, you need to measure it. If you've picked a channel that directly drives online conversations (many in fact do), then you can use Blogsearch or BlogPulse or a similar tool to begin evaluating the acceptance of your message. You may also have internal studies, or you may be able to tap your CRM system. You are looking for answers to these kinds of basic questions:

- Is your message getting picked up, and is it being reflected on the Social Web? How effective is it as a conversational element?

- Are you meeting, exceeding, or falling short on the expectations you've set? What is your performance versus expectation?

- How important is this specific touchpoint and its outcome (satisfaction versus disappointment) from the perspective of your customer or prospect?

To assign scores to each touchpoint, measure the visibility (talk value, *number of Social Web mentions*) of the message as applicable to your specific map. Add to this your own performance (consistency, importance, etc.) assessment against the expectations you've set. Your CRM data, customer service records, and *polarity* of Social Web mentions are all good indications of how well you are doing here.

Finally, how important is this touchpoint to your audience? If you asked new customers to name the top five factors that led to a purchase decision, is this touchpoint related to one those factors? While this last item does not appear on the map directly, this measure does set the priority on what you *might* do at a *later point* if it turns out that this touchpoint really matters. Importance, after all, drives talk value.

Wednesday's One-Hour Exercise

Today you're going to spend an hour building your touchpoint map. To do this, you'll start with a list of your touchpoints and then develop answers to each of the following questions. As a suggestion, implement a 10-point scale and assign a value to each.

Part 1: Assessing Touchpoints

- What is its relative contribution in regards to talk value? Rate this on a 10-point scale. For example, is your message getting picked up? Is it reflected on the Social Web? If this is a dominant message, its talk value is toward the "10" end of the scale.

- Rank your performance or similar selected measure, again on a 10-point scale. For example, are you meeting, exceeding, or falling short on the expectations set? If you are hitting home runs, the rank is in the 8, 9, 10 range.

Tip: Put some time and mental effort into this step: The value of this exercise is very much set here. If you are working through this book in test mode, it's a great extension to prepare for a real case. If you are building a real plan now, then sooner rather than later you'll be asked to explain or substantiate each of your measures. In either case, responding with "It seemed about right to me..." is not enough. Take the time to develop your scale, your basis for grade assignment, and the metrics used.

Although this exercise may seem simple, you are setting up your processes for longer term trends that you'll uncover, track, and use to guide your social media efforts. Take the time now to get them right. They do not need to be perfect, although they do need to be reasonable, and you do need to be able to explain them to your colleagues.

Part 2: Plotting Touchpoints

With measures and grades in hand, rank each touchpoint by its relative performance (or your similar measure) in the marketplace against its relative importance as a talk-generator to your customers. I generally use the y-axis (vertical) for "performance" (higher is up) and the x-axis (horizontal) for "talk value." (More important is to the right.) What *should* emerge is a cloud that is oriented "up and to the right." In other words, you should be doing the best (performance) — meaning that you're working hardest and/or succeeding most — against the touchpoints that most often drive purchase (importance) or whatever your hoped-for conversion as a result of these efforts may be.

Figure 6.5 shows a *hypothetical* touchpoint map, with touchpoint performance plotted against talk-value. Note the "Direct" touchpoint that is high in performance, yet low in talk-value importance. This suggests — but obviously does not in itself make the case for — overspending or over-allocation of resources *in relation to generating social conversations.* There may be very valid reasons for the effort applied to this touchpoint — direct response marketing may be a very important part of your program. However, as currently implemented, it is relatively unimportant as a *social* touchpoint. This underscores the importance of identifying business objectives, selecting touchpoints, and choosing an organizational method. Looked at a different way, "direct response" may be your best performing tool. Don't lose sight of that.

Next look over to the right at "In-Store." You'll see that this data point is lower on "performance" yet high on talk-value. If this were real, you'd really want to pay attention to this one. Again, this is a hypothetical chart, but if your map looks like this, the suggested remedy is spending some time on the in-store experience as a way to improve the conversation that is occurring on the Social Web. This is the kind of insight you are after as a result of completing your touchpoint work.

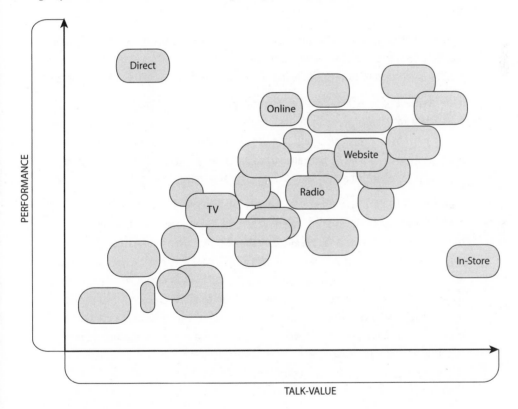

Figure 6.5 Example of a Touchpoint Map

The touchpoint map will show you a couple of things. It will identify places where spending is out of line with performance: This includes spending too little on touchpoints that matter as well as spending too much on touchpoints that don't. Like any other analytical tool, it's up to you to decide how to use it: The map is simply one view that will help you. Your touchpoint map will also identify the "favorite" or default channels that you are using. You'll quickly see any "pets" that may be used even though they really aren't performing in line with their expected results. To be sure, there may be strategic reasons or considerations for which the touchpoint process fails to account. Again, the touchpoint map is but one of the tools that you'll use in building your overall marketing plan and integrating social media into it.

Wednesday's Wrap-Up

Today you created your touchpoint map. If you're lucky, it is a cloud that tilts up and to the right. If not, you've got some work ahead. But hey, that's why you're reading this book!

My Map Is a Useless Blob

What if your map doesn't look like the one in the figure? In particular, what if all of your touchpoints are "very important" and "high performance?" If that's accurate, then hats off to you. You are clearly a Quadrant II marketer. Of course, you can still get more out of the touchpoint map.

It may well be that everything is working reasonably well: In this case, you'll have a bunch of points in the top-right of your map. Go through the following steps, however, and uncover the opportunities to improve single points. By doing so, you may be able to raise your entire level of performance when it comes to generating favorable talk on the Social Web. What I'm about to show works for maps that are concentrated at the lower-left, too.

First, set your current map aside: You'll still need it. Make a new one, but this time refigure your grades. It is essential that you use a numerical scale: For this exercise, use 1 to 10, where 10 corresponds to "best." Here is the big rule: For each axis, there must be at least one touchpoint *that is rated "1"* and at least one touchpoint *rated a "10."* To achieve this, rank your touchpoints according to talk value. The most important gets a 10, and the least important gets a 1. Now do the same for the performance. Note that your lowest talk point may be your highest performance point. The relative orders of the lists may not be the same. For each list, rate the points in the middle by comparing them with the points at the ends, and then replot your touchpoint map. Doing this will force you to increase the resolution of your map so that you can see differences in quality across your touchpoints, making it possible to increase the overall level of touchpoint performance. Combine this with your first map in the exercise tomorrow.

Analyze Your Data

Take a look at your map (or maps if you made more than one). Which are the touchpoints that you can *consider* trimming back, or at least need not focus on right away with regard to social media? If you made two maps, how are you doing overall? A concentration in the upper right means "doing pretty well." A concentration in the lower left means you've come to the right place. Which touchpoints do you need to pay more attention to? Your effort today is key to getting the most out of any social media program that you may launch.

With social media, what *you* are saying is only part of what drives the actual conversation. On the Social Web, it's your lone voice versus many. What happens *after* message uptake, purchase, or whatever your "conversion" is defined as can often be the larger part of the conversation. If you are overspending in one area when trying to generate favorable conversations, at the least you are not being as efficient a marketer as you could be. At worst, you are actually consuming resources that could be better applied elsewhere. While some particular touchpoints may seem inconsequential — and others self-evident as to their fundamental correctness — the real value of the touchpoint map is recognizing that channels you may not have been active in are actually driving the conversations that you have to clean up after or otherwise account for at the point-of-purchase. Jump back to the previous chapter on the social feedback cycle if you are unclear on how these concepts relate.

Thursday's One-Hour Exercise

For today's hour, make a list of the candidate efforts to cut and candidate efforts to boost. Along with each, identify the teams, products, customers, and vendors that are likely to be on the receiving end of your decisions. Pay special attention to the high-importance, low-performance touchpoints. *These are your big opportunities.* For each opportunity, identify specific internal constituents — the people, teams, departments — that you will need to engage in order to bring about the changes you think need to be made.

- What are your lowest talk-generating touchpoints?
- What are your highest talk-generating touchpoints?
- Which of your high-talk touchpoints are low-performing from your customer's viewpoint? Make a note of these.
- Which of your high-talk touchpoints are high-performing from your customer's viewpoint? Take care to identify and preserve these.

As you work this information into your plan, prioritize it: Focus first on the high-talk/low-performance touchpoints, as these are generating negative word-of-mouth and detrimental social content. Focus next on the low-talk, high-performance touchpoints: What could you do to make these more visible on the Social Web? Examine each of your touchpoints in this way.

Thursday's Wrap-Up

In today's exercise, you took your map and extracted insight. If your map affirmed everything you are doing — if all of your touchpoints that matter are being reflected positively in conversations on the Social Web (as well as borne out in your CRM and customer service and community management data) — then this a truly valuable exercise: You've established your readiness to implement social components in your marketing program. Your map is essentially saying that you can step up to the conversations without fear or hesitation. More likely, you've uncovered some touchpoints that are working well, and some others that are not. That's a great outcome too: You've now got a map to guide your preparations as you set up to use social components in your overall marketing program. Your map will help identify the places where social media can be applied effectively and where it is most likely to get noticed.

Plan Your Next Steps

I'm going to assume that your touchpoint map and subsequent analysis revealed at least one point where you can improve. I'm also going to assume that this point is associated with a marketplace outcome that you'd like to *improve* rather than simply a touchpoint that indicates an area of overspending. In other words, I'm assuming that you've got some work to do before you roll social media into your marketing programs. If this is not correct — if everything is truly perfect with regard to your touchpoints — then congratulations: You are exempt from the next challenge, and may leave the stage.

Friday's One-Hour Exercise

Take your number-one opportunity: The most important touchpoint from the perspective of generating talk that you are simultaneously performing poorly on. Today you're going to outline a plan to address this touchpoint and its performance. Here are the key things to focus on as you develop your plan:

- What is the issue? Is this the wrong audience or a poor customer experience?

- Did you set the right expectation? Did you over-promise? Or under-deliver?

- Who else is involved? Who are your primary internal constituents when it comes to moving this touchpoint up and to the right (or down and to the left) on your touchpoint map?

- Which of the required actions are directly within your control?

- How are you going to fix this?

Pull these answers together and set them aside for now. You will use these when you get to Chapter 13, "Objectives, Metrics, and ROI" and Chapter 14, "Present Your Social Media Plan" where you'll be completing your social media plan.

Friday's Wrap-Up

Today you took your first steps in building a social media campaign. Even if the primary impact of the actions you've planned are aimed at Operations versus Marketing proper, you've taken steps toward impacting and influencing the conversations on the Social Web. More importantly, you're setting about it in the *right way*. Remember, on the Social Web, you can't directly control the conversation. Instead, you influence it by setting an appropriate expectation and then delivering on it. That is the simple, time-tested formula for the effective generation of beneficial word-of-mouth, and by extension that same approach works on the Social Web. The touchpoint map you developed is the first of the trending and analysis tools that you'll use to chart your work on the Social Web.

By looking at the places your customers — and potential customers — come into contact with your brand, you identify all of the places you can influence them. By plotting performance against importance, you can evaluate the suitability of your current marketing efforts as an agent of influence in a *social* versus traditional media context. This combined action — measurement and trending, and then folding the results back into your marketing and operations programs — is your only effective assurance of sustained winning on the Social Web.

Chapter 6: The Main Points

* Touchpoint analysis leads to an understanding of the core elements of the experiences that will be talked about on the Social Web in conversations relating to your brand, product, or service.
* The touchpoint map is a systematic representation that quantifies the contribution and performance of individual touchpoints.

Week 4: Influence and Measurement

*If you could ask your customer just one question —
and your business depended on the answer —
wouldn't you want to ask that question? The Net
Promoter score, developed by Fred Reichheld, is
based on one simple question: "How likely is it
that you would recommend [name of company,
product, service] to a friend?" It turns out to be a
fundamentally important metric and central to the
successful implementation of social media. Think
about it: If your own customers would not recommend you...well, you can see the problem.*

*This chapter starts with an in-depth look at
the Net Promoter score. It continues and covers
existing metrics, some of which you are probably
already collecting, and then it shows how these
metrics can be used to make a case for the utiliza-
tion of social media and used to create a basis for
the determination of success.*

7

Chapter Contents
Influence and the Social Web
Applying Influence: Social Media
Metrics: Influence to ROI
Quantifying the Conversation
The Main Points

The Net Promoter Score

In this chapter, I refer to the Net Promoter score, created by Director Emeritus and Bain Fellow Fred Reichheld. Although there are other methods for computing social performance, I believe that this method is by far the best. It is easy to understand: Based on one question, it can be added to existing surveys that you are doing now. It is easy to build an action plan based on it: Knowing how likely your customers are to recommend your product or service takes you straight into the kinds of product or service changes that lead to the increased likelihood of a strong, powerful recommendation. Most importantly, the Net Promoter score takes into account the powerful impact of *detractors*. On the Social Web, the detractor — positioned opposite the evangelist — plays a pivotal role. For a complete treatment of the Net Promoter score and how you can apply it to your business, please read *The Ultimate Question* by Fred Reichheld (Covey, 2006). I highly recommend it.

Influence and the Social Web

Measurement and the Social Web go hand in hand, although it's not always obvious how to go about measuring something as dynamic as a conversation. Further, because the Social Web is a relatively new medium, many of the measures you'd like either aren't available or aren't yet proven as fundamental indicators of success as it applies to marketing. Reach and frequency, developed for mass advertising over a period of years and refinement, are solid mass media indicators. As a largely — but not exclusively — online phenomenon, social media measurement borrows heavily from existing online metrics. At the same time, questions like "How likely is it that you would recommend me to a friend?" are rooted in the principles that drive social media.

In the opening sections of *The Ultimate Question*, author Fred Reichheld makes two fundamental points:

- Customers who are willing to evangelize, based on direct experience, are the only sustainable source of long-term profits.

- Profits earned through any form of coercion, trickery, or misleading advice are at best short term and will — if left unchecked — ultimately destroy the firm.

Look at these two items and think about the Social Web. Customers who are "willing to evangelize" are precisely the customers that I identified as actively talking in Chapter 5, "The Social Feedback Cycle." These are the customers who have tried your product or service and have something to say about it. What they have to say may be a different matter, but nonetheless these are the customers that are both inclined and able (i.e., have the online tools and skills) to talk about the experience you have delivered. At the same time, you've (hopefully!) earned a profit on these customers. Running a sustainable, healthy business requires a profit, after all, and for most businesses the only source of that profit is your customer. Yes, you can spend less, and you can be more efficient with resources. These kinds of disciplines and activities can improve your profit margins and help you establish a long-term competitive cost advantage. At the end of the day, however, the cash flow you need to operate comes from exactly one place — your customers' wallets.

If you buy into the idea that your customers are both informed and inclined to make smart choices, then the Net Promoter score makes quite a bit of sense. The direct implication for generating long-term profits, according to the principles Fred defines, is that if you have generated your revenue through any activity or business practice that doesn't delight your customers — or wouldn't if they fully understood it — your days are numbered. The precise number of days may be large: Some businesses run for a long time all the while abusing their customers in one way or another simply because their customers have no other choice. However, eventually those firms either change or fail.

Think about mobile phone companies, who often give *new* customers a better deal than *existing* ones. Automobile dealers — who have long made the bulk of their profits on service and parts sales (not car sales) created price floors for the quick lube and replacement parts providers and in so doing gave rise to the businesses that now undercut them in these areas. Full-cost airlines who long enjoyed near monopolies in heavily regulated markets gave rise to upstarts such as Southwest Airlines that made customer satisfaction in the context of efficient, affordable travel their primary goal. Not coincidentally, Southwest Airlines is consistently profitable, has never accepted a government bailout, and depending on the day is worth about as much or more on the stock market than all other airlines combined.

Building a winning brand and maintaining one are two different things: Dell built a commanding position in the personal computer (PC) market by offering a better way for its customers to buy one. When its customer service floundered, however, Hewlett Packard (HP) gained and retook the global market share lead in the third quarter of 2006. Dell is now pushing hard to regain its top spot, and not coincidentally social media and the positive practices that drive it are part of Dell's program. In all of these cases, the role of the customer recommendation is central to the rise — or fall — of the brand.

Put these two concepts together — the evangelist as the key to long-term growth, and that profit earned by means that fail to delight your customers threatens your long-term viability — and you have what is essentially a formula for success not only on the Social Web but in businesses as well. On the Social Web — made up of social media applications such as blogs, photo and video sharing, collaborative event planning tools, ratings and reviews, and more — the conversations that stem from actual, delightful experiences with products and services are the key to driving and sustaining evangelism and hence long-term growth. Traditional marketing programs are essential in driving awareness and seeding markets. Evangelism — the impact of which is shown in Figure 7.1 — causes a steady amplification that builds over time through the combination of word of mouth and digital content on the Social Web. It literally creates markets. Contemporary brands and their social reputations are being built through practices that encourage evangelism.

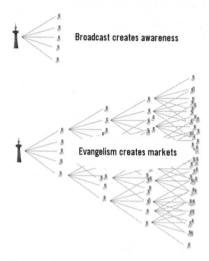

Figure 7.1 Evangelists Driving Sales

You can counter that price, or some other single killer feature, rules in the creation of evangelists. To be sure, I don't know anybody who doesn't like a deal, and attributes such as price do get talked about. But at the same time, a good chunk of your customer base will enthusiastically promote you for a variety of reasons if you'll only give them the means. This desire goes beyond any single characteristic — for example, price — associated with your brand. There are a few million people out there who do not want Southwest Airlines to go out of business and who are *willing to pay extra* to make sure it doesn't. This was made clear following September 11, 2001, as *customers* literally wrote in to support the airline, offering *cash contributions* and emotional support to keep the airline in the air, and to keep *all* of its employees working. That's love, and that's a key ingredient in the development of evangelism with regard to a brand, product, or service.

This connection to the brand, based on actual experience, is the reason the Net Promoter score is so powerful in social media applications. It treats equally what you are perceived as doing right as well as what you are perceived as doing wrong. *This is where most satisfaction surveys fail.*

Here's an example: Suppose that 60 percent of your current customers were highly likely to recommend you, while another 20 percent were reasonably satisfied but perhaps not moved to the point of offering spontaneous recommendations. The typical satisfaction survey asking the analogous questions directed at satisfaction rather than likelihood of recommendation will often group both of these, and conclude that 80 percent of the customers surveyed were basically satisfied or better. Who wouldn't be happy to learn that the majority of their current customer base considers the product or service acceptable?

The problem with this type of analysis is two-fold. First, it lulls everyone — including the CMO, CEO, and COO — into the false sense that everything is fine. Eighty percent sounds like a lot, and in truth it is. It's "almost everyone." The problem is that on the Social Web, which is where your social media campaign will play out, *100 percent of your customers are present.* "Eighty percent satisfied or better" is *not* "fine" if it means that 20 percent of your customers are walking around *actively* telling people not to buy your stuff. The typical satisfaction survey and conventional analysis can and often does conveniently hide this fact. What do you suppose will happen when you invite *all* of your customers to talk about you? The Social Web, by definition, is open to all participants. Do you think these 20 percent will stay home that day? They won't. If you don't know that they are there, or what they are likely to say, or what you will say when they start talking, that 20 percent will quickly become your worst nightmare.

Satisfaction surveys — unless they differentiate influential respondents — can also fail by missing the "key" social participants. Suppose you have equal numbers of lovers and haters, for example. That's good data, but it's not enough. It is also important to know the makeup of each group: Which group contains more of the "A List" bloggers? Which group reflects the comments of people participating in the 100,000- or 1,000,000- versus 1,000-member forums? Which bloggers are your potential customers listening to? This same caveat applies to your Net Promoter surveys, so be sure that you consider this. You may not be able to get this data right away; but if you ask for it, you can build it up over time and gain valuable insight into your audience on the Social Web.

The Net Promoter score helps you in three ways. First, it correctly identifies the share of customers that will stand up and recommend you. A score of 7 or 8 out of a possible 10 means they think you're OK, but it doesn't mean that they'll go out of their way to actively recommend you. A score of 9 or 10 means they will. So right off, you've got a big leg up in preparing for and managing social campaigns: You know what kind of *active* support you're likely to have. Second, you know what share of your customer base is going to give a negative recommendation.

In our simple survey, we asked only one question: In practice, you'll probably have more information available to you, including the type of customer, purchase history, demographics, and more. You can use this information to pinpoint issues, which brings us to benefit number three. Using the Net Promoter score and the methodology Fred has developed, you can put a plan into place that reduces the number of detractors while you also work on building the number of promoters. This is a huge gain for you: Actively working to reduce both the influence and the number of detractors takes you deeper into the operational aspects of your brand and can get at things that are often passed over and dismissed with excuses such as "We can't fix that" or "It's not my department." If detractors are beating you up about it, whatever *it* is *does* matter, and you *must* fix it. Looking at promoters versus detractors can also expose internal practices considered sacred: "At Jones & Jones, we simply don't do things *that* way." Maybe this a good time to start! Seriously, while I am making light of what can be real challenges, when tracked over time the Net Promoter score is an invaluable yardstick for social media practitioners. It is easy for your colleagues to understand, share, and internally promote. Most important, it gets directly at what drives the conversations that occur on the Social Web.

 Tip: You influence conversations on the Social Web by simultaneously *increasing the share of promoters* while *decreasing the share of detractors.*

Spend a minute thinking about this: It's the fundamental essence of social media management from a marketing perspective. You cannot "control" the social conversation in the same way as you can control your advertising message. Look at it this way: Yes, you can control the ad campaign. But, you can't control the *response* to it. Social media is an articulation of the *response*, to your brand, product, or service in actual use. The ad or PR campaigns you create set the expectations against which that response is generated. Fundamentally, the Social Web is built on conversations *that do not belong to you but instead belong to someone else.* Instead of trying to control the conversation (or worse, the participants), you have to change your product or service experience that drives the conversation. This, along with your behavior on the Social Web, is the only element of a social media campaign over which you have full control.

If you've got a great product that is delivering a superior (delightful) experience, then use social components such as blogs or video sharing that encourage more talk: Use the Social Web as a platform to spread your message. If you've got work to do, use tools such as support forums to identify and correct issues: Use the Social Web as a listening tool and take the conversation to the COO where you can fix the problems. Above all, participate, and be open and honest about what you are doing.

Quantifying the Conversation

This week is about establishing some basic metrics and using them to gauge influence. On Monday you're going to set up a call sheet and questionnaire and start calling. Hopefully you're not scared to call your customers. No customers to call? If you are working in a prelaunch startup, or are a student or in some other role that does not provide access to customers, then pick a brand and call your friends or colleagues and ask them the questions posed about that brand instead. On Tuesday you're going to make more calls, and continue to ask your customers (or friends) how likely they would be to recommend whatever it is you are calling them about. By Wednesday you'll be wrapping up the results. There's a chance that you won't have connected with everyone on your list by Wednesday: In that case, continue on with the exercises and move into the next chapter. However, keep working on this exercise until it is complete because what you learn here will be critically important in developing your actual social media campaign.

> **Tip:** A set of worksheets covering this week's exercises can be found in the appendix of this book. In addition to these printed worksheets, you can also download electronic copies and access related resources at the website accompanying this book. Complete information regarding these resources and the website is included in the appendix.

Influence and Metrics

Turn back to Fred's "ultimate question": "How likely are you to recommend Company X?" Embodied in this simple question is everything that powers (or destroys) a brand on the Social Web. This one question is the basis of a very simple — but powerful — measure of influence.

When your customers willingly support you through a pricing structure that provides a profit based on satisfaction, and are at the same time willing to evangelize your brand — to *recommend you* to others — you are in a very good place. Applying social media will be a very straightforward and largely risk-free proposition. After all, your customers are already talking about you favorably, and you have a business model that will stand up over time. Are you worried about "managing the conversation"? In effect, you already are. Through the experience of delight that you already provide, you are influencing the conversation in a way that is favorable to your position.

The experience of delight is the only way to positively influence the conversation on the Social Web. Delight can arise as the result of great experience, or, because you handled an experience that was less than great…in a great way. Provide a great experience, and the conversation will take care of itself. In contrast, provide a poor one, and the conversation will reflect that instead. The measurement of influence, and in particular tracking it over time, is key to managing your social presence and fully tapping the Social Web.

Today you're going to spend an hour identifying a set of customers that you can call. You'll be putting together a basic call sheet. I've provided a starting script that you can follow: You are, of course, free to improvise as long as you still ask your customers how willing they'd be to recommend you. Note that asking them if they like you, if they are happy with your relationship or with the last order, or if everything is going OK, is not the same as asking them how willing they'd be to recommend you. Liking someone is different than personally vouching for them. There is a higher degree of commitment implied, and it is for exactly this reason that a *recommendation* and the measure of likelihood is worth so much.

A Sample Call Script

"Good afternoon, this is _____ from _____. We've been doing business for _____ years and it occurred to me that I've never asked you about whether or not you'd tell others to try us. So, I'm calling today to ask you: On a scale of 1 to 10, where 1 means "no way" and 10 means "absolutely, without hesitation," how likely would you be to recommend our firm to your colleagues or others who you feel could use our _____ (product or service)?"

Your script can be as simple as that. You'll want to say "thank you" at the end of your call, too. You may well find that this call opens a dialogue, especially if the answer to your question starts out along the lines of "Well, I'm glad you called because actually....there are a couple of issues that would prevent me from recommending you." Structure your call sheet like the one shown in Figure 7.2. If your call does open a dialog about challenging issues, be sure to note these issues. Add these to your notes for use later when you build your plan.

In the call sheet shown in Figure 7.2, I want to call out one specific attribute: *influencer.* As you are calling, or through research that you do ahead of time, identify the role that each of your contacts plays in generating influential social content. It may be, for example, that the customer you are speaking with also runs a well-read blog or is a moderator in a popular forum. The recommendation metric is unchanged, but knowing that this person is more or less influential than your average customer is valuable when you are looking to stem negative conversations or quickly communicate positive developments that you initiate through social media later on. To get a handle on influence, look for blogs authored by the person you are calling: Use Google and search for the person's name and company or title, for example, or ask questions like "Have you ever recommended us or one of our competitors?" If the response is, "Yes, all the time. In fact, just last week..." then go ahead and check "Influencer."

Contact	Phone	Date	Score	Influencer	Notes
Drew Smith	867-555-1324	5/2/08	7		surprised that we wanted to know this
Diane McNish	328-555-2781	5/3/08	9	X	participated in business summit last fall
Pilar Mouten	888-231-5555	5/2/08	5		need to schedule follow-up with Ops
Ed Crocker	878-444-2387	5/2/08	8	X	referred APX account; industry blogger
Diane Elison	999-231-1989				
Larry Page	878-231-8765				

Figure 7.2 A Typical Call Sheet

Depending on your organization, you may need to work with sales or an alternative team when compiling a list of customers. Most importantly, do not call only those clients you know will tell you what you want to hear. Don't avoid "problem" customers. They can be your greatest source of insight. Sure, you can stack the deck, but then the only thing you'll learn is how to make a call, and you probably already know how to do that. Instead, pick customers randomly: You want a few who you know are tough and some with whom you have a great relationship. Approaching this week's exercise in this way is sure to produce some new learning, and after all isn't that why you are taking the time to read this book?

Now it's time to make your calls. Create a list of customers, and enter them into a list like that shown in 7.2 Next, pick a random subset to call. I suggest calling at least 10 customers, so you want to start with a list of 20 or more.

> **Tip:** To pick customers at random, sequentially assign numbers to each of the customers in your initial list. Then, jump over to www.randomizer.org/form.htm. Generate a list of random numbers and call the customers corresponding to those numbers.

Figures 7.3 and 7.4 show how the randomizer tool can be used to make picking customers easy and truly random. In the figures, I have asked for 10 random picks from my list of 50 customers. I will be calling the customers numbered 26, 44, 34, etc., from my list of 50 customers.

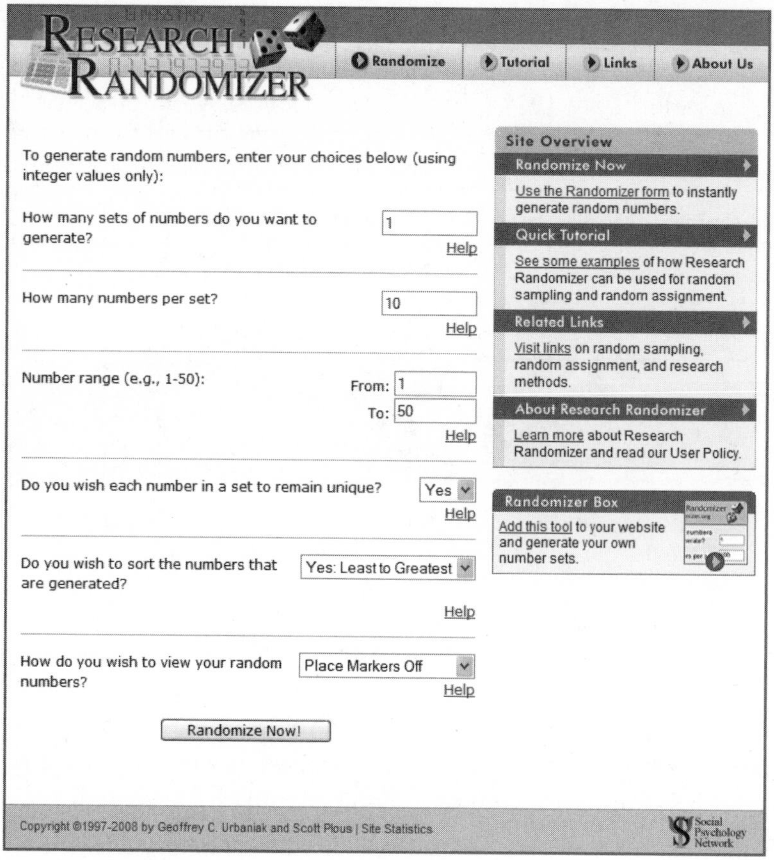

Figure 7.3 Randomizer.org Input

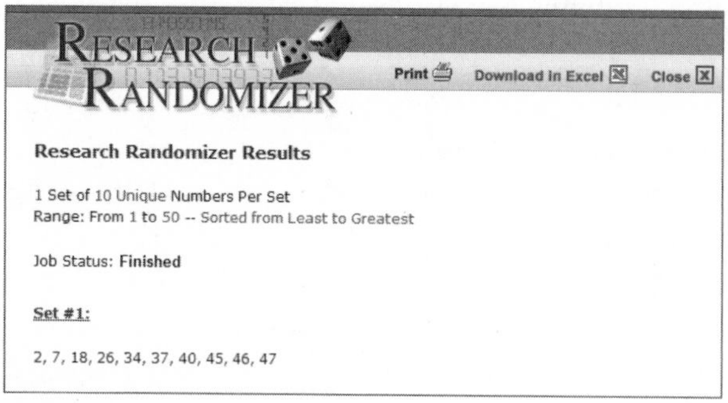

Figure 7.4 Randomizer.org Output

The randomization process may seem like extra work, but it's actually quite important. When you do a survey, you always want to take that extra step to push bias, however unintended, out of the system. Besides, when your colleagues start peppering you with questions about how you did your survey, won't it be nice to be able to look at them and say "We used a standard randomization method to select our sample population from our current customer base." That usually impresses the nay-sayers, helping you to successfully win support for your program when the time comes.

For the next hour, work through the following items. Don't rush — take the time to talk with your customers. You've got tomorrow as well to finish any calls you don't get to today.

- Using your script and call sheet, make your calls.
- Using your call sheet, record notes from each call.

> **Tip:** Though it may take longer, you can use an email or other type of survey instrument if this works better in your specific case. Use the same randomization method when determining who to include and adapt the script for use in these alternate survey tools.

Monday's Wrap-Up

Today you set up a basic call sheet and even made a few calls. What new things did you learn? Most people have a preset expectation of what they are likely to encounter. You may, for example, expect that a certain feature or competitive lack thereof, or a recent price increase is going to come up in every call. Did it? By calling customers at random and then asking about the likelihood of a recommendation rather than "How's it going?" or "Do you like our new products?" you focus the conversation on the issues that really drive the conversation on the Social Web. No one "likes" a price increase. Real business issues may prevent you from matching a competitor's offering feature for feature. But neither of these necessarily stands in the way of a strong, positive recommendation.

Looking at your call sheet, is it working for you? You may want to modify your call sheet to fit the kind of information you are getting. If you have time and the inclination, replace the sheet altogether with a simple database so that you can expand the questions down the road and track the results over time. This would be a great project to get a larger team involved in, too, and thereby build support for your social media program.

Tuesday's One-Hour Exercise

Today you're going to spend an hour finishing your calls and making any final notes based on what you have learned. Tomorrow you'll use the information you've gathered today and yesterday to determine your Net Promoter score.

Go back to the call sheet you set up yesterday and work through any remaining clients. Here are some helpful points that will ensure you get the most out of this exercise:

- If you're getting all "tens," do a quick reality check. Have you picked your "ten best" customers, or did you choose them randomly? Are your customers being frank with you?

- If they say they're very likely to recommend you, can you think of a customer you have now that was such a referral?

- It may be that you need to do the survey anonymously, too. In that case, go ahead and do that: You can set up the survey and then move on in next week's exercises while waiting for the responses to come back.

Central to both yesterday's and today's exercise is getting the information that you *need*. If the people you are talking to are saying nice things about you — that they like doing business with you, or that you have been one their longest-running suppliers — push harder. Don't upset them, of course, but do make sure you get the information you need. The question you want answered — the *only* question you want answered for this exercise — is the question pertaining to the likelihood of a recommendation. More information is great, but make sure you get the answer to this one question.

Although it will take a bit longer to set up, an anonymous survey may be the way to go. Typically, you would employ an outside service provider and then work with them to set up the survey you want done. The results can be very valuable and quite telling. One of the teams I worked with talked with its customers regularly, and over time confirmed that they were indeed "well liked." However, when they ran the same basic survey anonymously and had the survey firm probe more deeply, it was clear that while they were *liked* they weren't necessarily seen as a *business partner*. Being viewed as a business partner more often than not results in a strong recommendation as compared with the significantly softer "being liked." What was subsequently learned about how to change the perception of the firm to that of a business partner was worth much more than the cost of the anonymous survey that identified and quantified the underlying issues.

Tuesday's Wrap-Up

If you were able to make 10 calls and talk with 10 customers, that's great. If you have a few more or a few less, that's fine too. As long as you called randomly, you'll be fine in this exercise. Ultimately, you'll be going out to the marketplace with a social media campaign: It's much better to learn about issues that are preventing recommendations now. Likewise, it will be very helpful in presenting your case for using social media if you can stand in front of your colleagues and confidently say, "I talked with our customers. They indicated that they would be very likely to recommend us." If you've called your favorite customers, your colleagues will see right through it. Even worse, if you have, *and they go along with it,* then when you do go out in the marketplace the customers you avoided are likely to chime in. More than anything else, you really want to avoid surprises on the Social Web. The best way to avoid unhappy accidents is through a combination of excellent customer experiences and advance knowledge of what your customers think of you.

Applying Influence: Social Media

On Monday and Tuesday you conducted a basic customer survey focused on the social media fundamental of "recommendation." Recommendations are a critical component of social campaigns — in fact, recommendations *are* social campaigns. When you deconstruct a traditional campaign, you find at its core a message crafted by a professional PR firm or agency creative team. You find a message that is aspirational with regard to the brand: It's what the brand manager and agency account executives *hope you will think,* which will then carry you all the way through the purchase funnel to the cash register. There is of course nothing wrong with this: I am not being judgmental here. Rather, it is simply how most consumer transactions are thought about from a purely business and advertising perspective.

This stands in contrast to a recommendation. Recommendations — whether in the form of a conversation or a video clip — power the Social Web. A recommendation, often appearing along with a review or a rating, is an expression by one person of what might be useful or helpful to another. Ratings quantify the strength of the recommendation: Five stars on Amazon means I really got a lot out this book. Reviews add depth. When Robert Scoble takes the time to create a multimedia presentation of his "social media starfish" on Kyte TV, part of his message is an implicit *recommendation* that you think about adding some of these components to your toolbox. You'll spend more time on those components in Chapter 11, "Reviews, Ratings, and Recommendations": For now, you are focused on the role of the recommendation in relation to its power as a conversation driver.

Unlike the aspirational or persuasive marketer-generated message, a consumer-generated recommendation is often a purely informational component in the purchase process: Consumer-generated messages are both positive and negative, and they are generally first-person, adding authenticity and urgency to the message. Think back to the social feedback cycle: The conversation — however it is expressed — enters the purchase process in the consideration phase, between awareness and purchase. Social media covers the range of emotions and views that are raised in the post-purchase experience. Consumer-generated content can sway, convert, *or dissuade,* depending on its polarity (positive or negative). By comparison, marketer-generated messages nearly always attempt to positively persuade. "You'll love our product because...." So much of what happens in advertising is positive (that is, encouraging and supporting a purchase), the general response has become "Nice, but you're really only giving me part of the story. What about the negative? What happens after I buy?" Of course, that question leads directly onto the Social Web, where it gets answered.

By comparison, political "attack" ads are one of the few examples of *marketing* communication where the *entire ad* (not just a feature comparison) is often negative: They are often deliberately styled to appear to be more like consumer-generated media in terms of (lower) production value and a more direct speaking style. This is not generally the case in mainstream traditional advertising, again separating that medium from social media. Ford, for example, would never run an entire ad directly attacking Chevy, whereas plenty of pickup owners will post emphatically in online forums about how they'd rather push a Ford than drive a Chevy. There are some things that consumers can get away with which marketers generally do well to steer clear of. When dealing with social media, and consumer-generated media in particular, you are dealing with the statements of individuals woven together into a conversation. Using social media, you can tap the emotional elements of consumer-generated media by *influencing* — but not controlling — what happens on the Social Web.

Influence on the Social Web — expressed through the diverse set of social media components — is indeed powerful. Trust — covered extensively in Chapter 2, "The Marketer's Dilemma" — is a big part of the driver. It is for this reason that being open and honest is critical: Any indication that integrity is in question causes an otherwise well-intentioned social campaign to weaken. At its extreme, it will wreak havoc on your brand. It is influence — not control — that you are really after in your social media campaigns. It is influence that can be applied tactically at the point of consideration in the purchase process. *This is the exact point where a purchase decision is being formulated and validated.* Understanding who is likely to recommend you (or who will not) and to what degree along with why (or why not) is critical in assessing your readiness for a social media campaign.

Wednesday's One-Hour Exercise

Today you're going to score your survey. Referring back to Fred Reichheld's Net Promoter score, the methodology you'll use is simple. A quick note is in order before you do this: The sample you have used is decidedly small. The intention is to show you *how this works* so that you can apply it on a larger and more rigorous scale as you build your social media program over time.

Here are the steps you will follow to compute your Net Promoter score based on some sample data. You'll calculate your actual score following this example:

1.   Add up the number of customers who gave you a nine (9) or ten (10) and compute the corresponding percentage. These are your promoters. If you called ten companies and six gave you either a nine or ten, the result of step 1 is a Promoter score of 60 percent.

2.   Add up the number of customers who gave you a six (6) or less. These are your detractors. If two gave a score of six or less, this is Detractor score of 20 percent.

3.   Subtract the Detractor score from the Promoter score: Your Net Promoter score is the difference. In the example used, the Net Promoter score is 40 percent.

Forty percent?! That's terrible! That's FAILING, right? And what about the sevens and eights: Don't they count?

First, 40 percent is pretty good. It means that you have more active promoters than detractors. When you are fighting for every share point, you want more people pulling for you than pushing against you. A score of 40 percent says that this is the case. That's good. What's a score that indicates problems that need to be corrected? How about *negative* 40 percent! A *negative* score means you have more detractors than promoters: Jumping into social media and expecting to use it *as an outreach tool* with a negative Net Promoter score is a lot like bringing a spoon to a knife fight. You're in trouble before you even walk in. With regard to the sevens and eights, no, they don't count, and here's why: A score of seven or eight means people think you're OK, but would not necessarily give you a strong recommendation. In a world driven by recommendations, sevens and eights don't count.

Now calculate your actual Net Promoter score, using the survey data you collected:

1.   Add up the number of customers who gave you a nine (9) or ten (10) and compute the corresponding percentage. These are your promoters.

2.   Add up the number of customers who gave you a six (6) or less. These are your detractors.

3.   Subtract the Detractor score from the Promoter score: Your Net Promoter score is the difference.

4.   Write down your Net Promoter score.

Wednesday's Wrap-Up

Today you determined your Net Promoter score and got your first real look at a metric that can guide your social media program. Understanding your current base of active promoters versus likely detractors is essential to successfully implementing social media. If your score was 40 percent or higher, that's great. If it was 100 percent, run through this chapter again with ten new customers. Seriously, if your score is 70 percent or higher, that's really terrific. And yes, you still can improve: If you eliminate your detractors (not in the James Bond sense…), you could achieve a score of 80, 90, or even 100 percent. However, put this into perspective: Bain studied a group of respected companies. Scores ranged from near zero to the low 80s. One stood out for me personally: Harley-Davidson. Harley-Davidson scored 81 percent. What kind of customer base drives a Net Promoter score of 81 percent? *Customers who will tattoo your name on their body!* Take a look at Figure 7.5: What would it take to get your name there, in *permanent* ink? Suffice it to say, 80 percent and above is indeed remarkable.

PHOTO AND TATTOO USED WITH PERMISSION OF TATTOO ARTIST DANIEL UPTON, GOLDEN APPLE STUDIOS, AUSTIN, TX.

Figure 7.5 Harley-Davidson Tattoo

Metrics: From Influence to ROI

So far this week you've worked exclusively with the Net Promoter score. Think of this as the foundation for social media metrics, certainly as they apply to understanding your readiness to engage in *promotional* social campaigns. If your score is relatively high (if promoters outnumber detractors, for example), then the Social Web ought to be reasonably receptive to your efforts, provided you follow the basic rules of etiquette and conduct as established: disclosure, transparency, and participation versus interruption. If detractors outnumber promoters, then engaging the Social Web directly — in other words, using social media as an outreach tool — is risky. Fortunately, even in this case you can still use the Social Web and social media. Using social media for outreach is just one of the two available modes: The other is *listening and feedback*. Particularly for brands, products, or services with a low (or negative) Net Promoter score, the Social Web can be a great place to quickly and at low cost *discover* the kinds of things that, if addressed, will prove themselves valuable over the long run.

In addition to the measurements like the Net Promoter score, there are a range of similarly quantitative metrics available to you. If you currently have a company website or blog, or are using basic social media channels already, you can tap these for data. For example, if you have a website, link your sources of traffic to the metrics you collect there such as page views and detailed site visitor information, including length of time spent, traffic patterns, and entry and exit pages. If you are operating support forums or basic discussion boards, you can collect this same information and use it to get a handle on engagement or stickiness. If you maintain a blog, you can count the number of subscribers versus unique visitors, and compute the ratio of comments to posts and generate an estimate of the interest that people who frequent your blog take in its content. Together, these give you a baseline from which you can draw conclusions about the level of participation that currently exists. This is important in developing a baseline against which you can measure future changes as you develop and implement new or additional social media efforts.

Featured Case: Cymfony SONY Blu-ray

Using the Cymfony social media metrics platform from a group of nearly 18,000 posts from blogs, discussion boards, and consumer review sites, a sample of 2,000 were pulled for detailed analysis early in the Blu-ray/HD DVD battle. Early on, HD DVD had the lead: 2.5 times more posts discussed being impressed with the *technology* of HD DVD as compared with the number of posts mentioning Blu-ray technology, while 70 percent more posts discussed HD DVD's *advantages* versus those that discussed Blu-ray advantages. There was little discussion of Blu-ray's larger storage capacity or more sophisticated interactivity, both of which are significant differentiating features in favor of Blu-ray. In retrospect, Sony could have shortened the Blu-ray/HD-DVD battle if they had paid attention to how their marketing communications were failing to engage early adopters and influential writers and then quickly zeroed in and focused on this very important audience.

You can also measure the conversations that are occurring outside of your own online properties: For example, you can measure the number of times your product or brand is mentioned in blogs, and even the context (favorable or unfavorable) of the mentions using tools like BlogPulse. With Cymfony you can quantify the conversations and measure uptake of traditionally delivered messages as well build an overall picture of your brand reputation. Figure 7.6 shows selected cultural expressions — *meme*s — trended over the six months ending May of 2008. Mentions of "green" (in all of its connotations) not surprisingly tops the trends — it's a common word, after all — with spikes on Earth Day (environmental green) and St. Patrick's Day (celebratory green). Conversations referencing Iraq are of course steady, with a spike on March 19 marking the fifth anniversary of the start of the war in Iraq. As a measure of the continued relevance of pop culture, conversations referencing Britney (Spears) command a continued share of all blog mentions, spiking on and after days of increased news activity.

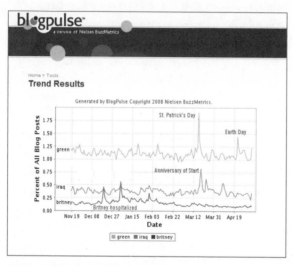

Figure 7.6 BlogPulse and Selected Memes

The challenge is of course to develop a way of interpreting and reporting these metrics that result in valuable insight or predict likely outcomes that are specific to your business. For this, I like to go back to the fifties, sixties, and seventies, and think about the kinds of empirical behaviors that, combined with data that was available or could be made available from networks, resulted in the robust metrics supporting traditional media today. In other words, while it may be true that there isn't yet an agreed body of "social media metrics," this doesn't mean there aren't some likely candidates. It certainly doesn't excuse social media marketers from measurement altogether. As I've developed in prior chapters, standing in front of the CEO and COO, it's going to be a tough sell on the part of the CMO or Marketing Director armed with only ideas and hunches about the value of social media. One way or another, some sort of quantitative basis needs to be advanced to successfully make the case for a social media budget, and more importantly to make the case for funding the kinds of *operations* efforts that need to be undertaken to positively influence the conversation on the Social Web.

Table 7.1 provides an index to the most useful metrics that are commonly available. They are presented in a grouped format, where the groups themselves are taken from the work of Robert Scoble and others. Note that you may not have access to all of these metrics: You may have only a website right now, for example. That's fine: You can begin with what you have and then build additional measures as you develop your social media program in upcoming chapters.

▶ **Table 7.1** Social Media Metrics

Target Knowledge	Interpreted Information	Underlying Metric
Audience	Who's reading	Aggregate profile data
Unique visitors	Page views, visitor info, blog mentions, click analysis, traffic patterns, sources of traffic via referrer measures	Web Analytics: Unique visitors
Influence	Memes (thoughts, ideas, pop culture artifacts like "Britney" or "green") and intensity over time (See Figure 7.6)	Time on site, blog context, review polarity
Engagement	Clicked on Length of stay Conversation	Time on site, pass-alongs, comment-to-post ratio, blog mentions, reviews, bounce rates
Action	Conversions	Pass-alongs, conversions, reviews
Loyalty	Trends: subscribers, repeat visitors, referrals	Pass-alongs, blog mentions, time on site, bounce rate

By taking the time to gather the kinds of data mentioned in Table 7.1, and then examining trends and patterns as you try discrete social media experiments, you can identify the metrics that are most valuable to you and that have the most potential for suggesting likely outcomes. You are a pioneer, and in the pioneer spirit you are looking for clues as to what lies around the next corner.

Thursday's One-Hour Exercise

Today you're going to spend an hour reviewing and compiling the metrics that you have available presently, and then supplement that using BlogPulse or a similar online tool.

Think as well about metrics that you may also have but that aren't listed. For example, how could you use your CRM data to refine or supplement the metrics suggested in the table? If you don't have this data handy — or don't even know where to start looking — take heart: By adding quantitative metrics to your social media program, you are simultaneously building a platform for success, and differentiating yourself from the many who will try social media *without* measurement. You may have to visit with IT, your webmaster, or your CFO to get the data you need. No matter, time spent on this now will pay big dividends later as you are sorting what works from what doesn't and making the case to increase your participation on the Social Web. The main point of today's exercise is this: Using the list in Table 7.1 as a start, find as many sources of data as you can that relate to how your customers perceive your brand, product, or service, and how they interact online with whatever digital assets — website, a blog, customer service emails — you have in place now. You'll sort them out in later chapters: For now you are simply identifying sources.

For the next hour, and using Table 7.1 as a guide:

- Track down the sources of as many of the metrics suggested as you can, at least as far as those that apply to your business;

- Note these sources of data in your emerging plan.

What you are looking for is the beginning of a measurement dashboard and "report card" — a standardized data presentation that you can build and sustain, and that you and those on or around your team can use to guide your social media program. Note that not all of these may apply directly to social media right now: Part of the objective of this exercise is to connect you with the sources of data that may prove useful in the future, or that may indicate the types of data you'll want to request later.

Then, having completed your basic list of metrics,

- Open your browser and go to the BlogPulse website;

- Look for posts about your company;

- Look for posts about your competitors;

- Look for posts about the companies you interviewed in your Net Promoter score exercise.

 Tip: You'll find the BlogPulse website here: `http://www.blogpulse.com`

Figure 7.7 shows a typical query: I looked for occurrences of the term "apple." Try it with the name of your firm, and see if any of them reference your company, or your competitors. Look as well for the competitors of the companies you called when conducting your Net Promoter survey. This exercise will show you how broadly the conversations that matter to you extend on the Social Web.

 Tip: When visting the BlogPulse site, click on the spikes in the BlogPulse Trend Chart (see Figure 7.7) to see the detail from the days of interesting activity.

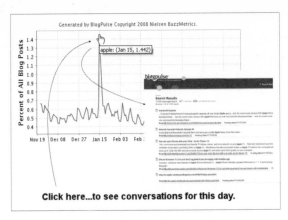

Click here...to see conversations for this day.

Figure 7.7 BlogPulse Trend Chart and Conversations

Blog Pulse will give you an indication of the blog coverage that you have currently. You can use this as a baseline as you take your current marketing program and expand it by adding social media. In the same way, move beyond the blogs themselves: Search Twitter, YouTube, and Flickr, along with other social applications that may be applicable to your business. As you do this, keep track of URLs or specific comments that are relevant to you.

> **Tip:** If you know of specific *support forums* that reference your brand, product, or service, you will need to search these separately. First, tools like BlogPulse index *blogs*, as the name implies. They do not typically index support forums and social communities. Second, many of the support forums — for let's just say technical reasons — are largely invisible to indexing and search services. Therefore, you will need to search these, often as a member yourself, in order to add this data to your overall results. Do take the time to do this — this can be the source of the some of the best data. The easiest way to search support forums is through the search tools supplied with the forum.

Thursday's Wrap-Up

Today you gathered a larger set of metrics, and then surveyed the blogs and social applications for evidence of conversations. The goal of this exercise is to begin putting together a map that connects the people that are most likely to be talking about you, or talking about others in your industry, with the actual conversation that they are having. This will reveal the types of recommendations that are occurring. When you combine this with the metrics you've identified in the first part of this exercise, these conversations and the references they contain will ultimately show you the value of influence on the Social Web.

Friday's One-Hour Exercise

Today you're going to spend an hour writing up what you've pulled together this week. Spend the next hour condensing what you've learned. Relate it to your social feedback cycle, touchpoint map, influence measures and metrics selected and to your current marketing plan.

Social Feedback Cycle

Pull out your social feedback cycle. Look at any specific comments you found using BlogPulse or when searching support or other private communities. The conversations you found are entering the purchase funnel at the point of consideration.

- Are these comments helpful, or are they creating obstacles that you have to overcome?
- How many of these specific comments can you relate to campaigns that you've run in the past?
- Is there a conversation that you found that references a customer service experience or a change in product design?
- Have any of your prior marketing messages referenced this same thing?

Touchpoint Analysis

Look at your touchpoint map and consider the following:

- How many of the touchpoints or experiences created have been reflected in your search of social content?
- How do your digital touchpoints drive social conversations?

Influence

Look at the Net Promoter score surveys you completed this week and at the overall score you calculated. You should see the beginnings of a cohesive view when you compare this with the notes you have added to your consideration cycle and touchpoint map.

- If your Net Promoter score and survey responses are distinctly middle of the road — sixes, sevens, and eights — then it's likely that you have also found relatively little talk or content on the Social Web.
- If you have nines and tens — or ones and twos — you probably found a lot more. This is a direct indication of how much the Social Web is impacting you.
- If you're in the middle, the impact is less notable: *This means you are missing out.* Raise the performance of your touchpoints, and participate on the Social Web to get the conversations going.

Metrics

Finally, look at the metrics based on Table 7.1 and integrate those with your Net Promoter score, social feedback cycle, and touchpoint map.

- While you may not have actual data at this point, create the shell for your report card based on the data you expect to begin collecting. Build relationships with the *sources* of that data.

Friday's Wrap-Up

You've covered a lot, and it is important to document and organize what you've learned. In the upcoming section of the book, you're going to start looking at specific social media components and applications. Based on what you've learned and documented this week, you'll be building selected components into your actual social media marketing plan.

What your customers have to say about you is where "the rubber meets the road." By talking with a small set of customers, you are seeing how to begin a systematic and ongoing evaluation of *all customers, current and prospective,* and how to use what you have learned or will learn to refine your marketing. Congratulations! You are now ready to confidently step onto the Social Web.

Chapter 7: The Main Points

- The measurement of influence is critical to successfully implementing social media. The Net Promoter score works very well for capturing and tracking this.

- Influence — rather than control — is the central element you have at your disposal on the Social Web.

- Taking the time to gather and distill quantitative metrics is essential: Speak with IT, your webmaster, media group, and your CFO to develop a comprehensive dashboard and report card that includes potential social measures.

- Integrate blog indexing services and any relevant online data that you have access to into your measurement platform.

Month 2: Social Media Channels

You've reviewed your current marketing plan and identified the specific points in your current campaign where post-purchase feedback and word-of-mouth generated on the Social Web might benefit you. Now, it's time to get a firm handle on the various forms of social media that are available to you. Part III covers each of the social media channels. It opens with a general approach for building your plan and then works through each of the channel groups — social platforms (e.g., Facebook), social channels, including both multimedia (e.g., YouTube) and ratings and reviews, and social interactions (e.g., social activity and status updates) — in turn. This is a long month — five weeks. You don't actually have to wait for one of this year's long calendar months to do these exercises. If you need an extra week, just roll the last exercise into next month.

III

Week 1: Build a Social Media Campaign

You've worked through the issues that drive social media and its acceptance by the people you want to reach. You've seen how you can use it to complement traditional and online channels. You've looked at the tools available to help you get ready to use it. Chapter 8 provides a quick dive into your emerging social media plan: Chapters 9 through 12 back it up with detail and channel specifics.

In this chapter, you'll develop a framework for your social media marketing strategy. You'll work through exercises designed to show you how to properly participate and influence the conversations that others use when evaluating your marketing claims and messages. Note that while traditional and online media are planned and controlled by you, your agency, or PR firm, social media is generated and controlled by participants.

8

Chapter Contents

How Is Social Media Different?

Does the receipt of your message depend on an interruption? If so, consider the following question:

If you couldn't interrupt people, how would you reach them?

For many marketers, interruptive advertising is very likely the basis of the marketing toolbox. I'd go as far as to say that most marketers don't even think of advertising as being an interruption: It is just *advertising.* Interruptions are so engrained across current marketing channels that a lot of marketers don't stop to think about the consequences of *not being able to interrupt.* It's a lot like air: It's just assumed to be there. Now, looking out across the Social Web, it feels like marketing on the moon. There is no air.

The question I've posed — asking what you would do if you couldn't interrupt — is indicative of where marketing is heading. As ad avoidance moves from an activity limited to those willing to install a pop-up blocker, email filter, or similar software into an expected condition that is adopted without further thought by everyone — the phrase *"all the kids are doing it"* definitely comes to mind — the way in which you reach and engage your audience will surely change. Presently, people not wishing to be exposed to marketing and advertising messages have to take an explicit action to avoid it: They have to *place their name* on a list to *avoid* calls or *install* a pop-up blocker to *prevent* intrusive ads. The shift from active to passive avoidance is happening now: Pop-up blockers are increasingly being built into browsers and browser *add-ons* (the little software applications that help people manage some aspect of Web use). Pop-ups as a result are routinely blocked unless specifically permitted. It's pretty easy to imagine the day when, as a marketer, *you* will have to get explicit permission to contact someone by phone, mail, in person, or through any other channel. Think about living in a whitelist world — where the only communication you actually receive arrives after having been accepted from a trusted source — instead of the current blacklist world where everything *except what's blocked* gets delivered. Think back to Gary Ruskin's quote:

> *"It is better for the industry to act voluntarily. Otherwise, after a long court battle, angry citizens will get rid of the commercial speech doctrine and replace it with the right to be left alone."*

If you doubt Gary's prescience, look at San Francisco and the naming rights for the city's baseball park at Candlestick Point. Following a set of corporate naming deals — first 3Com and then Monster — people became frustrated by the fact that the name of this and other similar landmarks was being sold. To start, it was a hassle: Try giving directions when the names of important landmarks keep changing. As well, many citizens who were proud of the roots of the original name outright resented this form of advertising, and simply refused to go along at all. Instead, they continued to refer to the park by its original name in print and especially conversation. Ironically, the latter — conversational use of the corporate name — was one of the prime benefits of buying the naming rights in the first place. Having had enough, the citizens of San Francisco voted in a mayor friendly to their cause. In 2004, a resolution was passed that returns the original name — officially — to the stadium after the 2008 season for evermore. On matters of intrusive advertising, if you push your audience hard enough, it *will* push back.

All of this is not to suggest that you stop doing what's working in your current programs. There are many formats — TV, radio, print — where interruptive advertising is largely accepted, particularly if something like GSD&M IdeaCity's "Uninvited Guest" credo is followed. The "Uninvited Guest," written by agency co-founder Tim McClure, holds that ads are interruptions: Ads are an *uninvited* guests. Therefore, a debt is owed to the person interrupted, and it is through the repayment of this debt — through humor, emotion, or similar — that your ad becomes an *invited* guest. With regard to social media, your message is an invited guest from the get-go. This is both an opportunity — your audience is picking up your message on its own — *and a challenge* — you *have to have that invitation* to get in! This chapter is all about earning your invitation, the right way.

I again want to stress that the use of social media is intended to complement and extend your current efforts, not replace them. As you consider the role of the participants who are talking about your brand, product, or service currently, think about techniques like spam and pop-ups. While most marketers have stayed away from spam, many have embraced pop-ups. Are pop-ups really any less offensive than spam? Marketers make extensive use of double opt-in email. While double opt-in is a very good practice, the further subscription option (often checked by default) that says something to the effect of "as well as our various and unnamed marketing partners now and in the future…" undoes about 99 percent of the benefit of double opt-in. Why not require that each marketing partner be separately approved? Why not offer a double opt-in for pop-ups, too? All of these interruptive and intrusive practices are viewed dimly by the majority of those online. Consider this as your chance to move forward. Offensive practices — attempted instead with social media — are unlikely to win friends in precisely the forum where you really want to win them: the Social Web.

On the Social Web, you have to take a different approach when creating your plan. When you first establish a presence on the Social Web, you're like any other newcomer. The fact that you've been marketing for 10 or 20 years doesn't mean nearly as much as your online social reputation. If you're new to social media, then by definition you don't have a social reputation beyond the carry-over from whatever you have built outside the Social Web. Building a solid online reputation is essential: Ultimately, it is your online — not offline — reputation that drives your results on the Social Web.

"If someone is mentioned by name and described as a non-Internet user, then that could be the sum of their online reputation."

— Nathan Gilliatt, Social media analyst/consultant

Your online social reputation is something that you build as you go — just as it was in the market square in your great-great-grandparents' day. Metrics like the ratio of blog comments to your blog post, unique visitors, dwell times, and quantitative assessments of social commentary about the content you create or the conversations that reference your brand, product, or service can provide an indication of your online reputation from a social viewpoint. Based on those measures, you can get an idea of what needs to be done to strengthen or improve your reputation, regardless of your starting point. If you think that some of the criticism and outrage levied on brands that trample the Social Web is severe, take a look at Figure 8.1. When it came to social transgressions, your great-great-grandparents had it worse. Much worse. This, incidentally, is exactly why disclosure and similar best practices are so important: Once caught, always a suspect. Tough love, that last one. But better learnt here than in public.

VILLAGERS IN STOCKS, CAPTION "WHEN MARKETS TURN UGLY" – PUBLIC DOMAIN, IMAGE FROM WIKIPEDIA, http://en.wikipedia.org/wiki/Image:John_Waller_in_pillory.JPG

Figure 8.1 Bad behavior is not tolerated on the Social Web

This week's exercises focus on building your social media plan. You'll pull your social feedback cycle and touchpoint map together, and at the same time add the data that you looked at in Chapter 7, "Influence and Measurement." This includes your Net Promoter score as well and the sources of discrete data — page views, dwell times, comment-to-post ratios — and any other measures you may have found.

By the end of the week, you'll have a complete framework for your social media program. Just in time, too. The next four weeks are going to be spent on the Social

Web, looking at both social applications and social media as applied by marketers for the purpose of business. By building your framework first, you'll be better able to readily spot the applications that are best suited to addressing the marketing challenges that you face. Think of what's coming up as walking into a grocery store: What you're writing out this week is a list of what you love, what you don't care for, and what you're allergic to.

Quantifying the Social Feedback Cycle

You're going to start this week by combining the metrics you've been gathering with the social feedback cycle and touchpoint map you created. In the section that follows, you're going to extend the metrics you looked at last week and tie them to the specific objectives that drive your social media campaign.

> **Tip:** A set of worksheets covering this week's exercises can be found in the appendix. In addition to these printed worksheets, you can also download electronic copies and access related resources at the website accompanying this book. Complete information regarding these resources and the website is included in the appendix.

Combining Touchpoints and Feedback

Your social feedback cycle shows you the "path" that potential customers take and the media and messages that they currently encounter as they learn about and evaluate your product or service. That much isn't exactly new: It's what marketers have been working through, in one way or another and across a range of media, for years. What *is* new is the consideration phase, and the way in which the conversations occurring on the Social Web enter the purchase funnel. This is what your social feedback cycle is showing you. Consumers routinely state that on the Internet, they can validate what they learn through TV, radio, or print. Recognize that it is *here* — the consideration phase, where the social feedback cycle connects to the purchase funnel — that this validation happens. Someone comes in contact with your awareness message and then turns to the Web for more information. This invariably includes asking others with whom they may be only loosely connected — or not connected with at all until this moment — but who themselves may have had direct experience with your product or that of a competitor. This is the Social Web at work in the consideration phase of the purchase process.

Turn next to your touchpoint map. Recall that this provides a very visual way of "seeing" the effectiveness of your various marketing efforts and the experiential points where customers come into direct contact with your brand, product, or service. Using your touchpoint map, you can see the relative importance of each of these as "talk-generators." If this seems a bit of a leap, consider that the intensity and polarity of consumer-generated content — positive (helpful) references versus negative (damaging) — is driven by the experience you create. In the case of "viral" advertising, the experience talked about is typically that of the advertisement: It is the ad (but not necessarily the product) that gets passed around. Of more interest to social marketers is the experience associated with the product or service itself. On the Social Web, people are looking for information, not promotion. When this experience is delightful, the service gets recommended. When the product delivers an experience that meets or exceeds expectations, it gets favorably presented to others on the Social Web. When it doesn't, it doesn't.

Taken together, between the social feedback cycle and the touchpoint map, you get a clear indication of the trigger-points for the important conversations that matter to you — as a marketer — and the way in which they are likely to play out through social media. As you review your social feedback cycle and touchpoint maps, think about and then answer each of the following questions. You'll be using these answers later this week when you develop the framework for your first social media campaign.

Monday's One-Hour Exercise

Today you're going to spend an hour looking at the social feedback cycle you created in Chapter 5, "The Social Feedback Cycle," and the touchpoint map you created in Chapter 6, "Touchpoint Analysis." Consider each of the following questions:

- What are you doing to generate awareness? Which specific awareness channels or media are you using?

- What channel is your top performer in terms of ROI? How did you measure this?

- What are you doing at the point of sale? Which specific channels or media are you using to ensure (or derail) competitive sales closures?

- Which of your identified touchpoints are working? Which are not?

- Which touchpoints represent your "top three" (or two or even one), the ones you absolutely count on to generate a talk-worthy experience?

- Are your strongest touchpoint experiences driven by marketing (the expectation you set) or operations (the product or service you deliver)?

- Which three could you do without? Which are the touchpoints that your customers don't really seem to talk about?

- Of the three that don't seem to matter, why do they exist? Are these left over from a prior selling paradigm, or just weeds that need to be pulled? Or, are they "neglected stars," the kinds of things that could be powerful talk generators if only ___ (and do be sure to fill in that blank!)?

Monday's Wrap-Up

Today you connected the social feedback cycle elements with your touchpoints. By understanding the contribution (or challenge) being introduced in the consideration phase of the purchase process, you can get an indication of the types of social channels that will most likely provide a beneficial effect and/or provide real insight. Social media is as much a forum for market study as social endorsement. By connecting your touchpoints, specifically ranking them, and then differentiating between the important versus optional touchpoints, you can pinpoint the places where social media is most likely to help you. After all, half of winning is knowing which fights to pick.

Applying Social Media Metrics

Yesterday you connected your social feedback cycle and touchpoint map. Today you're going to add your most robust metrics and hold the results up to your current marketing plan. Each day this week you'll build more: By Friday you'll have identified some very specific opportunities for social media and integrated these ideas into your emerging marketing plan. In the chapters that follow, you'll review each channel in detail to see which make the final cut.

In the first part of your working session today, you'll want to gather the metrics presented in Chapter 7. If you haven't yet completed your measurement exercises, you'll need to pause here and do that. The remaining sections of this chapter, and indeed most of the actual work that you'll be doing in subsequent chapters, depend on these metrics and the way in which they define the state of your current business. On this point one thing should be clear: Social media is as quantitative a discipline as any. Without "the numbers," you are flying by trial and error. One of my neighbors, now retired, was a commercial pilot. I was talking with him about the way that a lot of the "new marketing" seems to happen: He pointed out that from his perspective, trial and error is generally not the recommended way to fly.

In Chapter 7, you first encountered the metrics shown in Table 8.1. Table 8.1 repeats these metrics, this time connecting them with the social feedback cycle. This table shows you how to connect your available metrics to the activities of participants on the Social Web. This table links together metrics that you very likely already have — or could have relatively easily — with the kinds of questions that are of particular interest to you as a marketer.

For example, looking at page views, blog references, and click stream analysis, you can draw conclusions about who is participating and what they are reading and then look for ways to make that content more useful to them. This is important as a social feedback cycle best practice: By continuously reviewing and tuning your content based on its use you are continuously enhancing your relevance to specific audiences and thereby building your social reputation. For more on metrics and web analytics, refer to the sidebar "Web Analytics: An Hour a Day."

These Metrics...	Interpreted As...	Answer These Questions:
Page views, visitor info, blog mentions, click analysis, traffic patterns, referrers	Who's reading, and what (Unique) audience and habits	Audience: Who is reading and what is being read?
Time on site, blog context, review polarity	Memes and their intensity over time	Influence: What are people saying about your offer?
Time on site, pass-alongs, comment-to-post ratio, blog mentions, reviews, bounce rates	Items clicked on Length of stay Conversational qualities	Engagement: How involved is your audience; how likely is your message to spread quickly as a result?
Pass-alongs, conversions, reviews	Conversions, actions taken in support of your objectives	Action Taken: What happened as a result of participation?
Pass-alongs, blog mentions, time on site, bounce rate	Trends: subscribers, repeat visitors, referrals	Loyalty: How likely are people to return and to refer what you offer to others?

Take a look at the fundamental metrics and how they relate to the elements of influence, engagement, and more. Starting with the most basic measures — page views, click patterns, and referrers, for example — you can track and create a trend for unique visitors to your social content in the same way that you would do with any web asset. This gives you the ability to refine and improve the experience that you offer.

Featured Case: Product Pulse — Measuring Success

Product Pulse is a social marketing application, currently available on Facebook and MySpace. It gets brands, products, and services into the conversation on social networks and invites comments — both positive and negative — from members.

Recent campaigns have featured The North Face, Timbuk2, and Mountain Hardwear. These applications yielded very granular data and importantly data that are independent of the other existing metrics available for in-campaign and post-campaign analysis.

Beyond the reach-related numbers collected during the campaigns, detailed comments are generated by participants. The comment content is measurable. For example, the Mountain Hardwear program ran five weeks, engaged about 20,000 people in the campaign, and generated about 8,000 comments and 5 million social impressions across Facebook. According to Chris Strasser, Mountain Hardwear promotions project manager, "ProductPulse got people talking about Mountain Hardwear products on Facebook...something we couldn't do with banners."

This type of marketing/social integration is readily accepted by social network members, too: Product Pulse is in the top 3 percent of all Facebook applications.

Tracking additional metrics — for example, time spent across different social media assets, or the post-to-comment ratio if you are offering or tracking a blog or forum — will give you an idea of the robustness of the conversation. These are the metrics that relate directly to *influence* — the degree to which what is said in one forum will influence an action in another — as well as engagement. You may or may not have access to the data I've suggested: If not, ask around. Someone in your organization probably does. If you are working through these exercises without any data, for example, as a student or as someone interested in social media but not directly involved at the moment, then go and look at some popular blogs: Tally the posts and comments and create your own table of data so that you can see how this would be actually done, and why it is useful. If you maintain a personal blog, look at the data for that as you work through these exercises.

Web Analytics: An Hour a Day

If you are interested in digging deeper into web analytics, you may want to purchase *Web Analytics: An Hour a Day* by Avinash Kaushik (Sybex, 2007). Writing in the same style as this book, Avinash covers in detail many of the metrics that are referenced here along with the best practices relating to collecting and reporting on them.

Finally, add the number of content "pass-alongs" (e.g., "send to a friend") and more detailed information about the actual conversions. You can develop a very defensible position on how social media is being used with regard to your brand, product, or service using a handful of these measures along with a good deal of the intuitive expertise that you bring as a seasoned marketer. With this data, you can make a reasoned choice — based on quantitative and well-understood metrics — as to what social media components are likely to yield the most benefit in terms of augmenting your current efforts. By understanding which type of content or which social media channels are in play, you can define your influencers with regard to their role in the social feedback cycle. Are people sharing photos or videos of your product in action? Or, are they writing about an experience that they had? Are they creating and sharing positive or negative stories, or, are they creating content that shows new or novel uses of your product? These are things you want to capture and build on.

Tuesday's One-Hour Exercise

Today you're going to pull together a list of the metrics that you identified in your exercises last week (Chapter 7) and develop a basic framework for your *dashboard* and *report card*. Later, in Chapter 13, "Objectives, Metrics, and ROI," you'll come back to this and build on it. For now, focus on the basics and get the core data in place. If you haven't worked with dashboards and report cards, here's a quick distinction: The detail-oriented "dashboard" will organize and present the metrics you are collecting: page views, time spent, etc. The "report card" distills it all down into the smaller set of derived metrics that you track and use as a quick and ready performance guide.

As an easy place to start, consider making the Net Promoter score, a core social media metric that you worked with in Chapter 7, the centerpiece of your report card. You can back it up with the dashboard data that you'll begin collecting. The underlying dashboard measures provide a more granular view that is important to individuals and the departments they lead. Providing this data makes it easier for you to build an internal constituency.

 Tip: If you choose to utilize the Net Promoter score as a core element — and I highly recommend that you do — purchase a copy of *The Ultimate Question* and either retain an experienced consultant or personally develop any additional expertise required to implement this program fully.

To build your dashboard and report card, you can use just about anything, including pen and paper. My suggestion is that you use a spreadsheet or even a report card reporting package of some type. As you gain experience, you'll want to modify the design: If you've built your dashboard or report card in a text-based format, it won't easily scale or adapt. As a result, you're likely to quit using it, which of course defeats the purpose of creating it.

If possible, have the underlying reports you need that contain the metrics you want delivered in a format that you can import directly into your spreadsheet for quick and easy analysis. Your Information Technology (IT) department can help you with this — it's surprisingly easy and can make a big difference in the sustainability of your measurement efforts. It's social media after all: Get *everyone* involved! To create your data worksheet:

- Using Table 8.1 as a reference, identify the metrics that you have or can get. *There may be others as well that are specific to your business. Add those too.*

- Create a spreadsheet following the example shown in Figure 8.2, adapted to hold the data you identified. Create a list of the data you want: You aren't *collecting* it yet, but rather *identifying* it.

- For each item listed in your spreadsheet, identify the source of the data and work out a plan to either collect it or have it provided to you by someone in your organization.

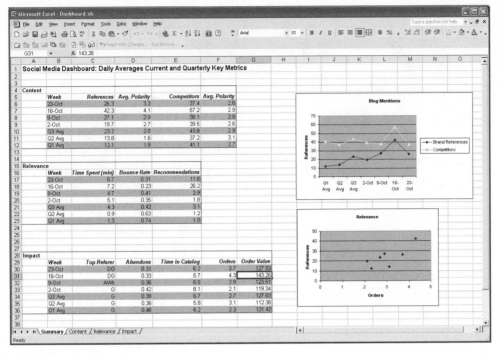

Figure 8.2 A Very Simple Dashboard

Tuesday's Wrap-Up

You now have two big pieces of your emerging social media plan in front of you. You have an analysis based on the social feedback cycle along with your touchpoint map, and you've added to that a reporting tool that will allow you to quantitatively track tactical results over time. In addition, you have a new metric, the Net Promoter score. It will help you over time by providing strategic guidance that effectively links your marketing efforts to operations. Additionally, the Net Promoter score will give you a solid starting point from which to plan your opening moves on the Social Web.

Social Media Channels

To make sense of the Social Web, I've found it useful to split social media channels into functional groups: platforms, content, and interactions, as shown in Figure 8.3. It helps me, as a marketer, to make sense of the dozen or so arms that Robert Scoble lists in his starfish model of social media. It also provides the nice side benefit of having ready buckets to catch new social media channels and content formats as they emerge. Finally, from a purely practical standpoint, it makes it much easier to plan a social media program.

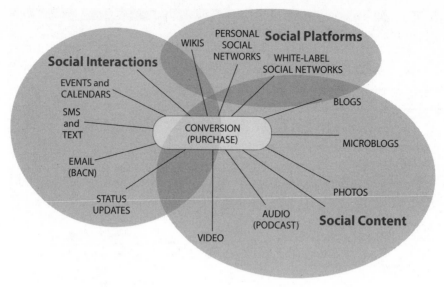

Figure 8.3 Social Media Channels and Groupings

Making Sense of the Channels

There is an underlying perspective shift when you move from participant to marketer on the Social Web. Looking at the starfish model and the groupings I have applied, for example, there are a number social media types spread around the central act of "conversion." From a participant's perspective, this makes complete sense: The participant (at the center) undergoes some sort of conversion — a persuasion or movement toward an action or a decision — as a result of interaction with or exposure to the surrounding social media ecosystem in which the participant spends time. From a marketer's perspective, however, what is of interest is how various channels can be used to increase the likelihood of a conversion on the part of a Social Web participant. The participant's question is "What do I need to know?" The marketer's question is "Through which channel or media type should I provide the answer?" From this perspective, it's a nightmare to try and plan a dozen or more channels, hoping to catch the right one in what is merely one element of a larger integrated marketing program. It is much easier to look at the integrated whole, find an opening or other indication of a need for social media, and then look for a tool within a specific group of social media channels that can be effectively applied given this need. Through the combination of your social feedback cycle and touchpoint map, this is exactly the approach you will be using.

Social Platforms

Social platforms, the first of the big groupings within social media, include social networks — MySpace, Facebook, LinkedIn, Plaxo, and more — as well as white-label platforms that can be used to provide community and support services. Also included in this group are wikis (collaborative platforms that drive consensus around ideas, externally with customers or internally with employees and partners). Wikipedia is the prime example, although there are lots of others. Social platforms will be covered next week in detail in Chapter 9, "Social Platforms."

Real-world examples — in this case from the publishing industry — of white-label platforms in use include Comcast's use of Lithium's community platform, Meredith Publishing Group's use of the Pluck Sitelife platform, and Jive Software's work with Condé Nast. Meredith Publishing also uses a wiki — served by wiki platform provider Wet Paint — in its *WOOD* magazine community. The wiki powers a "dictionary" of woodworking terms. Rather than tasking editors with maintaining the definition for a long (and growing) list of terms, the *WOOD* magazine editors seeded the wiki with the most important terms and provided a "starting" definition. After that, community members were invited to update, add to, and improve the definitions. Who better to maintain the dictionary of woodworking terms than the community that relies on it? This is a great example of the benefits of participation (on the part of the marketer or publisher) and simultaneous involvement of constituents made possible via social media. In this case, by applying a wiki, both marketer and consumer work together to do something great. Both participate, both benefit.

How can you do even more with these tools in marketing? Consider the personal or professional social networks (for example, Facebook). While you can always purchase banner ads or section pages on social networks, that's not really "social media." Compared with what is emerging on the Social Web, that's old-school, more akin to traditional interruptive online advertising. It's no different than buying 10 million impressions on ESPN or Yahoo. In the same way that targeting ads by itself doesn't makes them compelling, the fact that these ads are appearing on a social network does not make them social media. Make no mistake, those types of ad buys may well be an important part of your overall marketing program. They can work for building awareness, for example, and used correctly they have a proven return. But again, they aren't *social*, so used alone you are missing a big part of what the Social Web has to offer.

OK, that *sounds* great...but if not banners, then what? Take a look at the embedded *marketing* applications on Facebook. Beyond Vampire Bites and Sheep Throwing, there are some solid marketing applications that leverage the Facebook platform. American Airlines launched Travel Bag in March of 2008, and Product Pulse has been running contests featuring branded merchandise since 2007. Social Vibe — running in Facebook and MySpace — links marketers and social network members interested in the causes of charity. These applications directly involve the members of these networks and simultaneously promote the brands, products, and services of participating companies. The members are in complete control. The result has measurable marketing value: See for example the Product Pulse tip for more details.

There are a lot of working, integrated marketing tools that live inside of social networks. Take a look at these applications, or better yet, add them to your profile on these sites. You do have profiles on these sites, right? If you don't, take a few minutes and create them. If you'd rather, you can wait, and do this in Chapter 9 as an exercise. Either way — and quite seriously — even though it may seem at first a bit a of time waster, do participate in the online networks and content sites that I am presenting (or sites that are similar). Through participation you'll learn more about social media than by sitting on the sidelines. Social media is not a spectator sport.

White-Label Social Platforms

Beyond the personal and professional social networks, white-label platforms are available so that you can create your own social network. While this sort of undertaking is beyond the scope of what you can do in an hour, it is nonetheless an important channel for you to consider. *Not* recommended is creating yet another social network simply so that potential customers can come and hang out at your house. They probably won't.

When offering an online community, there needs to be an activity, a purpose, something to participate in or build together. One of the biggest differences in Web 2.0 (a.k.a., the Social Web) and Web 1.0 is the impact and importance of collaboration. Collaboration occurs visibly at the interpersonal level: Think about Wikipedia, or a discussion on Facebook, or your "friends list" on MySpace. Deeper than that, collaboration also occurs invisibly on the Social Web through the component parts that people use to create rich applications.

Social Content

The next big group is social content, the things that people make and share — photos, videos, comments, blog posts — that then circulate on the Social Web. This content is often consumer generated but just as easily can be marketer generated. Social content will be covered in detail in Chapter 10, "Social Content: Multimedia," and Chapter 11, "Reviews, Ratings, and Recommendations."

This type of content is already in widespread use. Even if you subtract the postings of "The Daily Show" (one of my favorites — aside from the Internet, where else would one even consider watching the news?) and other professionally generated content repurposed for the Web, there is still a lot of plain-old-made-at-home content that is being shared. According to Silicon.com and BBC News, estimates are that 8 hours of content is now uploaded to YouTube every minute, up from 6 hours every minute in 2007. You may be tempted to say "Yeah, sure, 8 hours of cats on skateboards!" Stop and consider, though, that a good chunk of the consumer-generated content is actually quite good — photos of national parks, snowboarding videos, and very useful hotel reviews to name a few. Even at its worst, a phone-recorded video of a baby eating spaghetti is still great content when it's your baby. More importantly, that content is taking away viewing time that just a few years ago would have been spent in front of a TV or reading a newspaper, potentially viewing your ad.

Social content is an area where you can play in several ways. You can use existing social content to gauge your reception and reputation as it currently stands. What are others saying about your company and what you offer? You can look for new ways to extend your products that tap the ideas and the applications being advanced through social content.

Enjoy the Lites

A great example of the idea of tapping existing social media ideas to power your marketing is found in the work of Carson Williams, an electrical engineer from Mason, Ohio, who in 2004 synchronized his residential holiday lights to music. Miller Brewing picked up on the idea, and created a 2005 holiday campaign around the concept, in the process providing a nod to the power of social media as a communications channel. You can experience Carson's most excellent work — as well as the Miller campaign it inspired, here: `http://www.snopes.com/photos/arts/xmaslights.asp`.

Instructional content, contests, and responses to customer issues are all ripe for your contribution of social content. The Social Web is yours to use as much as anyone else's. The big caveat is, of course, disclosure. If you're putting out a piece of video that shows the correct way to use your product, chances are it's "self-disclosing." After all, disclosure actually helps you in these cases. By making it clear that you are the Product Manager for the product being shown, for example, and that you'd like people to know about this specific safety aspect of your product or service, you not only build credibility for the social content you've created but you establish yourself as an expert.

Where disclosure is easy enough in instructional content like Home Depot's "Basics of Paint" video from YouTube shown in Figure 8.4, it is essential in promotional content as well. Do be sure to take the same care when putting out content that is intended to show why someone should *purchase* your product. When this sort of content is undisclosed, once discovered (and note, not *if* discovered but *when*) you will most certainly wish you had rethought that decision to market "under the radar." Failing to disclose is the number one reason for blow-ups on the Social Web.

Figure 8.4 Home Depot Painting Demonstration

Social Interactions

If social platforms are the containers for social content — the photos, posts, videos, and other content that people share — then how do Social Web participants keep track of what's going on? That's where the final group of channels — social interactions — fit. Think of these as the little pieces of content that fly around based on something that you or someone else just did, messages that notify you of what just happened or what is just now available to you. "Follow" notices on Twitter, status updates on MySpace, and Google alerts are all examples of these links. Social interactions will be covered in detail in Chapter 12, "Social Interactions."

> ### Making Sense of Social Information
>
> How do people keep track of all that goes on across the Social Web? More importantly, how do you as a marketer know where to look or what to follow? It turns out that the answer to both questions is the same: by tracking the feeds comprised of social interactions.
>
> Ten or twenty years ago the typical marketing program was a self-contained thing: a set of channels, planned and operated together to deliver a single message. Media fragmentation, along with the Web, made the planning process more complex but still left marketers more or less in control of the primary information channels — online media, direct mail, TV, radio, print, and similar. Now comes the Social Web: a dozen big social networks, private label communities, dozens of content sharing sites, and more. How do you keep track of it all as a participant? Do people really go out and check 100 different sites each day to see what happened? Or do they forsake all of the diversity in favor of one single site that they can manage effectively?

Social interactions range from quick notices — a new friend request, for example — to notices or requests for upcoming events that you and your friends are planning to see or would like to participate in. As a marketer, you can use social applications in this group to build your business. If you have a club, museum, or similar venue, make sure it's listed with or available through Dodgeball and Brightkite, for example. Utilize calendar and event listing services too, and especially the socially enabled tools that encourage rating and sharing. Where CitySearch and similar were the early leaders, Eventful, shown in Figure 8.5, is now one of my current favorites. Eventful is representative of the newest social calendars. While the newer sites include naturally social elements like ratings and reviews, they also include consumer-driven applications that draw events to specific locations. Eventful — through its "Demand It" service — gives local participants a direct line to event planners and organizers. Eventful includes tools that help performers plan tours based on local demand. Where the static or paid listings in typical local or online newspaper "weekend" calendars provide undeniable utility, the newer social event services help people choose based on the collective knowledge that drives the Social Web.

Figure 8.5 Eventful Listings

Wednesday's One-Hour Exercise

Today you're going to spend an hour looking at your social feedback cycle, your touch-point map, and your Net Promoter score so that you can select from the larger social media groups the specific channels through which you will want to engage your audience. You'll be doing the actual selection in the upcoming chapters: At this point, you are uncovering the opportunities that will inform your selection options.

Think about and answer the following questions:

- What are the top three objectives of your social campaign? What other forms of media are you using, and how will social media benefit you?

- Does your Net Promoter score suggest that you should start with an outreach campaign or a learning campaign? Are you looking to build on a positive reputation or to better understand how to go about improving one? Starbucks, following its "three-hour closing" in early 2008, rolled out a very social effort built around a blog and the simple question "How Can We Improve?"

- Think about social platforms, social content, and social interactions: Which is most likely to provide the support you need, and, fits into the marketing program you already have in place?

With your objectives identified, you can think about the kinds of applications that may be useful. Perhaps you're thinking about setting up a blog or launching a podcasting effort. If so, tentatively place these on your social feedback cycle and touchpoint map. Think through how these new marketing efforts will complement (or change or replace) what you are doing now. Tie back to the metrics you've identified as well: You may not be able to measure everything on Day 1, but do take the time now to note the measures you'd like to have. Then, locate the sources of as much of that data as you can and build it into your dashboard and report card. Importantly, don't worry about getting all of the channels identified at this point: You'll be working through each in detail in the upcoming chapters and then coming back to this exercise. The point for today is simply to make an informed choice now about what is starting to appear as a likely way to tap social media.

Wednesday's Wrap-Up

Today you identified the core social media channels that you'll be considering for your existing marketing program, based on the dynamics of your current customers and their interaction with potential customers at the point of consideration in the purchase funnel. You should now have a social feedback cycle that includes active listening or participative components: In addition to the awareness and purchase activities you are already engaged in, you should now have social elements that connect and amplify your messages if you are planning an outreach effort. If you are starting with a listening/learning effort, you should have a solid set of metrics identified that support tracking what you will learn over time so that you can use it to drive change within your organization, setting yourself up for success when you choose to add socially based outreach efforts to your marketing program.

Social Media and the Purchase Funnel

You're making good progress this week. You've identified some specific actions involving social media–based marketing that you can combine with your current efforts. Yesterday you identified one or more focus areas within the social media landscape that include the specific social media components. In the next section you'll look at how social media components can be applied to the purchase funnel in the consideration phase and then by extension to the tactical point-of-purchase efforts within your marketing plan.

The consideration phase of the purchase funnel is the focal point of your social media program. The consideration phase is the point in the purchase funnel where potential buyers make the most intensive use of social media in the context of a transaction. Word-of-mouth is the currency of the consideration phase: In the predigital marketplaces, word-of-mouth exchanges between people powered the referral and recommendation process. In the digital age — on the Social Web — word-of-mouth, in some form and especially social media, is part of almost every information exchange that takes place. To understand why — and to again underscore the importance of the combination of the social feedback cycle and touchpoint processes, consider two typical scenarios and the likely conversations that follow.

The first scenario, involving a hybrid automobile, is the classic expectation versus realization dilemma. This one centers on Environmental Protection Agency (EPA) mileage estimates. To be sure, instead of miles per gallon, the EPA really should have used either ratings stars or oil barrels — something that made it clear that these estimates were relative measures of fuel economy, not indicators of "your actual mileage," which in most case will definitely vary and, generally speaking, will vary unfavorably. No one on the planet believes that EPA mileage estimates have anything to do with what you will actually experience as a motorist. No one, evidently, except hybrid owners. *For hybrid owners, the entire purchase motivation is based on the expected mileage!* This is *not* a knock on hybrid buyers: Instead, I am emphasizing that what for many buyers is considered a relative guideline, used at best in passing, is in fact a fundamentally important touchpoint (a performance claim in this case) for hybrid buyers. In this case, variance matters, and a long, technically complex disclaimer does little to change that. In the "Hybrid" sidebar you'll see a relatively common post as the expectation of stopping for gas less often gives way to reality, as realizing fuel mileage that is only marginally better than many other vehicles sinks in. The shame here is that there are so many good reasons to buy a hybrid other than pure fuel economy. Yet, by asserting claims that no one — including the manufacturers — believes, consumers are left frustrated. As a result, they vent that frustration through social media and otherwise solid brands pay the price.

Marketer Introduces Hybrid, Claims 49/51 MPG

Consider the following excerpt from a typical conversation in a hybrid forum: "Civic Hybrid driver averaging 32 mpg city/highway files class-action suit; Honda claims 49/51. Frustration w/ actual mileage of hybrid versus advertised mileage; echoes that of other owners." What kind of marketing effort could be used to overcome this? While there is not an easy answer, this is the type of challenge that marketers face now on the Social Web.

The second scenario is reflective of a different issue: purchase envy. In the next sidebar, you'll see a comment from someone intrigued by the Nike+ running shoe with a built-in iPod transponder. Unfortunately, this person doesn't own Nikes. Hold that thought.

In the hybrid mileage and Nike+ examples, the social conversation is essentially word-of-mouth. The conversation flows around expectations, experience, frustrations, and joys — all elements of the basic conversation that you'd expect between two people discussing actual or potential purchases in real life. Word-of-mouth carries very naturally into social media. Whenever someone is posting or creating content that relates to a product or service experience, you can bet that an opinion or similar commentary will be present in that content.

Marketer Introduces New Running Shoe

Consider the following excerpt from a conversation in a health forum: "Looks way cool but it's missing a few things…you have to buy the special Nike shoes with the hole in the sole for the little accelerometer. Don't know that I want to cut apart my other shoes." What might Nike or Apple do in response? How could they capitalize on this?

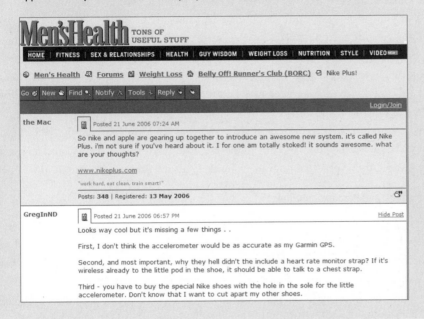

Tip: Tip: All of the rules that apply to word-of-mouth apply to social media. For a complete treatment of word-of-mouth, and to learn more about its proper and effective use, consider joining the Word of Mouth Marketing Association (http://www.womma.org).

The following sections provide specific guidance on how social media can be applied and used as a part of your marketing program.

Blogs

Blogs are one of the primary places where thoughts are collected and commented on. These are conversations that you can listen to, or jump into *provided you disclose your affiliation.* You are always able to create your own blog — a "corporate" blog — and to use it to talk about the things that are of interest to you. For maximum effectiveness as a marketing channel, be sure that what you talk about is also of interest to your customers.

Microblogs

One of the more recent tools on the Social Web is the microblog. Services like Twitter (text) and Seesmic (video) have become important components of social media. Microblogs facilitate short bursts of thought and communication, in particular in a context of people who are interested in the thoughts of specific others. You can create a profile and use these tools to tell others what's up, what you're working on, or to ask questions. Disclosure is essential. In particular, take care to understand the rules that apply in any specific forum, especially as regards spam. *Spam* in this context refers to using these channels as if they were your own corporate megaphone, creating post after post about what you are doing with relatively few if any that relate to what others are doing or talking about. On services like Twitter and Seesmic, others *choose* to follow you. If you spam them, they'll simply stop following your updates (they no longer hear anything you say) or in extreme cases will also block you, preventing you from seeing what they are saying as well. It's a lot like being told to sit in the corner, and as someone who got plenty of practice in grade school, I can tell you it is no fun at all.

Reviews, Ratings, and Recommendations

The Social Web is often characterized by terms like the "wisdom of crowds." Reviews, ratings, and recommendations are all tacit forms of the voting process through which the collective conscious arrives at consensus. These same tools can be used in a marketing context, both in a learning mode — for example, to see why your customers like or dislike something — or in an outreach mode where ratings, reviews, and recommendations play a direct role in affirming or derailing an impending purchase.

 Tip: Reviews and ratings are first and foremost a method of improving the purchase experience. Track them, pay attention, and use them to improve the current experience or to identify new features. Look back at the Nike+ sidebar and note the comment about adding the heart monitor to the system.

Video and Audio Podcasts

Podcasting can be an important part of your marketing program. The typical podcast episode is 15 to 30 minutes: What could you do if you had someone's attention for that amount of time? Because podcasts are episodic, you have the ability to build on more advanced or nuanced themes over time. You can use a podcast as an extension of a current program to deliver in-depth material about the use or application of a product, very much like the way the ProstateNet.org uses HearThis.com. Alternatively, look at shows like "Beach Walks with Rox" (http://beachwalks.tv/), shown in Figure 8.6, or Gary Vaynerchuk's "Wine Library TV" (http://tv.winelibrary.com/). Both have used podcasting to build the reputations of their respective businesses as their podcast subscriber base grows.

Figure 8.6 Beach Walks with Rox

Tip: Want to make managing your podcast and collecting the basic metrics really easy? Use Feedburner's online toolset. It takes a few minutes to set up, but it will provide the tracking and user data that you need. You'll find more information at the Feedburner website (`http://www.feedburner.com`).

The Point of Sale and Beyond

Thinking back to the role of social media in the consideration phase of the purchase process, it isn't surprising that social media can be applied at the point of purchase and even more so, *after* the purchase. What happens in the consideration phase almost always carries though to the point of purchase: The social conversations themselves likely begin post-purchase. This is because the conversations that are relevant to a potential buyer and, therefore, useful at the point of purchase are in general based on the experiences of those who have already purchased the product or otherwise had a direct experience with it and then talked about it. What goes around comes around, for better or for worse.

Common in marketing plans aimed at the point of purchase are keyword buys and search efforts, the use of case studies as "proof points," and post-purchase surveys. In addition, the social media components discussed in the following sections can be used.

Search Engine Optimization: An Hour a Day

If you are interested in digging deeper into consideration and purchase phase search engine optimization, you may want to purchase
Search Engine Optimization: An Hour a Day by Jennifer Grappone and
Gradiva Couzin (Sybex, 2006). Writing in the same style as this book,
Jennifer and Gradiva cover in detail the optimization techniques
that will additionally help drive these portions of your social media
program.

Online Reviews and Best Purchased With . . .

Amazon pioneered the online review and turned it into a marketing staple by extending the concept to the *reviewer*. By including the ratings of reviewers along with the
reviews themselves, potential buyers are able to more fully evaluate the applicability
of the review.

Like reviews, "best purchased with" is a form of social media applied to commerce that can drive overall satisfaction higher by making sure that customers have
everything they need to fully enjoy a purchase. When someone has a new dog bowl in
the checkout line at Petco, it's only natural for the sales associate to say, "Do you need
dog food, as well? I can get that for you right now." When I was buying spark plugs
recently at Auto Zone, the associate asked if I needed anti-seize or dielectric grease. I
started to say, "No, I have them in the shop at home," but I went ahead and purchased
those items as well. Guess what? I did not have either one of them at home. He saved
me an hour in traffic by avoiding a trip back to the store. He also increased his ticket
sales, which was fine with me.

The same principle applies online: If you offer e-commerce, use the knowledge
you have at hand — the items in the basket — and compare those with the last hundred
or last thousand baskets that had one or more of the same items. What else was in *those*
baskets? As a marketer, you can track and tap this knowledge, developing product bun-
dles or competing offers based on what your customers are already doing. Think of this
as free collective knowledge. Firms like Bazaarvoice can help you with this.

Tell-a-Friend

This social feature, perhaps more than any other, ought to be a "best practice" for
every marketer. Ask yourself this question: If you, through efforts that cost you both
time and money, brought someone all the way to your website where they happened
upon something that you sold…but that was perfect not for them but for someone else
that they knew…wouldn't you want that person to tell the other about it? Of course

you would! Yet, in practice, far too many marketing sites fail to include this simple feature. If you haven't implemented this, think about adding this one in particular as a social marketing tool.

Zappos is a great example of a company that "gets" social media and uses techniques like "Tell a Friend" to build their commerce. For every item that you look at on Zappos.com, not only is there an "Add to Shopping Cart" button but also a "Tell a Friend," as shown here in Figure 8.7. Sometimes a pair of shoes or a running jacket isn't right for your current customer but it is perfect for someone he or she knows. Tap that extended knowledge through social media.

Figure 8.7 Zappos Tell-a-Friend

Message Boards

I talked about white-label platforms yesterday: These platforms range from straightforward forums to full-featured communities. One of the ways in which the forums can be used (branded to your specification, of course) is as a support tool, linking customers with each other. Through these types of social applications, existing customers can exchange "best practices" and tips that both increase satisfaction among current customers and encourage and support potential customers as they evaluate your product versus competitive offers. The most active support community members, through rewards or status upgrades, will often become evangelists and further boost your return on your social media investment.

Refining Your Plan

Collect your current marketing plan and the work you've done so far, including your touchpoint map and your social feedback cycle. The objective for today is to look for points in your current marketing plan where you could connect with the feedback available on the Social Web. The connection points will either be touchpoints — in the form of something specific being done to create an experience — or a conversation (however short it may be) that results from an experience or perception of a touchpoint.

Thursday's One-Hour Exercise

Today you're going to spend an hour refining your marketing plan. Pull from what you've done in the prior three days and focus on the areas of your plan where you've identified potential social media components that can help you. Pay special attention to yesterday's selections of social media channels and today's discussion of the different specific types of social media touchpoints that are available to you.

One final note as you start today's exercise: Think about how your Operations department or function fits into this. For most social media applications, Operations will have much to do with the success of your campaign. After all, it's in Operations that the actual product or service experience is created.

Spend the next hour considering each of the following points, and write out your thoughts for each of them:

- What are the primary opportunities you've uncovered?
- Where do these opportunities fit into the social feedback cycle? Are they primarily awareness-, consideration- or purchase-related?
- Again looking back at the social media channels and groups, which appear most related to the opportunities you've identified?
- How do these choices fit with your current marketing efforts?
- What are the metrics associated with each of the above?
- What are the metrics that you are collecting now, and what are the sources for the additional metrics needed?

Thursday's Wrap-Up

You're now well on your way to an effective, practical social media program. You've got the data to back you up. You've got a start on your dashboard and report card, and you're adding some new tools to your marketing toolbox. Congratulations!

Putting Your Framework Together

Yesterday you connected your touchpoint map and social feedback cycle with your current marketing plan. To this you'll next want to add the key measures that define success, show progress, or indicate that perhaps a different channel might do better for you. You'll also want to address any remaining items (such as open surveys, data sources, or similar) that you may need to track down. Most important at this point is to have the basics in place to begin building a social media program that complements what you are doing now while addressing the specific business objectives that you have set.

Friday's One-Hour Exercise

Today you're going to spend an hour reviewing and finishing up what you started yesterday. Take a look at what you have in front of you now, and compare it with your "pre-social media" plan. Pay special attention to the following:

- Have you identified the sources of the metrics you need?
- Is your report card sustainable? Do you have the agreement of the data services team to provide metrics on an ongoing basis? Is this something you can automate?
- Do you have a plan in place to sustain your Net Promoter measurements?
- Which, if any, of the social media components you've covered are you using now? If you could add two or three more, which would you add next? Why?

When you reach Chapter 14, "Develop and Present Your Plan," you'll be presenting, defending, and then living your plan. This week you've developed a framework: Be sure to take the time today to make sure that you've established a solid footing.

> **Tip:** At this point you are not making a final selection of your social channels, but rather starting to link your business and marketing objectives with the social channels you've read about so far. The next four chapters will detail each of the social channels: It's not until you reach Chapter 14 that you'll actually be committing to specific channels.

Friday's Wrap-Up

Five weeks into this process, you've got a new appreciation for social media and how it works. You're looking at your marketing plan from your customer's point of view, and then picking the "competitive battles you can win" as seen through your customers' eyes. With each "win" you are giving your customers something *positive to talk about* relative to your competition. That has got to help.

Chapter 8: The Main Points

- Social media is most different from traditional media in that it lacks the option to force an interruption: Your message has to be invited in.

- Social media is fundamentally measurable.

- Social media can be organized as follows:

  - Platforms: This includes social networks along with white-label community and forum applications.

  - Content: This includes ratings, reviews, photos, videos, podcasts, and similar content that is created and shared on the Social Web.

  - Interactions: This includes the little bits of information that flow around through feeds, email, and SMS that tell participants what is going on across the Social Web.

Week 2: Social Platforms

In this chapter, you'll learn to evaluate the use of social networks in a business context and see how they encourage interaction and conversation. I'll show you how these networks provide quantitative information about how your brand, product, or service is being viewed. You'll spend time on community platforms, including support forums and the "white-label" community tools that you can use to build your own social presence. I'll make the case for why you should consider using social communities in support of your business objectives.

In your exercises this week, you'll gain hands on experience in online social settings. The exercises are designed to highlight the business oriented applications of these social spaces, and to provide you with ideas and a starting point when adding these tools to your social media campaign.

9

Chapter Contents

Social Networks

White-Label Platforms

Working with Social Platforms

The Main Points

Social Networks

In the opening section of this book, I talked briefly about the very early online social communities. Services like Prodigy catered to commerce and casual interaction while CompuServe focused on serving the needs of specific interest groups. The others that followed were likewise an early recognition of the kinds of interpersonal dynamics fostered by ubiquitous connectivity. When physical spaces no longer isolate people, common interests in very specific areas begin to emerge. Communities built around even the most obscure interests or fields of study are suddenly able to gather critical mass as those who share particular passions "find each other." Flash forward beyond AOL, then Geocities and Tripod, to the beginning of the broadband Internet. What changed wasn't so much the speed — sure, the Net is faster than it used to be — but rather the simple switch from a "connection event" to an always-on, always-around-us medium that gave rise to persistent and distributed communities. Prior to the widespread adoption of broadband, "going online" usually began with some purpose — to play a game, buy something, check a stock price or weather forecast — and involved a very deliberate "connecting" of the personal computer and the network. No more. Now, with mobile devices transparently navigating between Wi-Fi and cell networks, and personal computers in the vast majority of homes that are "always on" (meaning "always connected"), the Internet itself has become a sort of permanent place where things happen continuously.

Starbucks bills itself as the "third place," behind home and work. I'd suggest that all three are right now moving down a notch, as the Internet and the communities that ride on it become the "first place" for a whole lot of people. They may jump in and out of these online communities, but their information is always flowing through them and therefore available to others as if they were present. They disconnect briefly to breathe in real air in the same way a whale comes to the surface periodically. Then, they dive back into the Social Web, to what is becoming their first home. As a marketer, you really need to be there.

The contemporary social networks build on this emerging dynamic, and in doing so create a forum where conversation flourishes based in part on experiences with the things you sell or offer. Social networks form around general interests — think MySpace or Bebo — and around different cultural commonalities. The result is the global spread of online communities that manage to retain regional culture and behavior. Selected leading networks in representative locations are shown in Figure 9.1. As examples, MySpace is popular in the United States and LiveJournal is popular in Russia. In Latin America, it's Sonico and Orkut; in Asia a favorite is Friendster; and in the United Kingdom, it's Bebo. They form based on personal styles and interests: MySpace with its focus on music and personal entertainment versus Facebook and its Ivy League origin, both giving rise to demographic characteristics that remain today. Across all of them, however, the application is surprisingly similar: people meeting people and sharing experiences.

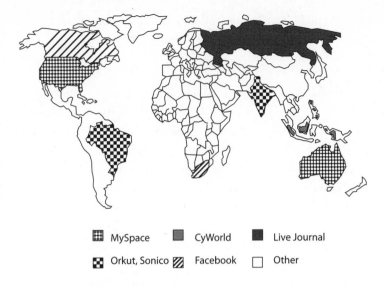

MySpace	CyWorld	Live Journal
Orkut, Sonico	Facebook	Other

Figure 9.1 World Map and Social Networks

If you step back and look at this, more than a few possible business uses for these networks jump out. In addition to the obvious application for interruptive advertising — buying a home page or feature banner on MySpace or one of the new left-column ads on Facebook — these networks are both sources of information and places where your brand can establish and show elements of its makeup that it might not be able to do otherwise. How can these elements help you? That's where you're headed next.

> **Tip: Simon Says ... Do *This*** The appropriate use of social spaces in business is critical to your success as a marketer. You are a guest, just like anyone else. The rules of conduct that apply to members of any given social network apply to you as well, with the additional requirement of full disclosure. If you're transparent, and genuinely helpful, you'll find that you will make allies within your communities, and that you will be in great position to begin building true community presence and connections.

Consider first the extension of your brand. On TV you are limited to 30 seconds give or take, and to a method of communication that is "one way." Online, through rich-media and interactivity, you can extend this a bit, but you're still limited by a context that is largely interrupt-driven. This means that the time your audience is willing to spend is limited as chances are whoever is engaged in your expandable banner right now was doing something a minute ago and probably needs to get back to it. In a social setting, this changes: participants are there to relax, learn, engage, or be entertained. They are looking for content. Compared with the limited time available on TV or even through online media, social networks are like being invited to dinner. The

BMW Facebook case study presented later in this chapter is an indication of what you can do when participants are willing to give you several *hours* of their time.

Personal Social Networks

Rules of etiquette apply on the Social Web and in social networks. Sure, there are rules that apply on TV as well, but in the case of social media and social networks in particular, *the other participants — and not the producer or programmer — by and large make the rules*. One of the issues that you will have to pay attention to when developing and implementing a social media-based marketing program is that social spaces are not always advertiser friendly. In fact, it's probably safe to say that until shown otherwise, they are advertiser *unfriendly*. But that's OK: you're going to see how you can get along.

Interruptive advertising — whether on TV, in print, online, or presented as a banner in a social setting works based on a trade-off between fundamental characteristics. It's interruptive. You schedule it, and it appears. Your message gets seen. As a sort of relief valve, the person viewing it is generally able to ignore it if interest is low or timing is off. Taken together, even though it's interruptive, most consumers accept TV advertising because they can always choose to ignore it. The same conditions exist online, though perhaps to a different degree. Most people understand that MySpace is free in exchange for the presence of advertising. At the same time, it remains to be seen how long this will last and, therefore, how long a marketing approach based largely on interruptions will remain effective. LinkedIn's April Fool's Day joke of 2008 — that it was planning to end its free service — may be closer to the truth than its timing would indicate. More seriously, just like on TV, if the audience makes a habit of ignoring the ads, then sooner or later the social networks will have to resort to some other means of generating income. If you *knew* that no one was watching, would *you* still pay for the ad? If interruptive advertising revenue decreases, something else has to replace it. If you couldn't interrupt...what would you do?

Figure 9.2 shows the first visible portion of two opening screens: on the top is my personal MySpace page, and right below is Weather.com. Surprisingly, the amount of space that is devoted to advertising — and which therefore interrupts my activities — is about the same on each of them. Weather.com isn't a social application, although it would be nice to share sunshine with friends. Weather.com is instead a simple utility that helps plan what to do over the weekend. It runs on interruptive advertising: to see the weather, I have to scroll down past the ads.

In the case of MySpace, where the share of space used for ads is about the same, the fact that they are purely interruptive really stands out. *There is no obvious motivation or mechanism for me to share the advertising content*. It's just there for *me* to look at. It's odd that a social network would start my experience — built around participation — with an interruption given that *sharing* rather than consumption is the basis of my belonging.

On the Social Web — banners on social networks included — the only way your message receives any real attention is through the interest of your audience. If you are *dependant* on the interruption, you'll find limited success, at best, through social media. Instead, adopt an approach of sharing and of influence, and of less control rather than more.

Figure 9.2 Ads on MySpace and Weather.com

How you conduct your campaign in a social context is critical to success. The key is not so much to "let the guests make the rules" but rather to work with those already in the community and to become part of it, to establish your value and develop a shared sense of respect. If you're a newcomer, watch and listen and then join in. Become part of the community. As a member you can certainly influence it through your own participation, just as each of the other members is equally able to do. In summary, be interested, and above all, be *interesting.* You spent time working on the touchpoint map and social feedback cycle *first* because the social components of your overall campaign are just that: the *social* components.

It's important to get the triggers for conversations — many of which are set at touchpoints and then carried into the purchase process at the point of consideration — established in a way that supports and amplifies your complementary use of other channels (for example, through in-store or traditional media). The social channels are only one piece of a larger whole, and though they operate differently than the others, they must operate in a consistent, supportive manner. Worried that you can't "strongly suggest" or "forcefully persuade" through social media? You have plenty of places where you can shout, persuade, and exert claims *outside the Social Web.*

Within the social networks, you've got the responsibility of conduct that comes with being a guest — and in particular a guest who would like to be invited back some day. In return, you have the opportunity to engage your audience at a level that you simply cannot match elsewhere.

So far I've focused on your presence in personal social networks. Whether you build a profile for your brand, or participate through discussion groups and similar, being a part of the community can be a great way to learn about your brand, product, or service and a great way to help customers get more value from whatever it is you offer. If you make kayaks, and are fully transparent about it, you are actually in a pretty good position to help someone looking to undertake the sport. You have genuine domain expertise: people who work at kayak or outdoor companies tend to be enthusiasts and therefore knowledgeable about these things. At the same time, the person considering the purchase has the whole rest of the Internet to check what you say.

Beyond a directly participative presence you can use marketing applications that are themselves embedded into the social platforms. Beginning with Facebook's opening of its API, firms like Slide and RockYou have developed and launched a wave of applications that ride on the social networks. While many of these are entertainment oriented — e.g., Vampire Bites, Sending Karma, and Truemors — there are also hard-working marketing applications like those built on Grafitti Wall or applications like Social Vibe, shown in Figure 9.3, and Friend-2-Friend's Product Pulse. Product Pulse and Social Vibe are supported on both Facebook and MySpace and will no doubt spread further. These types of marketing tools can help you establish a consistent presence in multiple settings.

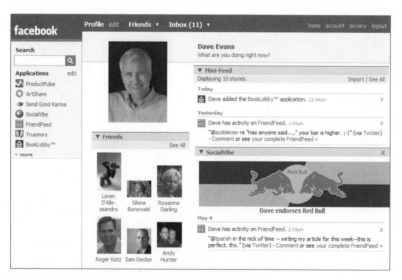

Figure 9.3 My Facebook Profile with Social Vibe Endorsement

OK, so you can develop a presence, and you can build campaigns on embedded applications with a marketing component. What else can you do? For starters, you can use social networks to attract and retain key employees. Having better people than your competitor gives you an advantage that often can't be bested by a lower priced competitor. As the Social Web takes hold — something that is happening as you read this — *performance* will become increasingly important across a growing range of products and services. Products that *almost work* — think back to the Net Promoter score and firms that consistently score 6, 7, or 8 — will face an increasingly tough sell. How many times do you really want to replace a cheap light bulb, regardless of how few people it takes? This same drive for quality extends to the floor or phone experience as well…and all of this comes right back to attracting and retaining the best employees. Walk into any Whole Foods Market and ask for Oscillococcinum, an absolutely fantastic flu and cold product. The associate you speak with will *walk* you — not point you — to the center section of the store and to the very shelf, and then hand it to you. If you ask, that associate will even tell you how to pronounce it! That is the kind of employee-customer experience that drives the unmatched success of Whole Foods Market as a grocer. For Whole Foods, its Associates and their passion around what they do give rise to a formidable competitive advantage.

Consider the popular objection to marketing on the Social Web, that "MySpace isn't for business. It's a place where kids hang out." Recognize that because the person saying this is usually about my age (fifty-something, I've lost track), it's a good bet that "those kids" are "twenty something" with a margin of plus or minus 5 or 10 years. In other words, the next bag checker — beginning a climb to CEO of your firm — is probably on MySpace or Facebook or Bebo or Orkut *right now.* Why not create a social presence that is maintained by *your employees*, a presence that makes the case for why this young man or woman should come to work for you instead of your competitor? Quality employees are becoming increasingly scarce, and networks are a great way to find them. There is good chance that you or someone working next to you found a job through a network. That's something to think about, and something that is most definitely related to your marketing campaign and to the way in which marketing, operations and human resources can all work together on the Social Web.

Social Vibe: An Alternative Approach to Charity

SocialVibe (http://www.socialvibe.com) is empowering people to generate contributions to charity to drive its business. SocialVibe understands that in social media, people are the publishers and therefore are a critical component of the value chain. However, the potential for ad-sharing at the member level — giving a portion of the advertising proceeds to these "micro-publishers" associated with the value they generate for brands — is likely to generate a few tens of dollars in a year, not much of a motivation for this new generation of content creators. Social-Vibe offers instead the ability for members to choose a charity and pool their resources.

continues

> ## Social Vibe: An Alternative Approach to Charity *(continued)*
>
> The result is the potential to turn a rather significant portion of media spending into a meaningful contribution to charity and to create a very favorable presence for the brands offering member-level sponsorships through SocialVibe in the process.
>
> This is a really smart approach to the effective use of social media. Not only can marketers achieve effective distribution in social media, but they can leverage direct connections with their consumers to improve their brand, product, or service. SocialVibe President Joe Marchese, puts it his way: "Advertising used to be all about how many people you could get to see your message. With the Social Web, advertising is all about how many people you can get to show your message. This means that, while the challenge with traditional advertising is creating an effective asset for consumer consumption; the challenge with social media is creating an effective asset for consumer adoption and distribution. Your consumers are your media. Reach out and engage them correctly and they will build your brand for you." SocialVibe is focused on helping marketers achieve just this result.

Business Social Networks

Next up are business-oriented social networks, where the network itself is designed to be used for what are generally business-specific purposes. LinkedIn, Plaxo, and more recent entrants such as Spock are part of this group. Facebook is in this set, too, as is Jigsaw, a socially driven contacts tool for business. Obviously, there are more. Each of these is designed to facilitate some aspect of a business transaction — a sales contact, a referral, or similar business purpose.

> ## Marketing on Facebook
>
> Wondering how to use Facebook effectively for marketing? You'll find the answer in the "Facebook Marketing Bible," which you can download at http://www.insidefacebook.com/.

Like personal social networks, these business-oriented networks can be powerful *components* of your marketing plan. For example, you can use the data-searching capabilities in LinkedIn and the contacts tools in Jigsaw to develop a very focused prospect list, against which you can apply a high-impact, highly personalized direct marketing campaign. Or, you could use a network like Facebook to develop a group around a new application that you are launching. You can grow your beta audience and engage them to elicit feedback, saving you development cycles and speeding your entry into the larger market. You can also use these networks to build your own organization, whether you are looking for marketing or related talent or for the kinds of general expertise or "raw materials" from which to build an excellent team. Any way you approach it, the use of business social networks is very likely a factor in some aspect of your marketing plan.

Monday's One-Hour Exercise

This week's exercises are intended to introduce you to social networks, beginning with a business presence. By starting with *yourself* and seeing the ways that *you* can apply social networks as a professional, you'll gain valuable insight into the broader range of applications of social networks in business, and of the role that social media plays within them.

> **Tip:** A set of worksheets covering this week's exercises can be found in the appendix of this book. In addition to these printed worksheets, you can also download electronic copies and access related resources at the website accompanying this book. Complete information regarding these resources and the website is included in the appendix.

Start with what you've got: yourself and the things that make you unique. Individuals are the core components of any social network — and a business network is no exception. By building your own network, you increase the number of people you can enlist when it comes to answering questions, asking about other's experiences with social media, and in general increasing the collective knowledge that is available to you.

Create a presence on a professional network, and invite a few colleagues to join along with you. Or, ask your colleagues which networks they are already members of and join one or more of those networks. Either way, the objective is to get involved and to participate. The goal of these next exercises is to increase your understanding of how people use social networks and therefore how you can — and cannot — use them for marketing. As a bonus, by doing this in the context of your current business network, you are actually learning and growing your business networking skills at the same time.

Make a list of the networks you are in, or would like to join for business or social purposes, and write out the purpose/benefit of each network identified. Include in this list the obvious: social networks like Facebook or LinkedIn. Also include support forums — Dell Support, for example — as well as fan clubs, social organizations (online and offline), and similar. For each, answer the following questions:

- Why do you participate in this network or social group?
- What do you expect to get out of it?
- In the past 30 days, what have you put into it?
- Also over the past 30 days, how much time (roughly) have you spent, and what have you done?
- Within the online social networks, how is advertising done? Who is advertising, and what are they advertising?
- What products and services are being talked about? What are members saying?

Monday's Wrap-Up

Today you looked at business-oriented social networks and noted the specific benefits you get through your association with other members. If you weren't a member of a business-oriented network, you should be now. If you have just joined, then be sure to spend some regular time — 30 minutes each day, for example — over the next few weeks so that you can get a good sense of what participation is all about.

As you develop your business social networking skills, think about the following ways to get more out of these networks and accomplish more as a direct result of your network memberships:

- Developing a presence to extend your brand
- Reaching out to potential employees
- Gathering feedback about what you sell or plan to offer
- Building a profile of your sales prospects

Participation Is Everything

The Social Web demands an active presence. On the Social Web, if your profile isn't up-to-date, if you're not commenting, if you're not making connections, you don't exist. "Lights on, but no one home" and you won't get the results you otherwise might. That seems obvious, but I point it out because I see a lot of profiles across a lot of social networks and communities that are evidently abandoned and are now home to what look like virtual zombies taking up residence in so many empty store-fronts. Chances are, that's not how you want to be perceived. Before you start building a presence on the Social Web, make sure you can commit to keeping it alive.

Look back at your exercise from yesterday: which are the networks that you get the most out of? Why? Most likely, these are also the networks you spend the most time in, and the ones you get the most value from when you do. In other words, like any other online endeavor, a social network has to perform; it has to do something for you. Unlike conventional TV programming — where someone else has done all of the work and you get to sit on the couch and relax — social networks are built continuously on the contributions of individual members. This partly explains why those members are also protective of the experience they have created, and why they tend to resist the presence of marketers. But it also raises the opportunity for marketers who show up with something of value, *ready to pitch in and lend a hand building the community.*

That is the approach you want to take when joining a network: just as you expect to get something out of your membership, you must also expect to put something into it.

From a marketing perspective, this means first and foremost following the rules of the community. Here is the basic credo for participation in a social network, as a marketer or in fact for anyone:

As a participant, I will add value to my community. I will not assume a false identity or post under a false name. I will not pretend to be something other than what I am.

A quick note with regard to the above: by "false identity" I don't mean "assumed name." In most of the communities I participate in, I use the handle "evansdave" as it is generally available. In others, I use "digitaldave," a name that I got almost 15 years ago when my wife and I launched our consulting company, Digital Voodoo. She is "voodoojen" and I'm "digitaldave." Obviously, "digitaldave" is not my real name. That's fine. What I mean by "false identity" is a profile name and description that would lead someone to believe you are "Joe Consumer" when in fact you are talking about your own brand or company. This is the kind of thing that can get you in trouble — real trouble, *legal* trouble — on the Social Web.

How do you avoid even a hint of impropriety? It's actually pretty easy. Be yourself. Whether I am "evansdave" or "digitaldave," I *always* include two things: a real photo (generally about 100 pixels square) and (where supported) a set of coded "XFN" links that point back to my primary website. Refer to the XFN sidebar for more about this emerging social protocol. The name you choose can often be enough by itself: A particularly good example is provided by Dell blogger and digital media team member Richard Binhammer. His profile name, "RichardatDell," makes it pretty hard to miss the connection between his posts and his employment to Dell.

Figure 9.4 Digital Voodoo and Related Contact Points

XFN: Showing Relationships on the Web

XFN — shorthand for "XHTML Friend's Network" — is a simple protocol that describes the type of relationship implied by an otherwise ordinary HTML hyperlink. You've seen the basic link and a usage such as "more info is here" — where "here" is the link to supporting content. What that link does *not* tell you is how the source of *that* information (the information being linked to) is related to the source of *this* information (the information in front of you now). XFN is intended to tell you: XFN is used to show how information sources are related to each other. For example, on my primary website, the links to my Facebook account are coded as "me," letting people know that the link to Facebook is a link to "more about me." Links to my family are coded as "kin," and links to people I work with are coded as "colleague." Using XFN, someone who finds me on Twitter can link back to my website and know that it is me in both places, and not just two users who happen have the name "Dave Evans." For more about XFN, search via Google for "XFN" or visit the XFN information page on `http://gmpg.org/xfn/`.

Through the use of a consistent username and a photo, it is always clear who I am. On top of this, I *always* explicitly disclose any relationship or interest that I may have, for example, when writing a book (as I did in the opening section of this one) or an article, or when posting in a forum about the virtues of social media! When your audience understands your full rationale and basis for participation, they can "discount" as needed, but they can also "credit" you for being an expert and having the personal integrity to take the time and disclose. *Disclosure is a net positive.* If you feel you can't disclose, you're pushing your message in the wrong medium.

Setting up for today's exercise — participation in social networks — the big points are the value of consistent participation and the imperative of transparency. Consistent participation in a social network is a lot like blogging: if you blog once a month, don't expect much of a following. Blog regularly (and blog well...) and you'll build an audience. Jive CMO Sam Lawrence offers this perspective on the importance of regular participation: the quote happens to have been made in Twitter; however, it applies equally well to any social network.

> *"Twitter should let you search by more criteria. Like, filter people (out) who haven't tweeted in X amount of time."*

On the Social Web, participation is important. To be sure, there's nothing wrong with being a spectator. However, if you *only* watch, you're not going to earn the credibility that you need when you start talking. If the only thing the community ever hears from you is "Let me tell you about this new product we have...," you'll get ignored. On the other hand, if you're a consistent source of useful information, the community is going to assign some credibility to you and by association to your brand. That is what you want on the Social Web. The Social Web is not an advertising platform per se, but is rather an adjunct to what you're doing elsewhere. You are building credibility, and then turning that into support for the marketing you do in the channels where more direct forms of marketing are appropriate.

Tuesday's One-Hour Exercise

Look back at your list from yesterday. After today you should be a member of at least two networks. I recommend joining Facebook specifically if you haven't already. Look at the social marketing applications like Social Vibe and Product Pulse within Facebook, and take note of how the level of involvement with the brands, products, and services is different from the interaction with the banner ads. Facebook, more so than many other networks, provides a number of excellent examples of marketing tools that have been integrated into the social experience.

For each of the networks you are in now as well as those you join today, do the following if you haven't done so already:

- Complete your profile
- Post some content
- Add one or more new friends

A few notes are in order. If you don't want to use your own picture, use one of your dog or your car or your city. Upload something other than the default image. For some, an actual photo might be problematic: a predatory ex-mate, a religion that precludes digital images of oneself, or simply your own preference. These are all valid reasons not to use a picture of yourself. In these cases, how about an icon? You can express your personality graphically even if you don't choose to show your face. Mikons (http://www.mikons.com) is a social site where you can create your own personal icon in just a few minutes. Complete as much of your profile as you are comfortable with, adding your name, email, personal and professional interests, and more. If you're in the Witness Protection Program, don't use your real name: use your authorized alias. It's OK in this case.

The point here is to give others something to go on when evaluating your posts, your content, and your contributions. Posting everything as "Mystery Guest" might seem acceptable, but for a marketer seeking to participate and gain influence, this just isn't going to work. Upload a picture or an icon. Post some video. Post a comment. Add a friend. Ask a question. The value of the networks that you are in depends on your participation. If you sign up and wait for the information to flow to you, not only is it going to be a long wait, but you will miss the essential element of collaboration and connection that powers social communities. You can see my LinkedIn profile in Figure 9.5: note the "100% Complete" indication.

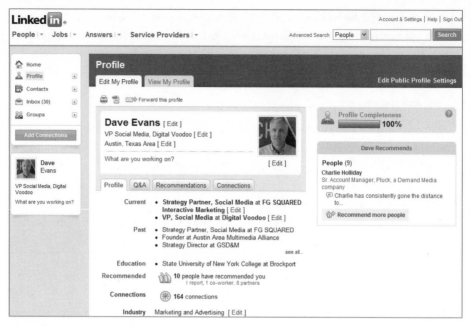

Figure 9.5 My Completed LinkedIn Profile

You may be wondering why I am asking you to do all of this — it might seem more like play than work, and after all the point of this book is work. What I am hoping is that you will experiment and learn, both as an ordinary participant and as someone interested in using social media for marketing. By getting to know how to use different networks while at the same time building an identity based on disclosure, you are setting a foundation for your participation as a marketer on the Social Web.

Tuesday's Wrap-Up

Today you took another step toward social media proficiency. "Joining a network" may seem trivial, or it may be a new experience for you. Either way, at this point you should be a member of a couple of a couple of social networks. Are you participating? Is your profile complete? Do you have online friends? Are you posting content? Participation — while following the rules of engagement — is the cornerstone of success on the Social Web.

It's in this sense that the value of the hour-a-day format emerges: you are moving through a series of small steps, getting each of the required elements in place to successfully participate in the next, to successfully tap the new forms of media in ways that complement the work you are doing through traditional channels now. Some days may take you less than an hour, others a bit more. But as you close in on Chapter 14, "Develop and Present Your Plan," you'll be in a great position to present a plan, handle objections, and lead a team or direct an agency in the effective use of social media as a marketing extension.

White-Label Platforms

On Monday and Tuesday you focused on the use of existing social networks. You covered the use of personal networks as participative forums where you can extend your brand, and business networks where you can gain intelligence and make connections. Today's topic — white-label social platforms — is all about extending your presence through your own support forum or community. A couple of caveats are in order: First, this is not for everyone, nor is launching a private platform something you can *complete* in an hour. You *can,* however, get a good idea of why or why not having your own social community makes business sense, and that is what you will focus on today.

There are, of course, a number of reasons why your own social space makes sense. Applications range from customer support to product development to customer engagement. The types of platforms that are available are further testament to the diverse nature of the application of community within a business context. In this chapter, you'll focus on support forums and customer-centered communities. Together these provide clear examples of how social networks can be applied to business issues of interest to marketers (and more) and how different the applications can be in the ways in which they involve customers and engage a larger audience.

White-Label Platform Listing

You'll find comparative listings of white-label social networking tools online, including a two-part series at TechCrunch. The easiest way to find this posting is through Google: search for "tech crunch white label." An additional listing is maintained by Forrester's Jeremiah Owyang. Using Google, search for "jeremiah owyang white-label social networking platforms" to connect with Jeremiah's blog and his comprehensive listing.

Support Forums, Message Boards, and Communities

As the name implies, support forums are intended to solve specific product or service-related issues, offer "pre-sales" advice, or otherwise extend the positive experience associated with actually using the product or service. Message boards are often geared toward supporting personal interests and hobbies, health issues, and similar. In all cases, the basic mode of interaction is largely the same: a focus area is defined, topics within that area are declared, and the posts begin. Underneath each post is a series of comments.

As an example, consider a software vendor with several product lines. Within the support community there would be a forum for each of the product lines, and then within each line there would be categories like "Installation" and "Application Development" and "Beta Release Program." Under "Installation," for example, there might be posts like "Can't open CD" or "Version 2.0 of plugin failed to install." Under the post are the comments of those who have encountered the same issue, and, solutions posted by those who have sorted it out. A typical support community — this one featuring Circuit City and built on Pluck's SiteLife platform, is shown in Figure 9.6.

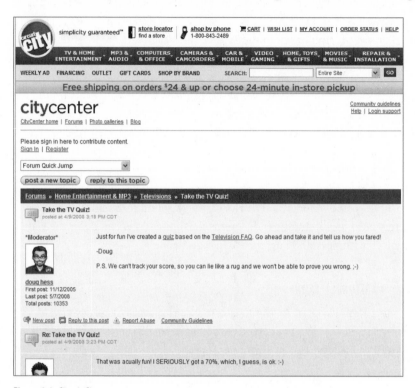

Figure 9.6 Circuit City

The benefits to the business making the product and their customers through the application of online support forums are obvious: The problems are solved more often than not by other customers, lowering the overall support costs. While product developers do a generally decent job of testing and anticipating issues, given the complexity of the "real world," they just can't match the range of application environments that are likely to exist. Unanticipated errors occur. Prior to online support the only real remedy was a call to customer service. The problem is, though, that not only is direct, personal customer support expensive and only minimally scalable, the customer support team is often unable to replicate the issue for the precise reason it occurred in the first place: they lack the particular setup or environment that their (now failed) product has been deployed in.

By contrast, there are likely other customers who have similar issues and have resolved them. The online forums allow those in need of an answer to get connected with a solution that has been developed by someone else. Seagate implemented just such a solution using the Lithium platform: the Seagate Support Community is shown in Figure 9.7. A case study is featured as well in the associated sidebar. When online support works — and more and more it does — it makes everyone happy. The business saves money, customers in need get taken care of quickly, *and the customers who have developed and offered solutions feel a sense of ownership for the well-being of the product and the support community to which they belong.*

Figure 9.7 Seagate Support

Consider that last point for a moment and your exercises of Monday and Tuesday: communities are built with the contributions of members. When a member of a support community posts a solution, kudos result. This is precisely why participation is so important, and why ceding control to members — who are then empowered to solve problems for themselves — is a winning community strategy. Of course, there is a role for guidance, and this is where the community moderators, either paid or volunteer, step in. Without going too deep into forum moderation — easily a book in itself — suffice it is to say that moderators play a key role in keeping conversations on track, checking that rules are followed, and that problems with regard to the use of the forums themselves are handled. Though it may surprise you, the best *technical solutions* often come from members.

Think back to what social networks are all about: call it the strength of the collective or the wisdom of the crowds. There may be, for example, a post that says "I've had this happen. What you need to do is…" and an explanation will follow. Underneath, comments such as "Thank you. That worked perfectly!" attest that this solution is in fact a good one. Future readers pick up on this very quickly, with little or no input from the moderator. In fact, it's actually easier and less costly in terms of moderation to manage a large community than a small one. Why? Again, turn to the "wisdom of the crowds." A larger support forum — one with more members and therefore more posts — is going to be collectively "smarter" and more able to take care of itself than a small one. In a community of two people, if they both have the same problem, they aren't going to be much help to each other. In a community of 2 million, there is a very good chance that at least one of them has already found the solution and has posted it for the benefit of the rest.

Wednesday's One-Hour Exercise

Tip: For today's exercise, you can do one of two things: you can do the following exercise using the example cited, or you can pick a favorite product or service and go and find the support for that instead.

Today you're going to visit Dell's support forum, built on the Lithium Technologies white-label forums platform.

Note: Unless you own a Dell and have a specific issue you'd like assistance with, please do not enter posts. These are real forums. If you have a Dell and have a question, then go right ahead: this is the place to ask it. Remember, this is an active community.

- Go to Google and search on "Dell support forums." The Dell forums are typically the first link that appears. You can also go to the Dell website and click into the Dell Community. From there, select "Support Forums."

- Once into the Forums, take a look at the First Time Users area. Here you'll find tips on how to use the forums, the importance of providing complete information, and similar guidance. This is actually an important part of a successful forum. After all, in any social setting — real or virtual — there will be a set of "mistakes" that all newcomers make and some established members that will get irritated as a result. Think back to the rules of etiquette I talked about: this is a good example of just such rules. It's therefore in everyone's interest to provide a "get acquainted" area so that the actual support forums run smoothly.

- After you've looked around a bit, jump into the photo/video discussions. Look at the topics, and in particular notice the number of replies to the various posts.

- Next, click on the poster's names and see what information is displayed about that member: you'll find this link in the Author column. Click on several, and notice how the status of the author changes as the number of posts and the overall usefulness of posts increases. In particular, notice that within the author's profile there are nearly identical personal attributes as you'd expect to find in any social network: name, friends, recent posts, contact info, and more. The support community is just that: it's a community. People get to know each other just they do in any other community.

- Finally, find and click the Who's Online link. This is an almost purely social feature — it is very much about being able to look into a social event and see who's there. Notice too that you can see who's there *without* being logged in yourself — like peeking through a window before deciding to join the party. Why do you suppose this feature is present? Most often, so that members who blab or rant excessively can be avoided!

As well, take a look at the content in these forums: the actual posts, the people involved, and the issues being discussed. Think about the last time you called (on the phone) a customer support unit. As you look through these forums, you'll almost certainly find issues that you've had with a laptop that you own or use, or one that is very similar. In other words, the problem that you waited for 10 or 20 minutes on hold to get help with very likely could have solved in less time through the use of a support forum.

> *"My daughter needed but couldn't find the Product Key for her Sims II game. She is recovering from surgery and is very cranky. She gave up trying to find it. I used Google, located a forum, and in it found the directions for retrieving it from the computer's registry. Voila! She thinks I'm a genius now."*
>
> — KATHY CARLYLE, freelance copy editor

Now put your marketing hat on. If your customers could benefit from similar access to online support, investing in a white-label platform might make senses. Talk as well with your Operations department: it may well be that online support is actually less costly. This is certainly the experience with Dell and many others.

Wednesday's Wrap-Up

Today you spent time in the Dell support forum. I picked this forum as an example for a couple of reasons. First, recall a few years back when Dell was dinged for its lack of effective support. Blogger Jeff Jarvis drove a good amount of press (albeit negative, though clearly well-intentioned) through his Buzz Machine blog. To its credit, Dell overhauled its support program and enlisted its *customers* in a big way. Building on this initiative, Dell added IdeaStorm — implemented to capture the ideas of customers as to how Dell might improve and add customer-driven features. More recently, Starbucks has added a similar tool, like Dell's Ideastorm also built on the Salesforce.com "IdeaExchange" platform. Support forums and the idea of reaching out to customers for guidance are a winning strategy and solid social media starting point.

Customer Communities

The support forum is a near universally applicable social extension for most brands. If you have a user base, you've got the opportunity to build a real community. It may be hard work, but the investment is worth it.

Social communities form around collective interests: in developing a social community — in comparison with a support forum, for example, where the motivation of getting support or assistance is clear, the initial requirement is that there is some activity that is both related to your brand, product, or service, and that this activity is better when undertaken in a social setting. In other words, like any other aspect of social media, from the member's perspective the community needs to fill a need *for them*. Given the investment that you will make — whether in time, costs, or both, the community will also have to fill a need for you. This is particularly true given that the majority of brand-sponsored social communities are free to the member. This generally means that the community is supported directly by advertising, or indirectly by a *verifiable* increase in sales or operating margin (for example, through support-cost expense reduction) as a direct result of online community involvement. When considering the implementation of a social community, there are a handful of key factors that can greatly impact your chances for "success."

The first of these is a definition of what "success" is. Though it may sound odd, this for me goes all the way back to 1994 and the focus of our initial consulting practice — working with companies interested in a website and what it could do for them. Some of our best referrals came as a result of showing clients — again, this is 1994 — why they really *weren't in a position to benefit* from having a website. The issue, from a business perspective, is the same now: social media and in particular the development of a dedicated, online social community can be a powerful element of an overall marketing strategy *in cases where there is a clear need to be met*. Ten years from now, online support will probably be the "front line" of support in most companies. But today, right now, the real question is "What do you want it to do and how will you know when your network is successfully doing it?" That means showing a measurable return on investment. As a prerequisite to doing that, it means knowing what you are going to build and being prepared to operate it. Next up, then, is preparation. It often begins not with your customers but rather with your lawyers.

> **Tip: Who You Gonna Call?** More than a few firms implementing active social media programs have placed legal resources either into or at the direct disposal of marketing teams *to facilitate participation* in social media. If your legal team is an obstacle, invite them to join the party. There are serious issues that can arise, and having knowledgeable, involved, and ready counsel can be a real competitive advantage.

Engaging in traditional media is for the most part "safe." You can plan, preview, and verify that any claims you'll make are based in fact. This largely minimizes the risk associated with the campaign itself. With social media, it's different. Just doing research — seemingly "safe" — can lead to real problems if you aren't prepared to properly act on what your customers share. Your customers might suggest changing something that you can't change. Now what? Originally, all they wanted to do was make a suggestion. Now, they are upset because, from their perspective, you asked for input and then ignored it. You've moved backwards. Or, your customers may suggest a new feature — and when you go to implement it, your legal team points out that "the customer who suggested it owns part of it." What is your response now?

These are the types of issues that you need to resolve in advance. As you start to move into outreach — for example, with a blog or other form of social media that involves consumer-generated content — the risks can go up further. Take the case of the pharmaceuticals industry, where regulatory compliance is a major factor in the development of any campaign, and no less so a social campaign. As you genuinely hand control of your message to consumers, what they say becomes part of what could be construed as *what you are saying*. It is therefore essential that you prepare for this: the seemingly innocuous "give your users control" isn't always the right answer — it's often instead about working with customer to build the right level of understanding as to what "participation in the process" means. It can be as simple as disclaiming or positively delineating the consumer activities from your approved corporate activities. Be clear that while you may not do everything that your customers suggest, you will consider everything. It may also mean forgoing some otherwise beneficial aspect of social media until such time as you can implement a rational plan. In any event, you want to be prepared for *what actually happens*.

Suppose you launch your community, and your members greet it with open arms. They love your product, and they say so on your new blog or in your community forums. Then you add or acquire a new product, and they *hate it*. You gave them the keys — you can't take them back now. You have to be prepared to use the tools you've put in place to correct the situation. This means you need to forge a tight alliance with operations — where the experience at issue is actually being delivered — ahead of time. Social media and owned-communities, in particular, require a holistic approach that combines the strengths of marketing, operations, human resources, and your technology team.

Oddly, your worst problems can emerge because you are too successful. I am reminded here of a campaign that I had seen where a free t-shirt was being given away on the company website. The marketing director and agency running the campaign had anticipated giving away a few hundred or a perhaps a thousand t-shirts to current and potential customers who visited the site and signed up to learn more about a new service being introduced. At first, things went fine. Then one day several thousand orders came in for t-shirts. The "free stuff" websites — communities in their own right — had linked to the request form. It happened again the next day, and the day after that, too. The website was quickly changed, but the damage was done: people who had been denied a t-shirt exchanged nasty comments with each other, all coming at a cost to the brand. At GSD&M, we ran a similar program: we had produced a free "coffee table" book for UnitedHealth with the intention of distributing the book free-of-charge. It was a straight-up "goodwill" piece. We printed a large number (hundreds of thousands) of books and ran TV in three markets. Through TV, we gave away a good number of books over the months that followed. Through the website, we had *days* where we were giving away in excess of *10,000* books. We were prepared: the whole point was to spread a message of a sensible approach to maintaining personal health as far and wide as possible. The "free stuff" communities drove the success of this program. In summary, be prepared, and think it out in advance. Going further, be doubly prepared for what "success" may bring.

Finally, have a forward-looking plan. You don't have to launch with everything — you can build your social media program as you sort out what makes sense and what doesn't. In fact, rolling out slowly is often the far better strategy, especially when working with new tools like social media. Start with forums, or a basic persona-plus-blog. Even simpler, start by encouraging your current site visitors to review and rate the content that you have put in place. What's helpful? What's not? Consider making registration a requirement for commenting, and start building an audience. Whatever your first step, though, have steps 2, 3, and 4 in the bag: be ready as you may find that your audience wants "more" right away. That ought to be a marketer's dream. By being prepared, and knowing what your "next step" options are, you can at the least avoid a marketing nightmare.

Thursday's One-Hour Exercise

Today you'll be reviewing selected social applications, built on a range of social platforms. You are welcome to visit any community sites that you currently use, or you can choose from the suggested examples. If you are not currently a member of a community site, pick one or two from the list that interest you and join that community. *You may need to create an account to fully participate.*

The sites that you will visit are:

- USA Today, built on the Pluck Sitelife platform (http://www.usatoday.com) Fair Isaac's FICO Forums, built on Lithium Technologies engagement platform (http://ficoforums.myfico.com/)

- Bank of America Small Business Community, built on Jive Software's Clearspace platform (http://smallbusinessonlinecommunity.bankofamerica.com)

- RealMadrid America U.S.A. Supporter's Club, built on KickApps social platform (http://www.realmadridamerica.com/vid/clubblanco.php)

For each site that you visit, make a note of the following:

- How visible are you, and what is the role of your personal presence?

- How easy was it to join? To sort out what to do?

- What tools are available? Blogs? Ratings? Comments? Friends? Which of these are appealing to you? Why? Which seem to be getting the most use?

- How is the platform being used? What are members doing?

Thursday's Wrap-Up

Today you spent time in social communities with a business purpose, an extension of the purpose-oriented support forums you reviewed yesterday. The distinction between the two is found in the degree to which the interaction between members is focused on a specific task — for example, completing the installation of a new router in a home network — versus building relationships between members through friend's lists, shared content items, or personal blogs around community-centric content. Sites such as Dell's support forums (with a more extensive personal profile) and tools like "Who's Online Now" fall in the middle.

As you finish today's exercise, think about how a social community might be used to develop a long-lasting connection between you and your customers *by providing them with a genuine purpose for developing long-lasting relationships between themselves.*

Working with Social Platforms

Social platforms are one of the three major groups of social media that exist when viewed from a marketing perspective. Shown in Figure 9.8 are the groupings and the components within each. These groups — social platforms, social content, and social interactions — provide literally dozens of options through which you can correctly add social media elements to your existing marketing programs.

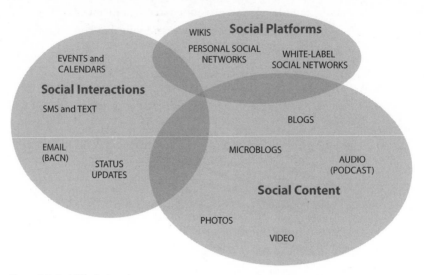

Figure 9.8 Social Media Groupings

If you are working through the exercises as you read this book, look at your touchpoint map and social feedback cycle. The social platforms you've covered this week are the "engines" of the conversations that power the social feedback cycle. Each of the touchpoints you've identified, combined with the actual product or service experience your firm delivers, sets in motion a conversation that informs *potential* customers as to what a relationship with your brand might be like while at the same time affirming (or calling into question) that same premise on the part of your *existing* customers.

It is in this way that the social spaces play a significant role within your marketing program. Along with your message, there is a conversation going on around you: it involves your customers and your potential customers. This is precisely the point that Forrester authors Charlene Li and Josh Bernoff make in their book *Groundswell* (Harvard Business School Press, 2008). Whether or not *you* choose to participate on the Social Web doesn't change this: what your decision *does* change is whether or not you'll benefit from these conversations. By engaging the audience within the social spaces, you can learn from what people are saying. Even if you don't like what they are saying, and more to the point, *especially* if you don't like what they are saying, the social spaces and the Social Web in general offer you easy access to the specific things that you have the power to change. If what they are saying is helping — if the conversations are largely having the net effect of building your business — then you have not only the opportunity to further improve (we can all do that) but also to put more distance between you and your competition by engaging the communities that are helping to drive business success.

Key to successfully doing this are a few basic rules: be transparent, be sure that whatever you offer is offered for a customer or member-driven reason, and measured either quantitatively or qualitatively. Figure 9.9 shows the BMW Facebook campaign developed by GSD&M IdeaCity and Dotglu. This campaign clearly delivered an experience that participants loved: referring to the associated case study, note that the average participant spent between 3 and 4 *hours* with the application.

Figure 9.9 BMW Series 1 Launch

Featured Case: BMW/Facebook Graffiti Wall

BMW's advertising partner, GSD&M IdeaCity partnered with interactive agency Dotglu to create and promote a Facebook "Graffiti" application contest (in partnership with Federated Media) as part of its introduction of the new BMW 1 series. This viral "build your own" application done in conjunction with Graffiti, one of Facebook's most popular applications, allowed users to express themselves while experiencing the design and beauty of the new 1 Series. The top 150 designs were voted on by Facebook members and the winner received a custom-painted model car by a famous artist. Within the first week of the application launch, over 8,400 Facebook members submitted entries, spending an average of 3 to 4 hours each to create and share their own personalized version of the 1 Series.

Friday's One-Hour Exercise

Grab your plan, look at your business objectives and your current marketing efforts, and think about how you might tap social spaces. Focus on the following questions that make up today's exercise: write out your answers.

Listening:

- What can you learn from existing personal social networks?
- How can you leverage existing business social networks?
- Add the above to your marketing plan: Create a specific initiative for each and connect it to the outreach elements of your current campaign.

Participation:

- Low-hanging fruit: Is there an opportunity to use a social tool like Product Pulse, Social Vibe, or a similar off-the-shelf, member-driven social media component? Take a look at the BMW/ Facebook featured case. It was a very smart campaign that used largely existing infrastructure — Facebook and the Grafitti Wall application — and then built on that.
- Add appropriate elements to your plan. Look for points where you reuse or build on current creative or brand assets and where you can integrate these new social elements with your existing program.

 Tip: The following takes more than an hour, but it's worth it.

Community Development

- Is there an opportunity to appropriately create a direct presence for your brand in a specific social network? Consider the following: Could your customers increase their own satisfaction through the implementation of a support forum or similar purpose-built community?
- Would your customers readily build durable relationships with you and with each other through a community experience relevant to your brand?
- Is there a current social space that falls short in meeting the needs of your customers now?

If the answers to any of the above are "yes," then you'll want to spend more time in considering an investment in an owned social space. For today, identify the connection points between a social platform and your current marketing plan: How would you use a community platform, and how would this change you current marketing efforts? What is the approval process that you would need to go through internally to make this a reality?

Most of the social platform providers either have or can put you in touch with developers able to assist you in developing and launching a social platform of your own. If a community platform or support forum is a promising next step, begin planning for it now and pull in your Operations, HR, and Technology departments so that you are ready to go when the time comes.

Friday's Wrap-Up

Pull together the following elements of your plan:

- Social feedback cycle map (Chapter 5, "The Social Feedback Cycle")
- Touchpoint map (Chapter 6, "Touchpoint Analysis")
- Dash Board and Report Card (Chapter 7, "Influence and Measurement")
- Building your Campaign (Chapter 8, "Build a Social Media Campaign")
- Social Platforms (Chapter 9, this week's exercises)

You should now have a solid start on a social media plan that fits into or alongside your existing marketing program. Looking at the social feedback cycle map and your touchpoints, look at the types of social media your customers are most likely to use when talking about your brand, product, or service, and the social media your potential customers are most likely to listen to when considering a purchase.

- What are the current metrics that you've identified for inclusion on your dash board or report card?
- Which of these lend themselves to the social media elements you've just listed?

For example, if your current customers are using video or photo-sharing sites to post content that shows your product in use, there is a good chance that they'd be receptive to a video series or podcast. If you're already collecting web metrics, you're in great shape to collect podcasting data, especially if you've chosen to use the Feedburner service.

Next, look at how you've started to organize your campaign.

- What are the first things you want to try?
- What is your forward-looking plan?
- Are you planning to use off-the-shelf tools to establish a marketing presence in existing social networks?
- Are you going to implement a forum or community of your own?

Add these elements to your touchpoint map, and start thinking about how you will develop a strategy to simultaneously address any touchpoint deficiencies as you add these new social media components.

You've covered a lot of ground now. You've got the basics in place now. As you head into Chapter 10, "Social Content: Multimedia," Chapter 11, "Reviews, Ratings, and Recommendations," and Chapter 12, "Social Interactions," you'll be building the rest of your plan. In Chapter 13, "Objectives, Metrics, and ROI," you'll finalize your metrics and reporting, and then in Chapter 14, "Develop and Present Your Plan," you'll build a presentation and present your plan.

Chapter 9: The Main Points

- Social networks lend themselves to direct participation.
- Participation and transparency are central to success on the Social Web.
- You can tap existing social marketing applications that operate within leading networks.
- You can use white-label platforms to implement your own community and support services.

Week 3: Social Content: Multimedia

This next chapter and the one that follows, "Reviews, Ratings, and Recommendations," are all about the content that people create and share on the Social Web. This includes content that relates to your product, service, and brand. In this chapter, you're going to look at pictures, videos, and podcasts, and at the tools people use to produce and publish them. For now, these tools are free — at this point, interruptive online advertising remains the primary business model. For how long is anybody's guess. As you work through this chapter, think about the difference between the content you are interested in and the ads that appear nearby. What if the ads went away? Who would pay for these services? Would anyone pay at all? Perhaps more importantly, who would use these tools to advertise?

10

Chapter Contents

Advertising and the Social Web
The Multimedia Channels
Your Social Media Marketing Plan
The Main Points

Advertising and the Social Web

Next to MySpace and Facebook, photo- and video-sharing sites such as Flickr (owned by Yahoo), Photobucket (owned by MySpace), and YouTube (owned by Google) are likely the next best-known social media related sites. To get an idea of the apparent business and marketing value of these sites, consider that MySpace was purchased for half a billion dollars (in really big, round numbers). YouTube, Photobucket, and Flickr together were sold for a combined 2 billion, again give or take.

The point that is often overlooked is that these values are primarily reflective of the *traditional media* valuation these sites. How so? At this point, the primary revenue model — for any of these sites — is the same model that has powered *traditional advertising* for 50 years. They all draw a big crowd, and they all feature — in some form — interruptive advertising. Some of the content platforms complement their basic (free) offering with premium services available for a fee, but the vast majority of users are not paying for these services with anything other than their attention. These are the new billboards, magazines, and TV stations. In this sense, using these sites as advertising platforms is *not* an example of "social media," though the *content* featured within the sites certainly is. It's an odd juxtaposition.

A new business model is coming. The conversations and media contributions powering leading social media sites aren't being directly monetized — nor are the acts of creating them. If you believe that interruptive media will become less effective as people further ignore it, or block it altogether, then *a business model based on some aspect of participation rather than eyeballs has to emerge*. Look back to the examples of the heat maps in Chapter 2, "The Marketer's Dilemma." If people ignore interruptive ads and at the same time install blockers to suppress more aggressive forms of interruptive advertising, then sooner or later advertisers themselves will force a change to the underlying business models of the majority of "social" sites. If an ad falls in the forest and no one notices...did it really make an impression? Probably not.

A Note of Caution

Throughout this chapter, and indeed throughout this book, I talk about the use of social media from the marketer's perspective. I cannot stress enough the importance of using social media *appropriately*. When the first websites were created, and the first banners were launched, the idea of using the platform for pop-ups and page takeovers wasn't on most people's minds, though clearly it was on the minds of a few. As pop-ups proliferated, so did pop-up blockers. People installed spam filters and pop-up blockers and the problems more or less went away, at least for those who installed such tools. The *Social Web will not be so kind*. Offend the collective, and expect a much more vigorous response than the installation of a filter. See the related sidebar, "Paid Blogging Gone Bad," for more about repercussions following the inappropriate use of the Social Web.

The Multimedia Channels

Presented in the following sections are the core content channels, built up initially around consumer generated media and now expanded to include the multimedia content that you can create. Channels covered include blogs and a section on corporate blogs, as well as microblogs, photo and video sharing, and podcasting.

Blogging

One of the easiest entries onto to the Social Web — and into the use of social media — is through a blog. No matter what your motivation or point of view, you have every right to create a blog. I mention this because blogging is one of the areas where a company-sponsored effort can be really effective, provided of course that you fully disclose the company connection. Think about it from a customer's perspective: The blog, properly identified and actively used (by you) creates a great channel through which you can tell customers what you're doing, and invite them to share their thoughts. It's a simple, easy, low-cost approach to social media..

Of course, this assumes that you are OK with whatever it is that people say: you really can't control the conversation on a blog other than through the limited enforcement of profanity bans or similar very basic and well-established policies.

"The Internet interprets censorship as damage and routes around it."

— JOHN GILMORE, 1993.

In fact you don't even want to control it: the point of the blog is to create a free exchange so that you can learn what your customers (and potential customers) like, dislike, value, etc. This drives directly back to the points I made in earlier chapters: the Social Web is a place where you can learn about current issues and opportunities, and where you can enlist the brains and emotions of your audience to help you develop your next-generation products and services. The basic requirements for beginning an effective blogging strategy are covered in the following sections. For more information about blogging, use Google and search for "How to Blog." You'll find plenty of good help.

Transparency

Transparency is key to an effective corporate blog. First, you want the benefits of your blogging program to accrue to *you*, and the best way to do that is by making sure that your name is on it. Second, by being transparent you prevent the kinds of very negative publicity that will (not "can" but "will") occur in response to the use of fake or paid blogs. With regard to paid blogs — a program through which you offer a payment or incentive in exchange for a blogger writing about you — this is a strategy to avoid. It will always almost always result in a disclosure problem.

Despite your best intentions, it is rare that a paid blogger actually discloses having been paid. As artisans, bloggers seek to increase the value of their reputations, and so there is always a tension around disclosure when bloggers are paid by those they blog about, just as there would be if a newspaper reporter was paid by the subject of an article. The result is that a forthright disclosure is often weakened, or skipped altogether. When outed, a predictable blowback results. In that event, *you* will inevitably be held accountable. After all, who do you suppose your critics will point the finger at: you and your flagship brand ...or "Joe up until now unknown blogger?"

Paid Blogging Gone Bad

The Social Web is quite effective when it comes to "outing" social campaigns that are not all what they may appear. A blog-based campaign such as Wal-Mart's "Wal-Marting across America" that I referenced in Chapter 2 is but one well-known blow-up.

Unfortunately, there are many others. These types of campaigns — in which what appears to be "neutral" content is actually sponsored — occur more often than you might think and by firms from whom you'd expect better. Cisco's "Human Network" campaign was called out for a lack of transparency by Jeff Jarvis. HP's compensation to bloggers won them a 'finalist' position in a SXSW panel featuring the worst social media campaigns.

Understand these are great brands with smart partners: if they can make this mistake, it's worth pointing out again here. Don't pay bloggers. If the blogger happens to be your own employee or contractor, that's fine. Just be sure that you always disclose the relationship. Don't create blogs that are less than 100 percent transparent.

Ironically, the practice of slipping sponsored content into neutral channels — for example, creating what appears to be news (and paying for it) isn't new. In August 2008, *Advertising Age* reported that the sixth annual MS&L Marketing Management Survey found 19% of the CMOs and marketing directors interviewed said they had purchased advertising in return for a news story. Moreover, 53% said "the marketing industry as a whole is not following ethical guidelines in the new-media realm." Social Web citizens expect a higher standard.

Willingness to Listen

From a marketing perspective, listening is a critical skill. This sounds so obvious, yet for many advertisers, listening is rarely the focus of the day-to-day work. Instead, the focus is on "tell," on making potential buyers aware of what you have to offer.

On the Social Web listening pays big dividends. Not only does listening — expressed, for example, through your blog posts that make an actual reference to what one of your readers said — help build a relationship with your audience, it provides you with a rich stream of information that you can use to gain a competitive advantage. Sam Lawrence, CMO for Jive Software, talks about the importance of listening:

> *Marketing needs to be released from being solely responsible for changing perceptions or driving leads. They should be enabling the organization to make meaningful, positive customer experiences and connections. This may seem like a subtle shift but when Marketing can feel comfortable becoming listeners instead of blasting sales messages, dramatic change ensues.*
>
> — SAM LAWRENCE, CMO, Jive Software

The change that Sam notes, moving from talker, from spreader of messages, to a *listener* is a key insight into getting the most from the Social Web. Again, think back to what you worked on in Chapter 6, "Touchpoint Analysis." Your marketing efforts on the Social Web are *just one part* of an overall, integrated marketing effort. If you only use the Social Web to listen — and then apply what you learn internally to make a better product or create a more delightful customer experience — how would *that* change things?

Operations and Marketing

You may wonder how the combination of Operations and Marketing within your organization relate to blogging. Building on the preceding discussion about "being a better listener," consider that one of the most effective uses of a corporate blog is as *a channel to effect internal change*, in the pursuit of a better customer experience. Properly implemented, a blog opens a channel between your customers and the people in your organization who can translate what is being posted into a better customer experience. The improved customer experience — whether moving from bad to good, or from good to great — will surely drive a stronger and more beneficial presence on the Social Web.

How do you leverage a strengthened presence on the Social Web? By linking Marketing and Operations, and by making sure that what your customers are telling you is being translated into action.

Willingness to Act

In the end, it's the translation into action that separates the winners from the "also-rans." Social media — precisely because it is "listener oriented" in a way that is dramatically different from traditional outreach channels — will surely raise the visibility of opportunities and challenges within your organization to new levels. While it may make good headlines for social media advocates, turning up the heat without a program to tap that feedback is a recipe for disaster. The goal is to use social media to drive business objectives and increase the effectiveness of your *entire* organization.

Before proposing the addition of a social media effort, and in particular using a channel like a blog that invites direct feedback, be sure to connect with and gain the buy-in of your Operations, IT, and HR teams. They are key constituents in the successful implementation of social media.

Corporate Blogs

Today you'll be reviewing a set of "corporate" blogs, looking at how they are used and getting a sense for the time commitment required to maintain them. I've picked three blogs from CMOs at firms involved in social media and from the companies themselves. The fourth blog you'll get to look at — The TED Blog — is included simply to give you something to think about.

The CMO blogs will give you an idea of how you can create a blog associated with the work that you do, and then use this to build relationships with colleagues and customers. This type of blog can be really helpful in increasing your social media knowledge, and will provide you with solid experience in using the blogging channel as a content producer. The corporate blogs selected are simple, straightforward examples. Some of the corporate blogs are handled and managed internally while others have been implemented through the use of a white-label platform — in this case, Salesforce.com.

Tip: Wikipedia provides two excellent resources if you're interested in learning about setting up a blog. The first Wikipedia entry listed below provides a comprehensive listing of blogging software. The second provides tips and typical uses in business, and includes a reference to a Technorati list of top-rated corporate blogs.

Blogging Software: `http://en.wikipedia.org/wiki/Blogging_software`

Corporate Blogging: `http://en.wikipedia.org/wiki/Corporate_blog`

There are additional resources and professionals as well. Using Google, search for "corporate blogging."

Monday's One-Hour Exercise

Tip: A set of worksheets covering this week's exercises can be found in the appendix of this book. In addition to these printed worksheets, you can also download electronic copies and access related resources at the website accompanying this book. Complete information regarding these resources and the website is included in the appendix.

Today you're going to spend an hour reviewing the selected blogs. You'll then develop a plan for including this channel — if applicable — in your social media marketing plan.

Note: These are active blogs serving current communities. Please do not leave "test" messages. If you see a post of interest, however, do participate. After all, that's why they are there.

GoBigAlways

http://www.gobigalways.com

Created by Jive Software CMO Sam Lawrence, shown in Figure 10.1, GoBigAlways is the blog Sam uses to post his thoughts on the development and application of social media. Note especially the disclosure that Sam provides:

> ### About Me
>
> *I am currently the CMO at Jive Software and a frequent speaker, blogger and work-a-holic. Although I write about social software, my opinions are biased in favor of Jive's collaboration and community solutions. I live in Portland, OR with my wife and two sons.*

This kind of disclosure not only prevents any appearance of impropriety, it actually gives Sam license to talk about Jive. Sam's credibility, therefore, transfers to the brand, just as the marketplace stature of Jive conveys a sense of "expert status" to Sam.

PHOTO BY ELLIOT NG, LICENSED UNDER CREATIVE COMMONS. LIKENESS OF SAM USED WITH PERMISSION OF SAM.

Figure 10.1 Sam Lawrence, JiveSoftware CMO, with the famed Enterprise Octopus

Bazaarblog

http://www.bazaarblog.com/

The Bazaarvoice blog is a straight-forward implementation of a corporate blog. Fully disclosed, fully transparent, and filled with useful information about Bazaarvoice and its key people, this blog is read by customers, potential customers, and importantly by the caliber of employees that power Bazaarvoice. Remember what I said about attracting and retaining the best talent? Here it is, in action.

Influence 2.0

http://blog.cymfony.com/

From Cymfony CMO Jim Nail, Influence 2.0 covers a variety of issues related to implementing and measuring social media and its impact on contemporary business.

The TED Blog

http://blog.ted.com/

From the annual conference, The TED Blog, shown in Figure 10.2, is a great series of thought-provoking posts by leading thinkers. Later this week, you'll visit the TED Talks podcast site. *Caution: I listed this one last as otherwise you could end up spending your entire hour here. Don't say I didn't warn you. To get the maximum effect of exposure to TED, consider staying at a Holiday Inn Express this evening. You just might wake as a brain surgeon.*

Figure 10.2 The TED Blog

As you review the blogs cited, consider the following:

- What is it that seems most useful about these examples?

- How is disclosure handled? How does disclosure strengthen the blog and its message?

- How often is new content posted? Which items posted generate the most comments (or the most passionate comments)?

- How does the company handle the discussion within the comments? Does the company participate?
- How could you use a blog as a part of your own marketing effort? Who would write it? Who would *listen* to it?

Monday's Wrap-Up

Today you reviewed three distinct examples of blogs related to marketing. Sam's personal blog is used as a sounding board for his ideas and often features the products of his employer. Bazaarvoice's Bazaarblog is an internally supported platform that features the ideas of its key people along with announcements of interest to current and potential customers. Jim's "Influencer 2.0" blog, along with the TED blog, are solid examples of the use of blogging as a way to extend your thoughts and then validate them based on comments and reader participation. These are the kinds of ways that you can implement and use blogging as an introduction into social media.

Microblogs

"Twitter is the gateway drug to social media."

— JIM STORER, Sr. Director, Social Media Strategy, Mzinga.

My friend Steve Golab, co-founder of the interactive firm FG SQUARED, spotted this on Twitter. At first, I didn't quite get it — I was new to Twitter at the time. (For the record, I was the 12,566,112th person to sign up for Twitter.) I have been using social tools and networks for a few years: most networks struck me as useful, but also possessing a distinct learning curve. Beyond the social norms and mastery of activities particular to Facebook, MySpace, Linked In, and other specific sites, the interfaces are generally complex, but then, so are real-life social interactions and conventions. Take Facebook as an example: you've got an inbox, notifications, applications, status updates, and more. This isn't a knock — simply a recognition that, like Microsoft Word, there is a lot there whether you use it all or not.

Not so with Twitter, shown in Figure 10.3. An input box, a submit button, 140 characters of your choice…and the whole world. I learned to use Twitter with relative ease. Seeing the value took a bit longer, but eventually I got it. Now, I'm hooked.

With *microblogs* you post quick, short bursts of text or video, as others around you do the same. You offer a new post, and others comment. You see something interesting, and you comment. Twitter has all the complexity of walking into a room full of people at a party. You start by listening, and then introduce yourself and get involved. Microblogs boil social networking down to its most essential elements: a post, a comment, and an indication of relationships. You choose to listen (or not) to people around you, and they do the same with you. In addition to Twitter, services like Seesmic, Jaiku, Pownce, and the status update tools in Facebook, MySpace, and similar are all forms of microblogging.

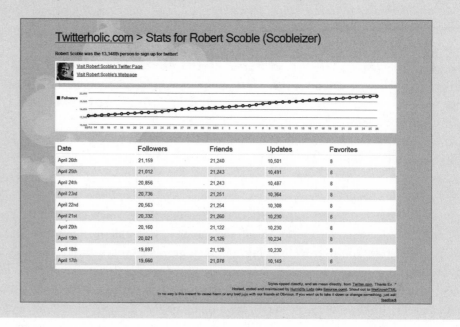

Figure 10.3 Twitter

Twitterholic: Quantifying the Chatter

If you'd like a quick look into the numbers of people using Twitter, look no further than Twitterholic.com. You'll find the most active members in terms of posts ("tweets"), friends, and followers. You'll also see the order in which members joined Twitter. For example, Twitter co-founder Biz Stone is member number 13; Robert Scoble is roughly number 13 thousand, and I am roughly number 13 million. (`http://twitterholic.com`)

Twitterholic.com > Stats for Robert Scoble (Scobleizer)

Robert Scoble was the 13,348th person to sign up for twitter!

Visit Robert Scoble's Twitter Page
Visit Robert Scoble's Webpage

Date	Followers	Friends	Updates	Favorites
April 26th	21,159	21,240	10,501	8
April 25th	21,012	21,243	10,491	8
April 24th	20,856	21,243	10,487	8
April 23rd	20,736	21,251	10,364	8
April 22nd	20,563	21,254	10,308	8
April 21st	20,332	21,260	10,230	8
April 20th	20,160	21,122	10,230	8
April 19th	20,021	21,126	10,234	8
April 18th	19,897	21,128	10,230	8
April 17th	19,660	21,078	10,149	8

Styles ripped directly, and we mean directly, from Twitter.com. Thanks Ev.
Hosted, coded and maintained by Humidity Labs (aka Emurse.com). Shout out to WeKnowHTML.
In no way is this meant to cause harm or any bad juju with our friends at Obvious. If you want us to take it down or change something, just ask! feedback

Using a microblog for marketing is pretty simple — but like anything on the Social Web, there are rules, and there are consequences for not following them. Spamming will land you in hot water in minutes. For example, while it may be tempting, do not randomly start contacting people to build a list of followers, only to then turn around and post about yourself and your products. This is considered "spam" and as noted will quickly get you (at best) shunned or (at worst) your account closed.

Twitter: Can I do business here?

Without a doubt, yes. Lionel Menchaca, Chief Blogger for Dell, reported on the Direct 2 Dell blog that "Not too long ago, we added @DellSmBizOffers to the mix. We recently surpassed $500,000 in revenue through Twitter."

Expanding the application of microblogs beyond text, multimedia is fast becoming a *conversational* reality. Seesmic is an international community built around a simple premise: discourse. Unlike blogs, social networks like Facebook, or Twitter — all of which are more or less text-based propositions, Seesmic is video. It's simple, too: if you want to get an idea of just how close we are to stepping from text (blogs) + voice (phone) to video (integrated motion and multimedia) as a conversational medium, Seesmic will give you a good indication. If your PC has a video camera connected to it, you can post a video conversation in just about the same time as it takes to write one. You can see my Seesmic account in Figure 10.4.

Figure 10.4 A Typical Seesmic Account

Like other forms of social media, microblogs can be used for listening (brand intelligence), talking (outreach), or both. Seesmic uses its own platform for video-based customer support. Firms like Comcast monitor Twitter, looking for references to their brand. They can spot problems, which is useful in and of itself. Even more important, though, is that they quickly spot problems being talked about in a highly connected social environment. Once a problem is identified, they can contact the originator of the post and work toward resolving it, *which also often occurs in public*. Because Microblogs are a "real time' stream, the problem can often be identified and resolved before the negative conversation has a chance to spread to more permanent media like a blog, a forum, or (gasp!) an *article or a book*.

Tuesday's One-Hour Exercise

If you're not using Twitter or a similar microblogging service, today you're going to start. In the first part of this exercise, the assumption is that you'll be using Twitter: you can adapt it to any microblogging tool you prefer.

 Tip: In addition to Twitter, check out Friendfeed, Identi.ca, Jaiku, Plurk, and Pownce. Each has its own following. You'll find a complete listing of these services in the references section of this book. If you're new to Twitter, TwitterHandbook.com provides a great starting point. Blogging Software:

http://www.twitterhandbook.com

Today, as you explore the suggested microblogs, consider the following:

- What is it that seems most useful about microblogs?
- How are marketers using these tools?
- Compared with a blog, do microblogs feel more like communities than publishing tools?
- How could you use a microblog as a part of your own marketing effort? Who would update it? Who would *use* it?

Twitter

If you haven't signed up, you can do so by going to http://twitter.com. It will take you about 30 seconds.

After you sign up, you'll be wondering what to do: this is normal. Search for friends using the built-in search feature, or let Twitter have a peek at your contacts list. The first thing you'll notice is the "public timeline" and a whole stream of posts marked "less than 5 seconds ago." Ignore this. It's like standing in the middle of the Astrodome and trying to make sense of the individual conversations of the 50 thousand people seated around you, made worse by the fact that on Twitter there are between a hundred and a thousand times as many people talking!

Having signed up at Twitter (or your preferred microblog), go to your Home tab. Search for the following:

- NY Times
- BBC
- Brooklyn Museum
- Southwest Airlines
- Zappos
- While you're at it, search for me! (Dave Evans)

Click "Follow" on anything that looks interesting (which is to say, any of the first five…) and you'll soon start seeing a stream (e.g., news updates) coming from these sources.

You can send email invites to friends, or search for friends or colleagues who are using Twitter already. Find them, and follow them. You can add your own thoughts to the conversation by simply typing into the box and clicking Update. Pretty soon you'll be part of what's happening on Twitter.

So what you can do? Post a question. Post a thought. Post an event. As a marketer, keep a couple of things in mind, though: Other than the public timeline, which as noted is not generally looked at, your generic posts will be visible only to those who have opted to follow you. If you post only about yourself and what you are selling, expect your list of followers to decline, all the way to zero.

Seesmic

Next, go to Seesmic. You can view all of the public videos without an account; there are many more that are visible only to members. You'll notice that the video conversations are in a variety of languages, too. What's that tell you? I'd suggest joining, simply so that you can follow the "askseesmic" video conversations, created by Seesmic staff and members. In these, you'll find a really interesting example of the way that video conversations can be used to provide a very nontraditional — and highly effective — approach to customer support.

Reference URLS

```
http://www.seesmic.com
http://www.seesmic.com/askseesmic
```

Tuesday's Wrap-Up

As with any social tool, the first step in learning to use it as a marketer is learning to use it as a participant. Get to know the rules, and take the time to understand why this particular channel exists. Look at what other businesses are doing. What seems acceptable? Follow their lead. Look especially at the kinds of actions that irritate people or get members ticked off…or kicked off. Don't do those things. Because *communities* — collections of followers and followees — are built voluntarily, you can actually use microblogs, just as with blogs, for business and promotional activities. If people don't want hear from you, they'll simply stop following or block you. Good conduct will minimize that.

 Tip: Go easy on posting until you've found your groove: with 140 characters—or a video camera—you may be thinking "What could go wrong?" Get too carried away and you'll find out.

Photo and Video Sharing

As the saying goes, "a picture is worth a thousand words." So it is with social content: a photo or video can convey very precise meaning and can engage an audience in ways that words alone will sometimes fail to do. This is particularly important when you consider the multitasking 'scan' oriented consumption of digital content. Adding visual elements transforms the conveyance of a message into a quick, scan-friendly experience.

What are the kinds of things that you can do — as a marketer — with visual content? For starters, you can simply show your products — although this is among the least effective applications of *social media*. To make the most of any social channel, start by creating content that involves your audience rather than simply talking at them. Then, extend this by integrating your content through cross channel campaigns that tap your other social efforts. Don't look now, but later in the chapter you'll see an example of this type of integration in the "Brooklyn Museum" Featured Case.

The Entertainer's Secret

Don't limit the use of your own content to photos and videos: you can use audio clips, too. In addition to written testimonials about its product, the web site supporting "The Entertainer's Secret," a throat spray for musicians and speakers, includes *audio testimonials* from its satisfied customers.

http://www.entertainers-secret.com/Testimonials.html

Want to "see" this product in action? Listen to these voices.

Got TV? You can use online channels — which are often more lenient with regard to their acceptance standards — to present a spot that has been made expressly for the Web. For example, you may have a special cut you might not have been able to show on TV but which — online — would generate favorable, appropriate exposure. Pictures and video are also helpful when offering instructional or similar content that shows a complex operation or otherwise illustrates written documentation. In that case, a photo or video that you make yourself can be perfect. When you do it in such a way that it can be passed around or easily picked up and dropped into a forum or blog by your customers, you further increase the likelihood that your message will be spread around.

When using social channels, you really want to leverage the "social" component and that usually means "audience participation." Creating what is essentially a catalog isn't necessarily a *social* experience. Look back at the list of channels available to you: TV, print, catalogs, and direct mail to name a few. You already have plenty of places to show and tell about your product or service. Don't short-change the Social Web by viewing it as one more "talk" outlet. Instead, use the combination of visual elements and audience participation to show your product or service *in action*. Let people see what other people are doing. Note here as well that I'm not talking about showing models or other artificial representations. Encourage real people, using content that they made, to spread the word about your products and services. *Tap your evangelists*.

Beyond the portrayal of your products and services (by you or by someone else), you can also use visual content to document events, parties, openings, cause related events, or product launches — all of which are things that you participate in at the brand level. This seems obvious, but it is still the minority of marketers that go beyond a single photo on the website of, for example, the CEO cutting a ribbon as next year's model is rolled out. How about uploading the entire set of pictures from the launch party to Flickr? What about uploading a video of runners crossing the line at a company sponsored charity run, and then tying that to your corporate blog or community newsletter to bring out the *stories* of the people involved? That is the social stuff that builds an audience.

Yes, you need to think this out in advance: you may need release forms, for example, to show an event video publicly. But it's worth the effort: if there was a video of *you* crossing the line after running a marathon, wouldn't you send the link to your friends? Most people would, and a simple Tell-a-Friend button would make this very easy. Combined, the value of your campaign or event sponsorship goes up as more people view the event and hear directly from the people who participated in it. This is the "social" part of "social media," and ironically the part that many marketers miss.

Wednesday's One-Hour Exercise

Today you look at some examples of professional and user-generated content that feature pictures and videos of products in use, instructional tips, and examples of the kinds of content that consumers will create to share with others. As you work through these examples, keep in mind that none of this social content exists alone: it is all supported in multiple other channels.

For today's exercise, do the following:

- Go to sites indicated and search for the suggested terms. Review each item, and think about how it is being used and who is viewing it.
- Having looked at the examples, imagine two video or photo programs that you could add to your social media program and then write these ideas down. For one, consider how you might use video to show your customers (and potential

customers) how to get more out what you offer. For the second, consider how you would encourage your current customers to create visual content that could be shared in order to create a positive "lift" element for your brand, product, or service.

YouTube

Search for: Instructional Video

Amazingly, and one of the best proof points for the impact that social media can have is an "instructional video" from Soulja Boy. If it isn't listed on the first page, then refine the search by adding "Soulja Boy" to the search terms. The instructional video that accompanies the track "How to Crank That" has been viewed over 30 million times. *This is Super Bowl caliber exposure, at considerably lower cost.*

> **Reference URLs**
> Soulja Boy - How to Crank That (32M)
> `http://www.youtube.com/watch?v=sLGLum5SyKQ`
> `http://en.wikipedia.org/wiki/Soulja_Boy`

The "Soulja Boy" video is a standout: most "social video" is viewed a few hundred, a few thousand, or maybe tens of thousands of times. That may seem small, especially in comparison to TV where millions of views is the norm. Remember, however, that online instructional videos are generally viewed by someone *seeking* that information: as a result, the number of actions that lead to a conversion can be much higher by proportion than you'd otherwise think. Consider the following as examples:

Search For: Home Depot DIY

Here you'll find videos ranging from the Home Depot-sponsored "The Basics of Paint" to Joe & Joe's "Making a Photo Backdrop." The relatively light viewership (in the hundreds to thousands of views range) reflects the relatively specialized applications. The "Backdrop" video has great information and is useful for any amateur photographer wanting to take better pictures in a home studio. Within that audience, the video has a solid circulation. One of the things to keep in mind when considering the production of a video series, or, encouraging or facilitating actual consumer-generated social content is the importance of knowing exactly who your audience is, and what *they* need.

> **Reference URLS**
> Home Depot - Basics of Paint
> `http://www.youtube.com/watch?v=r8DfgWjACNQ`
> Joe & Joe
> `http://www.youtube.com/watch?v=oJrH2Dj8oGc`

Moving beyond the basics of instruction, Home Depot leveraged the combination of its home makeover campaign centerpiece — a $25,000 gift card give-away — with consumer-generated media by inviting consumers to create a video showing why they should win the prize. With consumers involved, the number of videos — and the number of views — went way up. The video project then continued with the actual remodel. If you look around YouTube, you'll find lots of Home Depot-produced videos presenting its remodeling program.

Reference URLs
$25,000 Remodel Contest
`http://www.youtube.com/watch?v=U68J_TefJgs`

Flickr

Turning to photos, take a look at Flickr. If you are already using a photo-sharing site, you can adapt this exercise to whatever photo-sharing site you prefer.

Search Terms: Home Depot DIY

Here you'll find photos of projects as well as photos taken on "family days" at Home Depot where kids are invited to build basic wood-working projects. In this example, the permitted use of cameras in the store results in parents posting images of the kinds of family-oriented activities that typify these Home Depot construction days. Because these are posted to personal Flickr accounts, the assumption is fairly safe that they are being shared among family and friends, furthering the spread of the very positive aspect of the Home Depot brand. *This kind of content additionally serves to offset the posted content of Home Depot detractors.* Think back to Chapter 7, "Influence and Measurement," and the Net Promoter score: your online reputation is determined by the difference in the number of people talking positively versus those talking negatively. Without this positive content resulting from 'Family Days" at Home Depot, the instructional content and the contests, the *negative* efforts of the detractors would dominate the conversation. By participating in the social aspects of your brand as it is built online you can prevent that from happening. Again, you can't prevent detractors: they have as much right to the Social Web as you do. You can however, by participating yourself, *prevent them from being the sole social voice of your brand.*

In Figure 10.5, you can see photos taken in various Whole Foods Market and then posted online. I include this example here because it's worth thinking about the policies that your own firm may have when it comes to photography or video. Whole Foods Markets does not allow photography inside its stores without explicit permission. At the same time, it's quite likely given some of the comments that the people who took the photos were unaware that the policy existed *before* taking the photo.

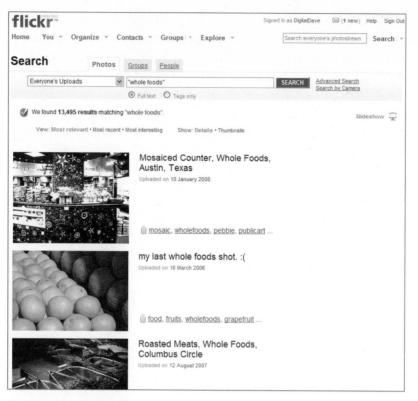

Figure 10.5 Whole Foods Market on Flickr

I'm not suggesting that merchants like Whole Foods — who go to great lengths to create an incredible customer experience — adopt and post policies like that for "Area 51," shown in Figure 10.6. The point is instead that it is becoming an experiential disconnect — think here in terms of touchpoints — for customers who are very used to creating and sharing content online — to be barred from doing the same thing in real life. When cameras are built into phones, and uploading taking one click, people want to document experiences. What people see...people share. Being told "no" works *against* your social media efforts.

Figure 10.6 Area 51 Photo Policy

The reality is that Flickr lists well in excess of 10,000 photos uploaded and tagged "Whole Foods." Many of them are interior shots, and many of the comments include phrases to the effect "as I was taking this shot, I heard a voice heading my way saying something about the prohibition of photos...." Individual policies are, of course, a matter for each firm to decide on its own. Suffice it is to say, though, that with over 10,000 photos at one photo-sharing site alone along with a number of comments that refer negatively to the photo policy, discouraging photos and the sharing of the Whole Foods experience is not likely to make the most of social media and what the Social Web can do. The Whole Foods experience is built on multiple touchpoints. For me personally, it's the passion of the Associates something that can't be photographed or easily copied — and not the way the oranges are stacked — that make the Whole Foods experience what it is. Even more important, though, is that policies that prevent the sharing of experiences *tip the content on the Social Web in favor of your competitors and detractors*. Unlike your loyal customers — who typically respect your wishes and put the camera away — your competitors and detractors are going to go into stealth mode and take the pictures anyway. The social conversation will be, as a result, decidedly one sided.

As a final example, look at this short instructional video for a niche, low-cost product that really benefits from a video. In this case, the product is a new type of in-line skate. This has been included simply to establish that you don't need fancy, professionally produced content to be *effective*. This casual video — viewed over 100,000 times — shows an easy way to get the hang of these skates — thereby encouraging mastery among new riders — and shows the proper use of basic safety equipment as well.

Reference URL
FreeLine Skates
`http://www.youtube.com/watch?v=fghOsqGacnU`

Wednesday's Wrap-Up

Today you looked at videos and photos, and added to your plan options with both an internal program and a consumer-generated program. Your emerging plan options now include a blog and/or microblog used for outreach, issue resolution, or product research, and visual components that directly involve your customers in the beneficial conveyance of your message.

As you are considering selected social components for your marketing program, another aspect of social media is likely emerging: it's about smaller numbers, added up, rather than larger numbers done all at once. Consider the Home Depot videos: most are in the 100 to 1,000 views range, with some reaching into the 10 thousands. Unlike "Soulja Boy," and certainly in contrast to TV, few are in the millions range. This is one the reasons that your creative agency or media buyers may be slow to roll out social programs: they are used to — and set up for — buying large amounts of exposure. There is nothing wrong with that, and large exposure campaigns are still an important aspect of an overall marketing effort for most marketers. It is, however, something to keep in mind as you move toward implementation.

Where traditional media is often centered on awareness or perception, social media is about *influence*. If you gain real influence, one person at a time, and that person tells three people, your social efforts significantly enhance your awareness and perception efforts. Think back to the purchase funnel and the social feedback cycle and the use of TV to build awareness or paid search near the point of sale to drive closure. Social media — active in the consideration phase — is about adding credible influence, suggestion, persuasion, tips, and new uses — the things that a potential customer will find most useful and, therefore, the things that are most likely to create an additional use (purchase) or help a "fence sitter" make a decision favorable to you. Both of these assume that the social content is positive: if the content is negative — recall the Kryptonite bike lock videos (search YouTube if you've never seen them) — then the result can be exactly the opposite of what you really want. In the end, social media is an adjunct, an aid, another tool that is part of your marketing toolbox. Like any other single tool, it is best used in combination — as an integrated element — with the tools used in the balance of your campaigns.

Understanding the *contributory* impact of social media — the difference between reaching a million people who may or not be thinking about repainting the living room this weekend versus reaching the thousand who actually have this task on their "to do" list right now — is critical not only to getting the most out of the Social Web but also to successfully "selling in" your plan. Where a traditional campaign can be presented in terms of "millions reached," a social campaign is typically presented in terms of a "thousand influenced." It will fall to you to make the case for the smaller, highly targeted social efforts that effectively convey your brand by allowing potential customers a direct and participative role in shaping and sharing a collective message about your product or service. Your social campaign — the false notion of "going viral" aside — is best built on small pieces that connect current customers directly with potential customers. These small pieces serve to amplify, extend, or bring credibility to your larger awareness campaigns. Added up, these smaller social campaigns (in comparison to the millions of eyeballs purchased via traditional media) are a significantly forceful component in your overall marketing program. If you couldn't interrupt... these messages would still get through.

Audio and Video Podcasting

Quick: What's the difference between an audio or video clip and a podcast? The answer is "Nothing, unless you count how it's actually delivered and consumed," which of course on the Social Web turns out make all the difference. The real importance of podcasting isn't the clip itself but rather *how it is delivered*. To be clear, the content does matter. The content itself has to do something for someone — it has to make your audience smarter, or laugh, or illustrate a point, etc. Note, however, that those are the same rules that apply to any marketing content that is expected to perform well, on the Social Web or anyplace else.

This point about delivery and consumption is again a fundamental indicator of the way in which the Social Web changes the rules of engagement for marketing, and again an example of the opportunity created for a savvy marketer. Start with a quick look at what makes a podcast a podcast. A podcast is after all, nothing more than a sequenced, subscription-based delivery container for content, generally audio or video. Podcasting is, at its core, an extension of blogging. And like blogging, podcasting is another application of RSS. Just like with a blog, your "readers" (here, listeners or viewers) subscribe to your podcast. Just like blogging, you publish regular posts, though in this case they are called "episodes." Finally, just like blogging, new episodes are automatically delivered to designated players — typically a computer, an iPod (from whence the name originates) or phone, or similar hand-held device. Once delivered, those who subscribe to your podcast can listen to or watch the episodes you've produced.

Podcasting: Numbers Don't Lie

If you've never listened to a podcast, you may be tempted to dismiss this medium as a fringe channel. It's not. Not only is it popular, it's also highly effective. Consider the following:

- Advertising in podcasts and online shows has a three-fold ad effectiveness increase over traditional online video and a seven-fold effectiveness increase over television. Unaided ad awareness across two years of studies was 68 percent compared to industry benchmarks of 21 percent for streaming video and 10 percent for television.

- Embedded ad placements are more effective than pre-roll across a range of audio and video formats, including varying spot lengths (:10, :15, :30 seconds) and across show formats (produced and host-read).

- Advertising in podcasts and online shows is effective in moving users from awareness to consideration to purchase. There is a 73 percent average increase in likelihood to use/buy versus a control group.

- Podcast advertising leads to a more favorable opinion of an advertiser after hearing or seeing an ad. Sixty-nine percent of those podcast listeners surveyed had a more favorable view of the advertisers following ad exposure.

Source: Podtrac-TNS Advertising Effectiveness Studies, 2006–2008.

With podcasting, beyond the content it's all about delivery. It's about giving your audience the absolute choice of where, when, and how to consume your content. Embedding a clip into a website fails on this count: it requires a visit to the website! If someone is on a mountain bike or hiking in Muir Woods, *they aren't going to simultaneously visit your website*. By allowing the people you want to reach to take your message to the place, time, and appropriate device of their choosing, you make your message accessible on an entirely different level. It means giving someone the ability to listen to an executive thought-leadership series while walking on the beach. It means making riding the train, working out at the gym, sitting in the airport (not that you ever do *that*) productive. In short, it means giving valuable gifts to your audience: the gifts of time, place, and choice.

By giving control over to your audience and then empowering them to set the terms of engagement with your message it signals that you are on their side, that you are a partner, and that you fundamentally understand the pressures and challenges presented in a multitask-oriented, information-driven world. If it sounds like I've gone off the deep end here, stop. Put the book down and continue through the rest of your day, but keep what you've just read in the back of your mind. Count the number of times today that you say or think "OK, hold on, let me finish this and I'll get back to you." Count the number of times that two or more "priority" events compete for your attention. Podcasting — and specifically giving your audience the choice over where, when and which device — *empowers your audience to shift the point of consumption of your message to a place where full engagement can actually occur.* As a marketer, isn't that what you really want? A great example of podcasting used effectively in marketing is Susan Bratton's "Personal Life Media," shown in Figure 10.7.

Figure 10.7 Personal Life Media

Featured Case: Cancer InfoLink and ProstateNet Podcast Series

I first met Dr. Krongrad working with ProstateNet.org, an outreach program created by prostate cancer survivor Virgil Simmons to provide men with information about the treatment available and the importance of talking with their doctor. A podcasting firm that I co-founded, HearThis.com, created a podcast series for Virgil: that series is a part of the cancer awareness and outreach program developed by Virgil. I was interviewing Dr. Krongrad about *laproscopic* — meaning "surgery without cutting you open" — *radical prostatectomy* (removal of the prostate). Dr. Krongrad pioneered the use of laparoscopic radical prostatectomy after witnessing first hand the needless blood loss and painful complications of traditional, open prostatectomy. The Krongrad Institute is the world's only private program devoted exclusively to laparoscopic prostate surgery. (http://www.laprp.com/)

Six months after we had completed the interview and published the podcast, I got an email from Dr. Krongrad inviting me to review his newest project, the community extension of Cancer Info-Link (http://prostatecancerinfolink.ning.com/). Dr. Krongrad had used the Ning social platform to create a discussion community around the outreach and awareness work that he is doing in conjunction with the podcast series.

Based on the initiative of Virgil and Dr. Krongrad, simple tools like podcasting and the free Ning community platform have been put to use educating men and their families about the issues of prostate cancer. The podcast allows men — who typically suppress emotions like fear, hurt, and pain — to educate themselves in relative privacy. The community groups on Cancer InfoLink give survivors a forum where they can talk with each other about beating cancer and talk with men who are just now recognizing that they too need to take action in order to do the same. These are powerful examples of social media, and testament to just how accessible and impactful this form of communication has become.

Thursday's One-Hour Exercise

Today you're going to spend an hour listening to and watching selected podcasts, and then picking a few for subscription. In this sense, you'll be doing part of this exercise today — sampling — and part of the exercise later when you actually listen and view the subscriptions. To satisfy the "immediate gratification" needs of a contemporary audience, one of the podcasting "best practices" is providing your audience with a "sampling" option that satisfies this need for immediacy. You'll start the exercise in the same way that your audience will typically experience your podcast program: by reviewing the descriptions of the podcast, and then continue by clicking the Listen Now button or link. Once you've found something that you like, subscribe to it. If you have a mobile device that can accept podcasts, set up your subscription to push the episodes to that device.

No Podcast-Capable Device?

If you don't have a mobile audio device, now would be a good time to get one. According to Podtrac, about 60 percent of all podcasts are listened to on a portable device, compared with 40 percent on a PC. The Apple iPod is by far the easiest to use. Shop around and look for a model that suits you. If you're on a budget, look for deals on "last year's model." Do you have an iPod savvy daughter? Offer to buy her a new one in exchange for her old one and a quick tutorial. Getting a decent podcast-capable device empowers you to take the content with you. This in turn allows you to explore the places where content consumption makes sense for you — and in so doing discover or imagine the places that your audience may choose to do the same. Try it. It's a great exercise, and one that is likely to change your view of your mobile device and of the potential venues for marketing content delivered via podcasting.

Here is a starting set of podcasts that you can sample. Some are personal interest, others are pure business. Note how each is monetized, and how each can be used to carry a persuasive message. With some, the content is the vehicle that carries a relatively traditional advertising play, they use pre- or post-roll ads, or video overlays. In others — like the series on men's health from `ProstateNet.org` — the message itself is the focus: the "marketing" objective is to bring information to men and persuade them to pay attention to their own health.

Already listening to or watching podcasts? If you're already a podcast consumer, then you can either do the exercise above — hey, you may find something new that you enjoy — or you can follow along, using your own podcasts in place of those above.

As you work through the exercise, note the following:

- The role of the description: how well were you able to judge the likely relevance of the content *before* you listened to it.

- The role of the "listen now" feature: did this help you make your decision?

- The presence or absence of "send to a friend."

- The presence or absence of a subscription option. Remember, if you can't subscribe, it's not a podcast. (It may still be great content, but it's not a podcast.)

- The overall quality of the podcast — how does it compare with other podcasts? With TV? What difference — if any — did this make? How good is "good enough?"

- What is the most important aspect of the podcast? For example, is it quality? Content? Accessibility?

   Personal Life Media/ Living Green
   http://blogs.personallifemedia.com/living-green/

   IBM Thought Leadership
   http://www-01.ibm.com/webcasts/podcasts

   Shell Global Solutions
   http://www.shell.com/globalsolutions/podcasts

   Slate Podcasts
   http://www.slate.com/id/2119317/

   Ted Talks
   http://www.ted.com/index.php/talks

Thursday's Wrap-Up

Today you explored podcasts and, hopefully, found and subscribed to a couple of them. More importantly, you gained a first-hand experience with a medium that is purpose-built for time and place shifting, in other words, the ability to take your content wherever you go and enjoy when it makes sense for you. If you're new to RSS subscriptions, as the podcasts you've signed up for begin arriving you'll get a real sense for the empowerment that choice over "where, where, and what" provides. If you're already subscribed to podcasts (and are consuming them on a mobile device) you've already experienced this.

By providing content in a portable format, you effectively increase not only the productivity of your audience (especially so with audio, which is built for multi-tasking), but you increase the likelihood that your content will be listened to in an environment with lower background noise (in both the physical and mental sense). That can be a significant factor in engagement, retention, and message reception. As a bonus, because the content can be easily shared, you've set your audience up to refer what they find useful among themselves, further adding to the effectiveness of your overall marketing program.

Your Social Media Marketing Plan

This week you covered social content — media created by you and your customers for the specific purpose of sharing uses, insights, and experiences among those interested in what you do. Applications include learning more, understanding purchase or use-related nuances, having fun, and a lot more.

Pulling Things Together

Now it's time to put this to work, and that means adding these elements to your developing social media marketing plan. As you work through today's exercise and the continued development of your plan, keep in mind that none of this social content exists alone: In Figure 10.8, look at the range of content — a blog, Twitter presence, video, photos, and event calendars — that powers the comprehensive online presence for the Brooklyn Museum.

Friday's One-Hour Exercise

To start off today's exercise, gather together the notes you made this week about video, photos, and podcasting. Review them, and then think through the following thought starters:

- What are the most challenging aspects of your current marketing program, in terms of overcoming objections, of driving new uses, or driving additional purchases?

- Which of the above lend themselves to assistance via video, photos, or a podcast?

- Which of these lend themselves to the kinds of content that your customers would create? Which would be best if *you* made the content, and then gave it your existing customers to share or comment on?

- What are the most promising multimedia applications that would add depth to the blog you created in the prior chapter?

Friday's Wrap-Up

You've now got a solid start on a comprehensive marketing plan that includes an effective component. To say it again, your social components are intended to complement — not replace — traditional media, direct mail, online media, and other marketing elements that you are using. Last week you stepped into networks. You saw how to create an effective marketing presence within social networks. You also got a look at the white-label tools that are available to quickly add an "owned" experience to your interactive programs.

As an example of how all of the channels you've seen come together to create a solid social campaign, go beyond Figure 10.8 and check out — online — the work of the Brooklyn Museum The Brooklyn Museum combines a website, blog, Twitter, YouTube, Flickr (along with an excellent photography policy!), and more to support its overall online presence and to connect the online audience to the museum itself.

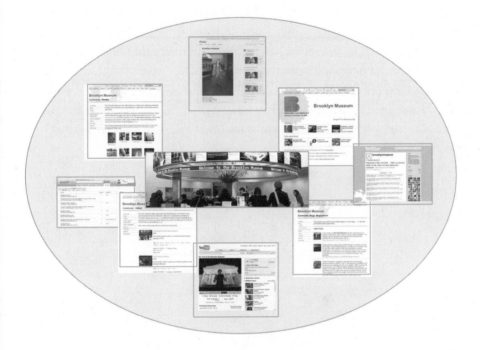

Figure 10.8 Brooklyn Museum: Comprehensive Social Media Involvement

Featured Case: Brooklyn Museum of Art

The Brooklyn Museum of Art has created an outstanding social presence for itself through the smart use of social media. Building off of the main website, which includes a blog, directory, and similar information resources, the museum's media team has added a presence on Twitter that is used to disseminate short bits of information. YouTube and Flickr are used as well: YouTube has videos of museum exhibits and promotions, and Flickr is filled with images taken by visitors and uploaded to the museum's Flickr group. Eventful, a social media-based calendar tool, lists all of the events coming up, along with a running commentary by people who have visited in the past. All in all, it adds to a solid presence, and one with multiple connection points. The museum's overall social presence is shown in Figure 10.8.

Chapter 10: The Main Points

- Blogs are an effective, easy way to build a credible social presence: Be prepared to deal with direct, public customer feedback.

- Microblogs are casual forums that can be used to quickly create a following.

- Audio and video content can be used to extend text-based information. When created by your customers, video can convey to them a real sense of participation in the brand.

- Podcasting gives those interested in what you have to say the ability to choose where, when, and on what device they will listen.

- Social media is one of the many tools that you have available when developing and extending your business presence. Like your entire toolbox, the more that your social components interlock with each other and with your traditional efforts, the better.

Week 4: Social Content: Reviews, Ratings, and Recommendations

Building on Chapter 10, "Social Content: Multimedia," you'll continue working through the social media content channels. In this chapter I'll focus on ratings, reviews, and recommendations. These are social content, just as much as blog posts, photos, and videos. They too are created by people based on an experience, and like a photo or video they are intended to be shared.

Ratings, reviews, and recommendations are an extremely important form of social media applied directly to commerce. For thousands of years, people have wanted to know whether others were happy with their purchases (or animal trades), and whether they'd recommend the merchant (or trader) at the center of the transaction. Once again, it's life moving in circles.

Chapter Contents

Building Consensus
Consensus and Marketing
Winning the Popularity Contest
The Main Points

Building Consensus

What's more basic than asking someone if they'd recommend for you what they just did. Did they like it or not? Did it work or didn't it? Are you likely to like it as well? The Social Web, especially when viewed from a consumer's perspective, is built on just such questions. To be sure, a lot of what appears on the Social Web might, from a marketer's perspective, be what you'd loosely call "personal entertainment" — photos of family, videos of community events, and similar material. But a significant chunk of the Social Web is also dedicated to commentary about the news, about politics, about commerce, and specifically about *the experiences of people following the purchase of a product, the use of a service, or an interaction with a brand*. This type of commentary definitely impacts your marketing efforts regarding awareness, persuasion, and ultimately conversion. This is one of you most fundamental connections to social media.

When your customers are positively recommending what you are selling, your work as a marketer is a lot like riding the perfect wave. Of course, there's no a guarantee the ride will last forever — even the best surfers still wipe out — but it sure beats sitting on the beach. Compared to paddling around by yourself, wondering where all the action is, having the Social Web working *for* you is pretty great. This chapter covers some of the most straightforward — but often overlooked — elements of the Social Web that you have at your disposal, social elements that can help you grab and ride that perfect wave.

Using multimedia content tools like those you've seen so far — Twitter, Seesmic, Flickr, and YouTube — people are telling other people "what happened." I'll extend these relatively informal channels with a focus on the tools that provide quantitative or otherwise structured information on "what happened," aka "ratings, reviews, and recommendations." Potential buyers are using this information to inform their pending purchase decisions. From your perspective, that has to matter.

Before getting too far into this chapter, I'd like to define a few terms. You may not agree exactly with them, but that's OK. These definitions are a bit arbitrary but useful nonetheless. I'd just like to be clear about the specific characteristics of ratings, reviews, and recommendations. Each is different, and each plays a different role in building and extending your Social Web campaigns.

> **Ratings** A *rating* is an indication of how well or how poorly a product or service performs in its intended application. It is typically indicated using a five- or ten-point scale: For example, a lot of ratings systems use five stars, where "no stars" (or one star) is bad and five stars is as good as it gets.

Reviews   A *review* is typically a written or visual description of what happened, of what was liked or disliked, along with supporting information that provides a deeper context. Videos are increasingly being used in place of text. Loïc Lemeur's review of the Schiphol Hilton presented in Chapter 6, "Touchpoint Analysis," is just such a review.

Recommendations   A *recommendation* is intended to quickly let someone else know whether or not something is, well, *recommended*. That's it: it doesn't denote quality or relative fitness for any specific application beyond the basic choices of "recommended, or not recommended." Two competing brands of tires may be recommended for use in the rain, even though one has a superior rating when compared with the other.

Ratings, reviews, and recommendations can be used as listening tools (for example, when following your own product or that of a competitor) to gather intelligence on the conversations that impact your marketing effort, either directly or via your competitors. Although it may surprise you, you can also use ratings, reviews, and recommendations as an outreach and marketing tool.

Let me explain that last line: As a marketer — or as any content producer for that matter — it's really *not OK* to review or rate your own stuff. You can't use ratings, for example, in the direct sense of promotion. I know that political candidates generally vote for themselves in an election, but that's a bit different. For a candidate *not* to vote this way would be really odd: It would be like saying "Hey, I'm not even voting for me…so you shouldn't either!" The correct analogy in marketing in this case is *buying and using* what you make. When you're a marketer, it's perfectly OK to *buy* your own products or eat your own dog food as the saying goes. It's *not* perfectly OK to Digg yourself or to write glowing reviews or to pump up your own ratings.

So how exactly do you use ratings, reviews, and recommendations as awareness or outreach tools? By offering these abilities to your customers! I'll assume that you make a decent product or offer a worthy service: if you don't, then think twice before turning to the Social Web to promote yourself. Giving your customers the option of rating purchases, of sharing reviews for recipes, or recommending your latest software widget is an obvious element of your marketing plan. Yet, this basic set of social media features is missing from way too many businesses with an online presence. Either a lot of firms make less-than-par stuff — which even in my most cynical mind I can't accept — or a lot of marketers have simply overlooked or actually chosen not to include ratings, reviews, and recommendations. Either way, it's an opportunity lost. The practice of social media is about opportunity found.

From a purely practical perspective, I understand that not every marketer will want to or be able to implement every social media or web technology feature, no matter how strong the case for that feature may be. At the same time, if you are reading this book, you clearly have an interest in understanding social media and how you might apply it to your business or extend or strengthen the social media programs you are running now. If that's the case, and if you don't currently have at least one of the tools featured in this chapter (ratings, reviews, or recommendations) enabled already, then you should consider doing so. If you are working on a challenging product and don't expect the Social Web to be supportive, then focus on finding all of the applicable ratings, reviews, or recommendations on other sites and track them. Use the Social Web for *listening* and for improving your product. If you have a best-of-class product, then add ratings, reviews, and recommendations so that your current customers can easily tell others why they love you. This is a point that Andy Sernovitz, co-founder of the Word of Mouth Marketing Association, made in a post to his blog, "Damn, I wish I'd thought of that" using the Bazaarvoice platform — on WalMart.com. Being able to rate everything changes not only the way in which your customers shopping for big ticket items (such as vacations or cars or HDTVs) make purchase decisions, but it also changes the way they shop for the little things, like a toothbrush. In Andy's words: "No consumer products manufacturer can avoid facing open, honest feedback." That is a hugely powerful statement with important ramifications for all marketers.

Damn! I Wish I'd Thought of That!

Looking for a list of unusually useful and socially savvy ideas for smart marketers? Look no further than Andy's blog: http://www.damniwish.com/

Consensus and Marketing

Ratings, reviews, and recommendations are the subject of this next section where I'll build on the basic definitions and provides examples and implementation guidelines. Along with discussions between consumers — think blogs and wikis — ratings, reviews, and recommendations enable consensus on the Social Web.

Ratings

The strength of a rating is in conveying how well a particular solution works given its claimed performance. It's more than 1, 2, or 10: it's a judgment of relative fitness for a specific application.

Ratings — typically shown on a multipoint scale — are used to indicate *expectation* versus actual *performance*. Figure 11.1 shows a typical rating of a photo posted in a wakeboarding community. Ratings, and in particular as applied to content, are an easy entry into the processes that drive the Social Web.

Figure 11.1 Wakesites' Content Ratings

If you are offering online commerce, in addition to rating products or services, ask your customers to rate their satisfaction with the checkout process or the condition of the goods they received. This is a touchpoint, too, and it has a big impact on conversions. These ratings will then indicate to others what to expect in checkout and shipping: if they are positive, potential shoppers will be encouraged to *buy from you* instead of a competitor. Internally, these ratings can be used to guide improvements as indicated or needed. For example, upon the opening of a certain dot com retailer,

I ordered a *wood maul* — a large, heavy, long-handled tool used to split firewood — and a designer bathroom scale, just to see what would happen. Both arrived on time, as promised; however, they had been shipped together rather loosely in the same box. I use the wood maul each autumn to when I stock up our fireplaces. The scale has never worked right. What do you think my rating of the fulfillment process would have been had ratings been available on this site at the time? It's actually too bad they weren't, because my feedback would have no doubt alerted someone within the firm whose job it (would have been) to monitor those reviews and see that the shipping process needed some work! Instead — because there was no feedback channel — my experience was probably repeated with other customers.

Tip: Use ratings to set expectations, to differentiate performance characteristics, and to guide internal quality efforts. Ratings are most effectively used in consumer-facing applications early in the Consideration Process, where competing options are being evaluated and additional facts are being gathered.

Reviews

Reviews are the most useful — and most problematic — of the group. Reviews are information rich: they provide great detail (thoughts, suggestions, and comparisons) that can be tapped and used by both you and your customers in evaluating a purchase option. An Amazon review — in fact, one of my own reviews of a book that I really enjoyed — is shown in Figure 11.2.

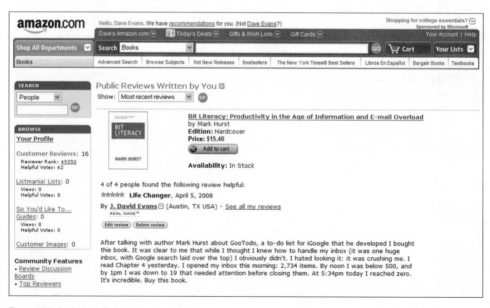

Figure 11.2 An Amazon Review

When Is a Review Not a Review?

A review is not a review when you write it for or under someone else's name! You may be thinking "We can create reviews based on our testimonials." Unfortunately, unless your customer writes the review *as a review*, it's not a review.

Useful though they may be, reviews also up the ante in terms of the issues around relatively uncontrolled user-generated content. To put it bluntly, if someone drops the f-bomb in an online review, what will your response be? In reality, dealing with profanity is pretty straightforward: nearly any review platform that you might consider implementing will have some form of input filtering. Profanity — at least in English and other common world languages — is pretty easy to screen out. The more difficult issue is controlling inappropriate references, hate speech, representations of profanity, slander, and similar expressions that you'd rather not have your customers exposed to — and certainly not on your website.

So how do you deal with this? Surprisingly, you enlist your customers. Enlist the members of your *review audience* — those people who write reviews based on experiences, those who read them, and those who use them to inform purchase options. Ask them to notify you when something is offensive, off-topic, or appears inauthentic or otherwise suspect.

Ensuring Safe User-Generated Content

Jake McKee (this book's technical editor) and Tamara Littleton of eModeration have developed a set of six easily understood and practical guidelines for ensuring safe content in a user-generated context. You can download the PDF here:

http://www.communityguy.com/six_techniques_for_safer_ugc.pdf.

Ultimately, the community that forms around the reviews is often your best defense against inappropriate or off-topic content. Sure, this means that one or more people will have seen the offensive item. But, if you act quickly, that's all who will see it. Plus, you get the added benefit of participating in a genuinely involved and responsive manner. The net result is an audience builder, not a business threat.

Tip: Use reviews when your audience has something to say that will itself aid potential customers in making a smart choice. Tap the audience, too, in order to keep content focused and appropriate. Consider implementing a "review of the review" to ensure quality.

Recommendations

Recommendations can be among the easiest of the three to implement. A recommendation itself can be as simple as a "thumbs up, thumbs down" or as complex as the ten-point scale presented in Chapter 7, "Influence and Measurement," where you saw the Net Promoter score. The basic two-point scale — thumbs up versus thumbs down or more simply, no thumbs given at all — is a very casual approach to a recommendation, something intended to be used quickly and without a whole lot of deep thought. "I think you'd like this. I recommend it." By comparison, the Net Promoter score is a much more considered approach to a recommendation. The Net Promoter score gets at the issue of how strong the inclination to offer a positive recommendation is and, therefore, how likely that recommendation is to result in the start of a beneficial social conversation.

An important clarification is needed here, and this is an example of the importance of understanding the difference between a rating and a recommendation. Looking back at the definitions I provided, a recommendation is an indication of whether or not I think this will benefit you. Consider two tires, both advertised as being suitable for use in the rain. Although both may have high ratings, they may or may not be equally recommended for any particular driver. One tire may be intended for use on a minivan, where ride quality and tire wear are important factors. The other may be intended for a sport or performance application: shorter life is a given as a trade off for a "grippier" tire that also transmits more "road feel" (aka, harsher ride). Both tires have high ratings, but you would recommend the $300 sport tire that is likely to wear out in 10 or 15 thousand miles for use on a family minivan? Probably not.

Digg, shown in Figure 11.3, is a basic recommendation service that operates on this simple premise. Online publishers of ezines, firms offering online product catalogs, and similar content and ecommerce site operators can add the Digg widgets and icons to the items on their sites. Visitors can then click and register "Diggs" — think popularity votes — on the Digg site where a larger audience follows the voting and thus learns about these items. This, by the way, calls all the way back to the opening definition of social media: "The posting of content…normally accompanied with a voting process to make media items become popular."

If you compare Digg recommendations with those underlying the Net Promoter methodology, there is obviously a difference. Digg is quite casual. *One* Digg isn't worth much, whereas a hundred Diggs (which gets you on the Digg home page) or 10 thousand Diggs (which lands you in the all-time tops) is. In the case of the Net Promoter, a single "1" or "2" is an indicator that there is a committed voice out there ready to speak out against you. Given the power of search engines and the lasting presence of content on the Internet, sooner or later that one voice will be heard. In the case of Diggs, it's a quantity thing: with the Net Promoter, every vote counts: your "9s" and "10s" are your best defense against detractors, provided you have given their bestowers the tools to easily share those thoughts and opinions. After all, these are the people who have indicated that they are willing to stand up for you. Help them out: make recommendations — along with ratings and reviews — part of your online presence.

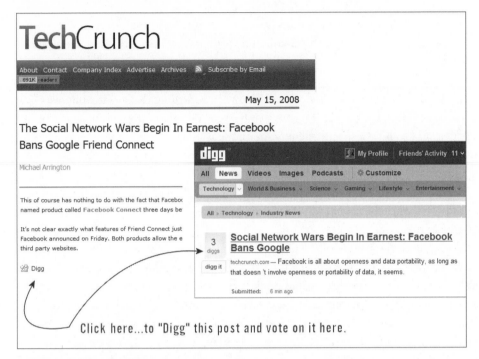

Figure 11.3 Digg Recommendations

> **Tip:** Use *recommendations* when the objective is to encourage a direct action. Recommendations are most effective when used in proximity to a clear call to action.

Putting It All Together

As you consider using ratings, reviews and recommendations in your social media efforts, take the time to think through the specific type of tool — or combination of tools — to offer in each distinct context.

Taken together, rating, reviews, and recommendations add considerably, not only to the social experience but to its usefulness to you and to your customers. (Recommendations in particular are an easy way to introduce participation into your online presence.) Adding this type of feedback increases the value of your online commerce or community sites because it provides information that is by definition relevant to your marketing and business objectives: your customers are in a direct way telling you what they think of your offers. Used purely as a listening tool (for example, to track the ratings and reviews on your own site, or on a competitor's site or blog), this type of actionable feedback provides you with the specific information that you need to make an effective case within your organization for needed change or the continuation of efforts that are winning praise in the marketplace.

Of course, there are more subtle issues that arise in applying ratings: what "one star" means varies from person to person, and varies in specific cases. Just as one star means something different when to applied to a light bulb that perhaps doesn't last as long it should versus an underwater shark cage with a slightly faulty latch, the number of stars awarded to identical products will also vary according the specific interests of the person providing the rating. Reviews can help in combination with ratings by adding the detail as to how a specific item is simultaneously rated "1" and "5" by two different reviewers. How you implement ratings, reviews, and recommendations, and in particular the combined use of them, can help your audience make sense of what you offer, get more value from it, and make better personal choices as a result. This helps you: customers who make smarter choices up front are more likely to post favorable reviews after the purchase.

As a practical example of the use of ratings, reviews, and recommendations, consider Amazon. As a pioneer of the use of "reviews" alongside online commerce, Amazon instituted customer-generated book reviews early on. While these were very useful, it soon became apparent that basic reviews could be "gamed," manipulated by those inclined to artificially raise or lower the rating of a particular book. In response, Amazon developed the "review of the review," shown in Figure 11.4. Although this doesn't eliminate the problem, it effectively turns control to the audience: if someone fakes a review, while the audience may or may not snap to the shenanigans, they will very likely conclude that this review is "less useful" than others. Either way, and as a direct result, the impact of the faked review is reduced, with the direct beneficiary being the potential buyer.

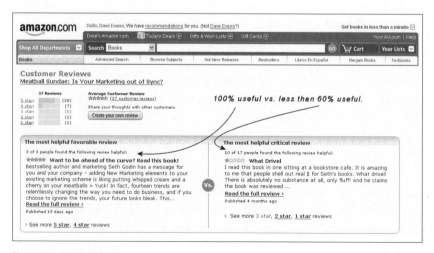

Figure 11.4 Reviews of Reviews

Going further, Amazon combines reviews, ratings, and recommendations to provide a very powerful combination that really helps people make choices. There are the *reviews* themselves: you can read about what others thought of a title that you may be interested in, as well as what others thought of the reviews. You can quickly sort out whether or not a book, CD, DVD, or anything else Amazon sells is for you by using the *ratings*: click on the fives and then click on the ones: look at the reviews and see if the things that you are looking for are praised or faulted. Then, look at the respective reviewers and see which are most like you. Finally, by participating and creating reviews and ratings yourself, you improve Amazon's *recommendation* engine as regards what it suggests that you might like.

Worried About Negative Reviews While Shopping?

Although it may seem counterintuitive at first, the presence of a small number of less-than-favorable reviews in a commerce setting can actually strengthen the value of the reviews overall. A recent Bazaarvoice study showed that conversion rates improved in the presence of a small number of less-than-excellent reviews, suggesting that the negative reviews add credibility to the positives. Make no mistake: if *all* of the reviews are negative…I think you can guess the outcome.

So what can go wrong when implementing ratings, reviews, or recommendations? For starters, you can offend people, not directly but instead through the actions of others. If you are implementing ratings, for example, on a craft site — where people are rating each others' work — take care that terms you use to describe "one star" aren't offensive. Requiring that people be logged in — in other words, disallowing anonymous ratings or reviews — is another way to avoid mean-spirited posts. To protect the integrity of the ratings system, do what Amazon does: require a purchase, require a log in, and limit reviews to one per person per item. Pluck's Sitelife, a white-label community platform, has a built-in feature that prevents ballot stuffing: Once you have given a "thumbs up" to a particular piece, you can't vote on it again. Ratings, reviews, and recommendations aren't perfect — no social media component is and sure enough there are tricks around most any measure. With reasonable care in implementation, however, these tools can be quite effective in adding real value to your online programs.

Monday's One-Hour Exercise

Tip: A set of worksheets covering this week's exercises can be found in the appendix of this book. In addition to these printed worksheets, you can also download electronic copies and access related resources at the website accompanying this book. Complete information regarding these resources and the website is included in the appendix.

Start today's exercise by making a list of at least five books that you've read in the past year. (Ten books would be even better.) The books can be about business, travel, personal interest, fiction, or anything else. For each book, write down your thoughts on the following:

- Did you like it? Why or why not?

- Did you recommend this book? Why or why not?

- Did you write a review — anyplace — for this book? If so, what did you say about it? If not, why not?

With the first part of this exercise done, go to http://www.Amazon.com and look up each of these books. I recommend Amazon because they have implemented the "reviews of reviews" feature I talked about. Also, and maybe it's just me, but compared with Barnes & Noble, the ratings at Amazon seem to cover a wider range, from "love it" to "hate it." As such, they will be more useful in this exercise.

At Amazon, compare what you've written (your experience) with the reviews you find. Record the results next to your comments: note both the rating associated with the review, and the share of people who found that review helpful.

Tip: While you're visiting Amazon, Barnes & Noble, or your favorite bookseller or online retailer, take the time to add your own ratings and reviews for books, CDs, DVDs, and other items with which you have direct experience. Get in the habit of participating and in the process increase your own awareness of the use and effort required with regard to social media from a consumer's perspective.

Monday's Wrap-Up

The reviews of the reviews offer an insight into the workings of the Social Web and the role of social media. You probably found some reviews in your exercise today where you agreed with the crowd and others where you didn't. It's also likely that where you differed significantly in opinion from the reviews, others did as well. There may even be one or two where you found yourself the odd man (or woman) out. This is how the Social Web and social media work: among people with a similar interest (for example, the audience for any particular book) there is a range of opinion that centers on a consensus. There are always a few outliers as well.

Note in particular the share of the number of people who found each review helpful: this *can* but doesn't *always* help you spot the suspect reviews. For example, on reviews where you did differ significantly, did the share of people who rated that review and found it helpful also dip? If so, for whatever reason, that review might be considered suspect: someone certainly said it, but no one else really believes or values it. In any event, it's clear that people are giving less credit to it than the more highly rated reviews.

At the extremes, and differing markedly from the consensus, are the genuine outliers: the people who just saw it differently. Importantly, also in this group are those who posted a review with a clear bias. In general, both groups will be de-emphasized by the collective. But don't dismiss them either: those with a genuinely different point of view are often predictors of the next wave. You'll be taking a deeper dive into the collective versus the individual versus mass in the next section.

> ### Bad Reviews...Are Good Information
>
> Bad reviews, while perhaps less desirable than good reviews, are still very valuable to you as a marketer. Bad reviews can provide a sense of reality: when you see only great reviews, you might still wonder what your customers are really thinking. When you see bad ones, you know. If you are seeing bad reviews, take note, address the issue, and then reconnect with the specific people writing the bad reviews. True detractors aside, they just might become your biggest fans.

Winning the Popularity Contest

Think back to Chapter 3, "What Is Social Media?" and the definition of social media from Wikipedia:

> *Social Media: Participatory online media where news, photos, videos, and podcasts are made public via social media websites through submission. Normally accompanied with a voting process to make media items become "popular."*

The last part of that definition — "normally accompanied with a voting process to make media items become popular" — is the focus of the next section. In the prior section, I covered the ways in which something that someone experienced is rated, recommended, and/or reviewed. In this section, I'm going to focus on *voting* and on the specific relationship between recommendations and voting. Voting is one of the mechanisms through which specific content items gain popularity and are, therefore, spread beyond their original audience.

The Voting Process

The process of voting content up and down in popularity is part of what drives the Social Web: if saying something is the cost of entry, then having others agree and affirm what you've said is the payoff. The voting process, when looked at this way, takes on a larger significance that is specific to the Social Web and the use of social media in marketing. Items that are voted up — and in particular those that include content that others considering a purchase might find useful — are being voted up based on collective experience and the desire to make sure that others do in fact see this content. *This voting process directly drives message spread.* As a marketer, your challenge is to create the kind of experience — and as result, the social media — that gets beneficially amplified through the voting process.

On sites like Digg, the voting process is part of the fabric. One Digg equals one vote. New items arrive and get voted up, and in so doing move from the "most recent" page *that the site opens with* to the "most viewed in 24 hours" or similar pages that reflect popularity as it accumulates over time. Hold the thought about new content appearing in a prominent place in your mind.

By comparison, in addition to subscriptions and recommended videos, on the opening page YouTube lists promoted (paid) videos along with featured and most active video content. It does *not* list the new content. On the home page of YouTube additional votes accumulate based at least in part on this prominent placement. Home page content gets more mention, and as a result more votes. You can see the cycle that sets up.

Where Digg brings new content to its subscriber base, YouTube presents and amplifies the content most appealing to a mass market. YouTube is the big dog chasing TV: Digg is the long tail.

Here's how it happens: Suppose five new pieces of content are posted today on YouTube: I'll assume that one person finds and Diggs each video, so all five are now referenced on Digg as well as on YouTube. Digg users will see each new video (or pointer to it) on the home page: YouTube users, unless they navigate to the Video tab and then select "Most Recent" *will never see these*. While YouTube is an archive for what is made popular on its own site and through sites like Digg, the YouTube home page is a *mass channel*. The net impact is that where Digg will tend to expose niche content, YouTube will suppress it. Put another way, Digg will tend to promote diversity while YouTube will reinforce stereotypical preferences. Look no further than the starting page of YouTube as proof: All of the expected content, given the user base, is present. Very little of the "richness of the Social Web" is presented. In many ways, YouTube *is* the "new TV" and is acting more and more like TV as a result. Highly popular (mass) content, featured on the home page, is used as a carrier for interruptive advertising.

There's nothing wrong with being popular, per se, and there are certainly a lot of reasons to offer the kinds of products and services that are attractive on a mass scale. However, if you agree that one of the promises of the Social Web is the realization of what Chris Anderson describes as the long tail, then one of the ironies of the Social Web and the emphasis on popularity is that the long tail can actually get cropped. Niche content — the long tail stuff which, by definition, will never be "most popular" — gets pushed further down in a relative sense as the mainstream rises to the top. The Digg and YouTube home pages are shown in Figures 11.5 and 11.6. Look at the content, and how different (and alike) what is presented really is.

This may seem like a nuance but it is actually a significant point for a marketer. If you are looking for a highly popular, interruptive (e.g., a typical online media buy) media property then YouTube is a great site. If you are providing a niche service or product, or if the content you are creating for the Social Web is highly focused, then for sure YouTube is still a place you want to be, but you'll also need to drive interest in and awareness of your content from sites or services with a niche focus. In this case, be sure to consider the role of services like Digg in building awareness of your content in addition to simply posting it to YouTube.

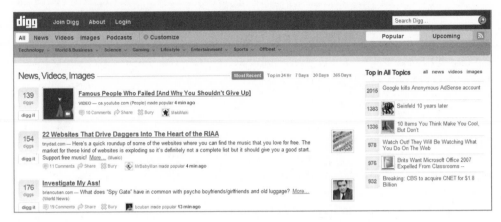

Figure 11.5 Digg

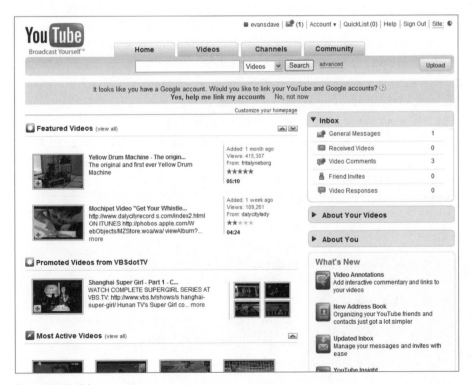

Figure 11.6 YouTube

Note: I have talked extensively about Digg and the role that recommendations play in driving popularity. Importantly, Digg is also very useful for sharing: by "Digging" something you are placing a link to whatever it is that you " Digg" in a public index, You are, in effect, sharing this content. Other popular sharing tools include Del.icio.us (covered briefly in Chapter 4, "Web 2.0: The Social Web") and Stumbleupon, a browser toolbar that taps the wisdom of crowds to suggest content that you might like based on what others with similar interests have themselves liked.

Tuesday's One-Hour Exercise

The point of today's exercise is for you to get an idea of the degree to which the major social media content sites are — or aren't — creating a place for niche content.

Tip: If you're not a member of Digg, take a minute and join. While you can review Digg content without joining, in order to add your own vote to content that you like you'll need to be a Digg member.

For today's exercise, first visit Digg and then visit YouTube, and do the following:

- Look at the home page content: by default, is it the newest, or the most popular content that you see first? How does this change the mix of content that you actually view at each site visited? Take the time to look into the items themselves, and explore beyond the home page.

- Looking at the top 10 items on each home page, which has more content covering topics you've never heard of? How many of the topics — on either site — are also present in the headlines on your favorite news site?

- If you had to pick, which site offers the most unexpected versus expected content? There is no "right" answer here — again the point is to experience the differences in the ways that different content sharing sites share and promote content.

Tuesday's Wrap-Up

Today you looked at the impact of social consensus, in both positive and negative lights. What does this say about diversity? What does this say about niche versus mainstream products, services, and the lifestyles of your audience? The take-away from today's exercise is simply this: if you are marketing a mass-appeal product or service, you are likely to see things like your TV commercials and other forms of content that you create picked up and repurposed on the Web. You can build on that, by either making this content available (e.g., posting it yourself so that those watching TV online can find it) and/or posting "outtakes" or bloopers, content that you could not show on TV but which might become popular online. By comparison, if you are in a niche segment or are creating content for a very focused audience, then you will definitely want to promote these items and make them accessible to these specific communities. Dropped loosely on the Social Web, they will surely get buried.

Online Performance Rights

To properly repurpose and monetize content for the Web, you may need to secure online performance rights from participants. The best time to do this is before you create your content: you can often negotiate more favorable terms by creating a package of rights and usages as compared with seeking Internet performance rights by themselves, after the fact. Always respect copyright and performance laws. Not only is it the right thing to do, but this is the Social Web: if you disregard performance laws, for example, expect to hear about it *in public*. It goes without saying — but I'll say it again anyway — that a public dispute will generally reduce the net benefits of your social media programs.

Applying Recommendations

So how can you as marketer, tap the basic *recommendation*? If you're selling a consumer product or service, and especially if you're selling it from your website, let your customers recommend specific items to others, making sure that the supporting materials on the site provide a context that answers the question of "why" the recommendation is being offered. But what if you don't have a retail or similar site? What if you offer editorial content or consulting services? What if what you do requires a lot of thought prior to the purchase?

You can still use recommendations. In these cases, use the recommendations to drive awareness and interest in the supporting materials that lead to a sale or to suggest that certain types of editorial content might be applicable to "people like you." Figure 11.7 shows a typical news article — in this case from the *Wall Street Journal*. The marketing application of Digg is to drive more readers to the *Wall Street Journal* based on the popularity of this article and hence boost ad sales. This is actually a very common application of Digg, so much so that Digg has a dedicated news section where recommendations for articles of note, taken from a wide range of sources, are posted.

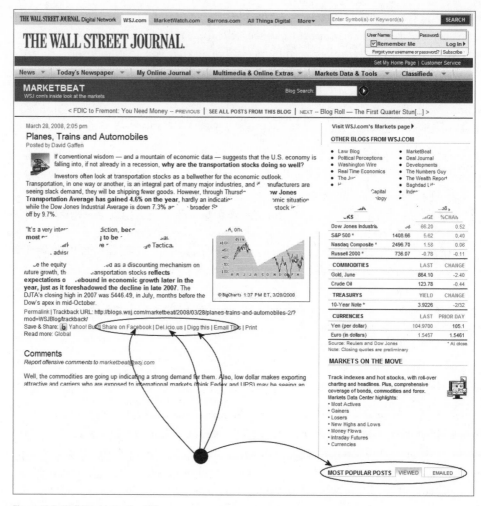

Figure 11.7 *Wall Street Journal* and Digg

Wednesday's One-Hour Exercise

Today you're going to visit sites that do — or at least could — utilize recommendations and content sharing tools like Digg. For each of the sites listed, look for things that you are interested in or would simply like to read more about. Your task is to find things that you'd like to share with friends, and then do that.

- *Wall Street Journal*
- *Ad Age*
- Amazon
- Edmunds
- iVillage

As you work through these sites, consider the following:

- Which sites made it easiest to share content? To rate content? To share the ratings?
- On which sites did you actually share the most content?
- If the tools on the sites that made it easiest to share content had been available on all of the sites you looked at, would you have shared more content?

Wednesday's Wrap-Up

Today you looked at the role of the combined impact of recommending and sharing content, and at a sample of top-tier sites across a range of applications for which content sharing — in the sense of driving awareness, generating members, or building at least some aspect of community — is essential. Yet, the tools to do this ranged from very visible to nonexistent. Think carefully about the impact of *not including* basic content recommendation and sharing tools: as it turns out, they matter.

The best way to do this is to put your consumer hat on: think of a few things that you want to buy and visit sites that offer information. Compare the sites that include consensus tools such as recommendation indicators with those that do not. To really drive this home, pick a product that you want (in my case, a new TV) and one about which you know relatively little (so, for me, that would be digital and HDTV). The recommendations — call it the wisdom (or even just "casual knowledge") of the crowd — can be really helpful in making a choice.

Getting There Faster

In Chapter 9, "Social Platforms," you read about white-label social networks and community platforms. A white-label solution, simply, is a set of services or capabilities that can be branded and offered as if it were your own. The downside of a white-label solution is that you get what you get. The services offered range from "everything you need" to a somewhat smaller feature set than what you had in mind, limited for example by what the majority of a particular platform vendor's customers need, or by that vendor's view of the market and its demands. The *upside* of a white-label solution is that you get what you get...today!

From my perspective, having it today trumps having the wish list.

I say this for three reasons: First, unless your core business is building and maintaining social software, don't stretch your limited resources by building what you can buy and therefore competing in a business at which you cannot be the best. Not only will it distract you, but your customers will start leaning on you to match the features and performance of firms like Jive Software, Pluck, Lithium, KickApps and many others. Jive Software builds world-class collaborative tools: Jive Software uses its own tools internally and with its customers. That makes sense: they learn by using their own tools. When Seagate — a company with no doubt more than a few tech-savvy employees who know how to build a website — decided to add a support community, they enlisted Lithium, a white-label service provider. The resulting success story was a case study featured in Chaptered 9.

More important though, especially in the short run, is *time to market*. While not impossible, it is very difficult to match the time-to-launch that you can achieve by using a best-of-class software services provider. The race to the Social Web is on: your business is likely facing this pitched battle on multiple fronts. Whether attracting and retaining key employees or attracting and retaining key customers, part of the challenge you face in tapping the Social Web is in getting it done *today*.

Finally, any advantage to getting exactly what you want often erodes over time as new technologies — think helicopters — marginalize the value of the effort that you've just put into blazing the first trail on foot through the jungle. The reality is often that as tasty as your wish list looks, there's probably a 5 percent advantage to doing something custom against a 95 percent chance that having "almost everything" would in fact get you where needed to be. Your audience won't miss many of the features you end up skipping, particularly if you do your work up front and skip the right stuff. In the end, grabbing a lift in the chopper and being in the market sooner rather than trekking through the jungle means you gain more *market* experience, and gain it faster. That's experience that you can use to crush the competition.

In this chapter, you are exploring one of the most fundamental and easiest to implement social elements: ratings, reviews, and recommendations. If you see this as a competitive advantage — *meaning your competitors likely see it the same way* — then this means that you need to *quickly* add these components to your plan. Otherwise, your competitors will get there first.

I'll feature Bazaarvoice (see sidebar) and its Ratings & Reviews platform as an example. I highly recommend looking at Bazaarvoice and using this platform along with services like Digg. By using these tools in combination, you can have a powerful social presence — and more metrics than you thought possible — up and running and building your business *very quickly*.

Bazaarvoice: Ratings and Reviews to Go

Bazaarvoice, launched in 2005 by CEO Brett Hurt, offers a plug-in ratings and reviews platform. Brett's prior venture — Core Metrics — provided the background and insights needed to make the step from *measuring* to *generating* metrics. Amazingly, 50 of the top 100 retailers — including Wal-mart, Home Depot, HP, and Dell — use the Bazaarvoice platform to power their ratings, reviews, and recommendations services.

A full-featured ratings, reviews, and recommendations platform — however you choose to implement it — should provide tools beyond the ratings, reviews or recommendations themselves. Specifically, any inclusion of ratings, reviews, or recommendations *within your site* should also provide you with quantitative data that you can use to guide successive efforts. In Chapter 7, I presented the beginnings of the measurement of influence. This led to the presentation of a basic dashboard and report card. In Chapter 13, "Objectives, Metrics, and ROI," you'll be pulling together more of the data — including data from sources like your community and ratings, reviews and recommendations platforms — and developing a more comprehensive dashboard.

Ratings, reviews, and recommendations are obviously important tools for consumers when shopping. They help guide purchases, and tend to increase satisfaction with the item ultimately purchased. From a brand point of view, many consumers now expect this as basic commerce functionality. This is an important point to note when you factor in the role of word of mouth in driving the Consideration Cycle and the creation of social media. The more satisfied (or dissatisfied) the customer, the more likely it is that a conversation will start. Think back to Chapter 7 and the Net Promoter score: the sixes, sevens, and eights are tossed out. These are the people that were OK with the product. If pressed, they would say things like "Yah, it worked well enough." That kind of word of mouth doesn't count for much.

Adding ratings and reviews provides your customers with the information they need to make an *informed choice based on the actual experience of others*. The result is not only an often increased spend at the time of purchase, but a lower return rate after the fact. In other words, the result is *higher satisfaction*. In Net Promoter language, sixes, sevens, and eights become nines and tens. Threes, fours, and fives that drive your Net Promoter score *down* often arise out a lack of information that would have resulted in alternative purchase. When ratings, reviews, and recommendations are present, these misinformed and hence highly unsatisfactory purchases *never occur*. Your Net Promoter score goes *up* as a direct result. The economic benefit alone of dropping the product return rate is a huge — and often overlooked — benefit that again points to the linked dependencies that exist between Marketing and Operations when working with social media. Take a look at the featured case study — Petco's implementation of the Bazaarvoice platform: the results speak for themselves. The Petco website, including the Sort by Ratings search option, is shown in Figure 11.8. Figure 11.9 shows a close-up of the ratings tools available at the product level on the Petco site.

Figure 11.8 Petco's Website

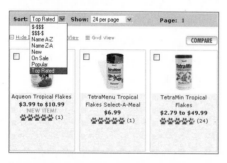

Figure 11.9 Petco Product Search: Top Rated Sort

Thursday's One-Hour Exercise

For today's exercise, go to the Bazaarvoice website and look at the Clients list. Pick several that interest you: for example, look at Petco, Circuit City, and Dell. Look at more than three if you have time.

For each of the sites you've selected, do the following:

- Look at the product reviews. You may have to navigate to a specific product, or there may be a link to "top rated" items present on the home page. Think about the advantages and disadvantages of having direct access to top-rated products.

- If a Sort by Ratings feature is available, use it. Think about the impact of the role of ratings and your ability to navigate them in terms of contribution to shopping-cart value. If this feature is missing, ask yourself what difference it makes to your overall shopping experience.

- Look at the reviews associated with the various ratings: do the reviews tend to support the ratings, and vice versa? Is the combination of ratings and reviews more valuable than either alone?

Featured Case: Petco and Bazaarvoice

PETCO is a leading specialty retailer of premium pet food, supplies, and services: its stores offer more than 10,000 high-quality pet-related products. Given the complexity of these offerings, adding product reviews and supporting information designed to help consumers quickly arrive at the best choice given their particular needs was a natural choice. Among the features installed was the Top Rated search-sorting option: this option allows customers to sort search results by "top rated" in addition to sorting by name, price, and other typical choices. With the Bazaarvoice ratings platform in place, the results were tracked over time. The results indicated a 49 percent boost in conversion rates and a 63 percent higher average order value when the Top Rated option was selected. In fact, the Top Rated results-sorting option is now the number 1 option at Petco.com.

The benefits didn't stop with sales, however. The overall customer experience was improved as well, as evidenced by the reduction in return rates. Return rates were just over 20 percent lower for products with reviews versus those without. For products with at least 25 reviews, the product return rate was reduced by an incredible 45 percent. These two improvements — increased conversion and reduced return rate — benefited Petco's business.

Thursday's Wrap-Up

Today's exercise centered on two primary concepts: the benefits to the consumer of a full-featured ratings and reviews platform, and the simultaneous requirement for consumer participation in creating this valued content. I point this out because it is too often the case that technology leads the social effort, rather than the business objectives that suggest a role for a social effort leading the technology. It's easy to get blinded by the allure of a quick solution: "If we only had this, we'd be all set."

In reality, it is seldom the case. Instead, by directly experiencing a sample of commerce sites that use ratings, reviews, and other forms of social media, you can see first-hand the requirement that the consumer be directly involved. What does this mean to you? It means that your plan needs to begin with the *consumer's role* in creating social content rather than your desire to sell more. To be sure, I'm not suggesting that the consumer's desire to generate content is the driver for your business. Your business objectives clearly come first. The point is this: given your business objectives — whether launching a new product, increasing sales by *X* percent or changing attitudes as measured by the Net Promoter score — the choice to add social media to the mix is tightly coupled with your view of your customers as sources of information. If you see in your customers the answers to your questions, you're in good shape. If you don't, take a quick walk around the block and clear your head. When you come back, take another look at your customers.

"If you have a question, go to the store. Your customers have the answer."

— SAM WALTON, founder, Wal-Mart.

This means getting very clear about how much you trust your customers as conveyors of your message to others. The underlying truth of social media — and in particular as evidenced through simple additions like ratings, reviews, and recommendations — is that *consumers are turning to each other to get the information needed to make an informed choice.* By providing the forum to do so and integrating it into the purchase process (or into the content ratings for publishers and noncommercial applications), you signal your implicit trust of your customers. This is how you win the popularity contest.

Building Your Plan

You've now got two of the three big social media channels under you belt: you've seen social spaces (two weeks ago), multimedia content (last week), and now ratings, reviews and recommendations. In addition, you've got a solid handle on the social feedback cycle as it applies to your business, the touchpoints that drive it, and the beginning set of metrics that define it. It's time now to start pulling things together.

Friday's One-Hour Exercise

Today you add ratings, reviews, and recommendations to your developing social-media marketing efforts and to your larger marketing plan. Here are some guidelines and tips on how to approach today's exercise:

- Think holistically. Ratings are not a purely digital technique. Use the ratings you collect in other media. Figure 11.10 shows how President's Choice taps its ratings in its print circulars.

- Involve customers. Customers have the answers, but they don't always know where to go or what to do with them. Tell them. Figure 11.11 shows a receipt from Wal-Mart advising electronics customers to rate their purchases at Walmart.com.

- Don't reinvent the wheel: look at existing services and solutions. Take advantage of the options and custom programming tools that are already offered to make your implementation as unique as your brand.

- Look at the data that is available to you: if your customers are sending you a message, be sure you're listening. Collect the numbers, and take the fight to Operations, where you can do something about it.

- Involve Operations directly. Social media is driven by conversations, and conversations result from experiences that are driven by Operations. If your customers are your external allies, Operations is your internal life partner.

Figure 11.10 Ratings in a Flyer

Figure 11.11 Invitation to Rate on Receipt

Here are your actions and objectives for this exercise. Consider each of the following and write out your responses, adding these elements to your developing social media plan.

- Look for the low-hanging fruit: based on your current digital marketing efforts, could you add Digg or Del.icio.us buttons to encourage recommendations and sharing?

- How do ratings and reviews apply to your business? If you offer goods and services online, it's a fairly straightforward application. If not, then what? For example, if you are offering expertise and you write a blog, is a Digg button part of each post? If you sell through a channel, are you pulling content that channel partners produce, packaging it with Digg, and adding it to *your* site to help your current and potential customers see the value of your channel partners?

Identify the specific uses of rating, reviews, and recommendations and add them to your plan. If you are planning to use a white-label platform, or planning to build your own, make a note of the data that you expect to collect. Keep that handy, as you'll need it in Chapter 13.

Friday's Wrap-Up

You're building a plan that begins with your business objectives and is rooted in your current marketing program. This is evolution, not revolution. Through the Hour a Day approach you are building this in stages. You can roll it out the same way.

At this point, you've got a social media program that potentially includes a community space, content that you or your customers create and post in places like YouTube, Flickr, Seesmic, and Twitter, a good start on fundamental measurements, and now the immediate feedback and content sharing capabilities of ratings, reviews, and recommendations. With about a month to go before your presentation (I did mention that you'll be presenting this plan to your colleagues, right?), you're in a very good place.

Chapter 11: The Main Points

- Ratings, reviews, and recommendations are different elements: each has a specific sweet spot.
  - Use recommendations to encourage direct action closer to the point of purchase in the consideration cycle.
  - Use ratings to provide information that will set expectations and address performance questions earlier in the consideration process.
  - Use reviews to provide detailed information needed to make an informed decision that can be "passed down" after a purchase experience: implement reviews of reviews and community policing to maintain review quality.
- Voting, typically via simple recommendations, both drives and hobbles the Social Web: it indicates consensus, typically based on experience. However, it can also drown out diversity as mass interests overwhelm niche content.
- Consider building or adopting a ratings platform to provide both the capability to customers to inform each other, and to provide the data that you need to drive your business. If you don't have an online store, you can still tap ratings and reviews by adding them to print campaigns and end-aisle displays.
- Help your satisfied *offline* customers tell their story. (The dissatisfied ones will figure it out on their own.) Look at Wal-Mart as an example: include a simple note on the cash register receipt.

Week 5: Social Interactions

In Chapter 9, "Social Platforms," I presented personal and business networks along with white-label services through which you can build your own social spaces and applications. In Chapter10, "Social Content: Multimedia," and Chapter 11, "Reviews, Ratings, and Recommendations," I presented the content that people create on the Social Web, content ranging from casual, short-burst conversations on Twitter and personal reflections like ratings and recommendations to more thoughtful blogs, reviews, conversations, and multimedia.

You can think of these as the nouns of the Social Web, the people, places, and things of interest to those who posted them and as well to those who commented on them and shared them with friends. This chapter is about the verbs, the connective threads that tell you what's happening.

12

Chapter Contents
Connecting the Dots
Managing Social Information
The Main Points

Connecting the Dots

Social Interactions — the third big collection of channels making up social media — consist of the messages, feeds, and emails that flow as social content is created, discovered, consumed, repurposed, and shared. I used the expression "connective threads" in the introduction: on the Social Web anyone can make something and put it out there. But if no one knows about it, how social is it? The updates, feeds, and emails — the connective threads — tell you to go look, that something new is waiting for you.

Taken together, these activity indicators become social content in and of themselves. They not only represent and carry information, in many cases they *are* the information. For example, consider Seesmic, a video conversation service. Using Seesmic, you create and post a new video or video reply, and instantly it's also pushed over to Twitter where people see the title of your video as if it were a post like any other. This secondary notice tells the participants in communities *outside of the one you are in right now* — in this case Seesmic — what you are doing at this moment, but somewhere else. *That is social content, just like any other post on Twitter.* This kind of information is what increasingly powers the Social Web, pulling people together and driving conversations, including those that you are interested in as a marketer.

As a more general example of the tools that make it easy to follow what's going on around you, consider FriendFeed. FriendFeed simultaneously aggregates, organizes, and then directs information about social content from those who create it toward those who want to know about it. FriendFeed provides pointers to nearly all of the content that those around you create — Twitter posts, Flickr uploads, and more.

Note: I have used Friendfeed in this chapter as an example of the services that simplify the use of social updates. Ping.fm and SocialThing are worth looking at too. If they're in beta, request a beta code from a friend. You can usually find someone in your Twitter following who can set you up with an access code.

FriendFeed: `http://www.friendfeed.com`

Ping.fm: `http://ping.fm`

SocialThing: `http://socialthing.com`

What's the benefit of a tool like FriendFeed to you as a Social Web participant? Instead of visiting a dozen places to see what someone that you may be interested has done recently, you subscribe to them via FriendFeed instead. When you see something new that interests you in the feed, you can jump directly to that content. Otherwise, if not interested, you just continue doing whatever you were already doing,

Through tools such as FriendFeed, Social Web participants are able to manage very large amounts of information: the updates literally flow to them, as they happen. As a marketer, you can efficiently follow the influencers that matter to you. It's a lot like fishing, but in this case the fish are jumping into your boat while you pay attention to more important things, as if there were more important things than fishing.

In the previous section, I talked about using tools that make it easy for you to keep up with the diverse activities of others. Using these same tools, you can also make it easy for others to keep up with you. By creating a feed of your own social actions, you can make it easy for your friends and followers (read "customers") to discover the content you are creating. Through social interactions and the messages that carry the information about what is going on across the Social Web, niche content percolates out through the Social Web and finds its way to the specific individuals who are interested in it.

Managing Social Information

Chapters 9, 10, and 11 were dedicated to "things" — virtual social objects such as networks, communities, photos, and conversations. That's the stuff that makes up the Social Web, right? Isn't that social media? Yes, it sure is — but it's only part of it. To be sure, social content matters — think for a minute about a post in a company blog relating to product safety. What matters as much or more than the post itself, however, is how that post comes to the attention of someone who needs or wants to know about it. The typical 20- or 25-year-old Millennial, no doubt an active member of multiple social networks, is also uploading pictures and videos, maintaining running conversations on Twitter, and monitoring a few dozen blogs and event sites for information on sports, music, films, and more. How do people keep track of this?

The common explanation is *multitasking* — the ability to perform multiple tasks or simultaneously divide one's attention between seemingly disparate, parallel activities. Multitasking is part of it, and a lot of Social Web participants do exactly this as they hop from site to site — or window to window — to see what's happened recently. Better, however, than "brute force" techniques such as individually checking a dozen sites each day or even tracking the specific updates that each site sends out is the ability to *manage* social information effectively. This means simplifying and making sense of a dozen sources information — each multiplied by the number of friends present, each of whom is also contributing their own content. That's a lot to keep up with.

Think back to Chapter 4, "Web 2.0: The Social Web." Most people live in a town with one or perhaps two newspapers, and probably some type of local entertainment publication. It used to be that when you wanted to know what happened yesterday — or was going to happen this weekend — you grabbed one of these papers and looked it up. Perhaps you checked with a local TV station or tuned into the local news radio. The point is that you needed to check with only a relatively small number of information sources to get a complete picture (or, at the least, as complete as you could get) of what was going on. Now, in the technical vastness of the future, there are hundreds, thousands, *millions* of *active* blogs, a good number of which reference news, entertainment, sports, and so on. What if they'd been implemented as websites instead of blogs? The analogy here is that a newspaper, like most websites, is an isolated, unconnected document that assumes *you* will be visiting *it*. It would be literally impossible to go out and monitor a large number of sites — and difficult to do so for even a small subset — on a regular basis to see what's new. So, you'd pick your favorites, and having done so *you'd be limited to whatever they knew about* and chose to share, just as *you'd be influenced by their opinion* regardless of the thinking of others around you. Blogs, thankfully, aren't implemented like that.

Instead, blogs are built around the idea of conversation, and use RSS to make publication and consumption efficient. As a result, you can subscribe to a lot of them: instead of one or two sources of information, you have 5, 10, 50, 100, 1,000 sources... it doesn't matter. When their authors post something new, RSS will see to it that you know about it. All you do is follow your subscriptions. RSS-aware tools like Google Reader make it a snap to keep up with lots of blogs and the hundreds of individual posts they contain.

The same concept applies on the Social Web. Instead of running about and checking each individual site of interest, savvy social participants set up feeds and then aggregate those into cohesive streams. Figure 12.1 shows how someone aggregates the social content of three friends and their activities across separate social sites into one easy-to-follow feed, in this example using FriendFeed. The same thing — scaled up — lets people aggregate hundreds of friends with activities spanning dozens of sites. Some take it one step further: they route subscriptions to their phone or handheld, reading and then tapping out a quick reply while on the go when something interesting comes their way.

What does this have to do with marketing? A lot, actually. To begin with, what you create on the Social Web competes with what everyone else is creating. If you think TV is crowded, consider that when you buy a spot, you at least have some degree of certainty that your audience will actually see it. With social media, there is no such guarantee. To be seen, your content has to be chosen, and that in turn means it has to be visible and that your audience has to know it exists. Beyond that, a lot of what you create is going to be modified or repurposed for presentation in some content form other than what you originally posted. Your awesome 30-second spot, repurposed for the Web, is going to come across Twitter as a simple text message that says "Check this out." That short message — limited to 140 characters in all — is what connects the rest of your potential audience to what one influencer has found worth sharing. Because your original information is condensed down into a short summary — "Just the facts, ma'am," as Sergeant Friday used to say — and because it is arriving with hundreds of other items, the recipient really needs to have a reason to notice it in the first place.

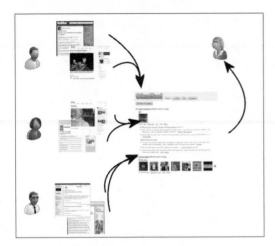

Figure 12.1 Feeds make following social activites simple.

Social standing — reputation — plays a role here. When your branded content is effectively wrapped in a plain brown paper, the social standing of the person who sent that content is the only basis that the recipient can use to decide whether or not to check out that content. Think about your well-meaning friends who routinely send emails with jokes: how often do you skip opening *anything* they send? On the Social Web, reputation is everything. It's not just the clutter you're fighting. On the Social Web, everyone, loosely speaking, is more or less equal. You'll find yourself competing with babies laughing and mispronouncing words like "spaghetti," or appearing to wield drums sticks to the beat, or talking in a deep voice with a Hungarian accent about world domination. Sometimes the babies win big, too, racking up a thousand times the views of your million-dollar spot. This is why building your own social credibility is so important.

All of this further suggests *not* using social media by itself. Social media is, in a larger strategic sense, a direct reflection of your business. Viewed this way, you might say it *is* your business. At a tactical level — where you are working here — the social media-based techniques that you decide to use are just one part of what is available to you for use in your overall, integrated marketing effort. The illustration in Figure 12.2 calls back to the holistic nature of social media and the importance of the marketing plus operations linkage. Applied, social media is an *accompaniment* to your existing awareness and point of purchase campaigns, not a replacement. Use TV, radio, direct mail, sports, and event marketing to seed the conversations, to set the expectations, and to create the beginnings of a demand. Then, like a 1-2 combination, tap social media and the conversations generated by direct *experience* with your brand, product, or service to reinforce your messages based on the genuine interest and comments of others.

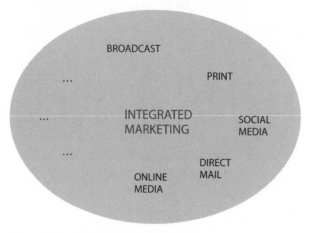

Figure 12.2 Social Media is but one component.

Understanding and using the social information flow that underlies all of this is becoming a fundamental marketing skill. Tap the Social Web and listen: understand your opportunities for improvement (and act on them) so that the conversation itself becomes increasingly favorable to you over time. Use social media to encourage and empower your evangelists so that they are more effective. These are the things you want to be doing: getting them done means keeping track of what is going on. Managing the information flows — for your own consumption — and understanding how others do the same to serve their own needs is key to fully engaging with your audience *and their friends* on the Social Web, and in the process to getting the most from your investment in social media. This where monitoring the feeds can really pay off. By using feeds to focus on influencers while at the same time paying attention to the larger conversation using tools like BlogPulse, Cymfony, Techrigy, or Google Alerts, you will stay in the loop. As a result you will find it relatively easy to guide your campaigns in ways that meet with public approval rather than rejection.

In earlier chapters, I presented social media tools, tips, channels, techniques, and other things that you can pick up and use in marketing. This week's work has a lot of that too, but as well includes several "survey" topics — things that may or may not be directly applicable to marketing but that you should know about nonetheless. The objective in presenting social interactions as a set of channels is to show you how the social content created through what I presented in the prior chapters increasingly finds its way to the recipients who will consider it when evaluating your offer. Some of this may not appear to tie directly to marketing, at least not at first. This is, however, an important matter, and in particular for marketers who may be used to being able to *direct* the message, for example through a paid channel and ultimately an interruptive experience. The Social Web doesn't work that way. This week's discussions and exercises show you why it doesn't, and instead how it does work.

Events and Calendars

The information in event listings and calendars is generally made up of discrete data — dates, times, places, prices, and similar — along with a description and detailed information about the event itself. The core information — who, what, where, and when — lends itself to a feed, to a stream to which people interested in specific events would subscribe. Turning back to the purchase funnel, there is an important distinction to note here between awareness and consideration: Building *awareness* often requires more than the "facts." The name of an artist and the performance date is generally not sufficient to pique interest in a new act that no one has heard of. A catchy name is as easy to come by as picking a character out of Dickens. A photo of the band is marginally better, a sound clip much better, and live video posted by a friend from prior shows is the best. Note the progression in the social components of the content, and the way in which that social factor helps drives real interest. Social content bridges awareness into the consideration phase — where social media is most effective. Combine this now with other information streams, for example, FriendFeed, Twitter, or a social calendar such as Eventful. If you know that your friends have a strong interest in seeing this new act, you may need little more than the date and the price to make a decision. In this case, you are tapping your friends collective knowledge, provided to you through the flow of social information, to support your own decision making process. Keep that in mind as you head into this next section.

In the consideration phase, the marketing challenge is often reduced in part to spreading the word based on what a small number of influencers in a social group may have stumbled onto. Subscriptions to what these influential friends are planning play an important role, as they can make it much easier for an extended group to keep up. The trick becomes getting people to talk about — in the digital sense — what they are doing. In fact, this too can be automated using socially aware applications, as listings of likes and dislikes can be generated automatically based on individual preferences as evidenced by choices and selections made through social sites. For example, Last.fm, a self-directed music service, will convey (with your permission) your recent musical selections and purchases to Eventful where this information can be used to guide what is presented to you.

Tip: You'll find Last.fm here: `http://www.last.fm`.

Shown in Figure 12.3, the Eventful service imports artists from popular listening services and then sends subscribers notices when those artists come to town. Because services like Last.fm themselves import — or "scrob," as they call it — music that you listen to through iTunes or Media Player in addition to Last.fm — your wider preferences in music become the basis for what Eventful is able to recommend. As a result, Eventful quickly figures out what you like and makes recommendations based on that. It may seem a bit weird or even scary at first: however, over time as you recognize that you and your friends are seeing more shows that you *like*, the benefit of these social tools becomes clear. At the same time, your decisions — and things you blog about as a result — make sharing your tastes and interests with friends as well as those who follow you online easier and therefore more likely. This is the collective at work (and at play!) through the social feedback cycle. This is a great example of individual preferences driving social content and ultimately commerce and, therefore, an example of how important being able to manage social information really is to marketers.

Figure 12.3 Eventful Imports and Notices

As a subscriber, event promoter, or artist, event feeds help you. Because feeds allow people to collect and manage information from a wide variety of sources, feeds can be of great benefit when trying to find specific information, or when trying to make others aware of it. This illustrates one of the challenges that marketers face transitioning from traditional or Web 1.0 online media to Web 2.0 and social media.

At the core of services like Eventful and Upcoming (now part of Yahoo!) is an information flow that potential customers can use when thinking about what to do, where to spend their time, and where to spend their money. As the amount of information in circulation on the Social Web rises, managing it and keeping abreast of what's happening gets harder. As noted, feeds summarize, consolidate, and carry and implicit social ranking (the events in many cases would not be included if you or a friend hadn't put them there) and in the process bring order to the social information flow.

MikonMixers: Real-life meetups made better.

Want people to meet each other faster at your next in-person meetup or event? Powered by the Mikons social drawing tool that helps people create and share personal icons, you can create sheets of iconic stickers specific to your event that attendees affix to their name badges. The stickers help attendees to quickly initiate conversations with others based on common interests and shared event themes.

http://www.mikonmixers.com

You can benefit from services like Eventful and Upcoming — as a marketer. You can use these services directly: make sure that your events are listed and that the listing is accurate. You can also use these services to plan or schedule your events. Eventful features a "demand" service shown in Figure 12.4. Eventful members interested in specific types of events can "demand" that a performer, show, or any other event come to their locale. You can use this to help sort out where the demand for your planned event might be highest and then build your event schedule around that.

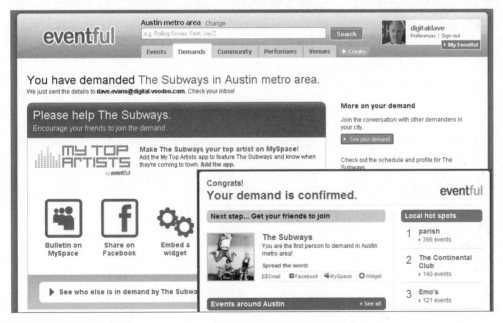

Figure 12.4 Eventful Demand

Tip: Don't forget: You can use these services yourself. Assuming you have a life outside of work (not always a given…) you can use all of the social channels presented in this book for personal use, and in so doing learn how to make more effective use of social media as a marketer.

Use the services you've seen here yourself. By signing up and using Eventful, or any of the other tools and services mentioned in this book for that matter, you can quickly gain experience. *Participating* will give you a first-hand perspective on what social media is all about and, thereby, make you better able to evaluate the tools likely to work for our business applications. Using what you've now seen — especially in a personal context — adds to your knowledge and gives you a jump start.

Monday's One-Hour Exercise

Today you're going to look at a cross-section of event and calendar services. Some feature a basic listing of events: this means you need to visit the site in order to see new listings. Others offer subscriptions to a feed or an email alert along with tools that generally help site visitors do more by more efficiently managing their information flow.

Spend the next hour visiting each of the following sites and answer the questions presented. Think of an artist or type of event that you'd like to see or go to and then try and find information about it on each of the following sites. You are, of course, free to look for whatever you want: make the exercise interesting and relevant to you.

Tip: This exercise isn't directly related to marketing: instead, it is intended to show you how various social management tools make it easier to find out about events that interest you. Consider using these tools as a starting point for your own exploration of social media.

For the next hour, visit the following sites:

- CitySearch (http://www.citysearch.com)
- Eventful (http://www.eventful.com)
- Upcoming (http://www.upcoming.com)
- The website for your local arts and events guide;
- Any other event or calendar site you'd like to visit.

As you visit these sites, consider and answer the following:

- How quickly were you able to find events?
- Was "sponsored" content presented? If so, how relevant was it to what you were actually looking for?
- How many pages did you look at in total? Was all of the information you needed presented on a single page?

- Which sites encouraged you to add your own ratings and reviews? Were the ratings and reviews of ordinary people presented more or less prominently than those of professional or celebrity critics?

- Which sites offered feeds or alerts?

- Which sites offered the ability to import your existing preferences related to the type of event you were looking for?

- How could you use the services you visited today to promote marketing events that you may be planning?

Monday's Wrap-Up

Having worked through the exercise today, you should see clearly that social commentary — reviews and supporting insight into the people who created it — is worth a lot when it comes to evaluating a choice. As well, being able to subscribe rather than having to come back and check makes it easier to keep up with what is going on. At Eventful, for example, if you search for "The Subways" you may or may not find information. The Subways may not be playing near you anytime soon. However, you'd be able to *subscribe to your search*. Even if nothing was found in your area today, when a listing for The Subways is added later, you'll be notified automatically, without having to come back and do the search again.

Today you saw examples of the way in which an individual's interests can be used to pull relevant information from the Social Web. This enables people to keep up with numerous, diverse content sources and therefore find the content that relates directly to the specific interests that they have. It is through the tools you used today and similar others that social content ultimately connects with the people — in this case, at live events — who really want it and who make purchase decisions based on it.

SMS and Mobile Communications

Yesterday you looked at events and calendars — services that tell you about things going on in the community around you. Today you'll turn it around. You'll be looking at services that operate primarily on mobile devices and let you tell others what you are doing — and where you are doing it — right now. As the notion of "community" increasingly shifts toward an inclusion of "virtual" — for example, the virtual community comprised of someone's friends at Facebook — it's a natural extension to combine the online and offline experiences. To be sure, you can always ask your real friends who also happen to be members of your favorite social network what they are doing this weekend. That is one way of linking online and offline activities and relationships. But what about people you know less well, or with whom you have only limited if any actual contact with even though they may be nearby and may share many of the same interests that you have? What about people *you want to meet*?

New, mobile social services are emerging that combine location-aware devices such as mobile phones with online social networking concepts like friending and privacy. The result is a network that combines online as well as offline behaviors. This happens informally on Twitter, a service you saw in Chapter 9, where I regularly see posts among the people I follow — for example, "Just landed in DC. Anybody want to get a coffee?" I've met more than a few friends from Twitter for the first time in person at ad-tech conferences this way.

Dodgeball is an example of the new mobile applications. Dodgeball, now part of Google, is a service oriented toward friends meeting friends, and one that let's you tell your friends where you are by posting a quick text message from your phone. Likewise, you'll be notified when they post their current location. Dodgeball helps you clue your friends in with regard to "knowing where the action is." Likewise, it helps them catch up with you as you roam from your office to a happy hour and on to a restaurant or a club. At the annual South by Southwest Interactive Festival in 2008, I used Dodgeball with friends and colleagues as I moved around Austin between conference venues. Each time I found a great party, I posted the location. Each time one of my friends found one, they posted that. Together, we covered a lot of ground.

 Tip: When considering the use of any of the mobile services—text or otherwise—be sure that you have a data plan for your phone that is appropriate given this increased activity. If not, you could be in for a nasty surprise when you get your next bill. I kid you not.

Brightkite, another mobile social service, takes the mobile social network concept one step further. With Brightkite, you "check in" (post your current location) by sending a quick text message: your friends with whom you have *specifically trusted* can then see where you are. You can post photos and share comments about that location, or arrange an in-person meeting, or "meetup." You can see some of my friends around the world via the Brightkite service in Figure 12.5.

Via these mobile, location-aware applications you can inquire about nearby business services. Sending "? Starbucks" as a text message after you've checked in at some location will instantly return a list of the closest Starbucks to wherever you happen to be right now.

As a marketer, compare this experience with Mapquest, one of the early leaders in location-based services. Mapquest offers many marketing programs and services: retailers can include the location of stores on its maps. Coffee shops, donut shops, casual dining restaurants, and electronics retailers have all used this. Although this works great on a device that reasonably supports a graphic interface, for many mobile users graphical interfaces simply don't work. By comparison, SMS/text-based services work on nearly every phone in existence. Even better, *text services are very fast*. You may be thinking that texting and SMS-based services will be replaced by better phone-based browsers. Try texting. It's so fast, and so easy that it is likely to be a mainstay medium for at least a while yet. By using Brightkite to locate the nearest Starbucks, you can be drinking a latte before Mapquest loads its first page. Sometimes less is more, and in the case of coffee, quicker is definitely better. Again tapping the collective, Brightkite has "seeded" its database with franchise and store locations; over time, as individual users check in and further define specific locations, the number and accuracy of listings will grow as the users themselves find and label specific physical points.

Figure 12.5 Friends Map on Brightkite

Tuesday's One-Hour Exercise

Today you're going to check out Dodgeball and Brightkite to get an idea of how people use location-based information services. Although you can obviously spend a lot more than one hour doing this, the exercise is focused on exploring a few of the basic features of two representative services.

Tip: To complete this exercise, you'll need an SMS/text-message-capable phone. Be sure to check your data plan: unless you have an unlimited or similar plan, you'll quickly discover that a la carte text messages are among the most expensive things you can buy with your phone.

During the next hour, you're going to sign up (if you haven't already) for Dodgeball and Brightkite. *The services are free: your messages may not be. This is your third and final warning.*

Tip: You'll find the sites for today's exercise here:
Dodgeball: http://www.dodgeball.com
Brightkite: http://www.brightkite.com

1. Sign up for Dodgeball and Brightkite.
2. Once signed up, go to the Brightkite website and log in to your account.
3. Check in on both services following the instructions they provide. In general, this is a simple process: You'll send a text massage like "@ street address" to the SMS number they provide.
4. Using Brightkite, see where you are after you check in.
5. If you have friends using Brightkite, add them: after they've accepted your friendship request, you'll be able to see where they are. (You may or may not be able to complete this part today.)
6. *Using your phone*, send a "? Starbucks" or similar request via Brightkite — note the response that comes back and how simple this is to use.
7. Go and enjoy a cup of coffee with your friends.

Tuesday's Wrap-Up

Today was a survey exercise: you took a very brief look at location-based services that connect people and link online and offline communities. The objective was simply to experience them and how they are used — to participate, however briefly, in the kinds of services that people spending time in social applications are using to meet up with each other, share information, and build more-durable relationships. Now that you are signed up, look for other ways to use these services. Again, the best way to understand the Social Web and social media is to participate.

Today you also got to see where location-based online marketing is heading. Rather than clicking through pages with sponsored locations that someone else wanted you to see, the services like those you looked at today allow you to quickly request the nearest location of the places you want to go and to quickly and easily arrange to meet up with your friends once there. As these kinds of services become more common — to be sure, they are still a bit new — creating an excellent experience so that your customers will take the few extra seconds to look you up rather than making do with whatever competitive service is nearby will become more important than ever. Read that last sentence again: as more complete information about competing options becomes easier to gather for purposes of making purchase decisions, the quality of the experience will gain in importance as the convenience of "I have a favorite, but this other place is nearby" ebbs.

Location-Based Marketing

In a decidedly real-world approach to location-based marketing, Applebee's locations outnumber Chili's by about 2:1. The strategy is evidently that wherever you are now, between you and Chili's is an Applebee's. Mobile services upend this: at your fingertips you now have the exact location of the nearest Chili's. Instead of driving around hungry and choosing Applebee's because you found it sooner, you confidently head straight for what you really wanted in the first place. More information — available when and where needed — leads to more genuine choices and less "making do." *This emerging mobile channel, as is the case with social media in general, drives product and service improvement.*

Status Notices and Bacn

Just how much wood could a woodchuck chuck? I have no idea, but if the varmint had a Facebook account, we'd all know the answer. People can and do post the strangest things in response to common social networking questions like "What are you doing right now?" "Chucking wood," says WoodChuck264.

On the Social Web, questions like "What are you doing?" are conversation starters — they get people talking. Whatever it is that people are doing right now, they post it and send it to their friends, through feeds or status updates. The thinking is that if you see a friend doing something that interests you, you'll respond with something like "Hey, I'm doing that right now, too." The result is a conversation. When someone makes a change to their account or adds a new application or makes a product recommendation, the fact that they just did that is often sent to their friends who can then act on this information, joining in the process and further spreading the underlying message.

Bacn, anyone?

Pronounced "bacon," *bacn* signifies the "email you want, just not right now." Think of bacn as being "better than spam." In the email world, there are the emails you know you don't want (spam) and the emails you know you do want, like the email you received from Google telling you they are interested in acquiring your new start-up. In between these two are the emails you've asked for but don't need to open right now: travel alerts, sale notices, and subscription updates. Added to this is the relatively large number of messages arriving in the Inboxes of the socially active: update notices from Facebook, friend requests from MySpace, follow notifications from Twitter, Brightkite check-ins, and many more. These are all examples of bacn.

How does bacn tie to social media? Put simply, bacn is the carrier of a lot of what happens on the Social Web. Bacn plays a social role by keeping you informed as to the activities in your various online communities. This in turn helps keep you involved, which is of course what drives these communities.

 Tip: One of the recommended best practices for the socially active is the use of Inbox filtering: setting up rules to automatically route bacn to a specific folder. It's easy to get a hundred social updates in a day. Even when it's bacn, that's still too much of a good thing. Route it off to the side and deal with it later.

Status notices are useful in a social context, especially so when they reflect things relating to what you have done — for example, posting new content, sending invitations to friends, or installing new Facebook applications. Like the whole notion of "feeds" and the consolidation and management of social information that they allow, status notices help you keep tabs on what is going on. Consider LinkedIn: members get LinkedIn requests — "so and so wants to join your network" — on an irregular basis as they are driven by the actions not of that member but by those of people who want to connect to that member. By sending these notices, members are made aware of these requests so they can deal with them in a timely and convenient manner, improving the membership experience for everyone.

So what do updates and the issues around bacn have to do with marketing? For starters, the increasing number of status notices — many of which arrive via email — raises everyone's awareness of the increasing burden of email. Outright spam is, of course, dealt with largely at the door — for example, through a personal, enterprise, or ISP-based spam filter. Spam filters reduce the level of incoming email to a manageable level automatically. With the increasing use of subscription services, networks, and similar — many of which send regular updates as activities occur — the number of inbound emails is creeping back up. As a direct result all of your email communication — sales notices, order tracking, new product announcements — will come under increasing scrutiny as the number of "status notices" coming from everyplace increases. Given the impact of status notices and other forms of bacn, it's evident that everything you do needs to be more relevant, more impactful, and in general more about *the recipient* and less about *you*.

> **Tip:** If you are shipping bacn, be sure that you think through the actual content and how it will be used. Getting a note that says "Some event just happened" that lacks a direct link to the action point—for example, a URL where whatever just happened can be seen and acted on—is maddening for the recipient. It's a lot like a voice mail that says "Hey! Important news! Call me."

Email Management

If you've got a pile of email sitting in your Inbox, you're not alone. Countless methods and practices espouse the virtue of reducing your Inbox to zero (nothing unread, nothing laying about waiting for action.) One of the most useful and practical books I've found is Mark Hurst's *Bit Literacy*. I reduced my Inbox to zero in the spring of 2008 and have held it there since: it's an amazing feeling.

Wednesday's One-Hour Exercise

The exercise today is about awareness: specifically, your awareness of how much bacn others are sending you. Getting a handle on how much bacn is really coming your way — I can almost assure you that you will be surprised — will raise your awareness of what your communications look like to your recipients. In particular, as you raise your social activity level while working through this book, you will gain an appreciation for today's exercise.

Using your own Inbox, look through all of the email you received last week. Using a tally sheet, mark off each item according to one of the following:

- Urgent: Read right away and acted on to the extent possible
- Important: Read, acknowledged, either completed or results in a new "to-do list" item
- Not Important: Filed; perhaps read, perhaps tossed
- Spam: Anything routed to your junk or trash that you never actually saw

> **Tip:** With regard to spam, you may need to look in your Junk folder and Trash for these items. If spam is automatically removed by your enterprise email system, skip this tally and focus on the first three instead.

When you have completed your tally sheet, add up the totals in each group. Then divide each of the subtotals into the total and compute the share of email in each group. For example, 87 spam emails out of 146 emails is about 60 percent. You may want to repeat this exercise once a month. As you become more active on the Social Web, the group marked "not important" will grow relative to the others. As a further extension of this exercise, repeat it, but this time do it at home, using your personal email. Compare the results.

Wednesday's Wrap-Up

Today you looked at the number of status notices, alerts, and similar emails *that you have asked for* in relation to the email that you know you must act on. Compare the percentages and think about the implications: chances are, the "not important" emails account for the biggest share, even after the spam has been removed. As your days get more demanding — as your need to be ever more efficient about how you manage your information grows — what are you going to cut out? Chances are it won't be the Urgent/Important email.

This same situation exists for your customers and potential customers. They too are swamped with information, and they too will need to prioritize what gets attention — and what doesn't — if they aren't doing this already.

Feeds

As you've been working through the exercises this week, it should be clear that in addition to creating and posting content — even to the extent that this is only done by a minority of Social Web participants — the task of keeping up with it all is significant. Further, this is a task that falls to everyone with more than a few friends. Quite seriously, dealing with bacn — simply knowing what to look at or what your friends have recently done — is a real challenge. Perhaps ironically, people are looking for ways to streamline the information that is being sent their way *even as they simultaneously choose to expand their social circles.*

Using Feeds to Monitor Twitter

Pete Blackshaw has integrated a Twitter feed on the site that supports his newest book. The twist that you should note is that Pete's feed, shown here, extracts *only company data* from Twitter. Instead of the normal personal conversations, this feed is exclusively "company posts." You could use this same technique to create an internal intranet-based Twitter feed that follows your competitors, and keeps everyone in your business current on competitive activity within this channel.

FriendFeed, shown in Figure 12.6, builds on this concept to make it easy for your friends to keep up with you. Rather than aggregating the content created and placed by others, FriendFeed aggregates your content — across the social sites that you participate in — and then makes it available to those who have subscribed to you. Through FriendFeed, people can publish a single stream that contains pointers to their content as it changes. Social media (specifically, content and actions) is thereby diffused through the Social Web, always being pulled in the direction of relatively more interest.

Figure 12.6 FriendFeed

Thursday's One-Hour Exercise

Today you'll spend time with FriendFeed. Beginning in Chapter 9 and continuing in Chapters 10 and 11, you've been signing up for and using social sites. You should have accounts now at places like Facebook, MySpace, LinkedIn, Twitter, Flickr, YouTube, Seesmic, Brightkite, and a half-dozen blogs and support sites. Using FriendFeed, you're going to create a single feed that consolidates your activities across many of these sites. With that done, people who are interested in what you have posted can subscribe to a single feed and be notified when you post anything new on any of the sites you've added to FriendFeed.

If you have accounts and have content posted to sites that you can use for this exercise, then proceed with the exercise. If you have or are about to set up personal accounts at the sites suggested, go ahead and do that now and then come back to this exercise.

If you'd rather subscribe to my feed, then complete steps 1 to 3 below and then check my FriendFeed feed periodically to see what I am up to. When you have ultimately set up your accounts, come back to this exercise and connect them to your FriendFeed account as well.

For the next hour:

1. Go to FriendFeed: http://www.FriendFeed.com.

2. Create an account.

3. Search for people whose activities and content you'd like to keep track of (search for "Dave Evans" to find me) and add them to your subscription list. You will now see the activities of these people.

4. Using the Services menu, add the services (social sites) that you have established to your feed. These people will see your activities.

5. Create an imaginary friend — this is a special friend at FriendFeed that allows you to track people who aren't themselves part of FriendFeed. Using the Imaginary Friends feature, choose a Flickr profile, for example, associated with a competitive firm that you are interested in and add this profile to your Friend-Feed. Even though this profile may not itself be a part of the FriendFeed service, you can still monitor activity via FriendFeed.

Thursday's Wrap-Up

Today you set up an account at FriendFeed. The objective was for you to see how people can easily manage the diverse activities of others on the Social Web, and how you can make your own activities easily accessible to others. From a marketer's perspective, the take-aways from today's exercise are the following:

- It's relatively easy to keep track of the activities of a large number of friends using services like FriendFeed. You can use this to track competitors or other content sites that interest you. Using FriendFeed's Imaginary Friend service, you can track the activities associated with profiles that are not members in FriendFeed.

- You can make it very easy for your customers to track what you are doing: simply offer a link to your FriendFeed profile and encourage them to subscribe to it.

Between these two applications of FriendFeed and similar services, you can significantly reduce the amount of effort required to keep up with what's going on the Social Web, and in the process make it easier for your customers, vendors, and suppliers to keep up with you.

Social Information and Marketing

In addition to social platforms and content, both of which are likely now finding an application within your marketing program, you have an additional set of capabilities that will help you track and manage social information. This week you worked through calendars and event listings along with mobile services through which you can connect virtual communities with things going on in real places. You looked at the issues around bacn and what it means for your current email programs, and finally at the use of feeds that allow you and others to consolidate large amounts of social data into very manageable streams. Taken together, the sources of information that define the happenings on the Social Web are as integral to social media as the content and networks that make up the more visible aspects of the Social Web.

As you're thinking through the application of social media in your marketing program, the challenge is to think beyond the photo or community or campaign: the challenge is to think through the entire life-cycle of what you are putting in place. At its core, the Social Web is all about relationships, and relationships take time — and information — to build.

Social Media and the Development of Relationships

Just as relationships take time to build, how you manage and end them is equally important. In traditional media, using a third party to build and manage your online ad programs is common. So to is running a campaign for a limited time period and then abruptly ending it.

On the Social Web, it's different. Yes, you can use third-party providers. But at the same time, it's essential that you stay involved: you are building relationships that will be associated with your brand *long after your campaign has ended*. Think about the campaign itself and about the end of the campaign: If there is a defined end-point, tell participants upfront. If their community simply "closes down" without warning, they are likely to experience this as betrayal and will then talk about it as such.

Don't write a check and walk away: get involved and stay involved. Think through the entire life cycle of your social media programs.

By participating, by using feeds, by connecting your virtual events to the real world and involving the *people* who make up your audience, you can build strong meaningful relationships over time, relationships that will in turn help you build our business.

> ## Featured Case: Vespaway
>
> In 2006, Vespa created and then terminated its "Vespaway" blog campaign. The campaign was great: it was transparent, it was engaging, and it was popular. Unfortunately, it was also abandoned, left to die a slow death, giving rise to what ClickZ Network then-editor-in-chief Rebecca Lieb called "derelict blog" syndrome. It was shame to see participants, who once powered the blog, slowly lose interest when they realized they were no longer supported. They turned negative, and the results are now forever captured in the Internet Archive's Wayback Machine. Preventing derelict blogs is easy: Craft a plan to continue the campaign if a real community takes hold, or set the expectation in advance that this effort will end at some point. Either way, have a complete life cycle plan.
>
> You can read more about this campaign and see the derelict conversation in my related ClickZ article here:
>
> http://www.clickz.com/showPage.html?page=3628705

Friday's One-Hour Exercise

Today you're going to go back through the services you looked at this week and sort out which fit, and how you can use them. The same caveat applies here as in earlier exercises: if you're reading through the book, or aren't actually working with a real brand product, then you'll have to tackle this last exercise theoretically. Otherwise, work through the following and note the results in your developing social media marketing plan.

- What events have you planned that could be listed and promoted through a service such as Eventful or Upcoming? If you added a link to Eventful's Demand It page, could you build a schedule around that?

- How can you use location-based services? You've probably seen the Wi-Fi "Warchalking" signs shown in Figure 12.7. Look at the symbol at the bottom of Figure 12.7: that one doesn't actually exist, but it should. What if you owned a café and posted that symbol on your door or on table tents, next to your Wi-Fi markers? Would more people remember to use their mobile phones to tell others to come and join them? You'll never know until you try.

- Finally, how can you apply feeds? As you look across the channels you are considering, how many of them have frequent updates? What if you create a feed and promote it on your website so that people easily follow all of the things you are doing as they go and look at what interests them?

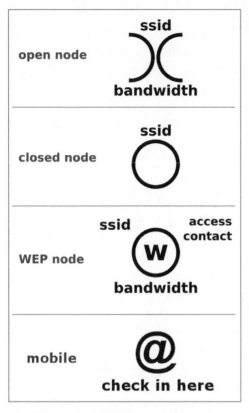

Figure 12.7 Mobile Warchalking

Warchalking: Early Social Media

Around the turn of the twentieth century, *hobos* (the men and women who traveled by rail seeking to find work) developed a code of ethics and symbolic language to make life on the road a bit easier. The symbolic language, typically drawn using chalk or charcoal, told others who were following what to expect. A triangle with hands meant "homeowner has a gun." Other symbols indicated dangerous dogs, hostile police, or fresh water and campsites.

This hobo language gave rise to the Wi-Fi warchalking marks that are used today. Interested? Read more at Wikipedia under "warchalking."

Friday's Wrap-Up

Three things should come out of your work this week. First, a lot of content is floating around the Social Web: You've seen some of the tools and services that help people manage it. By making the information about the content (the update notices, for example) more accessible, the content itself becomes more accessible. Second, mobile access to the Social Web is changing the way that people use online and offline communities. Someone can be sitting in a coffee shop, in the physical context of one community (the other people sitting around) and be equally present in a virtual community (those connected by virtue of the network). This happens frequently at conferences: Twitter, used as what social media and Web 2.0 change agent Ynema Mangum calls the "visible back channel," can beneficially shape or outright interfere with the actual conversation happening on stage by merging — very visibly — the conversation of the audience with the conversation of the panelists. Finally, the amount of information coming off the Social Web — update notices and status reports — is putting increased pressure on your existing communication programs, and especially email: the more email that comes in, the more likely people are to filter aggressively.

What all of these have in common — especially when you consider the idea of creating a feed to represent or point people to your social content — is that the way in which marketers must now approach messages and creative elements has changed. The typical TV or print ad is not meant to be manipulated by the recipient, nor is it intended to be shown in any form other than its original. On the Social Web, both of these presumptions fail. Social media belongs to the recipients the minute it leaves your hand. In the case of the feed data, while your content — for example, a product shot uploaded to Flickr — won't necessarily change, the description in the feed — which certainly will change — may be all that the recipient ever sees. How do you get your message across in that case? *By creating a delightful and durable experience.*

You've worked through each of the elements of the Social Media Starfish. Thinking back to my opening question in Chapter 8 — "If you couldn't interrupt me, how would you reach me?" — the answer ought to be getting clear.

Chapter 12: The Main Points

- By combining social knowledge with real-time presence, mobile social applications are changing the way people interact in real-world settings.

- Feeds make it possible for you to manage large amounts of information. You can use feeds to keep up with customers, competitors, partners, and suppliers.

- Feeds make it possible for your customers to keep up with you. As you create social content, consider adding a feed to make it easy to track and discover.

- Social media forces a rethinking of branded content: what does it mean when recipients have a hand in the creative and when the content itself is reduced to its purely informational state?

Month 3: Complete Your Plan

You've seen how basic techniques — touchpoint analysis and the integration of the purchase funnel and Social Web — can be combined with metrics to quantitatively indicate the degree of success of your campaigns. You've looked at individual channels — blogging, photo and video sharing, white-label and location-based social networking and more.

As you gear up for the final steps in developing your plan, the important best-practices come not from Parts II and III but from Part I: Campaigns will emerge on the Social Web that are counter to the long-term viability of social media–based marketing. How you choose to proceed — what you choose to do in response to others' questionable practices — will in large determine the availability of these important social channels for your future use.

IV

Week 1: Objectives, Metrics, and ROI

13

Walking into a ballgame, you'll often hear someone shouting "Programs! Get your programs! Can't tell the players without a program!" I can't think of a better analogy for this chapter: it's all about nailing down — in writing — what you are trying to do so that you know what to measure, so that in turn you'll know when you have achieved your goals. Knowing what to measure — and indeed what social media channels to apply — begins with your business objectives and your audience.

Chapter Contents
The Basis for Social Media Metrics
Choosing Social Media Metrics
Real-World Connections
Planning for Measurement
The Main Points

The Basis for Social Media Metrics

In any marketing program, it's usually safe to assume that the fundamentals of the program are at some level found in the business objectives of the firm or organization. For many marketers and the work that they do, this is in fact a valid assumption. However, it's not universally true. It should be. It may be that everything you do begins with a firm grasp or statement of business objectives. Just as likely, though, it may be that what you are doing as a marketer is actually distanced a bit from operations — perhaps by internal departments (aka silos), or control and ownership issues. The result is one or two degrees of separation between business objectives and marketing efforts. When applying social media, it is critical — and perhaps more so than with traditional marketing — that your business objectives and social marketing efforts be tightly linked.

Why? Think back to your touchpoint map and the social feedback cycle. Each marketing touchpoint — recall the airline advertisement speaking to on-time arrivals — triggers a conversation. So too, each operational touchpoint — recall the Chili's "to go" signage and separate entrance — results in a conversation that also follows the social feedback cycle. With traditional advertising and marketing, *you get to do the talking.* You get to tell your potential customers what to expect, why whatever it is that you offer carries value, and how your customers will benefit from choosing you over a competitor. If something goes wrong — for example, if an item is out of stock or a flight doesn't arrive on time — you can fix it after the fact by offering an apology, providing a future discount, or making some other similar gesture. The important point is this: not only can you make amends with your inconvenienced *current customer*, your next potential customer will still see your *original ad*, along with the original promise and implied benefit intact. With traditional media, preexisting brand or product issues aside, you are in effect always starting with a clean slate.

This is *not* the case on the Social Web. To be sure, you can make amends with a customer who feels wronged. It's also true that in so doing, that customer may tell others that you stepped up and addressed the issue, and the resultant word of mouth may in fact have a beneficial impact. But there again is the difference between social and traditional media: if you assume that this customer will tell others you fixed something, you've got to assume as well that any similarly disaffected customers (including any you may not know about) are also telling others that your *original* promise was *not met.* Unlike traditional marketing, where all potential customers see your original message, on the Social Web each successive wave of potential customers sees the actual experience of the last wave, at least to the extent that it is reflected in social media–based conversations. Your *first* customer hears "We have on time flights to New York." Your *second* customer, listening to the first, hears "They got me there late and I missed dinner, but they apologized and gave me a free flight coupon. They were nice about it, so sure, I'll fly them again." The second customer — as a result of that conversation — has a *different expectation* of your performance and, therefore, a different basis on which to evaluate a purchase or competing offer than did the first.

You are no doubt saying "Well sure, but that's a rather negative example. What about positive examples? What about flights that get in early?" Fair enough — flights do get in early, and positive conversations most certainly exist. According to Ed Keller of Keller-Fay and a recent Zenith Optimedia study, positive references outnumber negatives by about 7:1 in word-of-mouth conversations. One of the biggest reasons that you should be present in the conversations taking place via social media on the Social Web is to *ensure that these positive stories are told*, and that in the process the stories of the detractors are balanced or even negated. There is plenty that you can do to accentuate the positive, and do it you should.

That said, I'd also bet that your biggest challenge today is not looking at everything that is working perfectly and thinking about how great life is as a marketer! I'd bet that even if things are going well — really well — you are being pressed to do more, to deliver more traffic, to reduce expenses, and to improve margins, right? If so, I'd maintain that a lot of the gain you seek will come from improving what isn't working while taking care *not* to mess up what is in the process. So, yes, there is a proper focus on the "negative," or shall we say, the "opportunities to do better." That's why they call it "continuous improvement."

Define Your Objectives and Audience

What all of this adds up to is this: regardless of where your directives for *traditional media* come from, your directives for social media must be tightly coupled with operations-based efforts and your business objectives. This is a straightforward result of the basic social media dynamic that links experiences — not promises — with the resulting conversations and the development of your ability to *influence* these conversations. This linkage — shown in Figure 13.1 along with the conversations and resultant actions — is at the core of what social media metrics are all about.

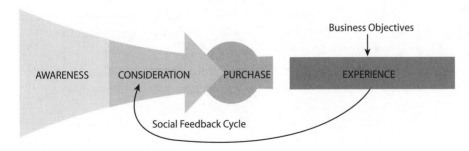

Figure 13.1 Objectives drive social media metrics.

On the Social Web, conversations are driven by actual experiences, which are themselves driven by operations policies and processes. Outside of conversations about your marketing campaigns — think "Subservient Chicken" and its impact on the Burger King brand — the conversations that directly drive sales are the ones that directly reference the things you sell. These conversations are rooted in product and service experiences. The corollary to this is that viral campaigns — especially those with conversations that focus on the ad rather than the experience — function much more like traditional media than social media. The ad may spread across the Social Web and that can impart a benefit, generally in terms of awareness. Awareness is a *traditional* media strength. Accepting that the conversations that really help you are ultimately based on what happens when people try your product or service means that your social media metrics must be linked to your business objectives.

So, before you start into a social media program, meet not only with your marketing team but also with your product managers, business unit leaders, and operations team. Review customer service calls and look at product returns and the issues that drive them. Talk to HR. Tie your social media objectives to the specific business objectives that drive improvement, and in doing so identify not only your choice of social media channels but also the metrics that will indicate success (or lack of) within those channels. Then — and only then — apply the social media-based marketing techniques covered in Part III as you work toward those objectives from a holistic marketing perspective.

Featured Case: Sony: Backstage101

Sony, working with social media provider Powered to market on social networks, placed interactive elements and widgets in these networks to create a branded experience within the community.

The branded experience, called Backstage101, centered on a social site that makes consumers smarter and creates engagement at the same time. Backstage101 is split into four categories: digital photography, digital video, home electronics, and personal computing. Not coincidentally, these categories line up with Sony products. From a consumer's standpoint, the connection to the brand is established through information that answers questions such as "What is HD?" and "What does 1080pi mean?" The program offers this type of information through a series of articles, flash tutorials, videos, and even free online classes. From a social standpoint, the site engages users by facilitating participant-to-participant interaction. As examples, participants can rate and review content, connect through profiles, and discuss issues through forums. For brands, structuring social programs around products can actually create a built-in measure of ROI.

Backstage101 has generated compelling results. Among them:

- Over 77 percent of participants are more likely to purchase;

- Over 62 percent of participants are likely to be "Promoters" as measured using the Net Promoter score methodology;

- Over 90 percent learned something they did not previously know about the categories;

- Nearly 91 percent of participants believe the program to be a satisfying experience.

There's a valuable lesson from this case for brands thinking about social media as part of their mix. Increasingly, social media practitioners are talking about a "build or join" decision around community and social. This case illustrates that a successful build effort should be accompanied by a compelling reason for a consumer to participate, especially when there are so many other social media choices on the Web. A way to create that "reason to participate" is to help a consumer spend smarter and be smarter about the products they own. To maximize engagement, the participants' experience should be built with a combination of practical and emotional rewards, such as learning (the practical benefit) and sharing that knowledge (the emotional benefit).

Behaviors that Drive Metrics

With your business objectives defined, next up is establishing the types of metrics that are both available to you (or could be) and that fit with your organizational or business culture. For example:

- If your business or organization is highly motivated by sales conversions, then tie your metrics into the pathway that leads through the purchase funnel to conversion;

- If your organization is all about visibility, then tie instead to the metrics that indicate your relative presence on the Social Web and its change over time within your specific audience.

In selecting your key metrics, it is equally important to think through the kinds of social activities that your audience — or various components of it — may be engaging in. Your audience may be actively *reading* blogs, but not at all interested in actually blogging themselves. These types of differences in behavior will certainly impact your choice in the activities you offer them and hence the types of metrics that are available for analysis.

Tip: In addition to measurements and the metrics you can identify and collect, be sure to tap resources like Forrester Research and eMarketer for baseline data and the trends that provide context to your quantitative objectives. Both Forrester and eMarketer offer a free newsletter in addition to subscription services. Featuring timely data and quick insights, both should be part of your regular reading.

eMarketer: `http://www.emarketer.com`

Forrester Research: `http://www.forrester.com`

What and Where to Measure

Measuring different aspects of social media allows you to evaluate what is happening at various points in the purchase process and on the Social Web, something shown in Figure 13.2. In the next section, you'll revisit the metrics tables from Chapter 7, "Influence and Measurement," and Chapter 8, "Build a Social Media Campaign." This time you'll select the metrics that are essential to you and then integrate them into your plan.

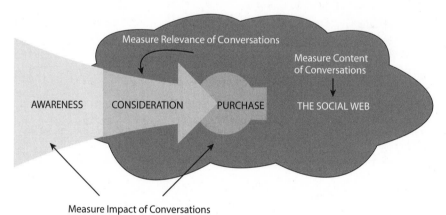

Figure 13.2 Metrics and the Social Feedback Cycle

Looking at Figure 13.2, you'll see various applications of metrics as they are collected at specific points. In the next section, I'll present various measurement points. You can use one or more, or all of them, to help build a robust measurement platform for your campaigns.

Tip: Because social media is a "moving target," you'll want to establish a baseline for each of the metrics you choose to collect and then track that metric over time. It is often the change — and not the absolute value — in a given metric that is important in establishing an ROI for social media-based campaigns.

The three types of metrics that I suggest collecting are those aimed at:

- **Quantifying *content*:** the social conversations and artifacts themselves.
- **Quantifying *relevance:*** the degree to which what is being said matters to you.
- **Quantifying *impact*:** the bottom line, the net benefit, the direct measure of the change in desired outcomes following exposure to a socially created and delivered message.

Just as social media is a complement to your existing campaigns, the metrics that apply to social media are a complement to your existing measures. For example, you looked at the purchase funnel and saw the social feedback cycle that links post-purchase measures of satisfaction and the likelihood of a positive recommendation. Recommendations and similar conversations are the drivers of what happens in the consideration phase, between awareness and purchase. The metrics that quantify them are just as much a part of your marketing program as rating points and market share.

Social Content Creation

The recommended starting point in gathering social media metrics is the Social Web itself. It's the most direct indication you can get with regard to understanding and tracking what is being said about you. If you measure nothing else, at least measure the relevant conversations as they occur on the Social Web. There are numerous platforms — I've talked about Nielsen|Buzzmetrics' BlogPulse and Cymfony's Orchestra platform. Techrigy and DIYDashboard and many others offer great tools as well that are geared toward the measurement of online conversations. Figure 13.3 shows the Techrigy Social Media Dashboard. Of course, you are always welcome to build your own. Beginning with tools such as Blogsearch and Google Alerts, you can go a long way toward gathering and tracking useful social data.

Beginning with content measurement has the nice added benefit of setting you up to *listen* to what your customers are telling you. If this is your first marketing effort outside of traditional media, this can be an especially insightful starting point. One of the most valuable aspects of the Social Web for marketers, and specifically with regard to the role of social media, is in its ability to provide a clear, detailed picture of what it is that the people who matter to you are saying about you and what they are telling others. There are an estimated 3.2 billion word-of-mouth conversations, worldwide, *each day.* About 2.3 billion reference a brand, product, or service, either directly or through a reference to associated advertising or media. The absolute number of conversations that reference *your* firm or organization directly may be small — but if you expand what you are listening to so that it includes your industry, suppliers, competitors, and customers, you'll find that a larger conversation is surely happening one that is definitely worth hearing.

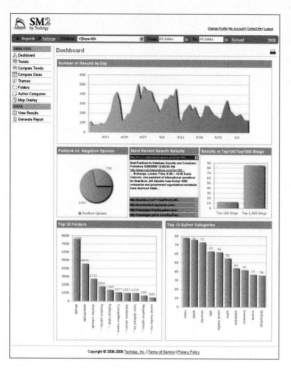

Figure 13.3 Techrigy Social Media Dashboard

 Tip: Attention B2B marketers: The potential for using the Social Web to follow not only your firm and your competitors but also your suppliers and customers is huge. They may not be hanging out on MySpace (or, depending on your industry, maybe they are!) but they are on the Social Web. Look for the communities that support them. Participate, pay attention, and take notes on what you find there.

One of the easiest ways that a listening program built on the Social Web can be started is by setting up and running private learning communities. Think of these as a sort of community/focus group hybrid: a place where a dedicated group — usually composed of a few hundred people — is regularly consulted *in situ* on a range of issues that often have relevance to marketers and product developers. Although these are not Social Web communities per se — they have been formed by design and are maintained primarily for purposes of research — they do represent a significant source of knowledge and are great step up from one-off focus groups. Firms like Communispace specialize in these types of listening applications. You saw two examples of Communispace applications, one for Hallmark in Chapter 3, "What Is Social Media?" and another for Glaxo Kline Smith in Chapter 5, "The Social Feedback Cycle." Naturally, these types of listening applications provide detailed metrics and are well worth your consideration.

Relating Social Content and Specific Offers

It can be useful to gauge the relevance of specific social media channels as the conversations they carry enter the consideration phase of the purchase process. By *relevance* what I mean is the degree to which the conversation helps a potential customer *relate* to your particular offer. This kind of measurement can be helpful in prioritizing social media channels. In prior sections, for example, I referenced the application of social media and *listening* to B2B marketers. Social media is applicable to suppliers and partners right along with customers and competitors. You are probably interested in what your customers are talking about if your business objectives center on boosting sales. Alternatively, if you are looking for a competitive advantage, you may find the conversations between your suppliers and partners to be valuable.

    This same sort of thinking applies to essentially any listening application involving social media. In all cases, you'll want to track the references to specific terms, or mentions of specific sources, as they show up in the conversations that your customers are having. For example, in order to locate the most useful social applications from the perspective of your customers, you need to know what they are participating in. This can help you to design and guide your own social media campaigns as well as provide insight into some of the marketplace dynamics that drive your business.

The Ultimate Goal: Conversion

Finally, social media can have a pronounced impact on the standard purchase funnel. In Chapter 5, I offered the following tip:

    To recap, if the Social Web is full of beneficial conversations about what you offer, you'll need to do less than you would otherwise to get a potential customer across the goal line and talking about you. If the Social Web is working against you,

you will have to work harder instead. You can actually tap your basic purchase funnel dynamics and use them to gauge the impact of your social campaigns, often without collecting any data beyond what you are collecting now.

Consider the assessment of effectiveness for traditional ad spending. By comparing changes in awareness with changes in conversions at the point of sale, classical marketing analysis draws a relationship between the spending required to achieve certain levels of awareness and certain levels of consumption. You've likely gathered (and will need to gather *before* launching social media campaigns) a reasonable base of just this type of information. You probably already know how changes in awareness drive changes in purchase behavior. You know the lower limits of "enough awareness," in other words the lower limit of ad spending below which the impact is roughly the same as not advertising at all, as well as the upper spending limits above which saturation occurs and incremental sales per dollar spent begins to slow or even drop. Between these points, if you've got the data, you can draw a fairly robust *baseline* relationship.

Enter social media. Beneficial conversations on the Social Web have a neutral to positive impact on the conversion rates for the portion of your audience that comes into contact with them. This, by the way, is why it's so important to establish both your business objectives and your audience behaviors *before* you start your campaigns. If you're all over YouTube — but your audience isn't — then your viewership metrics are meaningless and your business gains will be minimal at best.

Choosing Social Media Metrics

In the previous section, I presented a basic approach to the design of your social media metrics: Begin with your business objectives and the capabilities or social media-related behaviors of your intended audience. At the macro level, you looked at content, relevance, and resultant impact as a primary guide in what you want to be measuring. If you're starting out, focus on content and get a firm handle on what (if anything) people are saying about your brand, product, or service. If you've got a blog, or a basic support forum or community, if there is evidence of a meaningful conversation about your offer, focus on the consideration phase or your actual conversions and look for the impact of social media.

In the next section, you'll put all of this together as you define your starting set of social media metrics. Look at Figure 13.4. Recognizing a bit of a chicken and egg scenario, the logical flow of social media-based content that I'll assume — and the metrics that stem from that flow of content — begins on the Social Web with the *content* itself, with the conversations that are of interest to you. This is, essentially, a listening approach to collecting and tracking metrics: they talk, you listen, and then track the changes in what is being said over time and evaluate how it helps or hurts you. Your study of metrics continues with the *relevance* of this content and its entry into your world at the point of consideration: How are these conversations being used? Are the conversations central to the benefits of what you offer? For example, are people specifi-cally calling out a product feature that your competitors don't have, or one that your product lacks — or is the conversation more generic, more focused on the industry as a whole? The former tells you that your overall message — or that of your competitor — is getting through. The latter says, at least as viewed through these conversations — that either you have a "me-too" or undifferentiated product, or you are operating in a low-interest segment. *This is still very useful data:* it provides guidance on how to market. Your social media metrics help quantify the ultimate *impact* of these conversa-tions on the purchase funnel: the changes in conversion rates that result when social media — and with a bit of luck and lot of good planning, *beneficial* social media — is applied in a marketing context.

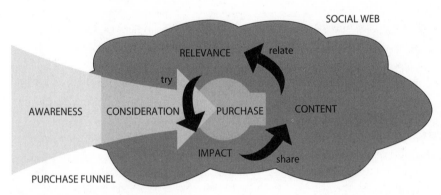

Figure 13.4 Metrics and the Social Feedback Cycle

Metrics in Motion

Social media metrics are evolving as the discipline of social media marketing evolves and the drive for robust metrics across a range of marketing and advertising applica-tions intensifies. As a result, developing a solid metrics base for your activities often involves a combination of well-understood data — for example, the time spent on your company website — along with trends that you develop over time based on the wider range of data available to you. This underscores one of the keys to establishing a solid quantitative base: measure and collect more than you think you'll need, and then dig into the trends you observe. In so doing, you'll uncover the key relationships that that matter in your particular business and your use of social media.

Content Metrics

Beginning with the metrics associated with Social Web content, Table 13.1 shows the relationship between *content* measures aimed at quantifying your audience — who is talking about you and your industry, and what they are saying. If you only do this much, you've made great use of the Social Web and social media. The metrics that you can collect will be used to indicate how the total of everything else you are doing — including the actual delivery experience — is perceived.

You can use this data strategically to isolate the contributions of your evangelists as well as the fallout from your detractors. Of course, you can also use this data in a highly tactical way (for example, to prioritize product improvements or schedule your response to competitive moves). Note as well the return of the Net Promoter score: while the actual Net Promoter score methodology involves directly questioning your audience and applying a specific ten-point scale, phrases that you can pick up and measure on the Social Web that begin "I'd highly recommend…" can certainly be used as a directional indicator in assessing the overall health of your brand. As well, you may find your own promoters being picked up on the Social Web.

 Tip: Do not skip the formal Net Promoter score, as presented in Chapter 7, in favor of an abbreviated assessment. You will not get the reliable data that you need in regard to this foundational social media metric unless you adhere to the methodology presented in the "The Ultimate Question."

▶ **Table 13.1** Content Fundamentals and Metrics with Suggested Sources

Fundamental	Metric	Source	Reveals
Audience	Blog Posts for Brand, Competition Product or Service Recommendations Tweets and similar Widget Views	BlogPulse, Google Alerts, Cymfony, Techrigy, Blog-search, Technorati Net Promoter Social Media Platform Provider	Who is talking about you; What people are saying about you and your industry

The collection method you use can be as simple as tracking Google Alerts, for example, and then making note of the source of the content referenced in the alert. This kind of analysis, though it may be a bit labor intensive, needn't cost you a ton of money.

 Tip: Consider using an intern if you approach the collection of data manually. The opportunity to explore the Social Web and extend some of the basic social media metrics tools aimed at content is rewarding and a great first step toward a marketing career. This can be beneficial to both you and your intern.

Alternatively, you can enlist any of a number of service providers to collect, distill, and report this data for you. Some of these service providers — in particular Cymfony — offer social media dashboards that include *offline* audience measures

in addition to online. By combining online and offline information, you can more effectively tie your social campaigns to your traditional marketing efforts. Cymfony's reporting module, listing online Hybrid conversations, is shown in Figure 13.5.

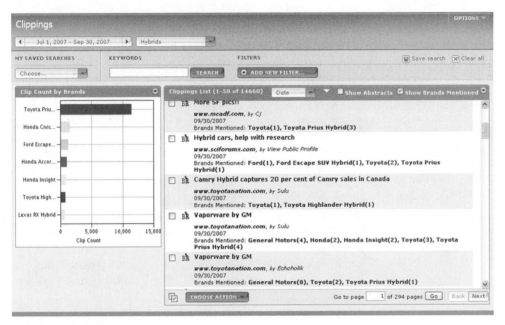

Figure 13.5 Capturing Content Metrics

Relevance Metrics

Continuing with the flow of content on the Social Web, the metrics associated with *relevance* — again, in the sense of social media experiences that link or *relate* the interests of potential customers with what you have to offer — are typically of interest to marketers. Although not perfect, the idea here is to link the metrics around the conversations on the Social Web that you covered in the prior section with the actual impact on your desired conversions, something you'll cover in the next section. Table 13.2 shows the relationship between the selected relevance measures that help quantify the contributions of social conversations in terms of influence, engagement, and loyalty.

Unlike the content metrics, many of the relevance metrics are associated with your own social media efforts — your company website, or other properties or assets for which you have access to the underlying analytical data. In evaluating relevance, what you are looking for in these metrics is an indication that the associated content is being used as a part of the decision-making process. You are specifically focusing on the application of these metrics and the weight given to the social media content as it enters into the consideration processes that support conversion. This can be a fairly subjective process, but even so it is worthwhile. As with nearly all social media metrics, the key is to track what you find over time. You will discover the elements that are most important to you and those that are most valuable in specific situations.

 Tip: Social media measurement is based as much on *heuristics* — using what is available to make the best of what you have — as it is more traditional quantitative and statistical analysis. Don't be afraid to go with your gut: your experience is worth a lot when it comes to making sense of these new channels.

▶ **Table 13.2** Relevance Fundamentals and Metrics with Suggested Sources

Fundamental	Metric	Source	Reveals
Influence	Time on Site Bounce Rate	Web Analytics: Google Analytics, Omniture, Web Trends	The value of the opinions and conversations to those interested in purchase.
Engagement	Pass Alongs Comment to Post Ratio Diggs, Stumbles, and bookmarks Podcast Listens and Views	Web Analytics, Google Analytics, Omniture, Web Trends, DoubleClick, Digg, StumbleUpon, Del.icio.us Feedburner	The interest levels in your message: Are customers willing to pass a referral along given a potential gain or loss of personal "social capital"?
Loyalty	Blog Posts for Brand, Recommendations Tweets and similar	BlogPulse, Google Alerts, Cymfony, Techrigy, Blog-search, Technorati	The context and intensity of blog posts. Are people sticking up for you? This can have a direct impact on whether or not this information makes it to the consideration process.

Impact Metrics

The prior sections — content and relevance metrics — covered information picked up by listening on the larger Social Web. This was then enhanced by gauging its relevance through the analysis of data available from social media tools that you may be using now (for example, a company blog or support forum). By taking an additional step — connecting the metrics associated with social media content and its relevance to the consideration processes *within the purchase funnel* — you can use the same tools you have in place now for measuring advertising and marketing effectiveness to assess the net impact of social media on your marketing program. Table 13.3 shows the relationship between content measures aimed at quantifying the impact of social media and indeed the entire social feedback cycle within your purchase funnel.

Fundamental	Metric	Source	Reveals
Audience	Referrers, Demographics	Web Analytics, Google Analytics, Omniture, Web Trends, DoubleClick	To whom your social media campaign is appealing.
Influence Loyalty	Time on Site Bounce rate	Web Analytics, Google Analytics, Omniture, Web Trends Repeat Customers	How involved your audience is with your message and brand, product, service as a result of exposure to social media
Action	Conversions Reviews Recommendations Tweets and similar	Web Analytics, Google Analytics, Omniture, Web Trends Reviews and Ratings Platform Net Promoter	The number of times a desired outcome occurs following exposure to your *holistic* campaign. Tweets or similar references to a definite purchase or action reveal this as well.

Looking at metrics from the point of the view of conversion impact brings the value (positive or negative) of social media home. When looking at your web analytics (for example, in evaluating your online commerce results, promotional offer uptake, or simply your incoming requests for more information), the first thing you want to establish is a baseline. If there is already some degree of social conversation happening then your current conversion measures reflects this. This is your baseline.

When you combine this with the additional historical data that you have around spending, awareness, and conversion, you can place bounds on the deviations from your straight awareness/conversion curve to account for competitive moves, economic conditions, and many of the other details that complicate the real life calculation of impact around any single media channel. Sure, this is a fundamentally empirical approach — that is to say, based on observation rather than hard science — but is nonetheless a valid approach. Precisely *because* it is empirical it has the nice side benefit of placing you in direct contact with the flow of social media and the data associated with it. The benefit of approaching metrics in this way cannot be overstated — especially for a relatively new discipline such as the use of social media in marketing — in an application where sales, market share, bonuses, and people's jobs are at stake. Take the time to work through the underlying metrics and build your baseline cases: this is, after all, the real show. This is not a dress rehearsal.

Real-World Connections

In the previous section, I presented the fundamental indicators and the associated social media metrics. The intent was to provide an explanation of how these metrics can be derived from conversational and analytical data. This is important because there is no social media sensor that you can wave over the Web to see what's going on — at least not yet. Instead, you have to measure what is visible, track it, and then derive the results based on what you see. In the next section I'll tie these fundamentals to five key areas of interest to most marketers: audience, influence, engagement, loyalty, and action. Within each of these areas, as shown in Figure 13.6, you'll see how the suggested metrics can be used to establish a baseline and then build on it as your social media program is put into practice.

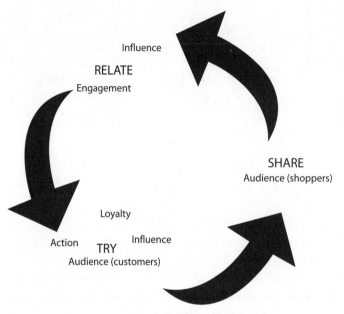

Figure 13.6 Connections to the Social Feedback Cycle

Audience

An understanding of your audience adds depth to the conversations you uncover by telling you who is leading them versus who is being led. What they are saying — the actual conversation — is only part of the story. Knowing who is saying it and who is listening gives you very valuable insight when planning your social media campaigns. By tracking not only the content but also its sources, you can pinpoint your influencers. The sources of conversations are available in most of the commercial tools referenced: this is a great feature to look for when selecting a metrics partner.

Taking audience measures one step further, once that audience arrives at your site — surely armed with whatever the Social Web offered up — what you are likely to be interested in is what they are doing. Here, you can turn to your own commerce or conversion analytics and supplement that with your web analytics (for example, referrer data which is good, but not always reliable) or tracking data from a third party like DoubleClick (which is much better) when and where applicable.

> **Tip:** Use audience measures to answer questions such as "Who are the influencers?" and "Are those they influence more or less likely than others to follow along?"

Influence

Influence, one of the key drivers of the interest in the use of social media in marketing, is present as a factor in both *relevance* — the likelihood that a conversation will lead someone to consider or reconsider your offer — and *impact* — the actual increase (or decrease!) in the likelihood of a purchase based on social media exposure. Influence is evident in two fundamental metrics that are easily obtained: time spent and bounce rate.

Time spent, as its name implies, indicates how much time people spend with your site, blog, or other online content that you maintain. More time spent generally correlates with higher interest: in the social sense, higher interest typically follows from an experience that has been relatively more influential. Think about this way: If a trusted source that you know to be a domain expert tells you to go and look at something, even if you don't understand *why* right away, you will tend to spend more time considering it, precisely because it's been recommended by a trusted source. That is influence.

> **Tip:** If you measure conversations that include strong indicators of active recommendations, look for increases in time spent at the destination point (e.g., your site or offer page).

Bounce rate is a sort of inverse indicator: generally, you want it as low as possible. Bounce rate measures the percentage of landing page terminations compared with all landing page arrivals. A bounce rate of 100 percent means that everyone who landed looked and split.

> **Tip:** More and more contemporary sites are built with AJAX and similar Web 2.0 technology that has a peculiar and significant impact on page views, bounce rate, and similar metrics that evolved in a Web 1.0 page-oriented context. A discussion of these technologies is beyond the scope this book, but do take the time to understand how your applications are built so that you can properly assign significance to the metrics you collect.

Unless your entire campaign is built on a single page and has no clickable call to action, the bounce rate is a clear indicator of arrivals who lost interest and moved on to some other search area or site rather than looking at your offer in further depth (i.e., clicking into your site). Like time spent, bounce rate is related to influence: higher influence in directing people to your site, all other things being equal, will lower the bounce rate.

 Tip: If you measure conversations that include strong indicators of active recommendations and your bounce rate is still high (e.g., over 50 percent) or is starting to climb, look at the landing page and check that the experience it provides is consistent with the likely interests or motivations of those arriving. If it's inconsistent, fix it.

Engagement

Often talked about but seldom grounded in hard numbers, engagement is one of the more elusive social media measures. Engagement, in the context of social media marketing means simply the degree to which someone feels attached to your product, brand, or service and the social media elements that are involved with it.

Engagement — or at the least, a very good surrogate for it — shows up in the consideration phase as *action taken*. Examples are the number of items sent to a friend and the comment-to-post ratio on your blog or those of others that reference your brand, product, or service. Send-to-a-friend actions are particularly good, as these indicate the degree to which someone spent enough mental energy to conclude that what you offer would be perfect...for someone else. If you are simultaneously tracking sources, then you can also get a sense for engagement as it regards *that source*. When you see a disproportionate share of traffic arriving from a certain site or community, you can conclude that a relatively high degree of engagement exists within that community. This is a point that Robert Scoble has made with regard to Digg. When your content generates Diggs, you get a lot of traffic. Digg is an engaged community. Look at Digg, StumbleUpon, and Del.icio.us as indicators of engagement for your own social media content. If you are using podcasts, look at the numbers of downloads using the great toolset available at Feedburner.

If you are maintaining a blog — or if you are evaluating a blog as a source of influence and interest in your content — the ratio between posts and comments indicates relative participation: More comments per post indicates that your audience is doing relatively more of the talking. That's generally good.

 Tip: Comment to Post or Post to Comment? You'll find this measure expressed both ways. While "posts to comments" is more popular, "comments to posts" is the measure that actually rises in value as the thing you are generally after — audience participation — improves. Either way, they both tell the same story. Be sure you know which measure you're looking at when talking about which way the needle needs to move.

Loyalty

Loyalty means spending time with something or someone on a repeat basis: coming back for more as a result of consistently choosing *this* over its competing alternatives. In the context of social media marketing and relevance, it means coming back to the point of consideration, moving consistently from the general conversations on the Social Web back to the social media-driven entry point into the purchase funnel. The more that someone is coming back to make or consider a purchase, the stronger the indication that this person has a relatively high degree of loyalty (or would be willing to develop a high degree of loyalty if you ultimately do your part). Once purchase intent is expressed, you can turn to things like cart abandonment, analogous in commerce to bounce rate in landing pages, and similar measures that indicate loyalty and ultimately conversion.

Repeat customers — and the conversations they provide through ratings, recommendations and reviews — are an obvious indicator of loyalty. Tracking an index based on your repeat customers along with what they are saying and then tying this to conversational metrics gives a forward-looking (i.e., predictive) metric with a timeline roughly equivalent to your sales cycle. How? Simplified, it works like this: if your sales cycle is 90 days and your typical repeat customer buys from you twice per year then when your repeat customer conversational index begins to dip, you can expect to see a magnified impact about two quarters from now. It's an early warning. You have 90 days to jump into the conversational data and find out what the cause is, and then develop a proactive response through a combination of efforts (for example, targeted email and social media) that are specific to your repeat customer base.

Action

Action is the bottom line: Did the conversion happen or not? Did social media play a role in this happening — or NOT happening? The most straightforward way to approach your development of action-oriented metrics is by looking at your conversion rates and comparing them with your benchmarks for conversion rates in the absence of social media. The best way to assess impact — and to get a handle on ROI (see related sidebar) — is to establish a robust baseline that describes the relationship between the marketing activities you are currently engaged in (spending levels, awareness, and sales, for example) and then compare this to what you observe as you introduce social media into the mix.

Many of the metrics you are likely to have at hand are related to both *conversion* and the number of people expressing *intent* versus the number who actually convert. Add to this the direct observation of social media: reviews, recommendations, posts on Twitter, and similar social forums, all of which provide guidance in understanding the role that social media is playing in driving (or dissuading) conversion. Look to your web and commerce analytics tools, your reviews or review platform, and of course to your Net Promoter score and its trend over time.

Assessing ROI

Fundamental to measuring or assessing ROI is determining what constitutes the return. You opened this chapter with the requirement of setting business objectives: this was no coincidence. You can measure conversions of nearly all types: subscriptions, purchases, requests for more information or a call, etc. Essential in developing a robust indicator of ROI is tracking all of this over time to measure the effectiveness of specific marketing activities as they relate to your business objectives. This gets to the heart of empirical measure. Ultimately, if you sort through the data you have — or could have — you can create a reasonable measure of ROI. Create a baseline for your current activities and a wide range of marketplace scenarios, and then use this data to separate the various contributions of specific marketplace efforts. As you introduce social media, look at the changes in what you observe, and from this make your case for ROI. As much as I'd love to say "just measure this," there is no single source for measuring as complex an environment as a marketplace. Data — lots of it — combined with your own skill and judgment as a marketer is your best way forward.

Planning for Measurement

Based on what I've presented in this chapter, the exercises this week will lead you through the identification of specific metrics — based on your business objectives — that are most useful in guiding your social media implementation. The exercises this week focus on setting objectives, evaluating the data sources that you looked into in Chapter 7 and Chapter 8. This week you'll be identifying a starting set of metrics to support your plan.

Featured Case: Jig-a-Loo: Grassroots Social Marketing

Jig-A-Loo is a silicone-based lubricant and water-repellent spray. It has been used in the commercial and industrial sectors in Canada since 1958. It was launched in 1998 to the Canadian mass retail market and launched globally in 2007. The campaigns' goals were to drive online awareness of Jig-A-Loo ideally resulting in consumer trial of the product and an increase in frequency of product use.

Fanscape's Grassroots department instigated strategic online buzz and fan activation in social online venues in 2008. The strategy behind Fanscape's approach was two-fold:

1. Focus on extremely targeted social media gathering places that would be responsive while tapping Fanscape's knowledge of the social media space and its relationships with site owners along with analytics tools such as Quantcast and comScore MediaMetrix.

2. Engage the target audience by presenting solutions to common problems that could be solved by the use of Jig-A-Loo *while being fully transparent with the messaging* as shown in Figure 13.7.

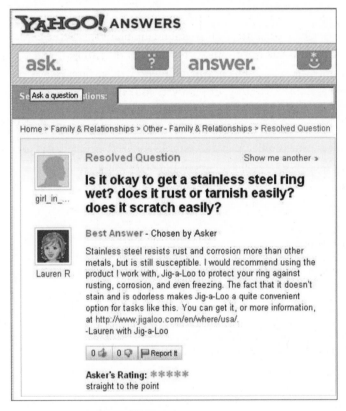

Figure 13.7 Jig-a-Loo Forums Participation

Monday: Your Business Objectives

Today you're going to spend an hour finalizing your business objectives. This is the opening exercise for the creation of the metrics portion of your social media marketing plan.

- Reach back to your exercise from Chapter 5, and look at the business objectives and success metrics you defined when you created your social feedback cycle. At the same time, pull together the larger business objectives that define your company or organization's success goals for the coming years.

- Connect each of your specific goals and success metrics set in Chapter 5 to one or more of your overall goals.

- Define each of the success metrics, and identify the source of the data that you'll need to support this metric.

Monday's Wrap-Up

Today you pulled your business objectives into your social media plan: this is the essential first step in setting up for success since it grounds your plan in the things that are valuable and as a result, actually drive your business. Don't worry that you haven't actually connected your business objectives to your plan yet: you will.

Tuesday: Your Audience

Now that you've defined your business objectives and established in them the basis for your social media campaign, today's exercise is all about understanding your audience. Knowing what they do online — reading, creating content, commenting or offering reviews, or doing nothing at all — is essential in developing a social campaign.

Featured Case: NBC's "Chuck"

Chuck is an American action-comedy television program created by Josh Schwartz and Chris Fedak. The series is about an "average computer-whiz-next-door" who receives an encoded email from an old college friend now working in the CIA; the message embeds the only remaining copy of the world's greatest spy secrets into Chuck's brain.

The supporting campaign, created and implemented by Fanscape, ran in two parts: an early creative build and a later online marketing effort. The overall campaign objective was to drive online awareness for the NBC series premiere of Chuck.

2007 Campaign: Creating a Social Presence

Fanscape created Chuckssecret.com, a Chuck online universe complete with every aspect of Chuck's personality and habits. The overall social campaign incorporated leading Web 2.0 sites through a series of "spokes," each designed to appear as icons on Chuck's desktop. These icons lead to real-world profiles of Chuck on sites such as MySpace, Facebook, LastFm, Twitter, Flickr, Stickam, YouTube, Geek2Geek, Ning, Delicious and more. Fanscape staff regularly maintained these 10 Web 2.0 properties for the fictional character "Chuck Bartowski," even sending regular tune-in reminders to friends who had subscribed. The site brought the character of Chuck to life

Featured Case: NBC's "Chuck" *(continued)*

and allowed viewers the opportunity to observe and interact with him online leading up to the show launch.

The graphic below and larger Figure 13.8 shows the Chuckssecret website sitting at the center of the social wheel: each of the spokes — the profiles and social presences created for the character "Chuck" — are shown around the central site.

The success of this approach was measured by the number "friends" and other WOM interactions (views, etc.) the profiles garnered (over 700 MySpace friends, over 300 Facebook friends, over 600 Twitter followers, 6,500 profile views on Stickam, 72 Last.fm friends with 30,000 profile tracks played) along with traffic to the website (74,000 visits).

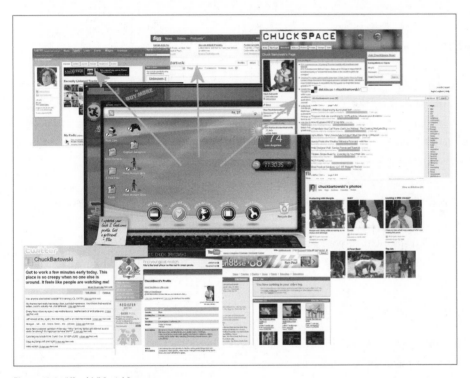

Figure 13.8 "Chuck's" Social Presence

Tuesday's One-Hour Exercise

Today you're going to pull together the data you need to make an informed choice about the social media channels that might apply. You are not going to pick them today; you'll do that in Chapter 14 when you make you plan.

In Chapter 9, "Social Platforms," I referenced *Groundswell* by Charlene Li and Josh Bernoff. The book takes a detailed look at the impact of social media and related technology, and the resulting transformation of consumers. Pulling from the extensive Forrester Research studies, they've identified fundamental consumer behaviors for various demographic groups. For example, they have separated people involved in content creation — making and posting a video or writing a blog — from those who would rather simply comment. They've identified active participants versus spectators versus nonparticipants. This is a solid framework for today's exercise, as well as for your regular use when mounting social media marketing campaigns.

Tip: An excellent — and free — profile tool that provides a quick snapshot of your audience with regard to its use of social media can be found at Forrester's Groundswell website:

`http://www.forrester.com/groundswell/profile_tool.html`

In addition to the Groundswell tools, the eMarketer newsletters referenced earlier in this chapter are an excellent source of high quality trend and behavioral data.

To complete today's exercise, do the following:

- Identify each of the audience segments — using standard age groups and demographic — that you are interested in with regard to your social media campaign.

- Gather internal data (or pull from your own knowledge) a picture of what each of your specific segments does when online.

- If you do not have this data — or if you simply want to check your data against the Forrester research studies — use the free profile tool found at the Groundswell website.

- For each segment in your audience, create a profile of the typical behaviors you expect: Are they content creators? Do they write reviews? Do they watch TV all day?

Tuesday's Wrap-Up

You now have a good handle on your audience and your business objectives. Keep this information in mind as you move forward this week.

Wednesday: Content Metrics

Now that your business objectives and audience behaviors are defined, it's time to look at the metrics open to you. Over the next three days, you'll work through the metrics that characterize conversations, the metrics that are indicators of interest and intent, and those that are directly associated with your purchase funnel. Each day, as you finish, you'll be adding one more set of metrics to your developing social media plan.

Wednesday's One-Hour Exercise

Today you're going to focus on conversational metrics: the things that define and indicate the intensity and polarity of what is being said about your brand, product, or service on the Social Web.

Today's exercise consists of the following items:

- Look back at Figure 13.1 and the definition of your audience and your business objectives. Confirm that there is something for people to talk about, and that the audience or audience segments you are focused on are themselves *likely to be talking about it.*

- List the specific features or unique attributes of your brand, product, or service.

- Create the same list, except do it for your competitors.

- Using Blogsearch, BlogPulse and Technorati, search for these items and write down (or summarize) what you find.

- Using Google, search for these same items on the Web and write down (or summarize) what you find.

- Trace the posts that you found back to their source. See if you can identify the type of audience member that contributed each item and ensure that you have accounted for this segment in yesterday's exercise.

When you have completed these items, integrate this data and its sources into the metrics section of your social media dashboard and report card that you created in Chapter 8. If you'd like to use this data to create your baselines for your selected measures, do so now. Otherwise, this should be your first action when you set up your metrics program and begin building your social media reporting tools.

Wednesday's Wrap-Up

The point of today's exercise is to create the beginnings of a baseline, and to validate the existence of conversations that reference the products and services you sell or offer. Importantly, you may or may not find your brand name or your specific feature. Very likely, however, you will find information that is useful to someone who is considering your product or that of a competitor. If so, and you begin to track it over time, you can develop a solid understanding of the things that potential customers are encountering when they are doing their online research. This can be very helpful in identifying other marketing opportunities, competitive advantages or disadvantages, and gauging the perception of your industry.

Thursday: Relevance Metrics

Today you are after the *connectors*, the metrics that help you link the relevant conversations on the Social Web with your actual conversion process. What you are looking for, as an example, is evidence that site visits resulted from an interaction with an element of social media. Clearly, you cannot do this in all cases. Unlike online advertising, where you can generally (and as a best practice) use tracking tags and similar tools, you can't always track directly the arrivals from a specific social media element and conclude that this visit was due to that exposure. What you can do, however, is tie the conversational metrics to your web analytics, for example, in cases where conversations are or should be driving people to your site. Similarly, you can track *pass alongs* — both inbound (people arriving via a direct referral) and outbound (people sending referrals to someone. Of course, if you *can* employ third-party tracking, do it. More data is better.

Thursday's One-Hour Exercise

To complete today's exercise, do the following:

- Look back at the conversational data you collected yesterday: does any of this reference your brand, product, or service? Is it positive or negative? Create a baseline that will help you establish a loyalty indicator.

- Look at your web analytics: do the metrics such as time spent and bounce rate exist? If they do, collect them and establish a baseline. If they do not, talk with your IT or web team and see if you can get them. Using the metrics you have, create a baseline for time spent and bounce rate so that you can track changes. These measures are surrogates for attributes like loyalty.

- To evaluate engagement and its contribution to connecting people to your offer, look at any metrics available to you that indicate a strong sense of participation or attachment: the number of send-to-a-friends (pass alongs), for example. If you maintain a blog, look at the ratio of posts and comments. Are people participating in the way you'd like them to? The same holds true for a particular blog that is important to you as a *source* of interest or traffic.

When you have completed these items, integrate this data and its sources into the metrics section of your social media dashboard and report card that you created in Chapter 8. If you'd like to use this data to create your baselines for your selected measures, do so now. Otherwise, this should be your first action when you set up your metrics program and begin building your social media reporting tools.

Thursday's Wrap-Up

By connecting the general social conversations with your purchase process, the measure of both the content and the content *source* relevance helps you prioritize your spending. Many of the dashboard products referenced include this data so that you can quickly see where it is that you should be spending your time.

Friday: Impact Metrics

Today you'll focus on the metrics that show the actual impact of social media where it counts: the conversion process. Whether you are asking people to try, buy or simply sign up for your newsletter, understanding the differences in behaviors between those who are exposed to social media versus those who are not is critical in tuning and maintaining your social media campaign.

Friday's One-Hour Exercise

Today you're going to do the following:

- Looking at your web analytics, review your referrer data. Add to this any applicable internal data you may have that helps you identify the arrival of specific audience segments.

- Again, look at the average time spent on your site and the bounce rate, but limit it to the commerce portions of the site and the informational pages that directly support commerce.

- Look at actual conversions, the number of reviews created, and recommendations. In short, look at anything that helps support the difference in people visiting your site with and without exposure to social media.

When you have completed these items, integrate this data and its sources into the metrics section of your social media dashboard and report card. If you'd like to use this data to create your baselines for your selected measures, do so now. Otherwise, this should be your first action when you set up your metrics program and begin building your social media reporting tools.

> **Tip:** The change in impact you observe can be positive or negative. If you are building a case for *fixing* something then one of the potential justifications for this effort is that the current conversion rates for those that have been exposed to social media is *lower* than for those who have not.

Friday's Wrap-Up

You've set your objectives, defined some basic behavioral parameters on your audience and its use of social media, and identified a core set of starting metrics. You are in the home stretch.

Chapter 13: The Main Points

- It is essential that you identify and clearly state your business objectives before deciding on specific elements of a social media program.

- The behaviors of your target audience are key in setting both the strategy and in identifying the metrics that will support your campaign.

- Conversational content can be measured, with the metrics leading to an understanding of who is talking about you and what they are saying.

- Metrics collected near and within your purchase process link the conversations to the actual impact on conversions. This is the data that can help you establish an ROI for your social media programs.

Week 2: Present Your Social Media Plan

This week you'll pull your plan together, collecting what you've developed in your prior exercises. You'll use this to define a set of social media–based components that build on your current marketing efforts. Whether starting with a purely listening approach like that of Hallmark or Glaxo Smith Kline, or with an integrated outreach program like the social campaigns of the Brooklyn Museum, this week you'll build your plan.

In this final chapter, you'll begin with your business objectives and a definition of your audience. To that you'll add your touchpoint and social feedback cycle, identifying your initial campaign goals. Based on this, you'll make your channel selections and identify the metrics that tie everything back to your business objectives.

14

Chapter Contents
Choose Your Path
Define the Opportunity
Select Your Channels
Select Your Metrics
Write and Present Your Plan
The Main Points

Choose Your Path

Setting out to create a plan means picking a suitable approach. You have a few potential paths. For openers, you can imagine the outcome you want and then just start writing. You can look at the work of someone else and do as they did, or you can lock squarely onto your goals and then just put one foot in front of the other until you get there. In this chapter, you'll be doing all three.

Social media as a formal marketing discipline is still relatively new. Perhaps you've been asked — or perhaps you volunteered — to look into social media and see what it's all about. As you work through this final chapter, think about the following points and *imagine* yourself running a marketing program in this context:

- A world without interruptions
- A world where the information needed to make an informed choice is readily available

I opened Chapter 8, "Build a Social Media Campaign," with the question about what you'd do as a marketer if you could no longer interrupt your audience. What would advertising look like, and how would you take your product or service to market in such a world? A real pushback is happening, and it involves not only interruptive advertising but the sheer amount of digital information to which we are increasingly subjected. This has an effect on the channels open to you, and on the ways in which you can use them. Contemporary playwright Richard Foreman, in an *Atlantic* article about Google and the impact of "search" on the collective intellect, had this to say about the way that the current generation and in fact all of us are *relearning* to think, manage information, and communicate:

> *"I see within all of us the replacement of complex inner density with a new kind of self, evolving under the pressure of information overload and the technology of 'instantly available.'"*
>
> — RICHARD FOREMAN, playwright

Simply put, we (all people) are being subjected to an increasingly intense data stream. Sometimes it is being pushed on us, and other times it's happening because we chose or asked for it. The end result, however, is the same: we are expected to cope with and make sense of increasingly complex global information, with multimedia (a significantly higher density form of information than text, that, a bit like potato chips for your brain, often requires *less* of your active imagination to fully process) and a continuous virtual presence (the always on "Blackberry" thing). *Some* Millenials, along with a number of GenXrs, Boomers, and seniors have mastered multitasking at a personal level and are able to operate in a mode best described as "continuous partial attention." Like aircraft controllers, AARP's online advocates — solidly in the "senior" segment — are managing incoming and outgoing data, often 24×7. At the same time, others, again across all demographic groups, are *pushing back entirely*, perhaps using technology for basic communication but little else, with some eschewing technology altogether. The Social Web — precisely because it is a massive connector — promises to elevate this discussion and bring to everyone involved, in some form, a reevaluation of what it means to be receptive to an interruptive message. A world without interruptions may not be that far off.

And so the question comes back: What would you do then? What if you could not interrupt your audience? You need to have an answer for that somewhat hypothetical scenario. At a fundamental level, how you view the role of the interruption and your ability to continue to reach your customers through interruptive media of any form will shape your social media plan.

What about the second of your plan-building options: *taking a cue from others*. Look around and see what else is happening. Extract the best practices and learn from mistakes. In Chapter 2, "The Marketer's Dilemma," I talked about Sony and their ill-fated street and blog campaigns. In Chapter 3, "What Is Social Media," I talked about Sony Tristar's successful launch of films using online and social channels. In Chapter 7, "Influence and Measurement," I presented the Sony/BluRay social media data that suggested the probability of a quicker end to the recent DVD format wars — which Sony ultimately won — had the Social Web been tapped sooner. Finally, in Chapter 13, "Objectives, Metrics, and ROI," I presented Sony's Backstage 101, a solid use of the Social Web built on Powered's social media platform. Sony's work on Backstage 101 has been very well received and resulted in a positive impact to recommendations of the brand as measured by the Net Promoter score. Likewise, the Sony Tristar results — impressive box office revenues generated using primarily digital and social media rather than traditional media — speak for themselves. At the same time, had social media been tapped earlier, Sony could have saved some money in the format wars. The mobile phone street campaign and PSP blog should never have happened at all. Taken together, these five campaigns — all from the same company — are a great example of the value of learning from others, in this case, from a market leader like Sony. Just because someone else did it doesn't mean you should. At the same time, if you see a best practice, write it down and think about how it might apply to you.

As you develop your plan — and just as importantly as you carry it forward — look around and take notes. When you see smart firms doing things that win praise, consider following. When you see them getting raked over the coals, don't walk — *run* — in the opposite direction. Recall my opening question for Part III: What will your response be when you see others using the Social Web inappropriately? If you copy their behavior in the hopes that you might get away with it, the Social Web will surely be spoiled for all marketers. Instead, learn and adopt proven, socially accepted best practices. The Social Web may just be your new best friend.

Finally — and to the core of this chapter and in fact the entire Hour a Day process — getting there means getting started, and getting started means taking the first step. Put one foot in front of the other until you reach your goal. You've been through 13 chapters and 10 sets of exercises: that's a lot of steps. Social media as applied to marketing is an evolving discipline, so there is yet a fair amount of leg work that needs to be done. During a panel discussion at Interactive Austin, an enterprise-oriented social media conference, fellow panelist and social media evangelist Giovanni Gallucci talked about the use of Excel as an alternative to the ready-to-use metrics platforms. It's a bit harder, but it's also a very good way to *get started*. Look carefully at the needs of your particular application: your way forward and the plan you create will be governed by the resources and constraints that apply in your particular situation. As you work through this chapter, you'll frequently choose between applying a ready-to-use solution or building one of your own. Perhaps you'll choose a ready-made platform, or maybe you'll start by building your own solution — and thereby gain an intimate knowledge of how social media really works. The knowledge you gain can be used later to write a specification for the use of a ready-to-use service that extends your core capabilities as you go for scale. However you proceed, it all starts by taking one step, followed by another.

Tip: New to marketing? Are you a sole practitioner, looking to understand social media and develop a practice of your own? You may want to look at this excellent "how to" for building your basic marketing plan, either before or as you take the final steps in building your social media program. This online planning guide, written by marketing expert Shama Hyder, is specifically designed for independent professionals and service firms. You'll find the guide here: http://www.afterthelaunch.com/

Affirm Your Business Objectives

In Chapter 13, I made the case for starting with your business objectives and then from those objectives developing the basis for your social media campaign. This is an essential step in planning a social media program. Ultimately, what plays out on the Social Web begins in Operations. Unless your program is tied directly to the fundamental goals and objectives of your firm or organization, there is going to be a disconnect between what you are doing and what your customers or constituents are experiencing. That disconnect will hurt you on the Social Web.

Your business objectives form the basis of your social media marketing campaign so this is where you will start. Today's exercise — as with all exercises this week — will be a matter of pulling together what you have done over the prior months. If you don't have your business objectives clearly defined — including quantitative success metrics — you'll want to take the time now to complete this.

Define Your Audience

Right along with your business objectives, you'll want a clear picture of who interests you the most. Different people do different things on the Social Web, ranging from not participating at all to being the social center from which much content flows in their online communities. This impacts listening just as it does outreach. For example, if you are looking at using a platform like Communispace or Passenger, the current behaviors of your target audience matter. If your audience is used to *participating* and creating content in online communities, this experience will be natural for them. If they've never participated in an online social setting — which may in fact make them the ideal audience for your study — then you'll have to take specific steps to help them up the learning curve. Be sure to account for this when you create your plan: plan *your own involvement* with as much care as you take in choosing your partners.

If you are using social media as an outreach tool, this requirement is compounded. You've seen a dozen channels as you've worked through this book — blogs, podcasts, photo-sharing sites and more. Each of these dozen channels has as many more options in terms of service or platform providers. Knowing what your audience is doing and using — or is likely to participate in — is critical to your success.

Choose Your Examples

In the previous 13 chapters, you saw in excess of 20 case studies and featured uses of social media. Additional references were presented in various sections as social media examples of what works on the Social Web and what doesn't. Which ones stand out? Which ones "feel" like the kind of approach to social media-based marketing that would work for *you* and would fit into or alongside the programs you have in place now? Citing established examples can help you identify best practices as well as avoid missteps; beyond that, as a part of your presentation, solid results that you can point to will help your colleagues who may be silently looking for some reassurance. After all, even though *you've* concluded that social media is a worthwhile addition to your marketing program, unless you're a sole proprietor you've still got to win support from everyone else involved.

Tip: Jeremiah Owyang, a Senior Analyst for social computing with Forrester Research, has compiled and now maintains a list of established brands that have adopted *and published* their social media strategies. This is a superb resource for you especially as you finalize the core elements of your social media plan and prepare to present it to your colleagues. You will find Jeremiah's list here:

http://www.web-strategist.com/blog/category/industry-index/

Monday: Build Your Foundation

Today you're going to spend an hour setting up your plan and framing your presentation. You'll be reaching back to the work you've already done, and thinking through the approach that you want to take in developing and presenting your campaign.

To develop your actual presentation or project proposal, use whatever tools you are most comfortable with: a document, a slide presentation, or a project-planning tool. Any of these will work well, but a quick note is in order:

"Power corrupts. PowerPoint corrupts absolutely."

— EDWARD TUFTE, professor emeritus of political science, computer science and statistics, and graphic design at Yale.

That's enough said about that. For more on the *effective* use of slide software in creating presentations, go here:

`http://www.edwardtufte.com/tufte/powerpoint`

 Tip: A set of worksheets covering this week's exercises can be found in the appendix of this book. In addition to these printed worksheets, you can also download electronic copies and access related resources at the website accompanying this book. Complete information regarding these resources and the website is included in the appendix.

Monday's One-Hour Exercise

Over the next hour, create the opening section of your presentation and project proposal.

1. Start with your business objectives. Clearly identify each, and include the success metrics associated with specific business objectives.

2. For each objective, identify the current marketing effort(s) associated with it, and provide a brief statement as to where you are now and how you are measuring this.

3. Define your audience(s) and provide a brief overview of the ways in which they are using social channels. Include any trend data that shows how they might be using this in the future.

4. Offer examples of best practices and things to avoid: because you haven't identified specific channels at this point of your presentation, focus on examples that show transparency, participation, or listening versus outreach. The objective is to give your audience a sense of what you are about to propose and why applying social media *correctly* is so important.

5. Finish this part of your plan and presentation with a statement as to how you will fundamentally approach the Social Web. Are you proposing a listening effort aimed at understanding why certain conversations about your brand are taking place, or are you proposing the use of one or more specific outreach campaigns to accomplish an identified growth objective?

Monday's Wrap-Up

Today you framed your plan. If this were the presentation itself, those in attendance would understand just how *your business objectives* are driving your proposal for the incorporation of social media into your marketing program. Even though they have seen a couple of examples of social media and related best practices, they may or *may not* understand what social media is yet. At this point in your presentation, you are putting your foundation in place: that foundation is your business-based rationale for properly adding this thing called social media to the marketing mix.

> **Tip:** Open your plan discussion or presentation with what your audience already knows: the business in which you all have a shared future. If instead you *begin* with a discussion of social media, your audience is likely to jump to MySpace or whatever their personal preconception of "social media" happens to be. You'll spend the next hour trying (and quite possibly failing) to overcome that. Start with your business objectives.

Define the Opportunity

How you set up your plan is as important as the information you present. The right idea — presented the wrong way — is unlikely to be approved. A case in point was the presentation to Congress and request for funding of the Voyager deep space program, a program which I joined later at Jet Propulsion Labs. The original plan, known as The Grand Tour, called for Voyagers I and II to visit Jupiter, Saturn, Uranus, Neptune, and Pluto. (At the time, Pluto was a planet. It isn't any more.) *The Grand Tour was considered too ambitious and was scrapped.* In its place, a scaled-back Voyager program — calling instead for two planetary visits, Jupiter and then Saturn, shown with one of the Voyagers in Figure 14.1 was offered. *This more modest plan was approved.*

> **Tip:** Take-away number one: When your audience perceives risk, they generally act in concert to reduce it or eliminate it, sometimes along with you and your plan.

Of course, I wouldn't be telling this story if that's all there was to it: we've all been shot down in presentations, and we've all come back to fight another day. In this case, the scaled-back Voyager program not only went forward, it *succeeded in accomplishing the Grand Tour objectives*: after visiting Jupiter and Saturn, Voyager II continued on to Uranus and then Neptune, with a visit to Saturn's moon Titan taking the place of the Pluto fly-by. The program, which ultimately included the successful visit of all four of the outer planets, was launched, as it were, into the history books.

Tip: **Take away number two:** Get *something* approved and you've preserved your chance to go big later.

What does this have to do with you? Avoid the appearance of too much, too fast. Instead, *under*-promise. The key is to make people comfortable with the ideas you are presenting and to help them see (and share in) the notion of success. Social media is disruptive. Be sensitive to that, and provide a solid footing that minimizes risks and the potential for failure. Make it easy for the decision makers in your organization to support you. Then over-deliver.

Source: Wikipedia. Licensed under Creative Commons Attribution 3.0. This image has been generated with *Celestia*; 3D model by ElChristou.

Figure 14.1 The Voyager Space Probe Passing Saturn

With the foundation of your marketing plan in place, the next step is to set up *why* you are proposing what you are about to propose. As I noted in prior chapters, "Because everyone is doing it…" or "Because it's the newest thing or the wave of the future" is not going to cut it.

Lots of people — me included — have made this mistake. At a recent conference on enterprise software, a number of social media platform and service vendors offered as strategies for gaining internal support amongst enterprise decision makers things like "Just give us $50K and we'll show you what it can do" or "Think of this as an experiment — try it and see what happens." They have a valid point: there aren't a lot of case studies yet, and somebody does have to be first. But at the same time, C-level decision makers typically require a bit more meat before biting.

I am as much a proponent of taking risks as anyone — I worked on the space program, remember? I also have a real bias toward rational motivations and measured progress. (Again, I worked on the space program.) Yes, social media is new, and there is definitely a reason to experiment and figure out how it applies to *your* business. At the same time, your risk-averse colleagues — your CFO and CTO, who have issues such as security, technical support and Sarbanes-Oxley to keep them up at night — may not be in love with the idea of seeing the brand plastered across MySpace, one click away from something scary or inappropriate. Which, by the way, is why I said to start with the business objectives.

Although MySpace is often the setting of the cliché example of inappropriate ad placement, it isn't actually all that scary, especially as viewed by its members who spend time there. Beyond that, social media-based marketing, rationally implemented, *offers very little chance* that your brand will end up in the wrong place, any more than your magazine ad will. But do you really want to begin your presentation with a defense of MySpace? By starting with your business objectives you *avoid raising that issue* until you've grounded your audience in what social media is really all about. By starting with your business objectives when you make your case for using social media, you've put yourself on solid ground.

Starting with the business fundamentals gives everyone a way to get on board and to establish a basic agreement with what you are presenting. Build on that by showing *how what you are doing now*, through your current marketing efforts, is delivering results. You'll also want to be very specific — as specific as possible — as to how adding social media to the mix can bring *additional benefits*. No one is going to argue with the core business objectives, and if you can show how you will improve the effectiveness of whatever is happening now, you'll have gotten yourself a good way through the presentation without being shot down. I've certainly experienced worse.

Ultimately, if you push too hard too soon, your colleagues and decision makers may love what you're saying, but then suggest a "wait and see" strategy. If that happens, it's likely game over. A better approach is to have a plan for the "big success" that you really believe in. Then break it into smaller pieces, and make each component of your plan accessible to your colleagues and decision makers. Help them help you.

Tip: Use normal language, the kind you'd use when explaining what you do all day when a relative or friend *outside* the industry calls and asks. Every discipline has a technical language of its own: it makes communication more precise and more efficient. At the same time, we all share some form of common language, the words and phrases we use when communicating in situations where the audience is more general. Stick to *that* language.

Social Feedback Cycle

Recall Chapter 5, "The Social Feedback Cycle." By overlaying your purchase funnel onto the Social Web, it's clear that social media is a product of an experience *and* it has an impact on your sales cycle. In Chapter 5, I noted the following quote, from a Forrester Research study:

"No matter what I hear, read, or find on TV, radio, or in a magazine or newspaper, I can verify it on the Internet."

This is the social feedback cycle, and it is exactly why the Social Web is so important to your business. As a marketer, you are tasked with telling customers and potential customers what they should expect, why they should buy from you, and what sort of value will be gained. At the same time, they are increasingly turning to others — and especially others with direct experience with your product, service or brand, and asking "Did this work for you?" If so, you're in good shape. If not, then you've got an opportunity.

The social feedback cycle shows the value of listening. Following a purchase, there is a continuous stream of conversation on the Social Web, and an increasing share of this is making its way — as social media — back into the purchase funnel. You can listen to the stream of conversations using tools such as Blog Pulse, Cymfony, Techrigy, Google Alerts, or using a tool that you have created.

Because the social feedback cycle is a loop, you can start at any point. You can begin by listening, and then use what you learn to drive product improvement and in doing so influence the next round of conversation. Or, you can start closer to home by implementing ratings and reviews using the Bazaarvoice platform, for example, applying this social media channel to drive additional sales. Wherever you choose to start, ultimately you'll want to measure and characterize the entire social feedback cycle as it applies to your specific objectives and application.

Tip: If you are running a commerce site, and looking for a low-risk entry into social media, think about using the Bazaarvoice platform. Fifty of the top 100 online retailers are Bazaarvoice clients: this is one of relatively few ready-to-use social media applications where you can directly point to top companies *using social media in business* and thereby substantially reduce the level of perceived risk when presenting your plan.

Touchpoint Map

It's time to pull out the touchpoint map you developed in Chapter 6, "Touchpoint Analysis." Your touchpoint map links what you are doing now with the experiences about which your customers are — or could be — talking. Your touchpoint map — on which you ranked touchpoint performance against talk value — tells you the following:

- What touchpoints are contributing to the conversations taking place in reference to your product, service, or brand?

- Which of these, based on touchpoint performance, are likely to generate favorable, neutral, or unfavorable conversations?

- Compared with all of your touchpoints, which are your outliers and/or most likely candidates for improvement?

Taken together, your touchpoint map provides you with a starting point in terms of knowing where to focus your efforts — what to improve, what to avoid messing up — and where your important talk-generators are. Knowing what to improve is obviously important: because your customers are free to talk about you, you want them to have the best experience possible before doing so. It's likely that you are focusing on this sort of thing now.

Less likely and, therefore, one of the items you'll want to emphasize in your plan and presentation is the importance of understanding your specific talk-generators. Using tools such as Techrigy's platform, Cymfony, BlogPulse, or Google's Blogsearch to locate and define your talk-generators is key to identifying the social media channels that you'll want to use.

> **Tip:** Your touchpoint map provides another very easy entry point into social media. If you have a touchpoint that is generating negative conversations, you can use it as a trial case within your organization. Team up with Operations and fix it. At the same time, use the suggested monitoring tools to track your progress. By showing that you can influence conversations — *the right way* — you can reduce the fear that social conversations are somehow completely beyond reach. Remember, you can't control these conversations, but you can influence them.

Net Promoter Score

In Chapter 7, I introduced the Net Promoter score. Again, the exercise you did — calling and surveying a relatively small number of customers — was designed *to show you how this tool works*. It may or may not be a statistically valid exercise. If it is — if your business has a relatively small number of customers or you've since called more — then you can infer quite a lot from the exercise. If your business has a large number of customers 100 or 1,000 times the 10 or so you called in this exercise, then you'll want to follow the Net Promoter methodology and obtain a statistically valid measurement. The good news is that you can start doing this immediately and establish a great social tracking tool in the process.

Tuesday: Choose Your Methods

Today you're going to spend an hour building the portion of your plan along with the presentation that articulates the drivers of what you will be doing and what will happen as a result. In other words, where yesterday was about establishing a foundation for your social media plan in your business objectives, today is about characterizing and defining the opportunity that exists, and your argument for why a social media-based effort is part of the solution.

Over the next hour:

- Based on your Net Promoter score — noting that this may simply be a directional guide — decide how this information will fit into your plan. If your Net Promoter score is reasonable, say 40 percent or higher, and your sample is significant, then you may choose to cite this as assurance that an outreach program carries only minimal risk. If it's negative, you may choose to use this as the basis for a listening program and a closer partnership with Operations.

- Based on your touchpoint map, identify the three most important talk generators. Note specifically the things you are doing now to capitalize on positive talk. Note the internal (Operations) efforts that are associated with any important talk generators that are negative.

- Develop a set of issue to explore with Operations based on any negative points that you know exist now. (Don't worry that you cannot resolve anything right now: you don't have the data for this yet. Part of your plan involves getting it.)

- Pull from your social feedback cycle the starting point for your campaign: are you proposing a listening effort that starts on the Social Web, an outreach effort that begins with your own content, or some combination of the two?

- Again referring to your social feedback cycle, decide whether or not your campaigns will involve your current conversion process. Are you looking to quantify what is being said and to then use that as a way to improve and thereby positively influence the conversations, or are you looking to directly impact conversion rates?

Tuesday's Wrap-Up

You now have the basis for your plan in hand. You've defined the central opportunity that you are pursuing, and you've fundamentally tied it to your business objectives. To begin influencing social conversations, you've identified areas where Marketing and Operations can work together to and improve the customer experience that drives these conversations.

Select Your Channels

On to the fun stuff! In this next section, you're going to pick channels and develop the objectives for the specific campaigns built around them. This section draws heavily from "Part III: Social Media Channels." In this section, you'll be referencing the objectives and choices you've made and built into your plan over the two preceding days.

The channels you choose for your campaign will of course depend on the campaigns themselves, so start there. The social feedback cycle is a loop, so the starting point is a bit arbitrary. What you hear should ultimately impact what you do, and what you do will likewise impact what you hear. So, instead of looking for the starting point to a circle, turn instead to the fundamental objectives of your campaign that you identified yesterday. Of these, there are two primary activities: listening and outreach. Pick one. You can use either as a starting point, and then based on your plan show how what you're proposing drives the entire feedback loop.

Listening

Listening is the single most valuable activity that you can engage in on the Social Web. As such, it's a great place to start your social media program. The Social Web is a place where you can learn about how every aspect of what you do is perceived, and then use that to improve.

When you consider that a leading frustration that consumers express involves (not) being listened to, it's a pretty safe bet that adding this capability to your marketing program will be well received. Just be sure that you are equally ready to act. Bill Fields, former CEO of Wal-Mart Stores Division, Hudson's Bay Company, and Blockbuster Entertainment Group (yes, all three), noted during our panel discussion at the 2008 Interactive Austin conference on enterprise social media that, "The biggest mistake a marketer can make in terms of listening is *not acting* on what your customer tells you." That is solid guidance.

In the following sections, the social media channels associated with listening are described, along with typical examples and suggested applications. Table 14.1 provides a summary reference.

▶ **Table 14.1** Social Media Listening Channels

Channel Group	Channel	How Applied	Representative Tools	Examples
Social Platforms	White Label Platforms Service Provider Platforms	Support Forum Research Group	Pluck, Jive Software, Lithium Communispace, Passenger	Lithium Seagate Support Hallmark, GSK, FOX, Chrysler
Social Content	Blogs	Gather feedback, ideas, suggestions	Wordpress, Blogger, Typepad, Pluck, Jive Software, BlogPulse, Cymfony, Techrigy, Google Alerts, Salesforce.com	MyStarbucksIdea, Dell's IdeaStorm
Social Interactions	Email and RSS Feeds	Gather competitive and market intelligence	Email, Google Reader	Competitive and Industry Group Newsletters and Product Bulletins

Social Platforms

Social platforms — whether through a presence on a public social network or the creation of your own branded community — offer perfect opportunities to listen. Support forums and efforts such as Starbucks' "My Starbucks Idea," presented as a featured case in Chapter 6, or Dell's "IdeaStorm" are examples of this type of listening application. I referenced Communispace and the listening platforms developed for Hallmark (Chapter 3) and GSK (Chapter 5). Each of these provides quantifiable information that you can use to your competitive advantage.

Tip: You'll find "My Starbucks Idea" here: http://www.mystarbucksidea.com
You'll find "Dell's Ideastorm" here: http://www.dellideastorm.com

Social Content

Whether through blogs, multimedia content, or ratings, reviews, and recommendations, people are creating and sharing a lot of information. A good chunk of that relates to products, services, and brands.

Ratings, reviews and recommendations implemented on your platform or through a service partner are an immediate source of feedback. You can track your own feedback, and you can track your competitors. You can track your suppliers and customers as well. If this seems like overdoing it a bit, go back to your touchpoint map: It's not uncommon that your performance — from the perspective of your customer — is itself *determined* by a partner or supplier, or viewed by your customers in the context of a competitive experience. The more information the better, at least at the outset of your program and until such time as you determine that one or more specific measures aren't adding to your understanding of your market presence and perception.

With regard to blogs, tools like BlogPulse and Cymfony can provide visibility into online and offline conversations that impact your brand. Dashboard products like Techrigy include blog content monitoring as well. You can use Google Alerts and Blogsearch and then import the data into K.D. Paine and Partner's DIYDashboard or your own tracking system. Aren't choices wonderful?

Tip: Metrics is the next expansion area in the business use of social media. Pay special attention here, and consider setting up a Google Alert for the topic of "social media metrics" and the products of the service providers I've referenced.

Social Interactions

If you want to know what your competitors are up to, sign up for their news feeds and email newsletters. Track them over time to keep tabs on the market as they see it. A lot of this comes under the heading of good old-fashioned competitive intelligence. Because your competitors are a part of the overall marketplace, they are contributing to the context in which your products and services are evaluated. Competitive activities most definitely impact touchpoint results and, therefore, drive Social Web conversations.

Always Be Testing

Author and online marketing expert Bryan Eisenberg released his latest book, *Always Be Testing*, with two covers. Why? He didn't know which one his readers would like the best. As the book begins to sell, Bryan will "listen" to his audience by watching the sales to see if one cover outsells the other. If so, expect to see a market develop on eBay for the discontinued ("collectors item") version. Better yet, buy both and have Bryan sign them. One of them is sure to be worth a fortune in the future.

Outreach

If you opt to create content or offer an environment in which social content can be created, then outreach programs using social media and the Social Web should be a part of your plan. By tapping social media for outreach, you can extend your brand and position it closer to the focal point of the conversations through participation in existing communities, or by creating a social community of your own. In the following sections, the social media channels associated with outreach are described, along with typical examples and suggested applications. Table 14.2 provides a summary reference.

Channel Group	Channel	How Applied	Representative Tools	Examples
Social Platforms	Social Networks	Presence	Facebook, LinkedIn, MySpace,	BMW, Product Pulse
	White Label Networks	Product Extension	Ning, Pluck, Jive, Broadband Mechanics	Ad Gabbr, Meredith Publishing, Condé Nast, Rodale
	Wiki	Collaborative Development	Jive Software, WetPaint, Twiki	Wikipedia, WOOD Magazine, FG SQUARED
Social Content	Photo Sharing Video Sharing	Common Interest, Product and service uses	Flickr, YouTube, Kyte, Photobucket	The Brooklyn Museum, General Motors (Volt)
	Podcasting	Information and Learning, Entertainment	Odeo, HearThis.com	Beachwalks with Rox, Personal Life Media, ProstateNet.org
	Blogs and Microblogs	Corporate Blog	Blogger, Typepad, Wordpress, Twitter, Plurk, Seesmic	Dell (@DellSmBizOffers) Zappos, Southwest Airlines, Mars Lander
Social Interactions	Event Services	Event Organization	Eventful	The Brooklyn Museum
	Location Services	Meetups	Dodgeball, Brightkite	Starbucks, Chili's Grill and Bar
	Update Aggregation	Pushing content streams	FriendFeed, Facebook, Minggl	The Roxy Theater

Social Platforms

Social platforms provide multiple ways to properly extend your brand onto the Social Web. Where permitted, create a presence in public social networks and use that presence to provide a bonding point with customers and potential customers. Alternatively, create a community around your existing content: Meredith, publishers of *Better Homes and Gardens* along with *Parents* magazine, has successfully done this as have Condé Nast and Rodale. *USA Today*, building on Pluck's Sitelife platform, has integrated its readership community through commentary on current events and then reflected that back by placing these reader-generated comments prominently on the homepage of the newspaper's online site. The newspaper includes a completely personalized community experience — powered through a member persona like that shown in Figure 14.2 — to further the notion of community and belonging, driving stickiness, use, and loyalty of the online newspaper.

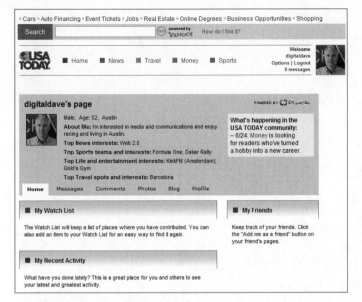

Figure 14.2 My *USA Today* Member Profile

Wikis and similar collaborative tools — Jive Software's Clearspace platform, for example, can be used to create places where customers, partners, and suppliers can work together and develop what Guy Kawasaki calls "curve jumping" solutions, built on the radically different ideas that occur when thinking is moved outside of existing constraints. Google and Reddit both offer best-of-class communities that support their respective developers and members: Through this kind of community and participation, applications that may not have been conceived of — much less developed — within the organizations themselves are brought into the market. Good ideas can come from anywhere.

Social Content

Using social media as an outreach component of your program means either making your own content, as Home Depot did with its YouTube-based "Basics of Paint," or alternatively, providing your customers with the direct ability to create their own content, as Home Depot did with its "$25K Remodeling Contest." Look as well at Seesmic, shown in Figure 14.3, and in particular the "askseesmic" support series that uses the company's own platform to create a video conversation between employees and customers seeking help or asking questions. Blogging, photo and video sharing, and podcasts can all be used effectively as *direct outreach tools* — meaning, you make or oversee production of content intended to be shared — or as tools that your customers are invited to use to create and share their own content.

Figure 14.3 Seesmic — Dave Evans on Social Media

Social Interactions

Services like eBay veterans Brian Dear and John Glazier's Eventful can be a natural social extension of your business. If you offer events, host conferences, or have a product or service that people like to do in groups — cooking, sports, or travel, for example — Eventful's customer-driven event services help make *them* it happen. How's that for delegation?

Location-based services like Brightkite and Dodgeball can be used in combination by facilitating *meetups,* casual get-togethers typically arranged on the fly, and similar gatherings. For your part, to get the most out of these services, you need only make sure that you are listed. If your business is centered around a social location — for example, a café or theater — encourage your customers to use these services to bring their friends and associates to you using the "warchalking" symbols I suggested in Chapter 12, "Social Interactions."

Wednesday: Pick Your Channels

Today you're going to select the channels that will form the core of your social media program. You have your businesses objectives and audience defined, and you've worked out your approach — listening, outreach, or a mix of both. You've sorted out where you want to focus: on the Social Web itself, at the point where the conversations are being picked up by your potential customers, or as a part of your current commerce or conversion pipeline.

Wednesday's One-Hour Exercise

For the next hour:

- Based on your selected approach, from Tables 14.1 and 14.2 select the two or three channels you'd like to use.

- Using Google, research each and find competing services: they change continuously, so do this regularly.

- After validation, decide on the actual channels you'd like to add to your plan.

- For each selected channel, write out the main idea you have for the use of this channel and add it to your plan.

- For each selected channel, develop or secure an estimate of the cost any an associated timeline for deployment.

> **Tip:** For some plan elements, you may not be able to obtain an exact cost at this point. That's fine. You may not be able to get a final signoff on your plan at this point. Understand that ahead of time, and go instead for the biggest "yes" you *can* get right now. For example, gain consensus on developing a formal specification and an RFP based on your plan and ideas. Remember, one foot in front of the other.

Wednesday's Wrap-Up

Today you added your first social media channels to your social media plan. It's limited to two or three by design: there is always more that you can do, and there will be more choices next month than there were last month. Having added a small number now you can always expand later. Tying your choices for your initial methods into your business objectives makes your work in selecting channels and partners that are likely to work for you that much easier, and makes approval that much more likely.

At this point your plan and presentation should have the following elements: check now to see that it does.

Plan Foundation (Monday)

- Statement of business objectives
- Marketing programs supporting each objective
- Current status and applicable success measure for each
- Audience behaviors with regard to online and social media
- Applicable best practices and examples of each
- Choice of approach: listening, outreach, or both

Statement of Opportunity (Tuesday)

- Net Promoter score and interpretation
- Touchpoint analysis and key findings
- Opportunities for collaboration with Operations
- Social feedback cycle and campaign points

Selected Channels (Wednesday)

- Specific channels you plan to use
- Preferred provider or method for each

If your plan does not contain each of the above, go back to the section of this chapter that applies to the missing or incomplete sections.

Select Your Metrics

With your channels and social media selections set, the remaining step in developing your plan is identifying an appropriate set of baseline and ongoing metrics so that you can track your progress. The point of the metrics you select is twofold:

- First, you want to know if you are moving toward your goal, and if you are improving your present market position or condition.
- Second, as your social media efforts get underway, some of your channels will perform better than others. You'll want to be able to capture this, and respond appropriately. Metrics are your guide.

New solution providers and social media options will emerge. By setting baseline metrics and then tracking the performance of various campaign elements, you'll know which are working and which need tuning or outright replacement.

Referring to Chapter 13, you will tie your business objectives to the metrics that you covered. I have split the fundamental business objectives into three groups: market position, brand health, and growth and profits. Most business objectives fall under one or more of these headings. In the event that your specific objectives do *not* fall neatly into one of these, look at the groupings and then find the closest group or groups and work from there. The objective is not to put your objectives into a bucket but rather to look at the types of metrics that are available and then to see what the best way to tie these back to your objectives might be. The groupings are merely a convenience, a starting point.

Market Position

If your business objectives include things like "establishing a leadership position" or "opening three new markets" or something similar, then measures of conversations along with the Net Promoter score can be very helpful in tying a social media-based marketing effort to your underlying business plan. In this case, you are using two measures: the overall conversational levels about your competitive set and the conversational levels of your specific brand, product, or service expressed as a fraction of the total conversation, and the polarity of the conversations you find.

Figure 14.4 shows the relationship between market position and the available measures of social media conversations. Table 14.3 lists each of the audience measures that are readily available along with the source of that measure. As with all social media measures, the recommended technique is to track the measure over time, and then interpret the change as you operate different portions of your social media campaign.

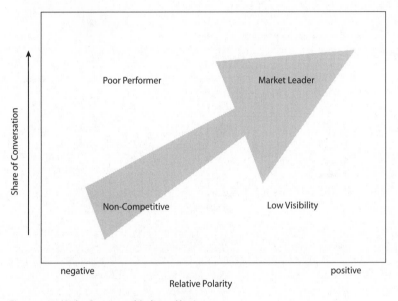

Figure 14.4 Market Position and Audience Metrics

▶ **Table 14.3** Market Fundamentals and Metrics with Suggested Sources

Fundamental	Metric	Source	Ties To
Audience	Blog Posts for Brand, Competition, Product or Service. Recommendations, Tweets and similar. Widget views	BlogPulse, Google Alerts, Cymfony, Techrigy, Blog-search, Technorati, Net Promoter score, Social Media Platform dashboard	Relative measure of interest and awareness in your brand, product, or service.

Brand Health

Your business objectives may include aspects of *brand health*, the relative value of the equity associated with your brand. Nike and Google have relatively high brand values, for example. Table 14.4 lists representative measures that are commonly available. Each of these is a surrogate for brand health. Note that bounce rate is inversely related: a high bounce rate is generally *not* good. It means people arrive but don't look into your offer in any sort of depth. Again, it is not an absolute value that you are looking for here, but rather a change (and direction of change) over time.

Tip: When looking at the Comment-to-Post ratio, more comments per post are generally better. Obviously, Post-to-Comment ratio — an equivalent measure sometimes cited — expresses the same thing but in an opposite way.

▶ **Table 14.4** Brand Fundamentals and Metrics with Suggested Sources

Fundamental	Metric	Source	Ties To
Influence	Time on Site, Bounce Rate	Web Analytics: Google Analytics, Omniture, Web Trends	The value of your brand in generating interest.
Engagement	Pass Alongs, Comment to Post Ratio, Diggs, Stumbles and bookmarks, Podcast listens and views.	Web Analytics, Google Analytics, Omniture, Web Trends, DoubleClick, Digg.com StumbleUpon.com Del.icio.us Feedburner	The value of your brand in maintaining and spreading interest.
Loyalty	Blog posts for your brand, Recommendations Tweets and similar	BlogPulse, Google Alerts, Cymfony, Techrigy, Blogsearch, Technorati	The value of your brand in retaining current customers and building long term relationships.

Growth and Profits

If you are concerned about sales and profits, you're not alone. It's hard to imagine a business plan and a set of objectives that don't directly or indirectly include some performance measure related to cash coming in the door along with a companion measure of how much of it actually sticks around.

Social media metrics — implemented near or very near your conversion pipeline — provide measures that both indicate a likely trend in sales, and tie activity on the Social Web directly into the sales pipeline.

Tip: Tying social media into the sales *pipeline* is not the same as tying social media into a specific sale. Tying to the sales pipeline provides a measure of influence. Tying to sales — very few and quite specific cases aside — isn't generally possible, any more than tying one car purchase to a specific TV spot is generally possible.

By tying activity on the Social Web into the sales pipeline, you can track the relative increase or decrease in conversion rates as you measure and observe various conditions on the Social Web. Understand that this is directly analogous to measuring the effectiveness of a TV spot or any other form of media — with the possible exception of some forms of direct response marketing — in that it assumes that the change observed is due to the change induced in the system. If you are changing seven things at once, then the changes in measures you observe are due to the combined impact of all seven changes you made. This implies the need to establish a baseline — as I noted in Chapter 13 — *before* you implement your social media campaigns.

This isn't as onerous as it sounds, but it does require some thought. For example, you probably already have a very good idea of how the changes in your marketing budget directed to the advertising you are doing now impacts sales. If so, and if you are careful about how you introduce your social campaigns — measuring each as you release it — then you can use your current knowledge as a baseline on which to build a quantitative assessment of the value of social media.

Tip: The Social Web is active and is currently impacting your marketing efforts. *This is part of your current baseline.* By beginning with listening, you can establish the current state of the conversations on the Social Web and thereby factor these into your initial baseline assumptions *before* you introduce any outreach programs that attempt to change those conversations.

Table 14.5 provides a listing of representative sales and profits related measures, along with the sources of each.

▶ **Table 14.5** Sales Fundamentals and Metrics with Suggested Sources

Fundamental	Metric	Source	Ties To
Audience	Referrers, Demographics	Web Analytics, Google Analytics, Omniture, Web Trends, DoubleClick	Uptake measures in key segments
Influence Loyalty	Time on Site Bounce rate	Web Analytics, Google Analytics, Omniture, Web Trends Repeat Customers	How likely customers are to buy from you; the degree to which you need to incentivize your sales
Action	Conversions Reviews Recommendations Tweets and similar	Web Analytics, Google Analytics, Omniture, Web Trends Review Platform Net Promoter	The number or dollar value of sales made

Thursday: Verify Your Metrics

Today you're going to spend an hour picking the metrics you need and adding them to your plan. For each, you'll start with your business objectives and then find an appropriate measure. Once you've identified them, you'll verify the source and availability of that data and add it to your metrics spreadsheet.

Thursday's One-Hour Exercise

During the next hour:

- For each of your stated business objectives, identify the social media metrics that are associated with this objective and the current success measures associated with this business objective.

- For each metric, identify the source and verify its availability.

- Create a place for this metric in your metrics spreadsheet.

Thursday's Wrap-Up

You've now completed the final step in building your social media plan and your presentation. Tomorrow you get to finish it up, and then you can review and present it. At this point, your plan and presentation should have the following elements: check now to see that it does.

Plan Foundation (Monday)

- Statement of business objectives
- Marketing programs supporting each objective
- Current status and applicable success measure for each
- Audience behaviors with regard to online and social media
- Applicable best practices and examples of each
- Choice of approach: listening, outreach, or both

Statement of Opportunity (Tuesday)

- Net Promoter score and interpretation
- Touchpoint analysis and key findings
- Opportunities for collaboration with Operations
- Social feedback cycle and campaign points

Selected Channels (Wednesday)

- Specific channels you plan to use
- Preferred provider or method for each

Metrics (Thursday)

- For each business objective for which you have identified a social media based marketing effort, an applicable metric and its source

  If your plan does not contain each of the above, go back to the section of this chapter that applies to the missing or incomplete sections.

Write and Present Your Plan

Your social media plan is essentially written. If you are building a slide presentation or written proposal, the primary sections should correspond to each of the exercises you've done this week. Of course, you can choose any organizational approach you'd like, but again, I recommend starting with business objectives and avoiding a head-long leap into social media.

Friday: Wrap It Up

Today you're going to spend an hour organizing, filling in gaps, and then assembling your plan and plan presentation.

Friday's One-Hour Exercise

During the next hour:

- Check each of the primary sections of your plan.
- Verify the facts, sources of data, and similar details.
- Set a future meeting time and then present your plan.

> **Tip:** Based on your plan, establish clearly in your mind the decision you will ask for in this opening presentation: it may be the outright approval and funding for your entire plan, or it may be a "go ahead" to the next step of writing a formal RFP. Understanding what you are requesting and ensuring that you are requesting something that your audience is able to give an approval for is a key presentation skill. Don't overlook this.

Friday's Wrap-Up

You are now ready to present your plan. Not only have you based it on your business objectives and tied in key constituents (e.g., Operations) but by following the Hour a Day process over the past three months, you have prepared yourself for any questions that are likely to come up. You have put yourself in a position not only to succeed personally, but to carry that success to your team and colleagues, and ultimately to your firm and its beneficiaries, including your customers.

Chapter 14: The Main Points

- Social media-based marketing begins with business objectives and an understanding of your audience.

- Social media as applied to marketing is fundamentally measurable in ways that can be tied to your business objectives.

- Understanding what you will be asking for and identifying the biggest "yes" you can get at each approval step is critical to selling in your social media plan.

Appendix: Worksheets

This appendix contains the worksheets for Parts II, III and IV of the book. They are arranged in sequential order. If you have questions on these exercises, please refer back to the corresponding chapter. The worksheets in this appendix can either be used directly, or as templates for a set of worksheets of your design.

Worksheets: Part II

Chapters 4–7

Chapter 4: Web 2.0: The Social Web

Monday: Using Blogs and Wikis

Blogs to visit: Check off as you visit.

- ❏ Boing Boing (http://www.boingboing.net)
- ❏ Social Media Today (http://www.socialmediatoday.com)
- ❏ Mashable (http://mashable.com)
- ❏ CommunityGuy (http://www.communityguy.com)

Questions to Answer:

For each of the above:

What is the central theme?

_____

Who would read this on a regular basis? Why?

_____

Are the contributors potential customers? If so, what other blogs do they read?

_____

What could you add to this conversation?

_____

Are you being "drawn in"? Are you starting to follow posts via comments and winding up in unexpected places?

_____

How could you use this in your business?

_____

Wikis to visit: Check off as you visit.

- ❑ Wikipedia (`http://en.wikipedia.org/wiki/Social_media`)

- ❑ One Laptop per Child (`http://wiki.laptop.org`)

- ❑ IBM Wikis (`http://www-941.ibm.com/collaboration/wiki`)

Questions to Answer:

For each of the above:

Are the entries evolving over time? Is there evidence of participation?

_____

Who is in charge?

_____

Is the Updates section or Discussion page visible? If not, does this change your view of the end result? If so, how?

_____

How could you use this in your business?

_____

Tuesday: Multimedia

Multimedia sites to visit: check off as you visit.

- ❑ Flickr (`http://www.flickr.com`)

- ❑ Photobucket (`http://www.photobucket.com`)

- ❑ YouTube (`http://www.youtube.com`)

- ❑ Seesmic (`http://www.seesmic.com`)

- ❑ Metacafe (`http://www.metacafe.com`)

- ❑ Personal Life Media (`http://personallifemedia.com`)

For each of the listed websites:

What services are provided at this site?

_____

Who would use this site on a regular basis? Why?

_____

What content could you add to these sites?

_____

Are you being "drawn in"? Are you following posts?

_____

What is the social motivation for the site?

_____

Why did the person who posted this content post it?

_____

What did you come away with as a result of reading this post?

_____

Wednesday and Thursday: Microblogs, Tagging, and RSS Feeds

Microblog services to visit: Check off as you visit.

- ❑   Twitter (http://twitter.com)

- ❑   Pownce (http://pownce.com)

- ❑   Tumblr (http://tumblr.com)

- ❑   Plurk (http://plurk.com)

- ❑   Identi.ca (http://identi.ca)

Questions to Answer:

What is the attraction to following the activities of others?

_____

How could you use these services in your business?

_____

Tagging services to visit: Check off as you visit.

❏   Del.icio.us (`http://del.icio.us`)

❏   Stumble Upon (`http://www.stumbleupon.com`)

❏   Ma.gnolia (`http://ma.gnolia.com`)

Questions to Answer:

What is the value of tagging and sharing tags with others?

_____

How could you use tagging in your business?

_____

RSS sites to visit: Check off as you visit and subscribe to these feeds.

❏   Twitter (`http://twitter.com`)

❏   Boing Boing (`http://www.boingboing.net`)

❏   Seesmic (`http://seesmic.com`)

Things to do:

❏   Locate the RSS/Atom subscription icons for each of the suggested services.

❏   Subscribe by adding these to your Feeds list.

❏   Take a look at your feeds tomorrow and see what's new.

Friday: Social Networks

Social sites to visit: Check off as you visit.

- ❏ Facebook (`http://www.facebook.com`)
- ❏ MySpace (`http://www.myspace.com`)

Business sites to visit: Check off as you visit.

- ❏ AdGabber (`http://www.adgabber.com`)
- ❏ LinkedIn (`http://www.linkedin.com`)
- ❏ Plaxo (`http://www.plaxo.com`)

Questions to Answer:

Look around MySpace in particular. What do you think?

_____

How is MySpace different from Facebook?

_____

For each of the sites you visited:

Who is advertising? What is being advertised?

_____

Beyond the ads, what is being talked about?

_____

Compare the social and business sites. What is the *common* element?

_____

How could you use the social sites in your business?

_____

How could you use the business sites in your business?

_____

Chapter 5: The Social Feedback Cycle

Monday: Campaign Objectives

Questions to Answer:

What is the name of the product or service (or brand) with which you will be working?

_____

What is the business objective of the social media campaign you are planning to create?

_____

What objectives are you setting for this campaign? For each objective, identify one or more metrics and note the success value, the failure value, and the current value (if applicable).

Metric	Success Value	Failure Value	Current Value
_____	_____	_____	_____
_____	_____	_____	_____
_____	_____	_____	_____
_____	_____	_____	_____
_____	_____	_____	_____
_____	_____	_____	_____

In a short summary, write out your definition of success looks like.

_____

_____

_____

Tuesday: The Awareness Phase

Questions to Answer:

Identify each of the awareness channels you are using currently or have used in the recent past. List them all and then for each channel identified, note the success value, the failure value, and the current value.

Channel	Success Value	Failure Value	Current Value
_____	_____	_____	_____
_____	_____	_____	_____
_____	_____	_____	_____
_____	_____	_____	_____
_____	_____	_____	_____
_____	_____	_____	_____

For each channel identified, what did you have to do to justify its use? When will this decision be reviewed?

Channel	Basis for Use and Next Review
_____	_____
_____	_____
_____	_____
_____	_____
_____	_____
_____	_____

Wednesday: The Point of Sale

Questions to Answer:

Identify each of the point-of-purchase channels you are using currently or have used in the recent past. List them all in the table provided here or make a similar one of your own. Then for each channel identified, note the success value, the failure value, and the current value.

Channel	Success Value	Failure Value	Current Value
_____	_____	_____	_____
_____	_____	_____	_____
_____	_____	_____	_____
_____	_____	_____	_____
_____	_____	_____	_____
_____	_____	_____	_____

For each channel identified, what did you have to do to justify its use? When will this decision be reviewed?

Channel	Basis for Use and Next Review
_____	_____
_____	_____
_____	_____
_____	_____
_____	_____
_____	_____

Look at Your List and Consider:

Do they all have quantitative success goals? Are they delivering?

_____

Which of the above are you using *offensively?* Which are used *defensively?*

_____

Which of the above are driven by direct market forces?

_____

What conditions would have to exist in the mind of your customers that would change the tactics you have identified?

_____

Thursday and Friday: Gathering Intelligence and Wrapping It Up

Visit each of the following, and search for information related to your firm or organization: Check the item off as you complete it.

- ❏ Google Blogsearch (http://blogsearch.google.com)

- ❏ Nielsen | Buzzmetrics BlogPulse (http://www.blogpulse.com)

- ❏ Planet Feedback (http://www.planetfeedback.com)

- ❏ YouTube (http://www.youtube.com)

- ❏ Set up an account at Google Alerts and request notices for terms or phrases that are important to you in the context of your business and marketing plan.

Based on the above, what did you find? Write out the conversations or phrases that stood out, and explain why.

_____

_____

_____

_____

Review what you've gathered this week: Check the item off when complete.

- ❏ Monday: Business objectives and success measures

- ❏ Tuesday: Awareness efforts and performance metrics

- ❏ Wednesday: Point-of-sale efforts and performance metrics

- ❏ Thursday: Summarized social intelligence

Create Your Social Feedback Cycle

Using the following funnel, note the placement of the various campaign elements you identified this week along with what you've learned through your social media intelligence efforts.

THE SOCIAL FEEDBACK CYCLE

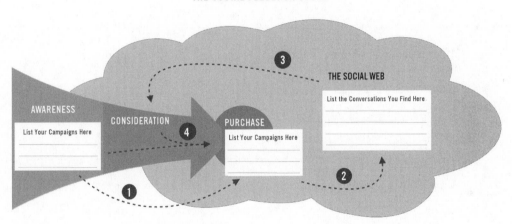

Figure A.1 The Social Feedback Cycle and Social Web

Chapter 6: Touchpoint Analysis

Monday: Gather Your Touchpoint Data

Questions to Answer:

What are your primary brand, product, or service promises?

_____

How are these promises related to the needs of your customers?

_____

How are these promises supported?

_____

What is the actual delivery mechanism that validates each promise?

_____

What are the actual customer experiences that demonstrate successful delivery?

_____

What channel has been used to convey each particular aspect of your promise or brand?

_____

How important to your customers are each of the promises and points and delivery?

_____

Tuesday: Organize Your Data

Structure Your Analysis: Check the box that applies to your choice.

❑   Organize by Channel

❑   Organize by Function

❑   Organize by Customer

❑   Organize by _____

Questions to Answer:

Why did you choose this organizational approach?

_____

How will the results be used to guide improvement over time?

_____

How can you tap the Social Web to drive this improvement?

_____

Wednesday: Evaluate and Rank Your Data

Part 1: Assessing Touchpoints

For Each Touchpoint Identified:

Rank its relative contribution on a 10-point scale in regard to talk value.
(1 = low value; 10 = high.)

Rank its performance or similar selected measure, again on a 10-point scale.
(1 = low value; 10 = high.)

Touchpoint	Talk Value	Performance Score	Notes

Part 2: Plotting Touchpoints

With measures and grades in hand, plot each touchpoint by its relative performance.

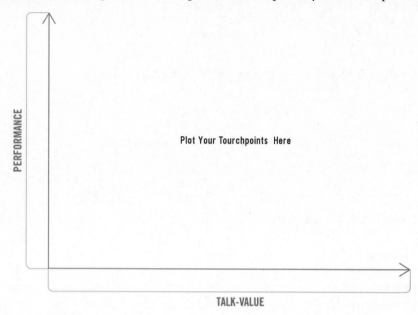

PERFORMANCE

Plot Your Tourchpoints Here

TALK-VALUE

Figure A.2 Your Touchpoint Map

Thursday: Analyze Your Data

Questions to Answer:

What are your lowest talk-generating touchpoints?

_____

What are your highest talk-generating touchpoints?

_____

Which of your high-talk touchpoints are low performing?

_____

Which of your high-talk touchpoints are high performing?

_____

Friday: Plan Your Next Steps

Find the most important touchpoints from the perspective of generating conversations on which you are simultaneously performing most *poorly*.

Questions to Answer:

What is the issue? Is this the wrong audience or a poor customer experience?

_____

Did you set the right expectation? Over-promise? Under-deliver?

_____

Who else is involved? Who are your internal constituents?

_____

Which of the required actions are directly within your control?

_____

How are you going to fix this?

_____

Chapter 7: Influence and Measurement

Monday and Tuesday: Make Your Calls

Using your script and call sheet, make your calls, and record the notes from each call.

Contact	Phone	Date	Score	Influencer	Notes

Wednesday: Score Your Calls

Calculate Your Net Promoter Score

1. Add up the number of customers who gave you a nine (9) or ten (10) and compute the corresponding percentage by dividing this into the total number of calls you made. This is your Promoter score.

2. Add up the number of customers who gave you a six (6) or less and compute the corresponding percentage by dividing this into the total number of calls you made. This is your Detractor score.

3. Subtract the Detractor score from the Promoter score: Your Net Promoter score is the difference.

> Your Promoter score: _____
>
> - Your Detractor score: _____
> ===============================
>
> Your Net Promoter score: _____

Thursday: Choose Your Metrics

Based on Table 7.1, track down the *sources* of the metrics that apply to your business. List these sources of data you need and your purpose for requesting them.

Metric	Purpose	Source	Notes

Open your browser and go to the BlogPulse website. Check off as you:

❑ Look for posts about your company;

❑ Look for posts about your competitors;

❑ Look for posts about the companies you interviewed in your Net Promoter score exercise.

Questions to Answer:

What did you find?

_____

_____

_____

_____

_____

Friday: Wrapping It Up

Social Feedback Cycle

Starting with your social feedback cycle that you created last week, look at the specific comments you found using BlogPulse or when searching support forums or other private communities.

Questions to Answer:

Are these comments helpful to your marketing effort, or are they creating obstacles that you have to overcome?

_____

How many of these specific comments can you relate to campaigns that you've run in the past? Are these recurring themes?

_____

Is there a conversation that you found that references a customer service experience or a change in product design?

_____

Have any of your prior marketing messages referenced or addressed this same thing?

_____

Touchpoint Analysis

Look at your touchpoint map and consider the following:

Questions to Answer:

How many of the touchpoints or experiences created are reflected in your search of social content?

_____

How do your digital touchpoints drive social conversations?

_____

Influence

Look at your individual Net Promoter *survey responses*: Check the most applicable box.

❏ If your Net Promoter *responses* are distinctly middle of the road—sixes, sevens, and eights—then it's likely that you have also found relatively little talk or content on the Social Web.

❏ If you have nines and tens—or ones and twos—you probably found a lot more. This is a direct indication of how much the Social Web is impacting you.

❏ If you're in the middle, the impact is less notable: *This means you are missing out*. Raise the performance of your touchpoints, and participate on the Social Web to get the conversations going.

Metrics

Finally, look at the metrics you've selected and complete the following:

❏ Integrate these with your Net Promoter score, social feedback cycle, and touchpoint map. How do the metrics you've selected provide quantitative insight into each of these items?

❏ Create the shell for your report card and dashboard based on the data you expect to begin collecting.

❏ Build relationships with the *sources* of the data you'll ultimately need.

Worksheets: Part III

Chapters 8–12

Chapter 8: Build a Social Media Campaign

Monday: Touchpoints and Social Feedback

Questions to Answer:

What marketing channels are you using now to generate awareness?

_____

What channel is your top performer in terms of ROI? How are you measuring this?

_____

What are you doing at the point of sale?

_____

Which of your identified touchpoints are working? Which are not?

_____

Which touchpoints represent your "top three"?

_____

Are your strongest experiences driven by marketing or operations?

_____

Which three touchpoints could you do without?

_____

Of the three that don't seem to matter, why do they exist?

_____

Tuesday: Dashboard Metrics

Questions to Answer:

Using Table 8.1 and the work you did last week, list the metrics that you will use in your dashboard and report card. For each, list the source. Use the following form, or create a spreadsheet based on the example shown in Figure 8.2. Adapt as needed to hold the data you've identified.

Metric   Source

_____   _____

_____   _____

_____   _____

_____   _____

_____   _____

_____   _____

Wednesday: Integrating Your Data

Questions to Answer:

What are the top three objectives of your social campaign?

_____

What other forms of media are you using, and how will social media benefit you?

_____

Does your Net Promoter score suggest that you should start with an outreach campaign or a learning campaign?

_____

Choosing between social platforms, social content, and social interactions, which is most likely to provide the support you need and fit into the marketing program you have in place now?

_____

Thursday: Refining Your Data

Questions to Answer:

What are the primary opportunities for social media you've found?
Are they primarily awareness, consideration or purchase related?

Opportunity	Awareness	Consideration	Purchase
_____	❑	❑	❑
_____	❑	❑	❑
_____	❑	❑	❑
_____	❑	❑	❑
_____	❑	❑	❑

Using the table below to record your answers, consider the following questions:

• Which social media channels and groups seem to be "best fits" given what you've seen so far?

• How do these choices fit with your current marketing efforts?

• What are the metrics that you are collecting now, and what are the sources for the additional metrics needed?

Social Media Channel	Relation to Current Effort	Metrics	Source
_____	_____	_____	_____
_____	_____	_____	_____
_____	_____	_____	_____
_____	_____	_____	_____
_____	_____	_____	_____

Friday's One Hour Exercise

This Week's Checklist:

- ❏ Have you identified the sources of the metrics you need?

- ❏ Are your report card and dashboard sustainable?

- ❏ Has the data services team or similar provider agreed to provide the metrics you need on an ongoing basis?

- ❏ Is the process for getting these metrics one that you can automate?

- ❏ Do you have a plan in place to adopt or continue your Net Promoter measurements?

Questions to Answer:

Which, if any, of the social media components you've now covered are you using now?

_____

_____

_____

_____

If you could add two or three more, which would you add next? Why?

_____

_____

_____

_____

Chapter 9: Social Platforms

Monday: Social Networks

List the networks and organizations you are in now and answer each of the following.

- For each, why do you participate in this network or social group?
- What do you expect to get out of it?
- In the past 30 days, how much time and effort have you put in?
- Within the *online* social networks you visited, how is advertising done? Who is advertising and what are they advertising? What products and services are being talked about? What are members saying?

Network	Motive	Ads and Member Conversations
_____	_____	_____
_____	_____	_____
_____	_____	_____
_____	_____	_____
_____	_____	_____
_____	_____	_____

Tuesday's One Hour Exercise

Complete the Following:

List the online networks you are now part of, including any you joined today:

_____

_____

_____

_____

_____

For each of the above, check when you have:

❑ Completed your profile

❑ Posted content

❑ Added one or more friends

Wednesday: Support Forums

Complete the Following:

Visit the Dell support forums, and check off the following as you complete the item.

❑ Take a look at the First Time Users area.

❑ Jump into the photo/video discussions. Look at the topics, and in particular notice the number of replies to the various posts.

❑ Click on the poster's names and see what information is displayed about those members: you'll find this link in the Author column.

❑ Find and click the Who's Online link.

Thursday: Branded Social Applications

Sites to visit: Check off as you visit.

❑ USA Today (http://www.usatoday.com)

❑ Fair Isaac's FICO Forums (http://ficoforums.myfico.com)

❑ Bank of America Small Business Community (http://smallbusinessonline community.bankofamerica.com)

❑ RealMadrid America U.S.A. Supporter's Club (http://www.realmadridamerica .com/vid/clubblanco.php)

Questions to Answer:

How visible are you, and what is the role of your personal presence?

_____

Which was easiest to join? Most difficult? To sort out what to do?

_____

What tools are available? Blogs? Ratings? Comments? Friends? Which of these are appealing to you? Why? Which seem to be getting the most use?

_____

How are these being used? What are members doing?

_____

Friday: Social Platforms

Questions to Answer:

Listening

What can you learn from existing personal social networks?

_____

How can you leverage existing business social networks?

_____

❏   Add the above to your marketing plan.

Participation

Is there an opportunity to use a social tool such as Product Pulse, Social Vibe, or a similar off-the-shelf, member-driven social media component?

_____

❏   Add appropriate elements to your plan.

Is there an opportunity to appropriately create a direct presence for your brand in a specific social network?

_____

Would your customers readily build relationships with you and with each other through a community?

_____

Is there a current social space that falls short in meeting the needs of your customers now?

_____

❏ Are answers to any of the above "yes"? If so, identify the connection points between a social platform and your current marketing plan.

_____

How would you use a community platform, and how would this change your current marketing efforts?

_____

What is the approval process that you would need to go through internally to make this a reality?

_____

Chapter 10: Social Content: Multimedia

Monday: Blogs One Hour Exercise

Blogs to visit: Check off as you do.

- ❑ Go Big Always (http://www.gobigalways.com)

- ❑ Bazaarblog (http://www.bazaarblog.com)

- ❑ Influence 2.0 (http://blog.cymfony.com)

- ❑ The TED Blog (http://blog.ted.com)

Questions to Answer:

What about these examples seems to be the most useful?

_____

How is disclosure handled? How does disclosure strengthen the blog and its message?

_____

How often is new content posted? Which items posted generate the most comments (or the most passionate comments)?

_____

How does the company handle the discussion within the comments? Does the company participate?

_____

How could you use a blog as a part of your own marketing effort? Who would write it? Who would _read_ it?

_____

Tuesday: Microblogs

Services to sign up for: Check as you create your profile.

❏ Twitter (http://twitter.com)

❏ Seesmic (http://www.seesmic.com)

Wednesday: User-Generated Content

Sites to visit: Check off as you visit.

❏ Soulja Boy – How to Crank That (http://www.youtube.com/watch?v=sLGLum5SyKQ)

❏ Free Line Skates (http://www.youtube.com/watch?v=fghOsqGacnU)

❏ Ben 10 Alien Force Alien Creation Chamber (http://www.youtube.com/watch?v=Y1AL84BLRrM)

❏ Joe and Joe Backdrop Project (http://www.youtube.com/watch?v=oJrH2Dj8oGc)

❏ Home Depot $25,000 Remodel Contest (http://www.youtube.com/watch?v=U68J_TefJgs)

Thursday: Podcasts

Podcasts to sample: Check off as you visit and/or subscribe.

❏ Personal Life Media/Living Green (http://blogs.personallifemedia.com/living-green)

❏ Beachwalks with Rox (http://www.beachwalks.tv)

❏ IBM Thought Leadership (http://www-01.ibm.com/webcasts/podcasts/channel)

❏ Shell Global Solutions (http://www.shell.com/globalsolutions/podcasts)

❏ Slate Podcasts (http://www.slate.com/id/2119317)

❏ Ted Talks (http://www.ted.com/index.php/talks)

Friday: Wrap-Up

Looking at your notes of this week, answer the following:

What are the most challenging aspects of your current marketing program in terms of overcoming objections, of driving new user, or driving additional purchases?

_____

Which of these aspects lend themselves to assistance via video, photos, or a podcast?

_____

Which of these lend themselves to the kinds of content that your customers would create? Which would be best if you made the content, and then gave it to your existing customers to share or comment on?

_____

What are the most promising multimedia applications that would add depth to the blog you created in the prior chapter?

_____

Chapter 11: Social Content: Reviews, Ratings, and Recommendations

Monday: Your Reading List

List five books you've read recently:

_____

_____

_____

_____

_____

Questions to Answer:

For each, did you like it? Why or why not?

_____

For each, did you recommend this book? Why or why not?

_____

For any, did you write a review—anyplace—for this book? If so, what did you say about it? If not, why not?

_____

Tuesday: Becoming Popular

Sites to visit: Check off as you visit.

❏   Digg (http://digg.com)

❏   YouTube (http://www.youtube.com)

Look at the home page: Do you see the newest—or the most popular—content first?

_____

How does this change the mix of content that you actually view at each site visited?

_____

Looking at the top 10 items on each home page, which has more content covering topics you've never heard of?

_____

How many of the topics—on either site—are also present in the headlines on your favorite news site?

_____

Which site offers the most unexpected versus expected content?

_____

Wednesday: Ratings, Reviews, and Recommendations

Blogs to visit: Check off as you visit.

- ❏ Wall Street Journal (http://www.wsj.com)
- ❏ Ad Age (http://www.adage.com)
- ❏ Amazon (http://www.amazon.com)
- ❏ Edmunds (http://www.edmunds.com)
- ❏ iVillage (http://www.ivillage.com)

Questions to Answer:

Which sites made it easiest to share content? To rate content? To share the ratings?

_____

On which sites did you actually share the most content?

_____

If the tools on the sites that made it easiest to share content had been available on all of the sites you looked at, would you have shared more content?

_____

Thursday: Case Examples

Pick three clients at the Bazaarvoice website:

Things to Do: Check off as you go.

- ❏ Look at the product reviews. You may have to navigate to a specific product, or there may be a link to "top rated" items present on the home page. Think about the advantages and disadvantages of having direct access to top-rated products.

- ❏ If a Sort by Ratings feature is available, use it. Think about the impact of the role of ratings and your ability to navigate them in terms of contribution to shopping-cart value. If this feature is missing, ask yourself what difference it makes to your overall shopping experience.

- ❏ Look at the reviews associated with the various ratings: Do the reviews tend to support the ratings, and vice versa? Is the combination of ratings and reviews more valuable than either alone?

Friday: Add to Your Plan

Questions to Answer:

Based on your current digital marketing efforts, could you add Digg or Del.icio.us buttons to encourage recommendations and sharing?

How could ratings, reviews, and recommendations be applied to your business?

Chapter 12: Social Interactions

Monday: Event Listings

Blogs to visit: Check off as you visit.

- ❑ CitySearch (http://www.citysearch.com)

- ❑ Eventful (http://www.eventful.com)

- ❑ Upcoming (http://www.upcoming.com)

- ❑ The website for your local arts and events guide

Questions to Answer:

For each site you visited:

How quickly were you able to find events?

_____

Was "sponsored" content presented? If so, how relevant was it?

_____

How many pages did you look at in total? Was all of the information you needed presented on a single page?

_____

Which sites encouraged you to add your own ratings and reviews?

_____

Were the ratings and reviews of ordinary people presented equally to those of professional or celebrity critics?

_____

Which sites offered feeds or alerts?

_____

Which sites offered the ability to import your existing preferences related to the type of event you were seeking?

_____

How could you use the services you visited today to promote marketing events that you may be planning?

_____

Tuesday: Location-Based Services

Services to visit: Check off as you visit.

- ❏ Dodgeball (http://www.dodgeball.com)

- ❏ Brightkite (http://www.brightkite.com)

Activities: Check as you Complete.

- ❏ Sign up for Dodgeball and Brightkite.

- ❏ Go to the Brightkite website and log in to your account.

- ❏ Check in on both services.

- ❏ Using Brightkite, see where you are after you check in.

- ❏ If you have friends using Brightkite, add them.

- ❏ *Using your phone*, send a "? Starbucks" or similar request.

- ❏ Go and enjoy a cup of coffee with your friends.

Wednesday: Email and Bacn

Questions to Answer:

How many "Urgent" emails?

_____

How many "Important" emails?

_____

How many "Not Important" emails?

_____

How many "Spam" emails?

_____

What is ratio of "Urgent" to the total?

_____

What is ratio of "Important" to the total?

_____

What is ratio of "Not Important" to the total?

_____

What is ratio of "Spam" to the total?

_____

Thursday: FriendFeed

Visit and check off as you complete.

- ❑ Go to FriendFeed (`http://FriendFeed.com`).

- ❑ Create an account.

- ❑ Search for people whose activities and content you'd like to keep track of.

- ❑ Using the Services menu, add the services (social sites) that you have established to your feed.

- ❑ Create an imaginary friend.

Friday: Build Your Plan

Questions to Answer:

What events have you planned that could be listed and promoted through a service such as Eventful or Upcoming?

_____

If you added a link to Eventful's Demand It page, could you build a schedule around that?

_____

How can you use location-based services?

_____

How can you apply feeds to your business use of the Social Web?

_____

Worksheets: Part IV

Chapters 13–14

Chapter 13: Objectives, Metrics, and ROI

Monday: Your Business Objectives

Check off each item as you complete it.

❏ Look at the business objectives and success metrics you defined when you created your social feedback cycle. Add to these the larger business objectives that define your company or organization's success goals for the coming years.

❏ Connect each of your specific goals and success metrics set in Chapter 5, "The Social Feedback Cycle" to one or more of your overall goals.

❏ Define each of the success metrics, and identify the source of the data you'll need to support this metric.

Tuesday: Your Audience

• Using standard age groups and demographics, identify each of the audience segments you are interested in with regard to your social media campaign.

• Briefly describe what each of your specific segments does when online.

• For each segment in your audience, create a profile of the typical behaviors you expect. Do they create content, comment on posts and articles, or is your audience the "read only" type?

Segment	Description	Expected Behavior
_____	_____	_____
_____	_____	_____
_____	_____	_____
_____	_____	_____
_____	_____	_____
_____	_____	_____

Wednesday: Content Metrics

Part 1: Talk Generators

Check off each item as you complete it.

- Look back at Figure 13.1 and the definition of your audience and your business objectives. Confirm that there is something for people to talk about and that the audience is *likely to be talking about it.*
- List the specific features or unique attributes of your brand, product, or service.
- Create the same list, except do it for one or more of your competitors.

My Product or Service

Audience Segment   Feature, Benefit, or Other Item of Interest

_____   _____

_____   _____

_____   _____

_____   _____

_____   _____

Competitor's Product or Service _____

Audience Segment   Feature, Benefit, or Other Item of Interest

_____   _____

_____   _____

_____   _____

_____   _____

_____   _____

Check off each item as you complete it.

❑ Using the services suggested, search for these items and write down (or summarize) what you find.

❑ Trace the posts that you found back to their source. See if you can identify the type of audience member that contributed each item and ensure that you have accounted for this segment in yesterday's exercise.

❑ Integrate this data and its sources into the metrics section of your social media dashboard and report card you created in Chapter 8, "Build a Social Media Campaign."

Item   Summary of Conversation

_____   _____

_____   _____

_____   _____

_____   _____

_____   _____

_____   _____

Thursday: Relevance Metrics

Check off each item as you complete it.

❑ Look back at the conversational data you collected yesterday. Does any of this reference your brand, product, or service? Is it positive or negative? Create a baseline that will help you establish a loyalty indicator.

❑ Look at your web analytics. Do the metrics such as time spent and bounce rate exist? If they do, collect them and establish a baseline. If they do not, talk with your IT or web team and see if you can get them. Using the metrics you have, create a baseline for time spent and bounce rate so that you can track changes.

- ❏ Look at any metrics available to you that indicate a strong sense of participation or attachment. Are people participating in the way you'd like them to participate?

- ❏ Integrate this data and its sources into the metrics section of your social media dashboard and report card that you created in Chapter 8.

- ❏ Use this data to create your baselines for your selected measures.

Friday: Impact Metrics

Check off each item as you complete it.

- ❏ Looking at your web analytics, review your referrer data. Add to this any applicable internal data you may have that helps you identify the arrival of specific audience segments.

- ❏ Look at the average time spent on your site and the bounce rate, but limit it to the commerce portions of the site and the informational pages that directly support commerce.

- ❏ Look at actual conversions, the number of reviews created, and any recommendations. In short, look at anything that helps support the difference in people visiting your site with and without exposure to social media.

- ❏ Integrate this data and its sources into the metrics section of your social media dashboard and report card.

- ❏ Use this data to create your baselines for your selected measures.

Chapter 14: Present Your Social Media Plan

Monday: Business Objectives

List and define your business objectives.

Objective	Current Efforts	Current Status and Measures
_____	_____	_____
_____	_____	_____
_____	_____	_____
_____	_____	_____
_____	_____	_____
_____	_____	_____
_____	_____	_____

List and define your audience.

Segment	Likely Social Media Channel	Best Practices and Notes
_____	_____	_____
_____	_____	_____
_____	_____	_____
_____	_____	_____
_____	_____	_____
_____	_____	_____

In your campaign, how will you *ensure* transparency?

_____

_____

_____

Tuesday: Choose Your Methods

Complete Each of the Following:

Net Promoter

Based on your Net Promoter score, indicate by campaign whether it will be a listening campaign or an outreach campaign.

Campaign	Objective	Listening	Outreach
_____	_____	❑	❑
_____	_____	❑	❑
_____	_____	❑	❑
_____	_____	❑	❑
_____	_____	❑	❑

Touchpoints

Based on your touchpoint map, identify the three most important *talk generators*.

Touchpoint	Positive	Negative
_____	❑	❑
_____	❑	❑
_____	❑	❑
_____	❑	❑
_____	❑	❑

Challenges and Opportunities

For each negative issue or challenge, briefly describe how you will engage other teams or departments to address it.

Issue and Action Needed | Requires Assistance From

_____ | _____

_____ | _____

_____ | _____

_____ | _____

_____ | _____

_____ | _____

Wednesday: Pick Your Channels

Selected Channel | Service Providers | Concept | Cost

_____ | _____ | _____ | _____

_____ | _____ | _____ | _____

_____ | _____ | _____ | _____

Thursday: Verify Your Metrics

Objective | Success Metric | Source Confirmed

_____ | _____ | ❏

_____ | _____ | ❏

_____ | _____ | ❏

_____ | _____ | ❏

_____ | _____ | ❏

_____ | _____ | ❏

Friday: Wrap It Up

Check off each item as you complete it.

- ❏ Check each of the primary sections of your plan.

- ❏ Verify the facts, sources of data, and similar details.

- ❏ Set a future meeting time and then present your plan.

Appendix:
Additional Social
Media Resources

*The following resources are included to help you
get started. You'll find a list of experts along with
some insightful blogs and online publications, as
well as links to all of the agencies and practitioners whose work has been referenced within this
book. You'll also find links to the social media
platforms, networks, and services that you've seen.
Remember, too: There are many more resources
available. Use the following as a starting point and
then build your own personal library of useful references. By the way, you'll find that Del.icio.us is
perfect for building, maintaining, and most importantly sharing the list you build.*

B

Industry Experts

Andy Sernovitz	http://www.damniwish.com
Bryan Eisenberg	http://www.futurenowinc.com
Charlene Li	http://www.charleneli.com
Ed Keller	http://www.kellerfay.com/management.php
Edward Tufte	http://www.edwardtufte.com
Fred Reichheld	http://www.theultimatequestion.com
Jake McKee	http://www.communityguy.com
Jake Nielsen	http://www.useit.com/jakob
Jeff Jarvis	http://www.buzzmachine.com
Jim Nail	http://blog.cymfony.com/
John Gilmore	http://www.toad.com/gnu
Josh Bernoff	http://www.bernoff.com
Nathan Gilliatt	http://www.socialtarget.com/company
Robert Scoble	http://scobleizer.com

Industry Blogs

AdRants	http://www.adrants.com
Boing Boing	http://boingboing.net
Church of the Customer	http://www.churchofthecustomer.com
Customer eXperience Crossroads	http://www.customercrossroads.com
Social Media Today	http://www.socialmediatoday.com

Industry Resources

ClickZ	http://www.clickz.com
eMarketer	http://www.emarketer.com
Forrester	http://www.forrester.com
Technorati	http://www.technorati.com
Yankelovich	http://www.yankelovich.com

Agencies and Social Media Practitioners

Bare Feet Studios	http://www.barefeetstudios.com
Brains on Fire	http://www.brainsonfire.com
Communispace	http://www.communispace.com
Fanscape	http://www.fanscape.com

Agencies and Social Media Practitioners *(continued)*

GSD&M Idea City	`http://www.ideacity.com`
HearThis.com	`http://www.hearthis.com`
Keller Fay	`http://www.kellerfay.com`
Modem Media (Publicis Modem)	`http://www.modemmedia.com`
Passenger	`http://www.thinkpassenger.com`
Powered	`http://www.powered.com`
SocialVibe	`http://www.socialvibe.com`
Tangent Design	`http://www.tangentdesign.com`
Wild Tangent	`http://www.wildtangent.com`
Zócalo Group	`http://www.zocalogroup.com`

Social Media Platforms

Bazaarvoice	`http://www.bazaarvoice.com`
BzzAgent	`http://www.bzzagent.com`
Jive	`http://www.jivesoftware.com`
Lithium	`http://www.lithium.com`
Mikons	`http://www.mikons.com`
Ning.com	`http://www.ning.com`
Pluck	`http://www.pluck.com`
ProductPulse	`http://www.friend2friend.com`
RockYou	`http://www.rockyou.com`
Salesforce.com	`http://www.salesforce.com`
Slide	`http://www.slide.com`
Small World Labs	`http://www.smallworldlabs.com`
Wet Paint	`http://www.wetpaint.com`

Social Networks and Services

AdGabber	`http://www.adgabber.com`
Bebo	`http://www.bebo.com`
Brightkite	`http://brightkite.com`
Del.icio.us	`http://del.icio.us`
Digg	`http://www.digg.com`
Dodgeball	`http://dodgeball.com`
Flickr	`http://www.flickr.com`
Eventful	`http://eventful.com`
Facebook	`http://www.facebook.com`

Social Networks and Services *(continued)*

FriendFeed	http://friendfeed.com
Friendster	http://www.friendster.com
Identi.ca	http://identi.ca
Kyte TV	http://www.kyte.tv
Last.fm	http://www.last.fm
LinkedIn	http://www.linkedin.com
LiveJournal	http://www.livejournal.com
Ma.gnolia.com	http://ma.gnolia.com
Metacafe	http://www.metacafe.com
Minggl	http://www.minggl.com
MySpace	http://www.myspace.com
Orkut	http://www.orkut.com
Personal Life Media	http://www.personalifemedia.com
Photobucket	http://www.photobucket.com
Ping.fm	http://ping.fm
Plaxo	http://www.plaxo.com
Plurk	http://plurk.com
Pownce	http://pownce.com
Seesmic	http://seesmic.com
SocialThing	http://www.socialthing.com
Sonico	http://www.sonico.com
Stickam	http://www.stickam.com
Stumble Upon	http://www.stumbleupon.com
Tumblr	http://www.tumblr.com
Twitter	http://twitter.com
Upcoming	http://upcoming.yahoo.com
YouTube	http://www.youtube.com

Metrics Platforms and Providers

A. C. Nielsen	http://www.nielsen-online.com
BlogPulse	http://www.blogpulse.com
BuzzMetrics	http://www.buzzmetrics.com
Core Metrics	http://www.coremetrics.com
Cymfony	http://www.cymfony.com

Metrics Platforms and Providers *(continued)*

DoubleClick	http://www.doubleclick.com
FeedBurner	http://www.feedburner.com
Google Blog Search	http://blogsearch.google.com
K. D. Paine and Partners	http://www.kdpaine.com
Omniture	http://www.omniture.com
Podtrac	http://www.podtrac.com
Techrigy	http://www.techrigy.com
Twitterholic	http://www.twitterholic.com
Zenith Optimedia	http://www.zenithoptimedia.com

Index

Note to the reader: Throughout this index **boldfaced** page numbers indicate primary discussions of a topic. *Italicized* page numbers indicate illustrations.

social media to spread, 41
trust in, 20, 43
Word of Mouth Marketing Association,
173, 240
world map, and social networks, *183*
written word, *57*

X

XFN (XHTML Friend's Network) Links,
191, 192

Y

Yellow Pages, *54*
YouTube, 64, 98, *104*, 104–105, 167, 210,
224, *251*
Home Depot on, **224–225**
promoted (paid) videos, 250

Z

Zappos, 87, 177, *177*
Zenity Optimedia, 43